IN THE SHADOW OF THE GREATEST GF

In the Shadow of the Greatest Generation

The Americans Who Fought the Korean War

Melinda L. Pash

NEW YORK UNIVERSITY PRESS
New York and London

NEW YORK UNIVERSITY PRESS
New York and London
www.nyupress.org

References to Internet websites (URLs) were accurate at the time of writing.
Neither the author nor New York University Press is responsible for URLs that
may have expired or changed since the manuscript was prepared.

LIBRARY OF CONGRESS CATALOGING-IN-PUBLICATION DATA
Pash, Melinda L.
In the shadow of the greatest generation : the Americans who fought the Korean War /
Melinda L. Pash.
p. cm.
Includes bibliographical references and index.
ISBN 978-0-8147-6769-6 (cl : alk. paper)
ISBN 978-0-8147-8922-3 (ebook)
ISBN 978-0-8147-6067-3 (ebook)
1. Korean War, 1950-1953—United States. 2. United States—Armed Forces—History—20th
century. 3. Soldiers—United States—History—20th century. 4. Veterans—United States—
History—20th century. I. Title.
DS919.P38   2012
951.904'240973—dc23   2012024954

New York University Press books are printed on acid-free paper,
and their binding materials are chosen for strength and durability.
We strive to use environmentally responsible suppliers and materials
to the greatest extent possible in publishing our books.

Manufactured in the United States of America
10 9 8 7 6 5 4 3 2 1

For Sid, Graham, and Sam

CONTENTS

When the first episode of the television series *M*A*S*H* aired in the fall of 1972 I was just shy of three years old, not exactly a member of the producer's target audience.[1] But, despite my age and a few flirtations with *The Dukes of Hazzard* and *Charlie's Angels* and in part because of syndication, I came to be a regular viewer and loyal fan of the 4077th Mobile Army Surgical Hospital in Korea and its collection of unusual doctors and support personnel. I tuned in every week to watch Hawkeye and Trapper John (or, after the third season, Hawkeye and B. J. Honeycutt—the B and J standing for "anything you want") cooking up trouble, Corporal Maxwell Q. Klinger donning a dress in his futile attempt to secure a Section 8 (mentally unfit for service) discharge, and Radar O'Reilly wheeling and dealing for supplies and equipment over the Army's archaic communication system. Decades later, I still chuckle when I think of Klinger decked out as the Statue of Liberty in honor of General MacArthur's visit or of straight-man Frank Burns ending up asleep at an aid station near the front with a toe tag reading "emotionally exhausted and morally bankrupt."[2]

Certainly, moments of bitterness and solemnity crept into the script. Who could ever forget that Lieutenant Colonel Henry Blake perished when the enemy shot down his helicopter over the Sea of Japan or that Hawkeye could never brew enough moonshine in his homemade still to forget the war (late in the series Hawkeye suffered a war-related emotional breakdown)? But, week after week *M*A*S*H* delivered to my television set and to millions of others across the country images of Korea as a war full of much more levity and entertainment than the conflict Americans had just watched play out in Vietnam. At the same time, the jaded and worldly attitudes possessed by the main characters belonged more to the generation that weathered the sixties and seventies than to the one that came of age in the years during and just after World War II. Yet, engrossed in the happenings of the 4077th, few viewers bothered to question whether or not the scenes meticulously crafted by Larry Gelbart and others and disseminated by the Columbia Broadcasting System (CBS) accurately reflected the experiences of the men and women who served in Korea. Strangely, in the American mind, *M*A*S*H* became much more than just another television program—it became the reality of the Korean War.

Not until graduate school did I begin to separate my own memories of *M*A*S*H* from the history of the Korean War—and then only because of a chance encounter with a group of "Forgotten War" veterans. Having decided to write on the Vietnam War, I attended a "veterans' prom" in hopes of making some connections. As the evening wore on, I settled in with a group of men discussing their wartime experiences. It did not take long for me to realize not only that these men were Korean rather than Vietnam veterans but also that the war they were describing had little in common with the one I had become familiar with through *M*A*S*H*.

That night I went home and began reading everything I could find on the Korean War—an easy task given the short supply of books and articles devoted to the conflict, especially in comparison to World War II and the Vietnam War. And, the more that I read, the more convinced I became that *M*A*S*H*'s 251 episodes spread over eleven years had not told the story of the men and women who rotated in and out of the Korean War. Maxwell Klinger had it right when he said, "I think it's the most stupidest thing in the world. You call it a police action back home, right? Over here it's a war. A police action sounds like we're over here arresting people, handing out parking tickets. A war's just killing that's all."[3] But, the show itself, while set in Korea, more closely mirrored the perceptions and realities of the Vietnam era and of that generation of veterans. Standing in the shadow of the "Greatest Generation" and shaded by the legacies of Vietnam, the Americans who served in Korea from June 1950 to July 1953 had yet to have their own narrative told. That realization became the genesis and driving force of this book.

ACKNOWLEDGMENTS

I could never have finished this book without the support of a number of people. Above all, my family provided years of encouragement. My husband, Sid, watched our two young sons, Graham and Sam, in Carlisle Barracks, Pennsylvania, Abilene, Kansas, Independence, Missouri, and Washington, D.C., while I did research, keeping his sense of humor even when things went awry, as when I got trapped in Ronald Reagan's funeral procession and could not get back to the hotel until long after our kids fell asleep or when our two-year-old, Sam, decided to un-diaper and go for a swim in the World War II Memorial pool. He also listened to ideas and proofread drafts. Both of my sons generously gave up spring and summer breaks to hit the road in search of another archive or another veteran.

My friend and mentor, G. Kurt Piehler, assisted me with every phase of the writing of this book. He also put me in touch with Captain J. W. "Buzz" Easterling of the Marine Corps, who kindly proofread the manuscript.

From the beginning, my editor, Debbie Gershenowitz, believed in this project and worked to make the book a reality. She guided it through the New York University Press process and contacted Professor John Whiteclay Chambers II of Rutgers University and Professor Lewis Carlson of Western Michigan University to read it. Both Professor Chambers and Professor Carlson provided valuable insights and offered helpful suggestions. I am indebted to them.

I am grateful to too many archivists and librarians to name them all, but archivists at the Eisenhower Library were especially helpful, as was Professor Paul Edwards at the Center for the Study of the Korean War at Graceland University in Independence, Missouri. At Fayetteville State University's Charles Chesnutt Library, Vera Hooks miraculously located the most obscure sources via interlibrary loan.

Lastly, many veterans sent me materials, answered questions, and proofread as I went along. Without their enthusiastic help this book could not have been written. I would especially like to thank Harry Matthews, Joe Scheuber, Stan Jones, and Ralph Cutro. These four shared their lives with me, gave depth to my research, and made this project a passion. If not for my own three boys, this work would be dedicated to them and to the many other Americans who heeded the country's call to serve in the Korean War.

Of course, while many people contributed to the completion of this book, any errors or inconsistencies are mine alone.

During the Korean War, the United States for the first time shipped home for burial the bodies of Americans killed in action. With little by way of ceremony or pomp, the remains of soldiers who died in Korea were interred in simple graves that merely identified the person's name, rank, and date of birth. Only later did Americans think to add "Korea" to the stones, ascribing a time and place, if not a meaning, to their deaths. More than thirty-six thousand American soldiers ended their wartime tours of duty in Korea this way while another 1.8 million returned home alive but alone and shrouded in the same anonymity, the forgotten soldiers of a forgotten war.[1]

Unlike their older brothers and cousins who served in World War II and returned to ticker-tape parades and welcoming bands, Korean War veterans returned quietly to a country that in their absence scarcely missed them. Though Americans initially rallied to the war drum when President Harry S. Truman called on the nation to defend South Korea from communist aggression, the lack of meaningful home front participation in the form of rationing or other personal sacrifice soon made Korea only a minor distraction for the American public. As soldiers still green to battle clung to the Pusan Perimeter, as marines fought their way out of Chosin Reservoir with frozen feet and staggering casualties, and as GIs tried to hold the line in a bloody stalemate half a world away, Americans at home went on with business as usual, concentrating on making the most of the prosperous post–World War II economy. Fearing wartime shortages, they snapped up furniture and televisions, refrigerators and cars.[2] In Fords and Lincolns and Chevrolets, the war drove right out of the minds of many Americans and into the middle and back pages of newspapers. Returning veterans could only wonder at the world that seemingly had forgotten them, surprised that "there was no evidence that the civilian population of the USA even knew (or cared) that those of us getting off the ship had seen desperate combat."[3]

Perhaps understandably, average Americans found themselves too busy to pay attention to the conflict raging thousands of miles away in Korea or to the soldiers trickling home, but movie makers, novelists, and even historians proved no better at acknowledging the sacrifices made by those American servicemen and women. Throughout the war and in the years following, Hollywood produced a number of war movies, but most of them looked back to the "good war," World War II, for inspiration. The silver screen showed John Wayne, Henry Fonda, Humphrey Bogart, Robert Mitchum, Randolph Scott, and a host of other stars heroically battling Nazis and "Nips" in such classics as *Flying Leathernecks* (1951), *Battle Cry* (1955), and *The Bridge on the River Kwai* (1957). To be sure, Korea did provide the backdrop for a number of films, but with few exceptions these failed to catch hold of the popular imagination and often simply reused themes and storylines from World War II pictures.[4] Movies, such as *Bamboo Prison* (1954), *Prisoner of War* (1954), *The Rack* (1956), *Time Limit* (1957), *The Manchurian Candidate* (1962), *The Young and the Brave* (1963), and *Sergeant Ryker* (1968), that broke from the World War II model tended to focus on Korean War POWs, feeding the public's appetite for tales of "brainwashing" and collaboration but doing little to educate the audience on the real war or to bring a measure of positive attention to those who served. Later films, like *M*A*S*H* (1970), which set out to portray the lives of doctors and nurses in a mobile Army surgical hospital during the Korean War, proved more adept at reflecting the values and issues belonging to the Vietnam War era than at depicting life in Korea. More recently, the trend remains the same—movie studios and television networks churn out new World War II classics like *Saving Private Ryan* (1998), *Pearl Harbor* (2001), *Letters from Iwo Jima* (2006), *Flags of Our Fathers* (2006), and HBO's ten-part miniseries *The Pacific* (2010), but largely ignore the Korean War and the men and women who served in it. When Paramount Pictures remade *Manchurian Candidate* in 2004, originally a movie centering on a prisoner of war brainwashed by the Chinese, they stripped the story of its Korean War setting, placing it instead in the Gulf War.

With its dependency upon public interest for earnings, one can readily appreciate Hollywood's reasons for paying such short shrift to the Korean War and its veterans, but academics and scholars also have shown great reluctance to tackle the first hot war of the Cold War. Historians have written hundreds, even thousands of books on Vietnam, the second major flare-up of the Cold War, but they have produced only a handful of volumes dedicated to the Korean War. The majority of these works concentrate on the military campaign itself or on the foreign policy that failed to prevent hostilities. Some look at the American home front during the Cold War, but generally these focus so narrowly as to preclude any real analysis of the impact of the Korean War on domestic life.[5] Elaine Tyler May's landmark study on the Cold War family, *Homeward Bound*, talks at length about the structure of the American family in the 1950s but never addresses the millions of families who sent husbands, sons, and fathers overseas to fight in Korea.[6] Not surprisingly, with so little attention paid in general to the conflict, the scholarly literature all but excludes Korean War veterans. Only a few works, like Rudy Tomedi's *No Bugles, No Drums*, Linda Granfield's *I Remember Korea*, and Donald Knox's two-volume oral history of the Korean War, take a close look at those who risked their lives on the peninsula.[7] While these books do a good job of allowing veterans to tell their stories, they provide little analysis, focusing primarily on wartime experiences and leaving the Korean War soldier turned veteran shrouded in mystery.[8]

With the sixtieth anniversary of the commencement of Korean War now past, the time has come for a fresh and more comprehensive look at the men and women who marched to the "land of the morning calm" from June 1950 to July 1953. Of the 6.8 million survivors of the Korean War era, only 3.9 million remained in 2000, and in that year the U.S. Department of Veterans Affairs estimated that by 2010 only 2.5 million would still be alive, none under the age of seventy.[9] The generation is passing and with it the opportunity to give a face to those who served and to understand the impact that this war had on veterans and on the world to which they returned.

This study focuses on the veterans of the Korean War, their upbringing, training, and wartime experiences, attitudes, and post-Korea lives. Chapter 1 explores these veterans' generational background. Raised during the Great Depression and the Second World War, the men and women who served in Korea learned first-hand the sacrifices that Americans might be called upon to make in the name of country. After the defeat of the Nazis and Japanese, however, few expected that one day Uncle Sam would ask them to participate in a ground war of their own. Still, situated between World War II and the Vietnam War, this generation patriotically heeded the call to colors as they had seen fathers and brothers do in the 1940s rather than seeking to avoid the draft and shunning volunteering like their sons and daughters in the 1960s and 1970s. Following up on these themes, chapter 2 discusses the various circumstances compelling Americans to accept military service and chronicles the experience of mustering into the armed forces in the early 1950s. This chapter also examines the Korean War draft, demonstrating that while the burden of military service fell fairly equally upon Americans regardless of socioeconomic status, it also set the stage for some of the draft inequalities associated with the Vietnam War era.

Chapter 3 evaluates the military training given those who served on the Korean Peninsula. Entrusting the nation's security to atomic deterrence and air power, President Truman pared down the military in the 1940s with the terrible result that the military had to secure manpower for Korea by calling up National Guardsmen and reservists and shortening the training cycle for new inductees. Effective at putting an army in the field, these measures also ensured that many soldiers and marines rotated into the war zone armed with a "can do" spirit but questionable and untested military prowess. However, military training as a whole did successfully begin preparing GIs to tolerate racial integration as the need for faster training outweighed the need for racially segregated housing and instruction.

Chapters 4 and 5 follow Americans as they entered the dirty, bloody war on Korea's hills. Wondering if the land and people on whose behalf they had been summoned could be worth the price, men fought not only against the enemy but also against frigid winters, blazing summers, terrifying scenes of brutality, and the lesser-known reality of life in a war zone, boredom. As the war dragged on, it became increasingly clear to those fulfilling their obligations overseas that the American public had little interest in the struggle over real estate in Korea, fostering a sense of isolation from the home front. Most rotated out of the war after accumulating enough points, but those unfortunate enough to have been taken prisoner either died in captivity or suffered months or years of torture and mistreatment. Chapter 5 chronicles the experiences of American prisoners of war captured by the North Koreans and Chinese.

Chapter 6 provides a brief interlude in the narrative to explore the lives of women and African Americans in theater. Seldom exposed to the war in the same way as soldiers or marines, nurses and female support personnel nonetheless learned the effects of battle and suffered the uncertainties of living in a war zone. African Americans, meanwhile, often viewed the struggle as an opportunity to prove their worth and achieve equality back home. Manpower pressures on the peninsula forced commanders in the field to integrate units there, and by the end of the war blacks and whites regularly served together at both training and duty stations. Men of different races came to eat, bunk, and fight together, with the result that biracial friendships and a newfound respect for each other developed. Few Korean War veterans returned home to become civil rights activists, but their wartime exposure to different types of people led many veterans to question the morality of segregation at home and to envision the possibility of an integrated America.

Chapter 7 details the process of leaving Korea and looks at what happened to veterans once they returned to the home front. In contrast to previous wars, service members returned home individually, rotating out after collecting a set number of points based on length and type of service in country. Some did arrive to parades or welcoming bands, but most experienced a quieter homecoming. Rather than celebrating the end of the war as in 1945,

Americans seemed anxious to simply put Korea behind them as soon as possible. Congress passed a Korean GI Bill in 1952, but it was less generous than that of World War II in its readjustment benefits, further acknowledgment of the country's tempered gratitude. So rewarded for doing their duty, many Korean War veterans, unlike their World War II predecessors, tried to forget their service and pick up their lives just where they had left off. Unfortunately, due to mental or physical injuries sustained in Korea, many found it impossible to return to normal life, suffering in silence for decades. Only after veterans of the Vietnam War began laying claim to expanded Veterans Administration benefits did Korean War veterans begin to seek and find available assistance in dealing with their own posttraumatic stress disorder (PTSD) and other war-related issues.

Pulling the narrative together, chapter 8 looks at Korean War veterans in recent years. Creating organizations such as the Chosin Few and the Korean War Veterans Association, these once "forgotten soldiers" rekindled their veteran identity and began to seek wider recognition for their service. Specifically, Korean War veterans successfully lobbied for a national memorial and for Veterans Administration medical benefits. Once labeled the "silent generation," those who served their country in the Korean War era have come full circle, from ignoring their status as veterans to embracing it.

To some, the Korean War must seem long ago and perhaps irrelevant to the modern world. Given the current wars in Iraq and Afghanistan and the cyclical return of veterans to American society, however, the endeavor to identify both the impact of war on participants and the impact of veterans on American culture remains a worthy one. More than sixty years since their war began, it is time to recognize the veterans of Korea, to move them out from under the shadow cast by the Second World War's "Greatest Generation" and into the light of the national consciousness. Relying upon such diverse sources as statistical data from the Bradley Commission Report, Korean War Veteran Surveys, personal memoirs, oral histories, archival records, public opinion polls, Project Clear reports, contemporary newspaper and magazine articles, and studies on the draft, this work seeks to give a voice to those who served in the Korean War and to carve for them a place in the larger context of American history.

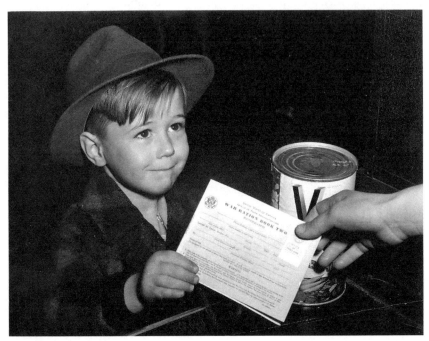

Americans who served in the Korean War grew up during the Great Depression and World War II. Like this schoolboy learning to use a ration book in 1943, they absorbed lessons of sacrifice and patriotism. Courtesy of the National Archives (photograph no. 535567).

1

Timing Is Everything

William Dannenmaier missed serving in World War II by just a year because of his age, but he did not fret over skipping such an important generational experience. Registering for the draft, Dannenmaier never expected to go anywhere, except maybe to graduate school. He reflected to himself on his luck, that the war was over and despite the legal requirement to register for the Selective Service, "young men's lives were no longer forfeit. We could plan our futures—and have them."[1]

Other young Americans shared Dannenmaier's optimism. By the early 1950s, Robert Baken had settled comfortably into the study of electrical engineering at the Illinois Institute of Technology, and Lynn Hahn and Rudolph Stephens had settled into something a bit cozier, both deciding to marry their sweethearts. Nothing in the seemingly placid and prosperous years after 1945 warned of the possibility that graduations, honeymoons, dinner parties, and maybe even a baby or two would not follow in short order.

Striking out in a different direction, Howard Matthias, Bill Anderson, Virginia Jennings Watson, and Betty Jo Alexander all enlisted in the military.

For the men, already draft liable, the peacetime armed forces seemed to offer uneventful service, decent pay, and perhaps a nice, dependable retirement at the end. Watson and Alexander probably gave little thought to retirement since every branch of the service mustered married women out quickly, making old maids out of those who built a permanent military career. For Watson, though, military service came naturally. Her father had served as an aviator in World War II and her mother, a naturalized American citizen, had served as a Navy yeoman in Estonia during World War I. Watson's enlistment in the Navy thrilled her father. Alexander's father reacted differently. Serving in World War II, he had come to think of military nurses as prostitutes and definitely did not want Betty Jo to enlist in the Navy, of all things! The alternative of staying in Altus, Oklahoma, and picking cotton, though, had little appeal, and Alexander did not let the weeds grow under her feet before marching down to the recruiter's office. While not subject to the draft like their male counterparts, Watson and Alexander found the promise of military service too alluring to resist.[2] After all, with the war over, both men and women could look forward to enjoying all the adventure of military service without all the wartime risks.

Across the country, the story was the same. In America's big cities and small towns, in the mountains, on the plains, and along the coasts, the young men and women who belonged to the generation after the "Greatest Generation" busily plotted the courses of their futures. But, somewhere in between all the dreams, engagements, weddings, births, college pins, careers, and carefully constructed plans, timing intervened. On June 25, 1950, North Korean forces invaded South Korea. To nearly everyone's surprise, President Harry Truman determined to resist this further expansion of communism and wasted no time in committing American servicemen to a limited war in Korea. As a result, many of those young men and some of the young women who had escaped the perils of service in World War II, along with many who had served, received a new "invitation" from Uncle Sam to come and fight (or nurse those fighting) in Korea. As Dannenmaier observed, "Now it was my turn."[3]

Despite whatever arrangements had been made for the future, the Korean War and the draft reconfigured the life blueprints of many Americans. Dannenmaier, Baken, Hahn, Stephens, Matthias, and Anderson all ended up in Korea rather than building lives back home. Dannenmaier enlisted in order to avoid the draft, replacing graduate school with basic training. Baken received his draft notice while on summer break in 1951 and left school for the military in September after the draft board denied his request for a college deferment. Stephens, believing that nothing could come of a romantic relationship interrupted by a long wartime separation, broke off his engagement, noting years later that he never got over his fiancée. Hahn and Matthias married their girlfriends, spending the last few months before shipping out as married men. On the eve of his departure, Matthias learned that his new wife was pregnant. The recipient of a Purple Heart wound, Matthias made it home in time to welcome the new arrival. Anderson, who intended to enlist in the Air Force, instead experienced Korea as a grunt in ground combat. Virginia Jennings Watson and Betty Jo Alexander received orders to report overseas as Navy nurses.[4] Like these, nearly two million other young Americans put their plans on hold or abandoned them entirely, shipping out to Korea, Japan, or hospital ships stationed in the Far East.

Born during the Great Depression and sandwiched between the "good war," World War II, and the "bad war," Vietnam, the men and women who served during the Korean War shared more than just the donning of military-issue olive drab.[5] They were a generation of their own, influenced by a childhood made common by the uncommon events they shared—a deep and nearly universal economic depression and then a war of unprecedented scale followed by what many hoped would be an enduring peace. Little did they know it then, but this historical backdrop served to uniquely prepare them to accept their roles in Harry Truman's war over a small, squalid, maybe even insignificant piece of Asia called Korea.

Though most of the men and women destined to serve in Korea and the Far East Command would have been too young to remember "Black Thursday," October 24, 1929, they undoubtedly recognized the effects of that day on their lives. Throughout the country, banks closed, factories sat idle, farmers threw in their rakes as banks foreclosed on their properties, and average Americans wandered the streets or rode the rails in search of work. For the children born in these years of widespread poverty, there were tangible and sometimes terrible consequences. Poor diet and the inability to afford proper medical care led to malnourishment, diseases like rickets and pellagra, and lifelong health issues. The high rate of unemployment meant that many suffered eviction, hunger, discomfort, and parental absence as fathers or mothers hunted for jobs. Youngsters frequently had to suspend their schooling either to find employment themselves or to help at home or on the farm.

But, the Great Depression served as an effective teacher to these kids, even if most of the lessons were bitter to learn. If they were old enough, boys and girls learned to work hard without complaining or questioning. They plowed fields, hawked newspapers, sold apples, cared for younger siblings, and fed livestock. Like the adults around them, children of the Depression sacrificed and pulled together with their loved ones, their communities, and their country to survive hard times. They also learned a new American lesson, that the government could be their friend. President Franklin Roosevelt's New Deal, begun in 1933, did not pull the United States out of depression, but it did ease the suffering of countless Americans who benefited from its various programs aimed at relief, reform, and recovery. Children who had known only empty bellies and hardscrabble existences could see the difference that government assistance made, and they learned to trust and love their Uncle Sam.[6] For many it would be difficult to shake the image of a benevolent president wisely acting in the best interests of the country—even when shivering through icy Korean winters and ducking showers of Chinese artillery.

As babies and young children of the Great Depression, most of the Korean War generation sat on the sidelines during World War II, too young to be drafted or even to enlist. But, the Second World War nonetheless proved a milestone in their lives. Ten- and eleven-year-old kids when the Japanese bombed Pearl Harbor, they saw Americans join together to back the war effort, even if that meant making grave sacrifices. Sixteen million American men stepped into military uniforms ready to do their duty and lay down their lives in defense of the country and the values for which it stood. Those on the home front did their part, too. Whole towns turned out to say goodbye to their native sons being shipped off to war. Ordinary Americans, even young ones, grew Victory Gardens, saved scrap metal and paper, bought war stamps and war bonds, harvested milkweed pod for parachute making, and patriotically rallied behind their government.[7] In schools, club periods became "victory periods" and junior ROTC units picked up metal and other materials and loaded them onto trains bound for national collection points. Many students quit school altogether in order to enlist or go to work in defense plants.[8] With fathers and older siblings gone in service of one type or another, younger children took on adult responsibilities at home and within the community.[9] When asked to conserve, Americans accepted severe rationing of gasoline, meat, butter, sugar, and flour, and they continued to support the war. For hundreds of thousands of kids, the message must have been clear; in a time of war American citizens rally together, sharing the sacrifices and keeping the trust with those whom they have called to serve.

In addition to burdens, World War II provided a great amount of excitement for those growing up. Jack Orth remembers sitting around the dinner table when his family heard the news of Pearl Harbor. "Everyone was in a state of shock. Can you imagine how exciting this was to a ten-year-old kid?"[10] And if the real war proved insufficient to keep the attention of youths, the "reel" World War II often did the trick. Saturday matinees routinely featured John Wayne or Robert Mitchum in motion pictures guaranteed to titillate audiences with true or manufactured wartime heroics. Even after the war ended, Hollywood deluged young moviegoers with films glorifying the men who fought at the Battle of the Bulge or Wake Island. For many, Sergeant Stryker, the cool-under-pressure, bona-fide hard-ass marine in *The Sands of Iwo Jima* (1949), served a far greater purpose than simple entertainment. He and other characters like him became influential role models for the generation of men who had missed out on World War II. As one Korean War veteran put it, "I had been exposed to everything about warfare by Hollywood. These visions filled my head when I joined up for the Korean War. My intentions were to kill a few North Koreans or Chinese, maybe get a small wound and be taken care of by a June Allyson or Doris Day type nurse. Then I would return home to a hero's welcome and have nice things said of me for the rest of my life."[11] Others felt the same way, and when the Korean War rolled around, they determined to pay their debt to America and become heroes in their own right, heroes worthy of depiction on the silver screen.

If exposure to World War II influenced the young men of the Korean generation to enlist, it sometimes had a different effect on young women. The movies occasionally depicted nurses, WAVEs, or WACs as American heroines, but many returning fathers, brothers, and sweethearts sang a different tune about female military service. Rather than touting feminine heroics and the glamor of wartime nursing, protective fathers stressed the uncertainty of military life. Brothers offered favorable appraisals in general of "women in uniform EXCEPT that they do not think it is good for their sisters."[12] Boyfriends frequently went further, associating women in service with immorality and poor reputation. All in all, "they would say bad things about the women in the service."[13] No wonder, then, that by the Korean War, female recruiters faced a difficult task, to convince women to join the military despite negative feedback from family or friends. Still, women were not immune to the patriotism engendered by the Second World War, and the Korean War claimed its share of servicewomen who, like Margie Jacob, claimed "patriotic response" as an important reason for their enlistment.[14]

With the surrender of the Germans and then the Japanese, American patriotism soared to new heights, as did American gratitude toward those who had fought. Noisy parades, ticker tape, and a flurry of speeches and parties greeted returning GIs. Organizations like the American Veterans of World War II (AMVETS) sprouted to represent and pay homage to the new veterans. Unlike their counterparts from earlier wars, World War II veterans also received very generous support from the federal government. The Servicemen's Readjustment Act of 1944, or the GI Bill of Rights, allotted federal money to help veterans buy homes and businesses or go to school.

Within a few years, some eight million veterans had spent $14 billion taking advantage of these educational benefits. So many ex-GIs entered college, in fact, that many universities had to set up Quonset huts on campus to house them. Men and women entering college directly from high school could not help but be impressed with the older veterans in their midst. In his memoir, Charles Cole notes, "[We] were continually reminded both of sacrifice and patriotism. We seemed a humble minority in the flood of returning ex-G.I.s who shared our classes."[15] From the perspective of the generation just a few years younger, veterans had become a special group in society, revered, honored, and remunerated.

World War II caused some peculiar fallout for the Korean War generation. When it ended, it left America at peace, but it also left in place the Selective Service System of 1940. Though President Truman was dismantling the military at an alarming rate, males ages 21-36 still had to register for the draft and were liable for one year of active duty and ten years in the reserves.[16] After an aborted attempt to replace the Selective Service Act with a Universal Military Training bill, Congress passed the Selective Service Act of 1948, which lowered the ages of eligibility for registration to 18-26, set the age of induction at 19-26, and increased the tour of duty to twenty-one months.[17] Boys maturing during and after World War II found the draft an ever-present force in their lives.

The changed landscape of the world in the postwar years, however, made military service both less likely and more tolerable. The atomic bomb would eventually scare Americans right out of their homes and into underground shelters, but in 1945 the country's sole guardianship of atomic weaponry provided a certain "atomic security."[18] Russia loomed threateningly on the horizon, but it would not take American ground troops to quell any difficulties—nuclear weapons would do the trick. Especially after the Soviet Union exploded its own atomic bomb in 1949, few Americans suspected that American boys ever would be called to fight in another war with traditional weapons and tactics. Evidently, Harry Truman did not think so either. By March 1949, the organized reserves had been pared down to 746,000, and by the end of the year all branches of the military halted enlistments. The regular Army had a strength of only 591,000 by mid-1950, strange in light of Russia's recent explosion of an atomic bomb, Mao's seizure of mainland China for communism, Europe's dependence on the Marshall Plan to shore it up against further decline and the potential siren song of communism, and the fact that containment made military assistance to Greece and Turkey necessary.[19] Stranger still, young Americans continued to believe throughout these unsettling and turbulent events that they would never be required to perform the same kind of wartime service as veterans of World War II. They mistakenly assumed that any war would be a worldwide affair, fought with nuclear weapons rather than conventional armies.[20]

Unfortunately, the Korean generation soon discovered that the atomic security they believed in was no security at all. Despite organized demands by citizens in Shawnee, Oklahoma and elsewhere that the government drop atomic bombs on Korea and use nuclear weapons on the battlefield, this war would be fought like thousands of wars before—by soldiers mucking around on the ground with guns.[21] On the bright side, probably no generation of American youth before or since was better prepared to deal with such a reversal of fortune than that which grew up to fight in Korea. Despite ethnic, racial, religious, political, and regional differences, they all listened to the same baseball games at night on the radio, wore the same clothes, shopped at the local A&P, ate macaroni and cheese for dinner, and, most importantly, internalized from their childhood experiences the lessons of hard work, obedience, and duty to country.[22] Consequently, when the country called them to serve in June 1950 and in the months and years after, those selected from among their Korean War cohorts heeded the call. No strong, organized draft protest ever developed during the Korean War as it had in earlier conflicts and as resurfaced with Vietnam, and very few men attempted to dodge the draft. Out of the roughly two million men involuntarily inducted from 1950 to 1953, only 20,080 faced prosecution for violating the draft, and of those only 9,890 were convicted.[23] Like Jimmie Clark they understood, "It's your privilege to disagree, but not disobey" and so "off we went to unknown places to serve our country as our leaders suggested."[24]

Still, not all soldiers marched willingly or happily to the Korean War, and it is remarkable that so few resisted the draft or protested the war itself. Given that they were separated by only a little over a decade from the Vietnam War generation, why did Korean soldiers not burn their draft cards and line the street in front of the White House demanding an end to the conflict? The answer lies in part in timing. The late 1940s and early 1950s were years of conformity. The second Red Scare made Americans look carefully at anyone who stepped outside the political or social bounds, and the consequences for such deviance could be devastating not only to individuals but to their families. The government investigated homosexuals as security risks, accused peace advocates of being communists, and revoked the passports of outspoken critics of segregation. World War II might have stirred up some resentment against the status quo and restlessness on the part of African Americans, Hispanics, women, and others, but such disillusionment would not blossom into full-blown rights revolutions until the 1960s. For the time being, consensus about American life in general remained virtually unshaken. When men grew up, they became the man in the gray flannel suit, married June Cleaver, and raised a family.[25] And, when asked to fight on behalf of American conformity to the doctrine of containment, they marched to war.

Unknown to them at the time, these children of the Great Depression and Second World War would be the last of their kind, a generation characterized by unquestioning obedience and trust. Their war, the war for conformity, would turn out to be one of a series of pivotal events spinning Americans in a thousand directions and creating more questions than answers. The Cold War would harden and become ever more frightening, pushing Americans toward less consensual and more precarious conformity at home. Communism would be exposed as fractured and splintered rather than monolithic, leading many to question the necessity of fighting it at all. Joseph McCarthy would reveal himself as a Red-baiting, demagogic bully in the Army-McCarthy hearings, sickening those who watched it on television. Segregation would end and the national civil rights movement would gear up, dividing the country on questions of race. Women, Native Americans, and Mexicans would challenge the status quo, redrawing societal expectations. Government leaders would prove untrustworthy, paving the way for future generations to question authority. Worldly and jaded GIs taking advantage of the World War II and Korean GI Bills would transform education, generating new lessons that bred less optimistic, more critical students. And Korea would become a reference point for those summoned to fight in Vietnam, leaving many young men and women unable to find a successful patriotic answer to whether or not the new war was worth it. Twenty years after the Korean War, the country was the same but the people had changed—they were still all Americans, but the old homogeny and agreement born of the Great Depression, World War II, and the early Cold War had vanished.

The men who fought in Korea and the women who served in theater were no braver than the soldiers or marines at Khe Sanh, Grenada, Panama, Mogadishu, Iraq, or Afghanistan. In the history of American veterans, they can claim no monopoly on that active love of country labeled patriotism. But, a different America had produced them, and more than the draftees of Vietnam or the all-volunteer force of recent years, they carried into battle and overseas duty the certainty that where they led the country would follow. In 1950 or 1951, they were too young to remember other American wars fought for lesser motives with less enthusiasm on the part of citizens than World War II. Perhaps naively, they imagined that they were marching to the beat of the same drums that had carried their fathers, brothers, and older sisters to France or Germany in the Second or even the First Great War. They could not yet hear that the tune was changing and that those values embedded in them during a childhood of economic trouble and war were becoming, if not outdated, at least less universal. When they returned, Korean War soldiers and servicewomen discovered that the country they thought they were leading had outpaced them and moved on, and they felt forgotten. Timing, it seemed, had not worked in favor of those Americans called to serve in Korea.

Captain James A. Vittitoe, a World War II veteran, goes through his second swearing-in ceremony in 1951 as his wife Janet looks on. Courtesy of Janet and Craig Vittitoe.

2

Mustering In

"You'll be soooorry!" The taunt from those who knew, who had already been there, usually came just a little too late—after raw recruits or inductees had already signed away a year or more of their lives to the military.[1] By then, many of those being warned already felt sorry. Entering the U.S. armed forces during the Korean War era, as in other periods, often amounted to nothing short of humiliation and hassle. For enlistees, the process began with a trip to the nearest recruitment office, frequently located in the local post office. Rural or small-town residents might have had to travel to a larger community, but that presented little hardship, unless of course one were black. In that case, special arrangements would have had to be made for travel, food, and lodging since segregation throughout much of the country, especially in the South, limited one's options.

Once at the recruitment center, the potential enlistee gave background information—age, race, educational level, marital status, number and ages of dependents, criminal record—to "fast-typing sergeants" who created a file for the applicant.[2] Prior to the outbreak of hostilities in Korea, one also had to supply three letters of recommendation written on one's behalf.[3] If everything looked good—age between eighteen and twenty-six for males (or seventeen with a parent's signature) and twenty-one to thirty-five for females (or eighteen, with a parent's consent), apparent good health, no evidence of an immoral character such as would warrant an administrative disqualification, and, in the case of women, being single with no dependents under age eighteen—the candidate moved to the next level, the mental qualification exam.[4] All took the Armed Forces Qualification Test (AFQT) or similar exams at the recruitment center or examining station. A hybrid aptitude-intelligence test consisting of one hundred questions covering vocabulary, math, spatial relations, and mechanical ability, the AFQT determined the fitness for service of the inductee or enlistee and indicated where a passing candidate best fit in the military machinery, what military occupational specialty (MOS) or job best suited them.[5] With less access to quality classroom education, minorities such as African Americans scored lower on the AFQT and had much higher rejection rates than whites.[6] A low score, however, though perhaps embarrassing, did not necessarily mean rejection. High school graduates "were automatically declared acceptable even if they failed to achieve the required score on the test."[7] And, before disqualification, low-scoring registrants with less than a high school degree met with personnel psychologists who conducted personal interviews to establish whether or not they had the mental ability to serve.[8] Also, as manpower needs went up, the minimum acceptable score on the mental exams went down.[9] In September 1949, one needed to score at least 49 percent to qualify for service, but by July 1951, one needed only 10 percent.[10]

Those found mentally acceptable had only one more obstacle to overcome before being sworn into their chosen branch of the military, the often dreaded physical exam. While female veterans rarely mention the physical in their writings and interviews, male veterans frequently describe it as "a very dehumanizing experience." Male inductees lined up naked or in their skivvies as military medical staff examined them one by one, checking, among other things, private parts for signs of disease, rectums for hemorrhoids, and feet for flatness. All that remained for physically fit recruits and inductees was to take their oaths and then catch a train or bus to basic training. For their troubles, these new marines, soldiers, airmen, and sailors received, after reaching their destinations and waiting in yet another line, their new military-issue clothing. Even many of those who had not wanted to join the service to begin with could not help but admire and be proud of their wonderful new uniforms. At the end of all the lines and red tape and after much anticipation or dread, entrants finally came to be officially mustered into the United States armed forces.[11]

This scenario played out millions of times during the Korean War as young men and women entered or reentered the armed forces of the United States in order to fill out the ranks. After World War II ended, President Harry S. Truman and his military planners focused on preparing for worldwide atomic war.[12] In the new era of superpowers, no one expected conventional weapons or troops to play much of a role. As a result, the various branches of the U.S. military had been pared down by 1950 to the point where the government itself conceded that more money would have to be spent rebuilding the armed forces if the country wanted to present a credible posture against communist aggression.[13] With the outbreak of war in Korea in late June 1950 and Truman's determination to use American troops to "police" the fray, the need for a bigger military became even more acute. Initially, General Douglas MacArthur pulled troops on duty in Japan for the Korean operation, but quickly realized that these would not suffice. Not only were the garrison forces there unprepared for combat after months or even years of easy duty, they were understrength as well.[14] Before long, American soldiers in Korea found themselves cornered in the Pusan Perimeter. Replacements and more units would be needed immediately. The Army, Navy, Air Force, and Marine Corps, only recently turning away enlistees, suddenly needed to fill uniforms and fast.

All branches of the service stepped up their attempts to attract voluntary recruits and to keep the servicemen they had on hand by offering enticements for reenlistment or by extending involuntarily enlistments that were due to expire. For its part, the Army made especially good use of the Selective Service System, the draft, to satisfy its manpower needs. But, new recruits, voluntary or otherwise, took time to train, time that MacArthur insisted U.S. troops in Korea did not have. By July 9, 1950, Congress authorized the recall of reserve forces to active duty.[15] Typically, these would have been used to train new recruits, but with the situation in Korea quickly deteriorating, many found themselves promptly headed for the combat zone. The combination seemed a winning one. MacArthur's daring mid-September Inchon landing secured South Korea, and by early October American troops were pressing into North Korea. The military's manpower needs should have fallen to near prewar levels, but, as luck would have it, a new and unexpected enemy entered the fight.[16] Chinese "volunteers" crossed the Yalu River on October 16, 1950, and by November 26 the Chinese had trapped and destroyed much of the United Nations force in North Korea, including about twenty thousand Koreans and Americans at Chosin Reservoir. The boys would not be home by Christmas. Instead, many more would be needed for what was metamorphosing into a much longer conflict than anticipated. The whole process of filling the ranks took on new life, and another generation of young Americans found it their turn to heed the nation's call to arms. Through enlistments, reserve recalls, National Guard call-ups, and the draft, over six million men and women mustered into the U.S. military during the Korean War period.[17]

The Volunteers

The Korean War rekindled a dying Selective Service System that in fiscal years 1948 and 1950 had not drafted anyone. But, even after the United States entered the Korean War, inductees rarely comprised more than 38 percent of those entering Uncle Sam's military.[18] Volunteers, guardsmen, and reservists accounted for the majority of those who served. When the war began in June 1950, career service members and leftover World War II volunteers or recruits from the interwar period made up the backbone of the armed forces. For these, the various branches simply extended expiring enlistments involuntarily.[19] But, in the three years that followed, a million and a half new enlistees joined the old salts. Why did these choose to enter voluntarily into wartime military service? Why had the older volunteers enlisted in the first place?

For males, the draft provided the most obvious reason to enlist. Under the Selective Service Act of 1948, men aged eighteen to twenty-six had to register for the draft, and those nineteen to twenty-six were eligible for a 21-month tour of duty.[20] Even noncitizens were vulnerable under the 1948 law unless they were willing to sacrifice the possibility of future naturalization.[21] In the pre-Korea years, the likelihood of being drafted remained low and few men received notices for induction. But, if one were drafted, the chances of entering the Army were high since only the Army and Marine Corps admitted draftees. The Air Force and Navy relied on all-volunteer forces. After Truman began committing troops to Korea in June 1950, draft calls skyrocketed and many more youths could expect their names to be chosen. Like Glen Schroeder, many young men enlisted in order to have a choice about which branch they entered. Glen joined the Navy to "avoid being a grunt. . . . I didn't want to crawl around in the mud, but go to sea instead."[22] Similarly, James Brady "rather liked the idea of being an officer, and the Marines had an undeniable cachet."[23] Many, like Huston Wheelock, "wanted to get it over with and serve my time."[24] Others, like Donald Bohlmann, chose to enlist in National Guard units even if they were due to be activated because they wanted to "be amongst people I knew."[25]

Many men volunteered for the National Guard, Navy, or Air Force in an attempt to either beat the draft or escape the war. Classified I-A (available for service), Frank Rowan discovered through a friend that he could fulfill his military obligations by joining the California National Guard, serving seven years and becoming exempt from the draft. It did not work out as he planned, though. Lured by extra "rations and quarters" pay and the privilege of wearing the uniform to work, Rowan went on duty as an "Active Duty National Guardsman," then got conscripted into the regular Army and shipped to Korea in the early months of the war.[26] Bob Carpenter, owner of the Philadelphia Phillies, encouraged two of his players, Charlie Bicknell and Curt Simmons, to avoid conscription by joining the Guard in 1949. A year later, their division, the 28th Infantry Division, got orders to activate and prepare for combat. Bicknell got sold to the Braves and sent down to the minors on waivers, only to play his last game on September 6, 1950, the same day he left for basic training.[27] Franklin Manzar, who "joined the Air Force with the intention of not going to Korea," ended up in the war zone anyway.[28] These cases were not unusual, and many men who joined the National Guard or the Reserves found these did not offer a safe haven from service in Korea. Nevertheless, draft pressure almost doubled the number of male enlistments per month.[29]

While the draft provided a potent inducement to enlistment, men and women volunteered during the Korean War era for other reasons as well. Leftover patriotism from the Second World War along with a sense of nostalgia or duty compelled many to answer the call to colors. Fred Smith remembers that after World War II, "patriotism . . . was an important part of our lives . . . and we felt we needed to do something for our country."[30] Arthur Smith agreed, "because all the guys went through World War II to do their thing to save this country, and I thought that's what we were doing."[31] Warren Grossman wanted to offer "service to my country in time of need."[32] Clyde Queen "felt a compelling obligation to serve my country . . . and to me that was the most important thing in my life."[33] Even women, who often entered service for what might be deemed "practical" reasons, remark that volunteering "had a kind of patriotic sense about it in doing something for my country."[34] For the same reason, Native Americans also rallied to the flag. In September 1950, Dr. Frank E. Becker, national secretary of the Indian Association of America, offered the government a plan to organize Native American military reserve units specializing in communications in order to channel the energy of six thousand military-age men on reservations for service to the country.[35] Gilbert Towner heard that Indians, as wards of the government, could be exempted from wartime service, but thought it a "high honor to fight, anytime, anywhere, to protect the country we love."[36]

Those too young to have participated fully in World War II enlisted in the interwar and Korean War eras because they could not shake the feeling that they had missed something significant. During high school, John Nolan's classmates disappeared as volunteers or inductees, leaving him with "this hang-up feeling that it was an experience that I wanted to share."[37] Anthony Herbert, determined not to miss out, tried to enlist for World War II service at age fourteen, but his high school principal ratted him out as underage. Three years later, he hurried to enlist again because he knew "that there would be another war, and I would be in it."[38] Arden Grover signed up because he was "not going to sit on the sidelines" if another war broke out. Jack Orth, who had felt cheated when World War II ended, thought himself lucky when Korea came along because, "Now I could go to war." He later reflected that "I must have been nuts," but at the time memories of what he had missed secured his enlistment.[39]

Financial need also prompted many to muster into military service. John Kamperschroer recalls, "Patriotic? I don't think so. There was a poor future for farm boys."[40] In the same vein, Wadie Moore asserts, "Patriotism never occurred to me. I had one desire. That was to escape degradation and poverty. I mean clapboard, two-room, chicken house kind of poverty."[41] For Gilbert Towner, the reservation had little to offer, and he believed he could "take better care of my mother with a steady pay coming from the Marine Corps."[42] Joe Connors, a Chippewa Indian, George Hopkins, Joseph Morey, and Richard Ballenger all needed work and so volunteered.[43] On an internship at Philadelphia General Hospital, Hank Litvin had work but no pay. When a Navy captain came around offering ensign's pay in return for twenty-four months of service after completing his internship, Hank signed up.[44] Douglas Anderson joined when he ran out of funds for college, and Charles Smith, a Native American, signed up in hopes of getting GI educational benefits.[45] Similarly, Shirley Brantley "was looking for some way to continue my education and get to see something besides Pittsburgh," so she entered the Air Force.[46] Robert Chappell, a black sharecropper, viewed military service as his only ticket to getting any kind of education.[47] For numerous volunteers, service represented something very tangible—several pairs of shoes, nice clothes, a regular paycheck, and the chance for a better life.[48] Service "was a matter of necessity—the patriotism thing came along a couple of years later."[49]

In some instances, military service provided the only viable option for potential enlistees. Unprepared for college and uncertain about his future, Elmer Payne viewed military service as "an escape."[50] Johnson Slivers, a sixteen-year-old Navajo, turned to the Army because he "had nowhere to go."[51]

Melvin Rookstool, Elmer Bailey, and James Murphy had places to go, but
if they wanted to see beyond the bars of juvenile hall or the jailhouse, they
would have to enlist. Sixteen-year-old Rookstool had been "just knocking
around," getting "involved in some problems" when the judge offered him a
choice of either joining the Army or going to reform school. It did not take
Rookstool long to wish he had chosen differently, but by then he had already
enlisted.[52] Bailey, an African American, stood accused of engaging in a relationship with a white woman and his options suddenly narrowed to "getting
strung up by a lynch mob, going to jail, or joining the Army."[53] A judge made
the choice simple for Murphy: "Either join or go to jail."[54] For other law-
breakers, military service offered the easiest way to a second chance. President Truman issued Executive Order 3000 in December 1952 offering a full
pardon to "all persons convicted of violation of any law of the United States"
who served in the armed forces for at least a year and separated from active
service under honorable conditions during the Korean War.[55]

For those maturing during and after World War II, family military tradition frequently pulled them toward the recruiter's door. Like the character
Conway in the *Sands of Iwo Jima*, more than a few shipped in because they
were expected to ship in: "Seems every time there's a war the men in my
family join the Marines. . . . I'm simply here for tradition."[56] For Louis Lyons,
whose ancestors fought in the Revolution and Civil War and whose five
brothers all served in World War II, enlistment on his seventeenth birthday
came naturally.[57] James Boden, who lost an uncle in World War I, a cousin
in World War II, and a friend at Chosin Reservoir in Korea, heard the siren
song of the service as clearly and enlisted at age eighteen. Listening to the
stories of his father, a World War I soldier, and Old Man Caldwell, a slave
turned Union soldier during the Civil War, Charles Bussey "always wanted
to be a soldier." He was "prepared to live for my country, fight for my country, and if necessary, to die for it."[58] With a father who fought as a marine
in World War I even before he had citizenship, Native American Gilbert
Towner asked, "How could I be any different?"[59]

Many of the women who enlisted also had some sort of family military
heritage. The Marine Corps was a tradition for Mary Ann Bernard, whose
father and sister had both served in the Corps.[60] Jane Heins Escher's father
had been in the Navy, and she followed in his footsteps by becoming a
WAVE.[61] Valeria Hilgart, who joined the Marine Corps, had a brother and
sister already in the Corps, and her father had served in World War I.[62] The
family histories of both men and women who served in the Korean era, volunteer and draftee alike, reveal that a majority had relatives or loved ones
who served before them.[63] Military tradition might not have been the main

reason for joining the military, but no doubt it accounted in part for the will-ingness of many to seek out enlistments of their own.

Some foreign residents volunteered for service in hopes of expediting the naturalization process. After World War I and World War II, veterans with honorable discharges could be naturalized as U.S. citizens, as outlined in the Immigration and Naturalization Act. Initially, the government made no such provisions for the aliens who donned U.S. uniforms during the Korean War. Although willing to subject foreigners to the draft and to expect them to do "their duty on the battlefields of Korea and on assignments throughout the world," the House and Senate could not agree upon the terms under which to grant citizenship, leaving veterans to ask, "Why shouldn't they be accepted by the nation as citizen-soldiers?"[64] Finally, in June 1953, Congress passed Public Law 597, which entitled foreigners who had completed five or more years of military service to be deemed lawfully admitted to the country for permanent residency if otherwise qualified for citizenship.[65] This law expired of its own terms on December 31, 1955, but new legislation followed to per-manently amend the Immigration and Naturalization Act to favor Korean War veterans.[66]

In the late 1940s and early 1950s, a host of other things enticed youths to visit their local post offices and hitch up for tours of duty. The military, especially in wartime, offered unparalleled adventure for kids who craved a view of something more than their hometowns. Enlisting in the Navy or the Marine Corps seemed a fine way to see the world while performing a service the country would appreciate.[67] Those old enough and interested enough to fear communism thought the war tendered a unique opportunity to "fight it in someone else's country . . . [and] stop the Communists there."[68] Oth-ers, men who previously served, re-upped in order to increase their rank, be with old buddies, or simply fill their time.[69] Some, like Franklin Hodge, were already planning for retirement. He calculated that by rejoining the mili-tary and making a career of it he could retire at thirty-nine with over $150 a month.[70] Captain Helen Brooks reentered the Navy as a nurse because "they desperately needed help in Korea."[71] A few enlisted to avenge the deaths of friends or loved ones or, like Joseph Timanaro, to seek revenge for the North Korean atrocities they had read about in the newspaper.[72] George Pakkala, an American citizen raised in Finland, joined in order to learn English.[73] Many women, if not enlisting in general for the uniform, at least chose their branch of service because the uniforms looked sharp.[74] As many reasons to enlist existed as there were volunteers.

Interestingly, while women volunteered for many of the same reasons as their male cohorts, they more often stressed practical reasons over patriotic ones. Very limited in career choices, especially in occupations that paid well, many females desired a career in the armed forces. As one enlistee later put it, "I decided to join the military because I perceived my only options to be teacher, nurse, secretary, or the nunnery."[75] The passage of the Army-Navy Nurse Act in April 1947 and the Women's Armed Services Integration Act in June 1948 gave women a real incentive to enlist in military service.[76] While not abolishing restrictions on servicewomen, such as the requirement that servicewomen be unmarried without minor dependents, these acts created a permanent place for women in the military organization and guaranteed a pay scale similar if not equal to that of men doing the same kinds of work.[77] And, increasingly, military women could choose what work they did. Before the end of the Korean War, women in the U.S. Air Force achieved entrance into many aviation specialties and women marines broke out of strictly administrative jobs and could gain posting to overseas duty stations, privileges often denied them in the years after World War II.[78] Few other places in American society promised these same benefits. By 1952, the Navy concluded that women enlisted out of a desire to travel or have a career, gain education or self-improvement, receive job training, take advantage of educational benefits, or wean themselves from family dependency. The study failed to mention duty to country as a motivating factor at all. The Army decided that patriotism did matter, but came after the desire for overseas service, self-improvement and education, interesting work, and the opportunity to meet new people and make new friends.[79] As Katherine Towle notes, one did "not join the services primarily for patriotic reasons."[80] In contrast, studies conducted on male inducements for enlistment during the Korean War era placed patriotism at the top of the list, with draft motivation, choice of service, recruitment, and the Korean GI Bill weighing heavily on the decision.[81]

African Americans sometimes found choosing military service more difficult than their white comrades. They possessed the same love of country and personal and financial reasons for wanting to enlist, but they resented the idea of sacrificing again for a country that could not be depended upon to show gratitude. Many remembered that black World War II veterans returned not only to a climate of discrimination and segregation but to outright hostility. In 1946, World War II veteran Isaac Woodard, still in his uniform, had been pulled off a Greyhound bus and beaten and blinded by local law enforcement officials in Batesbury, South Carolina.[82] In the first six weeks of that same year, policemen in Birmingham, Alabama killed five African American veterans.[83] All over the country lynching increased after the war.[84] From the vantage point of some blacks, Korea looked no better. Numerous articles in the black press decried the unfair treatment of black soldiers facing courts-martial at much higher rates than whites and other pieces documented that white troops in Korea were flying the Confederate flag or that the white rapists of the wife of an African American soldier fighting in Korea had been let off easy in North Carolina.[85] No wonder that many began to question black participation in the war and to ask, "Why should Negroes die for second-class citizenship?" or to insist that "[t]he United States should bring its troops home to fight for democracy here in this country!"[86] They did not want to be on the front line in Korea and then return to the back of the bus back home.

Still, African Americans found plenty of reasons to volunteer for or reenter the armed forces in the late 1940s and early 1950s. In 1948, Harry Truman issued Executive Order 9981, which called for equal treatment and opportunity for all service members regardless of race, color, religion, or national origin.[87] The measure did not immediately desegregate the military (that came later, partly due to manpower needs in Korean trenches), but it did represent a sure step up from the Jim Crow South or even the North. Charles Bussey happily left his job as policeman in California, where he had been stationed in the black ghetto despite finishing first in his class at the police academy for a return to active duty in August 1948.[88] Similarly, James Allen, who grew up sharecropping in Florida, decided after a trip to New York that he did not want to go back to Ocala and Jim Crow and so enlisted at age eighteen.[89] Beverly Scott saw the Army as an honorable profession. "There was no better institution in American life . . . than the army for the black man in the forties and fifties. . . . You had more leverage in the army. You always had somebody you could go and complain [to] about bad treatment. A black man couldn't do that in civilian life."[90] Hundreds of others felt the same way and signed on, some for the rest of their careers. African Americans also volunteered because they believed that their service would help to change the racial situation at home. As Gerald Early notes, "They saw there was a connection, that you'd be able to make a stronger argument when you came back: 'We fought for this country, and we deserve to be treated as full citizens.'"[91] During the war, African Americans began to call for "unprecedented consideration." They wanted to do their duty, but in return, they expected "all of the rights guaranteed . . . by the Constitution."[92] After 1950, when racial quotas limiting black enlistments were lifted, blacks, like other Americans, would knock on the recruiter's door.[93]

Lastly, but very importantly, recruitment efforts by the military drew volunteers into the services. The process often started as early as the high school years. Recruiters visited schools, held career days, and served as models for the fancy new uniforms willing candidates might themselves wear one day.

After 1951, high schools throughout the country began to show a series of films produced by Coronet Films. With titles like *When You Enter Service*, *Military Life and You*, and *What It's All About: Your Plans, Service, and Citizenship*, these films ostensibly attempted to "help guide young people facing the difficult task of civilian-to-military adjustment" brought about by the draft.[94] The films cast military service in such a positive light that groups like the National Council Against Conscription urged people to write their congressmen and "tell them what you think of their [Coronet's] program for making America military-minded."[95]

In addition to preparing boys mentally for later enlistment or induction, the military offered programs in the 1940s aimed at enrolling younger men. Both the Navy (V5) and the Army (ASTRP) had programs for seventeen-year-olds that allowed them to enlist but go to school until they turned eighteen.[96] College men could join ROTC, a program designed to produce military officers. For blacks this presented a problem as segregated schools did not always offer ROTC courses and not all ROTC programs accepted African Americans.[97] But other options were available. Charles Bussey joined the Citizens' Military Training Camp (CMTC), another system for developing Army officers that was open to men of color. Before Korea, these recruitment efforts bore enough fruit that not everyone who wanted to enlist could get into the military. High school diploma in hand, Richard Bevier tried the Air Force, but he and a score of others were released after physical exams revealed elevated pulse rates due more to the fact that no billets existed for new enlistees than to anything else. He then offered himself to the Marine Corps, which, also out of quotas to fill, cut him loose for dental reasons. Not quite eighteen, Bevier found himself rejected by two branches of the armed forces.[98]

Once the Korean War broke out, recruiters had billets aplenty and began soliciting male enlistments in earnest. They promised an assortment of benefits—ranging from free lifetime health care for those who served twenty or more years to educational assistance under the 1952 Korean GI Bill—whether or not they had the power or authority to make good on their word.[99] The armed forces also spent loads of cash on advertising and other efforts, so much, in fact, that Secretary of Defense George Marshall and Assistant Secretary Anna Rosenberg felt pressured to defend their budget.[100] Posters appeared in schools and post offices touting the merits of service, and recruiters made the rounds as the armed forces tried to lure young men into service and perhaps to Korea.

Even in the slow years after 1945, the military targeted men for recruitment, but most branches of the service ignored women, having little use for females within their ranks. By June 1950, the WACs numbered only seven thousand, the WAVEs thirty-two hundred, and the Women Marines under six hundred.[101] Suddenly, the new mobilization seemed to demand a far larger female presence in all the services. The Navy wanted female hospital corpsmen to replace men sent overseas.[102] All branches needed women to tend to nursing and administrative tasks so that men in Korea could hope for rotation out, future scientists could continue college training instead of mustering in, and families could remain undisrupted.[103] Enlisting females did not necessarily save men from being drafted, but it could free men up for other things. To these ends, a flurry of recruitment activity ensued. The Navy announced its intention to enlist ten thousand women, and after August 1950 raised its female enlistment quota so that by March recruiters were pressing to enroll 528 women per six-week period.[104] Assistant Secretary of Defense Anna Rosenberg asked Congress to raise the 2 percent ceiling on women in the military and prompted Secretary of Defense George Marshall to form the Defense Advisory Committee on Women in the Services (DACOWITS) to assist with and advise on female recruitment.[105] Posters and even television commercials advertising the services to women appeared, as did a much increased number of female recruiters.[106] By December 1952, the Army, Navy, Air Force, and Marine Corps combined had close to 250 women in forty-four stations exclusively assigned to recruitment.[107] As early as July 1951 these efforts were paying off. The WACs could claim 12,000 women in uniform, the WAVES 6,300, and the Women Marines 2,065. Both encouraged and driven by these numbers, in October 1951 Rosenberg announced the biggest campaign for female recruitment since World War II. President Truman personally launched the appeal to women, and rumors circulated that unmet quotas could result in a draft on women. In October 1952, 48,700 servicewomen reported for duty, but that was still well short of the military's goal of 112,000, and a number of these proved unqualified for service. Scrambling to meet quotas, recruiters sometimes falsified test scores, educational records, and references.[108] In the early months of 1953, the Defense Advisory Committee on Women in the Services launched a new program to recruit quality female citizens, aged 18-35, in excellent physical condition, with a high school or college degree, and of high character. In addition to the usual tactics, potential female enlistees would be treated to slogans like "There's a job for you—and you're needed for it" and "I'm set for life" (with all the job training opportunities offered by the military).[109] Just as it did for men, the increased pressure of recruitment prompted many women to enter one of the services.

During the Korean War, as in other wars, voluntary enlistment for whatever reason did not ensure that new enlistees would remain satisfied with their decision to enter the military. Soon after mustering in, a great many men and women, like Raymond Delcambre, could not help but ask themselves, "What in the world did I get myself into!? And how could I get out?"[110] Travel, which seemed so exotic before, became less glamorous when one was stuffed with two hundred other people on an ancient, unheated train with hard wooden seats headed for a college gym or training barracks.[111] Instead of adventure, many youths found only homesickness and regret as their tours of duty began—regret that sometimes deepened as news and casualty reports filtered in from Korea confirming that this "police action" was in fact nothing less than an old-fashioned war. Also, families did not always support their loved ones' decision to muster in. When Joe DeMarco joined the Marine Corps, his father responded, "In the old country they say you gotta go in the army, you go. But here no one says you gotta go in these Marines. Why you go? You don't like your home, your family, whatsamatter?"[112] Along with the fact that volunteers frequently had less education and scored lower on mental and physical tests, buyer's remorse helps to account for the low retention and increased delinquency rates of enlistees when compared to draftees. Despite claims by Secretary of Defense George Marshall that volunteers had higher morale and served longer than inductees, volunteers throughout the Korean War proved less likely to complete their terms of service than those forced into uniform by the draft.[113] While 95 percent of draftees received honorable discharges, only 62 percent of volunteers did. Still, the majority of enlistees eventually came to terms with their situation, and more than a few grew to feel that "the Army was home" or that "there's something about the Army that I like."[114]

Regardless of long-term satisfaction, motives for enlistment stayed constant throughout the Korean War. Their volume, however, dropped with each year of the war. In fiscal year 1951, 630,000 Americans entered the armed forces by enlisting, but by fiscal year 1953 only 397,000 entrants could claim voluntary accession.[115] No doubt personal reasons weighed heavily on the decision of whether or not to enlist, but so did the home front climate. In the early months of 1950, potential volunteers had no reason to suspect that the Korean War would command any less of the public's attention and patriotic support than did World War II. Aside from a few naysayers who wrote President Truman to complain that American intervention in Korea differed little from the "naked aggression" of Hitler's regime, a handful of folk singers like Woody Guthrie, communists, and Jehovah's Witnesses, most Americans supported military efforts in Korea.[116] An August 1950 Gallup poll showed 65 percent of Americans firmly behind the war effort.[117] Even the Socialist Party's National Action Committee voted unanimously to back the action.[118]

As the war dragged on, however, public interest and support waned. By the first week of January 1951, after Chinese intervention, only 38 percent of Americans still thought that Korea was not a mistake, if they thought of the war at all.[119] The buying frenzy that had characterized 1950, when people still worried that war would directly affect their ability to purchase sugar, shortening, or televisions, had drawn to a close, leaving Americans free to concentrate on things other than the war effort.[120] Headlines concerning strikes, domestic events, and even UFOs, rather than war news, monopolized the front pages of most newspapers. Servicemen and women stationed stateside appeared invisible as Korea's police action status allowed them to wear civilian duds instead of uniforms when off post and not on duty.[121] In October 1951, *U.S. News and World Report* labeled Korea the "forgotten war," not surprising given that in a poll that same month 56 percent of Americans agreed that Korea was an "utterly useless war."[122]

But, Korea was not totally forgotten. Few people bothered to protest the Korean War vocally, but antiwar demonstrations did take place, if only on a small scale. On June 25, 1951, the first anniversary of the Korean War, a half-dozen or so Catholic Workers joined David Dellinger of the War Resisters League and Bayard Rustin of the Fellowship of Reconciliation in Times Square to call for peace. Despite some public confusion—in this case an angry spectator mistaking the pacifist Catholic Workers for communist Daily Workers and punching Dellinger in the face—activists planned and executed protests throughout the war.[123] Also, folk artists churned out antiwar songs for the duration of the conflict. In "I Just Wanna Stay Home," Irwin Silber opined that he didn't "wanna die for the stock exchange." Boots Casetta's "Little Bronze Medal" tried to stir pacifism by lyrically dramatizing a mother's plea to save her son after she had already lost a husband and son to war.[124] This negativism took its toll on the American public and by extension on enlistments. Support for the war bobbled up and down from 35 percent to 37 percent through 1952 and 1953, finally settling at about 50 percent in January 1953, but potential recruits seldom could have imagined that the same patriotic impulse existed for this war that had materialized during World War II.

Throughout the Korean War era, men and women did not necessarily flock to enlist as had their cousins and brothers of the Second World War. And, in general, however much they liked to believe that they were answering the same glorious call, they marched to the recruiters' offices without the same single-minded purpose as their recent forebears. For the men and women who volunteered for Korean service, there was no Pearl Harbor, no Nazi regime, and no sacrifice universal enough to be endured by all Americans whether at home or abroad. Instead, there were a variety of personal needs, a pressing draft, and the country's call to colors. Raised to be people of grit and sacrifice, the boys and girls of the Great Depression and World War II volunteered to do their duty, perhaps not happily, but with determination and in greater numbers than their sons and daughters when the next war started.

The Reservists and National Guardsmen

June 1950 turned out to be a bad month for National Guardsmen and reservists. Budget crunches early in the month led to a series of early discharges among active personnel, who then had to find other means of employment and income. While perhaps disappointed, few protested the decision. Most reservists, while joining up for the same reasons as regular military enlistees, expected to be used only in case of emergency and took their move to inactive status in stride. But the month was not over yet. Sitting in front of his girlfriend's house on his way to another town and a new apprenticeship with Monterey Optical Company, former active guardsman Frank Rowan heard news of North Korea's invasion of South Korea on the radio. "Oh shit," he said. "In a month I will be in the Army."[125] It took a little while for the news to really sink in, but all over the country guardsmen and reservists had the same startled reaction. The impossible had happened—peace had been shattered and Americans were about to march to war again.

Within days of the United States entering the fighting, Congress granted President Truman the authority to call units or individuals of the National Guard and Reserves to active duty for up to twenty-one months.[126] The military first sought volunteers from among the reserve components, but when few appeared, involuntary reserve call-ups proceeded, and in August 1950, six hundred reserve units shifted to active duty.[127] For the first time in history, women reservists, especially those in critical ratings such as hospital corpsmen and supply clerks, were involuntarily mobilized along with the men.[128] National Guard units also felt the pull, and from August 1950 to February 1952, some nineteen increments of them would be taken, totaling 138,597 guardsmen.[129] Under normal circumstances, all of the reserve troops would have trained raw recruits and inductees, but low manpower levels in Korea demanded replacements double quick time and many of the recalled guardsmen and reservists shipped out for the war zone soon after activation.[130] As a result, despite the opposition that developed to calling up National Guard and reserve units, even more had to be called to active duty. When the Korean War ended, between seven hundred thousand and one million reservists and guardsmen could claim service through recall or activation.[131]

A handful of reserve personnel accepted their orders or even welcomed the chance to go on active duty when called. Hank Buelow, who had enlisted in the National Guard at age fifteen, rejoiced when his unit got activated during Christmastime 1950. Though a full-time student at Colorado A&M, Hank wanted to muster into active service.[132] For the inactive Reserves, the perks of being involuntarily recalled often softened the blow of activation. Unlike reservists who volunteered for active duty, those forced back into uniform against their wishes retained their termination promotion rank, giving them an advantage over everyone else and prompting complaints by jealous regulars and draftees.[133] For Martin Markley and others it seemed a sign that they should not only willingly fall in for service but should make a career out of the Army or Marine Corps, where no better avenue to advancement existed than combat.[134]

Many guardsmen and reservists, though, complained bitterly about their recall to colors and refused to come quietly. One unhappy California guardsman waiting for his ship to the Far East told a newsman, "I thought I was signing up to fight Oregon! I didn't know Governor Knight was mad at Mao Tse Tung!"[135] Others pointed out the inequity of calling older reservists who had jobs and families while younger men without children could apply for deferments and exemptions.[136] Writing from Korea, a group of reservists asked, "Why should John Doe be exempted from the draft because he has a wife, when 36-year-old Reservist Richard Doe, veteran of World War II, who has a wife and two children, is now fighting in Korea?" Similarly, Carl Vinson, chairman of the House Armed Services Committee, wondered, "Why should you have one rule that fits the (inactive) reservist, and another rule that fits the inductee?"[137] And, many of those being tapped for duty had already given a chunk of their lives to Uncle Sam.[138] Wallace Donaldson, drafted during World War II, had just finished school and finally reached the position where he could make money when he received his Korean War recall notice.[139] Thomas McLain fulfilled his obligation to the Army and became a civilian again on June 25, 1950, just three months before being pulled back into olive drab and put on duty at Camp Breckinridge, Kentucky.[140] Scott Defebaugh, a World War II hospital corpsman who had worked several jobs and used the GI Bill to train to be a teacher, got activated the very day he was supposed to begin teaching ninth grade in Woodward, Oklahoma.[141] Disgusted with their plights, retreads and other individuals called up for the Korean emergency wrote their senators and congressmen, as well as President Truman. The backlash prompted Major General Lewis B. Hershey, the Selective Service director, to declare, "Everyone wants out; no one wants in."[142] For its part, the Army pointed out that those being summoned to service had drawn the pay as guardsmen or reservists. Washington officials failed to note, however, that many of those being called to duty served only in the inactive Reserves and thus had received no monetary compensation at all. Fearing a broader conflict with Russia or even total war, the military decided to save its better trained, paid active reservists for later.[143] Ultimately, the military could argue only that reservists and guardsmen had entered their contracts voluntarily and concede that in calling up the Reserves, "military necessity overrode considerations of equity and justice."[144]

For scores of guardsmen and reservists, recall to service caused more than a minor inconvenience. The initial uncertainty of just who might be called up caused employers to refuse jobs to reserve personnel, and to deny promotions to or even fire those already employed. Such discrimination persisted despite the pleas of Marine Brigadier General Melvin J. Mass and others to employers to "put a premium on their [reserve officers'] employment as a step toward making the nation strong enough to avert future wars."[145] Banks and insurance companies turned down loan and policy applications, and the offended party had no legal recourse.[146] For veterans, the July 1951 expiration date of the World War II Servicemen's Readjustment Act of 1944 could not be put on hold, and more than a few worried that another stint in service would deny them their benefits.[147] Once orders came, men and women had to report regardless of their personal or financial situations and before any effort toward exemption would be entertained by the military. Regrettably, records of inactive reservists had not been updated in years, in some cases since World War II, and men with ten children and nurses with babies and toddlers of their own became at least temporarily caught in the country's manpower net.[148]

Countless others had their whole lives disrupted by the new call to arms. John Saddic, a World War II Purple Heart recipient and Marine Corps reservist, had a wife and family to support but found himself forced to reenter the Marine Corps at too low a rank to be granted a family allowance.[149] Welfare told him to sell his furniture, the Red Cross advised him to go on welfare, and only after he went to the newspaper with his story did he garner any assistance at all. When he returned home from Korea with frozen feet, the Red Cross hounded him to repay the "loan" he had received![150] Harry VanZandt, another World War II veteran, got his notice to report while lying in bed with pneumonia. He managed to get a deferment due to illness, but in the end it did not save him from leaving his wife and son and heading out for another overseas tour of war.[151] A Texas Reserve sergeant who had worked to set up a prosperous plumbing business in the years after the Second World War worried that his absence would result in the repossession of all his tools by the bank, leaving him without much to return to. Professional men fretted over lost promotions and opportunities, doctors wondered if after service they would be too old to pick back up again and build a private practice, and recent graduates felt uneasy about waiting years to apply their education to real-life work.[152] Fathers, husbands, and World War II veterans, both male and female, felt punished for their loyalty to country and cheated that so many Americans were escaping military service altogether while they were plucked from their civilian lives, many for the second time. Defense Secretary George Marshall agreed, but at least for a while reservists and guardsmen continued to muster in for the Korean War.[153]

Mustering in for a second time proved easy enough for most guardsmen and reservists, but the actual process varied from place to place and unit to unit. For all, it began with notification. Usually guardsmen and reservists received an official letter with orders to report, but military police visited a lucky few to break the news, and some guardsmen got word in person while at summer camp. Not surprisingly, guardsmen, who held weekly meetings, trained on weekends, and attended summer camps, were better prepared for the news than inactive reservists who never participated in drills and many of whom did not even belong to a particular unit. After receiving notice, reserve personnel had to report without much delay. Harold Mulhausen, a Marine Corps reservist, remembers that he was allowed about a week to quit his job and make arrangements for his family before checking in at the Reserve Center for transportation to Camp Pendleton, California.[154] George Tsegeletos got activated into the Marine Corps while at his first summer camp, and his unit was ordered home only briefly to "get your things in order" before returning to Camp Pendleton.[155] Aside from a few who were too ill to report immediately or who were still in high school, reservists and guardsmen found it difficult to garner any extra time before reporting.[156] Men and women scurried around to un-rent apartments, resign from jobs, withdraw from college, store possessions, move up wedding dates, and kiss their loved ones goodbye. Some units required members to fit physical exams or vaccinations into their already hectic schedules or to participate in recruitment drives when units were understrength.[157] Then, they gathered at the same armories as their World War II forebears not so many years before, and the same townspeople collected to wish them well and to memorize the faces that might never return.[158] Boarding buses or trains or cramming into cars, recalled servicemen and servicewomen headed out toward active duty and camps and bases all around the country.

Once settled at Fort Lewis or Camp Pendleton or wherever else they ended up, guardsmen and reservists had much to do in preparation for regular military service. Occasionally medical exams were administered, but more frequently candidates were found "physically fit for duty" without even being seen by a doctor.[159] Those not yet immunized received their vaccinations, and then it was on to the business of making ready for war. At camp, some reserve units classified their members as older veterans who were "combat ready," men who needed a refresher in "combat training," and new recruits who needed boot camp or basic training, sending them to either the war zone or training accordingly.[160] However, early in the war, when manpower shortages in Korea necessitated more troops immediately, many reservists, regardless of experience, spent only days or weeks drilling before shipping overseas.[161] Sometimes, men who recently had joined the reserves boarded the troop ship without ever having been taught to handle a weapon.[162] One reservist complained that after he had fought at Inchon, Seoul, Chosin, and the Guerilla Sweep, the Marine Corps wanted to send him back to the States for boot camp.[163] Nurses especially found themselves quickly mustered in and deployed, so quickly in fact that they had to borrow uniforms. In more than a few cases, the Navy and Marine Corps discovered married women or mothers within their ranks, but by then the women were already at their assignments and had to wait to be formally discharged until replacements were found.[164] National Guardsmen faced much the same general process as reservists, but sometimes took longer to leave the camps. In the fifties, the Guard did not require recruits to take basic training and as a result many guardsmen started active duty in basic training.

As they mustered in, many guardsmen and reservists felt that they followed in the footsteps of the reserve personnel called to service in World War II. In 1950 as in 1941, Guard and reserve units mirrored the communities they were leaving behind. The faces of brothers and cousins filled the ranks as they set out for destination points unknown. But the Korean War proved a very different experience. Those who left together did not always remain together as many units were either broken apart or reconfigured before they ever reached battle. Recruitment drives plumped up units with new people, the classification of individuals in different categories of combat readiness splintered units, and often individual replacements were plucked from the ranks and sent over separately.[165] While some units did reach Korea intact, many others contained totally different personnel by the time they boarded the ship.[166] Reservists and guardsmen summoned for the Korean War expected to be among friends and relatives when it came their turn to soldier, but instead a great many faced the task alone. Many couldn't help but feel "when we slipped our lines at the dock, and later as we passed under the Golden Gate Bridge, that perhaps this was not quite working out as we had planned."[167]

The Draftees and the Deferred

"Greetings from the President of the United States." Millions of young men around the country cringed when they read the words that prefaced Harry Truman's letter informing them that their time to report for the Korean War draft had come.[168] Within sixty days of hostilities in Korea, monthly draft calls spiraled upward from the post–World War II doldrums, reaching fifty thousand by September 1950 and eighty thousand by January 1951.[169] Calls averaged about half a million a year throughout the war and might have risen higher had MacArthur not emptied training units in order to provide combat units in Korea with replacements, making it impossible to prepare a larger number of draftees for service.[170] Local boards, made up of unpaid civilians, scrambled to sift through millions of Selective Service registrants and classify them as fit for selection, deferment, or exemption.[171] Amazingly, these boards managed not only to meet the calls but to produce more names than requested every single month of the war.[172] As a result, draftees accounted for over 30 percent, or about a million and a half, of those who mustered in for the conflict.[173]

Upon receiving draft notifications, potential inductees had only ten days to report to the local board for classification. Those who failed to appear for any reason risked having their names turned over to the United States attorney general for prosecution for delinquency.[174] One fretful woman appealed to Senator Robert Taft on behalf of her husband, a merchant marine aboard a transport ship delivering supplies to the Far East, because the local board had turned him in to the federal authorities for not reporting or appealing his I-A (available for service) status in person.[175] Others failed to report for less innocent reasons. Some had been careless about updating address information and had no idea they had even been called, but others deliberately side-stepped the draft board.[176] That World War II sense of participating in something important had vanished, and registrants were sometimes driven to become no-shows by their lack of enthusiasm for military life.[177] As hostilities dragged on, a kind of malaise about the war also played a role. Again and again local boards found themselves having to explain to draftees that "they have an obligation to their country that they must perform."[178] But not all registrants agreed that they owed such service. Minorities pointed out the irony of the country expecting them to fight abroad for rights and freedoms they were themselves denied at home.[179] One Native American woman wrote President Truman in disgust, saying the Navajos "have not been helped and you ask for our boys."[180] Many African Americans felt the same way, and some men, like Roosevelt Ward Jr., executive secretary of the Labor Youth

League, and James Lawson, a future Nashville civil rights movement leader, chose prison over Korea.[181]

Still, delinquencies ran low throughout the Korean War. Many might have felt like Rudy Stephens that they "wanted to run away, assume a strange name, and get lost in this big country of ours."[182] They might even, as Mickey Scott asserts, have known the way to Mexico or Canada.[183] Probably more than a few of them thought the draft board unfair in forcing them into service while others went free.[184] But on the whole, the men summoned to report for the draft came when called. In 1950, the Justice Department prosecuted only 4,490 men for draft evasion, convicting 1,750. Even fewer inductees attempted to evade the draft in 1951, the first full year of the war, and of 3,680 facing charges, only 1,560 were found guilty. By 1952, the number of cases rose to 5,610 with 3,130 convictions, leading up to 1953, the most popular year for skipping out on the Korean War draft, when 6,300 trials resulted in 3,450 guilty verdicts.[185] As months of war lengthened to years, the number of draft dodgers increased, but never to the levels of the Vietnam War or even of the world wars. The numbers remained low and manageable. Few veterans can even remember men who sought to avoid the draft by fleeing to another state or country. Tom Clawson notes, "I had no thought, and I knew of nobody in high school or college who ever said to me, 'We're going to try to avoid the draft,' or go to Canada or any of that stuff. It just wasn't heard of back then."[186]

Why did Korean War era inductees, especially those receiving their notices after it became clear that Korea would never be a popular war like World War II, not stage demonstrations, burn their draft cards, or flee to someplace safe, somewhere where they couldn't be brought back, dressed up, and shipped off to war? Given the draft resistance of World War I, which in some instances required the dispatch of federal troops to quell armed bands of deserters, and in the wake of Vietnam, it seems inconceivable that when faced with the prospect of being sent overseas to fight in the inhospitable landscape of a country most Americans neither knew nor cared about, most young men accepted their fate.[187] Many scholars argue that low draft calls provided little opportunity for delinquency or incentive for organized resistance.[188] While compelling, especially with regard to the two world wars, this thesis has severe limitations when applied to Vietnam. The Vietnam War posted far higher rates of delinquency than the Korean War, but draft calls for Korea consistently outpaced those of the Vietnam era by some two hundred thousand annually.[189] Also, Selective Service inducted 1,529,539 men from June 1950 to June 1953, almost as many as during the entire nine years of the Vietnam War when 1,857,304 draftees marched into the Army.[190] And, if draft calls themselves were to blame for delinquency, the rates would remain steady even if the raw numbers fluctuated by going up with high calls and down with low calls. Something other than low draft calls must explain why more Korean War draftees did not choose to evade the draft.

The veterans themselves, when asked to explain why they decided to report for duty, cite a number of reasons, with patriotism of one sort or another crowning the list. Called only a few years after the patriotic fervor of World War II, the men of Korea believed then and still believe "it was our duty to serve our country."[191] As Joseph Fabiani relates, "I was a very proud young American going off to serve my country in a time of war."[192] Unlike many of the next generation, they would not turn the United States down when it needed men.[193] Additionally, while the draft could present a financial or career opportunity, draft evasion in the fifties would end in nothing less than humiliation and time in the penitentiary. Mickey Scott remembered the disgrace heaped by communities on those who tried to beat the draft in World War II, extending even to their families. "Weather stripping was the snickered name [given to babies born to draft-vulnerable men], the connection being to keep one out of the draft."[194] Rudy Stephens realized that if he tried to outrun his orders to report, "the military would be looking for me for a long time to come" and he "didn't want to take the chance of going to Fort Leavenworth, Kansas, to spend time behind bars."[195] As a generation, Korean War–era draftees, trained by the Great Depression to accept their responsibilities without question and hardened from witnessing the sacrifices made by many Americans during the Second World War, could not conceive that it might be possible to refuse Uncle Sam's invitation to the draft and get away with it. They "came from an era of 'It's your privilege to disagree, but not disobey.'"[196] For them, despite great public indifference to the Korean War, no Tet Offensive took place to rally the forces of opposition and make draft resistance seem a moral choice, and, unlike the Vietnam War, this war ended before average Americans had time to get tired enough of it to protest. And, if their determination to fulfill their duty wavered, the draftees, like the volunteers, had plenty of examples encouraging them to accept their turn as soldiers. Fathers, uncles, cousins, brothers, and friends had already served in one of the world wars or even in Korea. How could they refuse to do likewise? For most, the answer was clear, they could not.

Once deciding to report, potential inductees presented themselves to the local draft board of their community, where they received classification in the least liable category for which they were eligible.[197] Those without claim to deferment or exemption moved on to Armed Forces Examining Stations for preinduction exams, both mental and physical.[198] These tests determined whether a registrant would be rejected (classified IV-F for mental or physical exam failure) or classified I-A (available for service).[199] Rejections, however, like deferments, could be temporary. Throughout the war, Congress and Selective Service lowered test standards in order to widen the manpower pool, meaning that many who had been disqualified on the basis of test failure later had to be reclassified as acceptable.[200] Classification, even for those deemed I-A, did not end the suspense of the process. Low draft calls meant that not every person available for service needed to be called up. Local boards summoned eligible draftees in order, but could not predict the date when one would be required to appear for induction.[201] Dan Grimes complained that the draft board alerted him of his imminent call-up in November 1950, but kept delaying his entrance into the Army. Finally, he informed the local board that if they did not draft him quickly, he was going to enlist in the Air Force. Soon he found himself wearing the Army's uniform and "considering pros and cons of deserting."[202] Not everyone received such a swift response. Delays and uncertainties made it difficult for men, especially those with wives, to prepare for their departures. As one potential inductee wrote, he did not know whether to store his belongings and rent his house immediately or wait because neither the draft board nor he knew when he'd be leaving.[203] Eventually, when the call came, draftees went through a final induction exam, took their oaths, and prepared for shipment to basic training.

In theory, all young American men of draft age should have shared equally the burden of the draft, but Selective Service provisions and deferment and exemption policies worked to spread service liability unevenly. During the first few months of the conflict, mental test qualification standards led to a high rate of rejection among men from underprivileged backgrounds, allowing them to avoid service while leaving better-heeled and better-educated registrants stuck in the draft pool.[204] In fact, mental test failure became a major source of "deferment" or exemption during the war for African Americans and others who were too poor to attend college or to show that military service worked a financial hardship on their families.[205] By June 1951, the Universal Military Training and Service Act rectified the inequity by dramatically dropping the minimum allowable AFQT score and allowing many of those who previously had been disqualified to enter service.[206] Rejection rates based solely on the mental test fell from 16.5 percent from July 1950–December 1951 to 13.2 percent of those selected in 1952.[207]

Rejection rates as a whole, whether for administrative reasons or mental or physical exam failures, also fell as the war continued and manpower needs increased. In July 1950, Selective Service rejected 59 percent of all candidates for induction, but the percentage continued to drop to a low of 27.7 percent in February 1951.[208] Lower rejection rates meant that a broader base of males was eligible to be called into the country's service.[209] Eliminating one imbalance in the system, however, did not prevent others from forming or continuing. Eligibility to serve became more widely spread with each passing year of the conflict, but some boys remained more vulnerable than others to Selective Service and involuntary induction.

Throughout the war, ministers of religion and divinity students received exemption, but conscientious objectors did not.[210] Conscientious objectors were liable for either noncombatant service or civilian work, depending on how they felt about contributing to the war effort.[211] Ted Head discovered this the hard way. Classified I-A by the local draft board, Head attempted to avoid service by seeking reclassification as a "pacifist on religious grounds." Failing at that, Head went through all the in-processing until reaching the induction center, where he refused to "'step forward' when his name was called to place him officially in the military service." Convicted of draft evasion, 22-year-old Head faced three years in a federal penitentiary unless he agreed to muster in as a noncombatant.[212] Since no distinction had been made for COs who served during World War II, many conscientious objectors found themselves drafted for a second time during the Korean War as if they were registering for the first time. Such was the case with Robert Dudgeon, who had already served twenty-two months in the Second World War. The local board classified him as IV-E (conscientious objector opposed to both combatant and noncombatant role but available for service), rather than as exempt for previous service.[213]

In general, exemptions also went to military veterans who had served for a minimum period of time and been discharged under honorable conditions.[214] Timing could be cruel, however, and a great many men missed exemption by only days or weeks of service. Raymond Johnston served in the Pacific from August 1945 to August 1946, racking up enough terminal leave to earn him a cash settlement from Congress, but found himself nineteen days short of the one-year mark that would have gotten him a Korean War draft exemption.[215] Marvin Beech Jr., a World War II Navy veteran who served thirty-three months of his three-year enlistment before being discharged in the congressional effort to reduce manpower, also found himself called up for Korea. Though willing to serve, Beech could not "see why I have to do my duty twice."[216] Similarly, Doug Brown, who had served ten months in the Navy during 1945-46 and been drafted again in November 1950, wondered why he and others like him could not be at least "given credit on a month for month basis for previous service toward the present requirement of 24 monthly."[217] Men who had risked their lives in Italy or on islands in the Pacific could not believe that they would be subject to the Korean War draft simply because they had been discharged before six months or a year of active duty. They had wives and homes and new college degrees, and as a group they felt that their obligations to country had been met. In the end, the pleas of veterans failing to meet the minimum service guidelines for exemption went without further action on their behalf, but a majority of World War II veterans and a sizable chunk of those who began service after that war did obtain immunity from the draft.[218]

In addition to exemptions, a number of deferment options offered temporary relief from draft vulnerability during the Korean War years. The 1948 Selective Service Act deferred for dependency reasons all married registrants as well as most men with children. In any given year of the war, about a million registrants held dependency deferments.[219] This policy caused much controversy, however. Angry reservists complained that they had been recalled without consideration of their marital or dependency status. Divorced, noncustodial fathers pointed out that even if they paid child support they could not be considered for deferment.[220] And, some men tried to take advantage of the system by stacking dependency deferments on top of other deferments. Louis Perrino, given a postponement of induction in order to complete school, married shortly before his time to report and tried to get a dependency deferment from the local board on account of his wife's pregnancy.[221] In actuality, cases of deferment pyramiding were rare, but the perception that men were evading service led to changes in the law.[222] As Private Gerald W. Long, whose wife was expecting triplets, learned, by 1951, married men without children could not expect a deferment unless they could prove hardship, and the policy of discharging soldiers with four or more dependents applied only to "civilian components of the army—such as the Oklahoma national guard" and not to draftees or volunteers.[223] In 1953 President Dwight Eisenhower issued an executive order ending deferments for fatherhood altogether.[224]

Despite surpluses in government warehouses, many farm workers could thank political lobbying and leftover World War II protections of agriculture for qualifying them for II-C classification (deferred for agricultural occupation).[225] For some, like Bill Dallas, who got to stay home only until crops could be harvested in the fall of 1950, the deferment proved only temporary.[226] For others, faced with local boards either indifferent to or antagonistic toward removing farm hands from the draft pool, the deferment turned out to be elusive. One 55-year-old farmer with six hundred acres to work bemoaned the fact that his eldest son had been drafted in September 1950 and his younger son was set to be called in early 1951. He asked, "How will I farm? . . . We cannot send both boys to service and farm."[227] Another man had 139 acres of corn to harvest but couldn't be assured by the board that his 22-year-old son would get an extension to see them through the season.[228] In tens of thousands of other instances, though, farm types did get deferred, often for the duration of the conflict.[229] Ultimately, a higher percentage of agricultural laborers received deferment than any other occupational group during the Korean War.[230]

Selective Service sought to protect other occupational fields as well. Classes II-A (deferred for occupation) and II-B (deferred as government official) existed to defer men employed in any one of a number of professions deemed essential to the national health, safety, or interest.[231] The government especially concerned itself with protecting industrial manpower, science, technology, and production. Petroleum drillers, microbiologists, engineers, geophysicists, machinists, millwrights, patternmakers, saw-smiths, shipmasters, tool and die makers, mathematicians, government officials, and many others could count on staying home instead of mustering in.[232]

Lastly, large numbers of students enjoyed deferments during the Korean War.[233] Under the Selective Service Act of 1948, high school students under age twenty and some college students received I-S classification (student deferment to complete high school or the current academic year) so long as they continued to do satisfactory schoolwork.[234] This system, however, which really only delayed induction for a short while, proved inadequate to mollify many Americans. Students halfway through their degree programs wanted time enough to finish college before beginning military service. Professional and scientific groups warned that drafting college students would deplete the country's personnel resources in the very fields crucial to winning the Cold War. These elements pressed at the national level for more generous college deferments.[235] On March 30, 1951, despite his desire to avoid any type of "class legislation," Truman issued an executive order creating a new student deferment program.[236] College males wishing to postpone induction until graduation could do so by passing with a score of 70 percent or better the 150-question multiple-choice Selective Service College Qualification Test (SSCQT) or by ranking in the top half of their class, and then asking the local board for II-S (student deferred to complete college) classification.[237] Undergraduates and graduates alike were eligible, but those deferred could earn only a single degree under the system and their draft vulnerability extended to age thirty-five. This situation prompted one wit to lament,

Today in college
To gain more knowledge
More and More I strive.

A student deferment
Is my preferment
'Til I reach thirty five.
But Selective Service
Has me nervous
They grant but one degree.
Despite my plea
For a Ph.D.
They offer me a P.F.C.[238]

Hundreds of thousands of men took the SSCQT during the war, and about half a million Selective Service registrants succeeded in getting II-S deferments.[239] By 1952, three-quarters of the nation's male college student population had secured some kind of deferment or exemption to shelter them at least temporarily from military service.[240]

No matter the reason for exemption or deferment, few of the millions of men shielded from the draft thought of their draft status as privileged treatment, and many expected to take their turn if or when the time came. College students in particular viewed deferment as merely a postponement of military service—and for good reason.[241] Amendments made to the Universal Military Training and Service Act in 1951 extended the liability for service to age thirty-five for men deferred for reasons other than hardship or dependency.[242] When sociologists questioned a sample of students at eleven universities in 1953, 91 percent of them said they anticipated serving at least three years in the military after completing their education. Overwhelmingly they acknowledged military service as a duty of citizenship and frowned upon deliberate attempts to evade it.[243]

Americans outside of draft protection, however, viewed things differently. Draftees noticed just who failed to turn up at basic training or, more revealingly, in the foxholes of Korea. College-deferred men often talked of their willingness to serve after completing their schooling, but few rushed to enlist after receiving their degrees. Of 11,079 men classified II-S in April 1951, only 20 percent had entered the military a year later, with 50 percent still II-S and the other 30 percent reclassified but not yet mustered in.[244] Some university students went to great lengths to legally avoid military responsibility. William Dannenmaier marveled that both a football player from the University of Missouri and a basketball player from Washington University in St. Louis failed their mid-1951 physicals while he passed with flying colors.[245] James Brady watched the son of "some big noise in Washington" get off the troop ship in Japan while everyone else went on to Korea.[246] Mothers wanted to know "why college students have any more right to be deferred than a young man . . . working and waiting until financially able to take the training for his life's work." They asked, "Isn't this country, the college boy's country and hasn't he just as much right to defend it . . . as the less fortunate ones who were nabbed before they were financially able to enter schools?"[247] Other Americans, sensing that draft policies failed to share service obligations fairly among draft-age cohorts, insisted that "the rich should go as well as the poor" and that "some men should not get to go to college while the rest go [to Korea]."[248] Foreshadowing the troubles of the Vietnam era, charges of class and race bias followed the draft throughout the Korean War.[249] No matter what registrants with exemptions or deferments thought about their classifications, average Americans and inductees often believed that middle- and upper-class white men had managed to get a better deal from Selective Service.[250] So widespread was this notion that President Eisenhower's assistant secretary of defense, John Hannah, labeled Korea "a poor man's war" and various draft board members resigned their posts "in protest against a deferment policy that was seen as 'un-American and represented class discrimination.'"[251]

In reality, the draft probably did catch more men from Harlem or Muskogee than Manhattan or Tulsa, with high school rather than college diplomas.[252] But, Selective Service provided only one avenue to military duty during the Korean War period, accounting for far fewer accessions than voluntary enlistment. If one considers that college-educated men joined up in numbers roughly proportionate to their percentage of the population, and that regardless of income factors the military participation rate for the draft-age cohort averaged 70-75 percent, the Korean-era military seems quite equitable in its manpower procurement.[253] Also, though the regular draft slanted in favor of the rich and educated, Selective Service targeted doctors, dentists, and others with the 1950 Doctors' Draft. All males under fifty in medical, dental, or allied fields had to sign up, even those already in the draft pool.[254] Like regular inductees, they could try for deferments or exemptions, but in 1952 shortages of qualified personnel led the Department of Defense to decree that anyone fit to carry on a private practice was fit for military duty.[255] The Doctors' Draft resulted in few inductions, but it did pressure tens of thousands of men into enlisting, picking up commissions and bonuses, and serving twelve months.[256] And, it helped to remedy some of the inequalities inherent in the Selective Service System. Even so, college deferments had an impact in the field, where they helped to deprive units of potential officers and, in some instances, of quality leadership.[257]

Like draftees of the Civil War, World War I, and World War II, most of those who appeared for induction during the Korean War would have preferred to stay home. Few draftees relished the idea of stomping around in military-issue boots, especially if those boots marched them into a war zone. Even fewer wanted to leave behind everything and everyone familiar. Unlike many of the boys of World War I or World War II who served alongside friends or neighbors, the draftees of Korea rotated in and out of service alone.[258] They tried for exemptions and deferments and they blamed local boards or appeals boards or the "damned" Selective Service when it came their time to muster into the Army. But they did not riot like New Yorkers conscripted during the Civil War or attack federal officials enforcing the draft as men did during the First World War, and they seldom ran from the draft as did many of their brothers in the Vietnam era.[259] They groused and griped and grumbled, but draftees did the job Uncle Sam asked them to do, and they did it better in many instances than those who willingly signed up for military service. The draftees, though, by and large remained civilians at heart. They wore the uniforms, but it was the value that they placed on citizenship, the acknowledgment of duty drilled into them during childhood, that caused them to pack up and go "to unknown places to serve our country as our leaders suggested."[260]

Who Mustered In during the Korean War Era?

The men and women who mustered in for the Korean War looked much the same as those who entered the armed forces during other American wars. But, as scholarship has shown, the composition of the American military has never remained constant, the color and kinds of faces in uniform changing from generation to generation. And, Korea was a war between wars—between World War II, when participation in the military became a generational experience, and Vietnam, when service grew into an issue of socioeconomic class.[261] So the question arises, just who served in the armed forces during the early 1950s, and what characteristics did they share with each other or with veterans of other eras? Was the Korean War military a middle ground between World War II and Vietnam?

As military personnel go, those who served during the Korean War were young. Conditions in Korea demanded the quick mobilization of manpower, but unlike in World War II or the Civil War, the armed forces did not need every able man, young or old, to slip into uniform. Initially, the Department of Defense recalled reservists and guardsmen for shipment to Korea, but as the war continued, Selective Service and recruiters targeted younger men for induction and enlistment.[262] Despite the efforts of local boards to call up older registrants first, the draft pressured enough teenagers to enter the Army and Marine Corps that mothers complained about being "sick and tired of this child draft" and asked "when did this country get so bad off it has to take our children directly out of schools to protect us?"[263] By 1952, troops in the field noticed the "youthful homogeneity" of their platoons and noted that most of their comrades seemed to be between the ages of eighteen and twenty-one.[264] In all, the average age of American soldiers was twenty-three during the Korean War, three years younger than in World War II and the Civil War and two years younger than in World War I.[265] But, if one considers that this number includes the typically older reserve personnel called up during the first year of the war, it is possible that the average infantryman in Korea, especially after 1951, was actually closer in age to his nineteen-year-old Vietnam War counterpart than the statistics imply.[266] Also, given the types of MOS's for which men with less education could qualify, great probability exists that younger men more often found their way to the war zone as front-line infantrymen than did older candidates who had more skills and experience or education to offer.

Though not subject to the same draft pressures as men, enlisted women and many female officers in the Korean War armed forces tended to be young. Perhaps because of regulations restricting married women and mothers from military service, teenagers made up 40 percent of new female recruits after June 1951. By December 1952, more than half of the enlisted women in all branches of service were under age twenty-six. In the Marine Corps 52 percent were 18-21 and in the Air Force 47 percent were 18-20. The Army and Navy retained greater numbers of older enlistees, but the Army still had 35 percent between eighteen and twenty in its ranks and the Navy had 27 percent under the age of twenty. Not surprisingly, nurses and women medical specialists in all the corps were older, having completed degree programs of one type or another before entering service. But, officers not infrequently fell into younger age groups. About 36 percent of female Army officers were age thirty or under, and in the Marine Corps 51 percent were age 21-25. Only the Navy could boast 67 percent of female officers over the age of thirty.[267] For women as for men during the Korean War, the faces behind the uniforms reflected a certain youth as service became the obligation of ever younger Americans, a trend that would continue into the Vietnam era.[268]

Despite their age, recruits and draftees in the early 1950s possessed educational levels favorably comparable to those of their World War II predecessors. America had changed in the interwar period, giving kids the opportunity to acquire more years of schooling than in the past.[269] Also, with manageable draft calls, Selective Service could be more selective in choosing registrants for active duty.[270] As a result, about 50 percent of Army enlisted personnel in the Second World War had completed at least twelve years of school, but 52.6 percent of enlisted military personnel in 1952 had high school diplomas and another 9.9 percent could claim some college credit though not a university degree.[271] In this way, the Korean War proved a stepping stone to the better-educated armed forces of the Vietnam War when about 60 percent of the troops had high school diplomas.[272]

While pressure from the Korean draft ensured the enlistment and induction of high school graduates, student deferment policies worked to reduce the draft vulnerability of college and university students, resulting in a decline in the percentage of servicemen with college diplomas. In World War II, 8.5 percent of the troops held bachelor's degrees or better, but by the Korean War only 3.9 percent did, and the rate slipped further to just 2.6 percent during the Vietnam War, when gross inequities resulted in protest.[273] Not surprisingly, however, officers had a higher level of education than enlisted men.[274] Some 46.6 percent of commissioned officers during the Korean War had college degrees and an additional 29.6 percent had at least some college. Only 4.4 percent of officers had not completed high school. This trend toward a better-educated base of officers continued after the war, and by 1965, over 70 percent of officers would possess a college diploma and less than 1 percent would lack a high school degree.[275] Among average GIs, though, college diplomas remained scarce.

Ironically, despite mental test qualification standards and the drift toward better-educated personnel, a large percentage of men with less than a fourth-grade education filtered into service, especially into the Army, during the Korean War era. Almost 150,000 men of two million receiving special training fell under the label "illiterate, non-English speaking, and below 4th grade educational level." More than twice as many men were so categorized during World War II, but they amounted to a small minority of the seven million trained.[276] By the Vietnam War, less educated men would again find it difficult to qualify for military service, and only about 21 percent of Americans with less than an eighth-grade education would muster in as opposed to the Korean War, when 35 percent did.[277] Still, as a whole, the 1950s military seemed to be moving away from both the uneducated and the highly educated and toward the vast middle ground of high school graduates.

Given the narrowing educational level of GIs during the Korean War, one might reasonably wonder if the social classes of the men and women answering the call to colors also changed. Did the burden of service fall to members of all social strata, as in the Second World War, or did the sons and daughters of the working class disproportionately carry the responsibility, as in Vietnam?[278] Increasingly aware of student and other deferments, many people at the time certainly believed that draft policies protected an economic or "intellectual elite" while pressing poorer folk into the military machine.[279] Assistant Secretary of Defense John Hannah even asserted that "there is too much validity in the statement often made that the son of the well-to-do family goes to college and the sons of some of the rest go to Korea."[280] Many scholars agree, labeling Korea a "poor man's war," but in reality the likelihood of military service had less to do with whether or not one came from a wealthy family than with other factors like reserve call-ups, draft pressure, and recruitment. Office managers, steelworkers, salesmen, and the unemployed all sent their sons into the Army or Marine Corps or one of the other branches of service in roughly proportionate numbers, with 67-76 percent of draft-age cohorts donning uniforms. Only the sons of farmers could claim a significantly lower rate of military service, with 56 percent of them joining up.[281] In general, service remained the obligation of all classes of eligible men.[282]

While social status had little effect on whether or not one entered the armed forces during the Korean War, it probably did affect how individuals served their time. Upper-class youths who had been able not only to complete high school but also to afford some college before entering service were well-positioned to move on from basic training to either advanced training or specialized units, while the sons of the lower classes, with their rudimentary schooling, shuttled off to the front lines as combat infantrymen.[283] A study of men from Detroit determined that the casualty rate dropped as the income level rose and that nonwhites suffered a rate twice that of their white counterparts.[284] While flawed in various ways, the study does support the conclusions of many scholars that combat units in the war zone had an unduly high concentration of soldiers from the lower and working classes.[285] Also, the Bradley Commission concluded that while 64 percent of accessions in the Army at home during the Korean War had tested above mental group IV, only 15 percent of men sent to overseas commands had.[286] The Korean War military might not have suffered from class bias, but the units in Korea quite likely did.

Unlike men, women came to the military from a more limited range of social classes. Regulations requiring a high school diploma or the equivalent effectively weeded out women who for economic or other reasons had failed to finish their education, possessed few work skills, or existed on the lower end of the occupational pay scale. At least in the Air Force and Navy virtually no domestic workers, food service personnel, agriculturalists, or horticulturalists left their day jobs to answer Uncle Sam's call.[287] Similarly, on the upward end of the scale, few coeds traded their textbooks for service stripes, and female managers and professionals steered clear of the recruiter's office. Of servicewomen claiming a previous career, the vast majority listed clerical or secretarial work as their mainstay.[288] Later, as days of war spun into months and years, all of the services accepted younger women who had not yet begun gainful employment, but nothing suggests that these teenagers differed socially from their more mature peers. The women who looked for opportunity in the armed forces belonged to neither the lowest station of society nor the highest.

Racially, the faces of the troops during the Korean War revealed a new and slightly darker American military. Before Korea, the armed forces employed a variety of means to limit minority and especially black participation in the military.[289] All branches of service established quota systems, allowing only a certain number of African Americans into uniform, and then shepherded the fortunate few into special segregated units.[290] In 1948, however, President Truman issued Executive Order 9981, calling for equality of treatment and opportunity for all servicemembers and the creation of the Fahy Committee, which would suggest and implement changes.[291] Ultimately, pressure from the Fahy Committee, along with manpower needs in Korea, caused the Army and Marine Corps to integrate troops in the war zone and abolish quotas.[292] By April 1950 the legal barriers blocking black enlistment had lifted. As a result, the percentage of African Americans entering the military began to rise, especially in the Army. In 1949, only 5.9 percent of those in the armed forces and 8.6 percent of Army soldiers were black, but by 1954, 7.9 percent of military and 11.3 percent of Army personnel could claim African heritage.[293] This trend continued into the next war. By 1965, 9.5 percent of military personnel and 12.8 percent of the Army were black.[294] And, unlike their brothers of the First and Second World Wars, the "tan" soldiers of Korea and Vietnam were more likely than others to do their duty "in country" and in combat.[295]

Every state produced recruits and inductees for the KoreanWar, but a lower percentage of draft-eligible men mustered in from the far West and South than from other sections of the country. Overall, 79 percent of eligible northerners and 76 percent of midwesterners served, but only 70 percent of men from the far West and 72 percent of southerners did.[296] In part, the rural nature of states like Mississippi or Wyoming helps to account for this disproportion. With a high percentage of their populations living outside of metropolitan areas or small cities, western and southern states had lots of men eligible for agricultural deferments, and a higher percentage of rural dwellers in these areas got deferred than in other regions of the country.[297] Also, especially in the South, the general health and educational level of residents prevented many males from entering the military. Mental exams like the AFQT had a provisional minimum threshold equivalent to about an eighth-grade education.[298] This presented a stumbling block for men in states like North Carolina, South Carolina, Georgia, Alabama, Mississippi, and

Louisiana, where the median number of school years completed by persons age twenty-five and older fell months or even a year short of the eighth-grade standard.[299] Consequently, these states led the country in IV-F classifications, with Mississippi suffering a higher rate than the Virgin Islands.[300] In all, the armed forces rejected only 11 percent of northern boys, but declared almost 18 percent of southerners unfit for one reason or another.[301]

Saddled with high rates of rejection, some southern states might have failed to shoulder their share of the manpower burden for Korea, but southern men were still well represented in the armed forces. West Virginia had ninety-five thousand men, or 4.73 percent of its total population, in uniform.[302] Only Maine, New Hampshire, and Vermont could come close to that rate of participation. Alabama alone of the southern section ranked among the ten states with the lowest rates of service, not surprising given that as late as the induction exam Selective Service rejected 6.5 percent of Alabamians.[303] Also, though southern states did not provide the sheer numbers of men that New York, Pennsylvania, or California produced, a high percentage of southerners ended up as casualties of the war.[304] Almost 1 percent of West Virginians in service died in action, as did .7 percent of men from Kentucky.[305] West Virginia, Kentucky, Arkansas, Oklahoma, Virginia, Louisiana, Tennessee, Mississippi, Missouri, and South Carolina all fell into the top twenty of states that suffered the highest percentage of population killed or wounded.[306] And, southerners supplied much of the leadership for the Korean War as men from the South were more likely to muster in as officers or officer candidates than men from other sections of the country.[307] Memoirs and scholarly studies alike make reference to the southern flavor of military leadership.[308] Despite entering service at a somewhat slower pace than their midwestern or northern counterparts, southern men did fulfill their duty to country throughout the early 1950s. Unlike the Vietnam War, which ironically would have a distinctly southern bent, no single section of the country during the Korean Conflict bore a strikingly disproportionate burden in providing manpower.

Like men, women came from all over the United States and from as far away as Puerto Rico to join up. Also like their male counterparts, many came from states like California, Pennsylvania, New York, and Illinois.[309] Overwhelmingly, though, female candidates hailed from small towns or cities rather than from sprawling metropolitan areas. In 1952, the Marine Corps determined that only 35 percent of its female recruits lived in cities of one hundred thousand or more, and the Army, Navy, and Air Force found that fewer than 30 percent of their enlistees came from cities that size. In all branches of service about another 25 percent of women called cities of twenty-five to one hundred thousand home, but 35-52 percent traded farms or small towns or cities for the military life. Except for nurses and medical specialists, who came from places large enough to have accredited schools, female recruits tended to come from places with smaller populations.[310] This pattern resembles the manpower paradigm of the next war, in which rural and small-town America provided more military personnel proportionately than central cities or even working-class suburbs.[311]

No matter what part of the country they came from, many veterans of Korea had already mustered into the armed forces at least once. Especially early in the war when manpower needs reached critical levels, the armed forces pulled World War II veterans out of reserve or National Guard units and returned them to active duty. Leading the return troops were the old salts, sergeants or lieutenants or other officers who had stayed in service after the Second World War, or in some cases the First World War.[312] Eventually, newly minted servicemen and women became the face of Korea's military, but at war's end 20 percent of veterans could claim service in at least two wars.[313] Close to a million men served in both Korea and World War II.[314] But, duty did not always stop in 1953 or 1954. Almost two hundred thousand of those who had served in both World War II and Korea went on to wear their uniforms for the Vietnam War, as did another 273,000 veterans of Korea alone.[315] For many young men, Korea turned out to be only one of their defining wars.

In the end, the men and women who filled uniforms for the Korean Conflict both resembled World War II's "Greatest Generation" and foreshadowed Vietnam's reluctant one. They came from all parts of the country and most sectors of the economy, and they shared the patriotism and willingness to serve of an earlier time. But, increasingly throughout the early 1950s the faces of the troops reflected the shifting demographics of postwar America. Younger, better educated, and more racially diverse than their brothers and sisters of World War II, these new soldiers became a generation of their own and a stepping stone to the armed forces of the next war. Not all who mustered into the military, though, would march to the beat of Uncle Sam's drum. First they would have to cross through that age-old rite of passage, basic training.

With the outbreak of the Korean War still a year in the future, Hershal Burns and Harold Mulhausen take a break from summer camp in California in 1949. Courtesy of Harold Mulhausen.

3

You're in the Army (or Navy, Marines,
or Air Force) Now!

When new recruits arrived at the train or bus station with duffle bags in hand, as ready as possible for the upcoming weeks or months that would transform them into "Government Issue," the oft-repeated ritual began. Anxious mothers and wives tried to keep from crying too hard, sweethearts planted kisses in hope that they not be forgotten, fathers gave last-minute pieces of advice, and babies squealed while older children clambered up and down the safety rails oblivious to the day's portent. Even a few husbands and boyfriends turned out to bid farewell to wives and girlfriends who either had enlisted or had been called up from the Reserves.[1] Then, when the order came, these soon-to-be servicemen and servicewomen piled into train cars and bus seats, waving goodbye and blowing barrages of kisses to their friends and families and civilian lives. The men and women who would serve during the Korean War belonged to the military now.[2]

It did not take long to wash down the last bites of a Red Cross doughnut with coffee or to smoke a few of the free cigarettes handed out by the various military service clubs, and it did not take long for those headed toward basic training or boot camp to realize that they had left much of the familiar behind and that more than miles separated them from home. The train ride alone often proved eye-opening. Young men and women who had been sheltered in America's small enclaves could only wonder at the multitude of vices indulged in by other trainees en route to their destinations. Still naïve if not just plain green when he left Oklahoma for Camp Pendleton, California, Harold Mulhausen had heard about "goings on" but never really witnessed such an abundance of drinking, gambling, cussing, dirty song singing, and smoking as when he boarded the troop train.[3] One can only imagine what he might have thought of fellow marine James Putnam, who joined other recruits in drinking and partying even before the train arrived at the station to carry them to Parris Island, South Carolina. Putnam and his cronies became so uncontrollable that the train conductor simply unhooked their cars, leaving them to party outside of Atlanta, Georgia, until they all ran out of money and the Marine Corps found and attached them to another eastbound train.[4]

These antics, while entertaining, usually turned out to be only one of many firsts experienced by troops along the well-worn train tracks carrying them toward military life. Many trainees had never traveled more than a few miles from home before and had never come into close contact with people from other sections of the country. Now they found themselves crammed into close quarters aboard troop trains with people who spoke and looked differently than they did. For northerners the journey could be especially unsettling as most training centers were south of the Mason Dixon line, where climate made year-round training more viable.[5] That meant that men and women accustomed to a more integrated world learned first-hand the rules of the segregated South. Years later, Mary Robinson, a white recruit, remembered her astonishment at seeing "White Only" sections in Virginia train stations and segregated barracks at Fort Eustis: "This was a surprise to me—a kid from the North."[6] For African Americans born and raised in New York or Philadelphia, the introduction to the South went beyond surprising—it was nothing less than traumatic. Despite their military status, blacks in the South had to obey the signs dictating where they could drink, eat, use the restroom, enter or exit train or bus stations, and shop for supplies.[7] Even so, these recruits and draftees had entered a world of noncivilians, and as time went by trainees accustomed to segregation had adjustments of their own to make. The military shipped and trained men and women separately, but ultimately all branches of the armed forces phased out racial segregation in troop training and transport. By March 18,

1951, all basic training within the United States was integrated.[8] Southern trains still enforced segregation, but once trainees entered the military reservation they left racial separation behind and inevitably had at least some exposure to persons of other colors.[9]

Many recruits got their first real glimpse of military life at reception battalions while processing in. Cadre at these centers greeted them by calling roll—mispronouncing even the simplest of names—and by assigning the bewildered-looking newcomers a variety of tasks and putting them to work right away. Depending upon an individual's luck or demeanor, one could end up "policing" or cleaning the grounds, standing guard at night, or pitching in on KP, or kitchen duty. Additionally, trainees had to attend to numerous other details. Piles of paperwork had to be completed, including medical history forms and the assignment of allotment insurance to wives or parents in case one died while in service to Uncle Sam. Written examinations had to be taken to allow the military to gauge whether or not one needed remedial-type training or to determine an individual's assignment within a particular corps.[10] Physical examinations, including tooth inspections and, in the case of men, genital inspections for venereal disease, had to be endured, complete with vaccinations for those not yet immunized.

More importantly, while at the reception battalions, trainees began the long and painful process of leaving their individuality behind and accepting their place on the lowest rung of the military ladder. Warned before leaving home to pack only the bare essentials—a toothbrush and razor, a pair of underwear or two, and maybe a change of clothes—trainees by necessity and instruction began to dress alike once they received their uniforms from the quartermaster. Only the fact that the military required trainees to stencil their names and serial numbers onto everything issued them distinguished one pair of fatigues or boots from another. In addition to dressing alike, all trainees made a mandatory visit to the post barber shop where the barbers invariably asked each customer how he or she wanted his or her hair cut. Most men wanted a little off the sides or top or perhaps a nice trim, but all left the chair with the same close, clean, standard-issue buzz cut. As Louis Baldovi notes, "In less than a minute I was practically bald."[11] For women, hair was normally cut to the bottom of the jacket collar, shorter hair being discouraged as unfeminine and perhaps a sign of lesbian tendencies.[12] By now, the trainees not only looked alike; they had learned to act alike as well, to conform to the military's demand that they obey orders. John Williams and his tent mates had internalized this lesson so completely that they complied when men came to their tents at three in the morning, ordered them to fall out, fall in, and double-time march for two miles in the cold. Told at the end to wait for the next soldier, Williams and the others did not move until morning came without anyone else appearing and they realized that they were standing on the road beside their tent.[13] Indeed, even before boot camp, military life could be filled with hardship.[14]

However educational the trip to basic training turned out to be, though, it still did not prepare most trainees for what awaited them on the other end. Regardless of branch of service, basic training or boot camp had one mission—to tear down the civilian and build up an effective member of the military machine.[15] And, the clock began ticking the moment that new recruits and draftees stepped foot on the military post. From that point forward it no longer mattered who or what one had been in civilian life—male or female, black or white, rich or poor, educated or unschooled. The only thing that mattered was that trainees learned to be homogenous if not interchangeable parts of their particular armed force, accepting of orders, disciplined, and prepared for whatever duty lay ahead.

Army Basic Training

Throughout the Korean War era, no branch of the armed forces strained harder to train new recruits and draftees than the Army. Of the 5,720,000 Selective Service registrants examined from July 1950 to July 1953 who went on to serve in the wartime military, 2,834,000 received their training from the Army. In addition, the Army accepted 1,475,700 or 94 percent of the era's draftees into its ranks.[16] Under the best of circumstances, training so many new soldiers would have posed difficulties, but the situation in 1950 made completing the task frighteningly burdensome. After World War II, the Truman administration significantly trimmed the military, reducing many units to below strength while paring others to zero strength. These postwar personnel cuts all but emptied the Army's pockets of qualified basic training instructors, and the immediate deployment of reserve troops to Korea in the early months of the war intensified that shortage.[17] Out of options, the Army simply shortened the basic training cycle so that existing schools and instructors could more quickly churn out overseas replacements and possible training cadre.[18] By August 1950, basic training for men had been reduced from fourteen weeks to only six weeks to be followed by another eight weeks of technical or unit training.[19] Even so, the Army continued to hunger for replacements and in October 1950 it shortened WAC basic from thirteen to eight weeks so that more women soldiers would be available to replace men in stateside jobs, freeing them to in turn replace men in Korea.[20] Throughout the war, high-ranking officers as well as various members of the press complained that six or eight weeks of basic turned out green troops, and commanders in Korea lamented that replacements did not have adequate training, but with few exceptions the Army stuck to its guns, producing an astounding number of new soldiers in a very short period of time.[21]

Regardless of when one entered the Army or how long basic training lasted, the experience remained fairly similar for Korean War trainees. Most men and women arrived at camp with strangers they had just met on the train or bus rather than with hometown friends.[22] In the years following World War II, the Army abandoned its policy of creating geographically based units. Instead, trainees from all over the country shipped in for basic training, only to be assigned to different units on the basis of individual skills after completion of the course. Not infrequently, these trainees approached training camps well after dark. Nighttime arrivals did not represent official policy, but when they occurred the Army took advantage of them to throw new arrivals off balance. In only a few weeks, the Army hoped to transform these undisciplined civilians into combat-ready infantrymen, and the sooner trainees could be mentally torn down, the sooner training cadre could rebuild them as soldiers.[23]

Most recruits and draftees did not find the Army welcoming upon their arrival at basic. Some drill sergeants made a point of immediately heaping abuse on men and women fresh from induction centers or reception battalions. Rudolph Stephens remembers that as soon as he got to basic, "a big black sergeant started cursing us and calling us foul names."[24] This particular incident "was hard to take because very few of us had even spoken to a black person in our lives." For men like John Kamperschroer, who came from homes where "4 letter words were not used," such language provided a rude introduction to military life.[25] Training cadre usually greeted newcomers somewhat more cordially than this, but trainees still felt a wave of regret. Homesick, frightened, and tired, they "didn't know what to do or why I was there."[26] Before long, though, most realized that they simply had to get used to things because "there wasn't anything any of us could do about it."[27]

No matter what time of the day or night trainees pulled into camp, they soon found their way to the barracks for a first look at their new home. Korean War–era volunteers and draftees did not expect luxury, but even so they could not help but be disappointed when they saw the buildings that would house them for the better part of two months. In order to accommodate the huge flow of trainees after the outbreak of the war, the Army reopened camps that had been mothballed or simply left to rot after 1945.[28] Troop quarters consisted of "temporary" wooden structures built cheaply to house the soldiers of a different war and they had the appearance of abandoned buildings.[29] Some had doors or windows missing, and almost all relied upon primitive coal furnaces for heat. At Camp Lee, Virginia, smoke from a local chemical plant permeated everything, including the female trainees' uninsulated living quarters.[30] But, "since their flimsy walls and floors had not yet collapsed, and their showers were still functional, they were deemed appropriate to accommodate the recruits for Korea."[31]

Inside the barracks, more surprises awaited the temporary occupants of these temporary shelters. Comfort and privacy had become things of the past. Rows and rows of beds, really just three-inch-thick mattresses resting on wire springs, ensured cramped, uncomfortable quarters for would-be sleepers.[32] In the bathrooms, common showers ruled the day.[33] Forty or fifty men or women might be expected to rotate through only five or six showers each morning before marching to the mess hall for breakfast. Toilets sat unshielded by stalls and not uncommonly faced the only available sinks. As one veteran recalls, "sometimes, depending on what was served for dinner, a trio or quartet would be performing for an uninterested audience of hand-washers or shavers."[34]

New trainees almost always received some type of orientation from company commanding officers, either at the reception battalion or shortly after arriving at basic training. "Your military career is about to begin," these lectures started. "Perhaps you think it has begun already, but you haven't seen anything yet. You're in the Army now."[35] Part pep talk, the speeches went on to detail all the benefits of Army life—free food, clothing, housing, and a steady salary, not to mention status. "Mama will be very proud that her boy is not a mama's boy any longer." But they also informed "rawcruits" that "in return, you are expected to work, and I mean work" and warned that some would never make the grade because "the going is too rugged." Trainees also learned some of the dos and don'ts of Army life, starting with "do not go absent without leave." Some camps issued information packets with admonitions against going AWOL printed repeatedly throughout.[36]

With introductions out of the way, training began in earnest. Designed to tear down trainees' civilian identities, inculcate them with military customs, and work them into physical fitness, the first couple weeks of basic training made even the toughest men and women question their abilities. Highly regimented, each day typically began before sunrise when reveille sounded. Trainees got up, showered, shaved, dressed, and got into formation to march to the mess hall for morning chow.[37] After eating, it was time to clean the barracks and latrines or head off to training.[38] Rain or shine, every day included not just classroom sessions on subjects like map reading, the achievements and traditions of the Army, and personal hygiene but also plenty of outdoor field exercises and calisthenics.[39] Occasionally, films on topics like the need for soap and how to use it broke the monotony.[40] By lunch, hungry trainees devoured whatever the cook gave them and then returned to the day's business.[41] After the evening meal, trainees finally had some free time to polish shoes, wash and iron uniforms, and "police" their living quarters. If they finished their chores quickly enough, they might slip down to the service club for a game of table tennis, a snack or beer, some live entertainment, or even a dance if women had been brought in by a local social group.[42] Lights out came around 2100 hours or 9:00 p.m., not a minute too soon for most of the exhausted trainees, but training cadre not infrequently awakened them in the middle of the night to inspect footlockers or wooden floors.[43] Around the clock, strict instructors demanded perfection from trainees who could not help but feel that "even by trying to do right, one could be humbled quickly and unfairly."[44] Luckily, most trainees adjusted fairly swiftly to military life as they were either too busy following orders to think about it or too tired to give any thought to whether or not they were happy.[45]

In between inspections and physical conditioning, the Army imparted a number of fundamental skills to trainees in the first few weeks of basic training. Men and women who came to camp slouching and dragging their feet became accustomed to standing up straight, lining up in an organized manner, and marching on demand, sometimes for miles. Through drills and classroom instruction they learned to find their way with only a compass and map, properly attach gas masks, sanitize living quarters, employ appropriate military jargon, and, in some cases, distinguish their left hand from their right.[46] Trainees also became familiar with the most important tool of their new trade—the M-1 rifle. No one would have the opportunity to actually fire this weapon until at least the third week of basic training, but by then all trainees would be proficient in disassembling, cleaning, and assembling it. Without exception, drill instructors and training cadre emphasized the M-1's centrality to battleground survival and told their trainees to "make it your friend, take it apart, oil it, keep it clean, and take it to bed with you."[47]

By the beginning of the third week, recruits and draftees were on their way to physical fitness and it was time for the real work to begin. Having beaten trainees into submission, drill sergeants and cadre now started to build soldiers. Some trainees participated in "confidence courses" to boost their self-esteem. Daniel Wolfe describes how his unit marched three miles before beginning just such a course where the men had to hop from tire to tire, crawl through puddles under barbed wire fences, scale a twelve-foot wooden wall, and cross a stream. After ten minutes' rest, the men embarked on a hike through the mountains that kept them out until almost two in the morning.[48] Tired or not, trainees still had duties, like KP or fireguard watch, to attend to, and they still had to get up early the next day ready to process all of the information that the Army deemed crucial to their survival. Specialists taught trainees elementary first aid, the art of camouflage and concealment, the proper way to construct field fortifications and dig foxholes, and how to effectively wield a bayonet.[49] Under supervision—or, more accurately, under scrutiny—trainees practiced hand-to-hand combat, obstacle courses, and foxhole drills where tanks rumbled above their heads.[50]

After the first few months of the Korean War, the Army added more realistic maneuvers to its basic training lineup. In general, the Army had done little to update training methods or technology since the Second World War and had become complacent in the belief that no reason existed for tough, realistic training.[51] When North Korean forces almost pushed American troops off the peninsula, however, the Army recognized that it had to better prepare its soldiers for the task of fighting.[52] As a result, basic training personnel began to develop infiltration and other exercises to familiarize trainees with and inure them to the sights, sounds, and smells of real battle.[53] At Fort Dix, cadre treated trainees to a course where they crawled under barbed wire obstacles dragging their M-1 rifles as buried explosive charges detonated around them and machine gun bullets "whizzed inches above our heads."[54] Then, officers examined the rifles for dirt, and anyone unfortunate enough to have emerged with a less than clean M-1 had to repeat the ordeal. At the end, drill sergeants gave the order to fix bayonets and charge dummies that had been strung up in the trees. Seymour Bernstein remembers one of his officers marking the occasion by shouting, "Scream, damn you! Scream as you go in for the kill! That's how you scare the hell out of the enemy!"[55] By 1952, Fort Dix also had added a maneuver taken straight from the hills of Korea. In their last week of basic training, soldiers charged "Ridge 102," using live ammunition.[56] Similarly, the Hawaii Training Center had trainees jog uphill behind tanks for almost a mile only to be assaulted with live ammunition at the base of Hill 904.[57] Such simulated battle conditions were thought by more than a few to be worse than those in the Korean war zone.

Whatever else trainees did at basic training, they spent the majority of their time after the first two weeks learning to use the Army's stockpile of weapons.[58] The M-1 remained the primary focus, and in eight weeks each trainee fired over five hundred rounds in an effort to achieve reasonable accuracy.[59] Cadre also introduced trainees to a host of other devices being used in Korea, such as M-30s, Browning automatic rifles (BARs), 60 mm mortars, bazookas, .45 caliber pistols, 37 mm recoilless rifles, and all types of grenades.[60] Not surprisingly, accidents and incidents could and did happen. At Fort Hood, a private gunned down a lieutenant saying he "would do anything to get out of the army," and at Fort Dix a corporal narrowly saved the day when a trainee froze after unlocking a grenade.[61] Private Charles Burrows died not long after his arrival at Camp Stoneman, California, when someone accidentally shot him.[62] Such occurrences, coupled with the amount of time spent firing different weapons, prompted many trainees to conclude that the entire object of basic training was to teach them to "forget thinking and learn to kill."[63] Like Rudolph Stephens, they believed they "learned the same thing over and over again, and that was how to kill, kill, kill. That's all you heard day in and day out, how to kill someone."[64] Whether this was true or not, if trainees managed to internalize the willingness to take another life, then they had in fact made the transition from citizen to combat soldier that the Army desired.

For both men and women, basic training ended the same way, in a long bivouac designed to expose them to everything they might encounter on a real battlefield. Just as they would have to do if sent to war, trainees left the security of their barracks and marched or jogged ten or twenty miles weighted down with full packs, heavy tent equipment, M-1 rifles, and the disassembled parts of various other weapons. Ambulances tagged along behind to pick up men who fainted from exhaustion, but otherwise no one could expect to hitch a ride on a truck.[65] As one Korean War veteran told trainee William Abreu, "In Korea there might not be trucks. It may rain all day, snow all day, and sweat may be running down your ass all day."[66] After setting up camp, trainees engaged in a number of different activities. Some cadre continued weapons training.[67] Others conducted more grueling exercises such as dumping trainees out miles from their new camp, handing them a compass, a map, and a book of matches and expecting them to find their way back alone. Usually, trainees participated in some sort of a mock battle. They assaulted hills, tried to infiltrate enemy lines, and dug foxholes. No matter how well individuals or units did, instructors quickly pointed out that "this was a piece of cake compared to what you'll find in Korea."[68]

For men who graduated basic training after the first few months of the Korean War, such warnings had great resonance. Army policy in previous years had been to assign new soldiers either to advanced training or stateside duty stations before shipping them abroad. As late as July 1950, the Army sought enlistments by promising "no present plan" to "use the recruits overseas."[69] However, manpower shortages in Korea increasingly pressured the Army to send men fresh from basic training to the war zone as individual replacements, and by September 1950 the press and others accused the Army of using green troops in the Korean theater. Army spokesmen denied these charges, but admitted that soldiers with at least fourteen weeks of individual and unit basic training could be sent.[70] Just over a year later and deeper into the war, the Army officially revised its system, allowing men entering service for the first time to be sent overseas directly after basic training, which by this time had been shortened to produce more soldiers in fewer weeks.[71] The FECOM (Far East Command) assignment became so common for new basic training graduates that the Army simply mimeographed the order and passed out copies when men returned from their final bivouac.[72] Some trainees managed to enter advanced training programs or officer candidate schools after their six or eight weeks of basic, but for many more basic training provided the only training they would receive before departing for Korea as "qualified killers."[73]

Both during and after the war, questions about the adequacy and effectiveness of the Army's basic training in preparing soldiers for battle surfaced. In 1950, a high-ranking officer complained about the "creampuff army," declaring "we've got to teach 'em how to fight, get rid of the non-essentials and get down to tough, hard bed-rock training."[74] He went on to say that basic training needed to be longer, at least fourteen to sixteen weeks, and that training needed to include more night training, reconnaissance on foot, and guerilla warfare tactics. A colonel in Korea told reporter Marguerite Higgins that soldiers had been "nursed and coddled, told to drive safely, to buy war bonds, to avoid VD, to write a letter home to mother, when somebody ought to have been telling them how to clear a machine gun when it jams." He reminded Higgins of the human consequences of making men "learn in combat, in a matter of days, the basic things they should have known before they ever faced an enemy." They became casualties because "some of them don't learn fast enough."[75] After the war, an Army panel found that the Army could have fought better in Korea and lamented that "the Chinese were tough . . . they knew how to endure . . . [while] we had to have three squares a day—and two of them had to be hot or junior would write his congressman or his mother." Mostly composed of Korean War veterans, the panel recommended major overhauls in Army training, starting with stricter discipline, off-post saluting, and a merit-based ranking system.[76] As prisoners of war began returning in the wake of "brainwashing" allegations, Army officers and psychiatrists targeted the training that had failed to inculcate the kind of devotion to God and country that would fortify soldiers during such an ordeal. The Army had been too solicitous of its trainees' welfare, such critics charged, leaving soldiers undisciplined and ignorant of American democracy.[77] Many Americans concluded that the Army had not provided tough enough training to its recruits and draftees and as a result had not produced men mentally and physically conditioned to fight.[78]

The troops themselves often agreed that their military schooling had holes in it larger than those made by their M-1 bullets. Exhausted, they missed out on information that could "spell the difference between life and death" in Korea and, while they reached a certain comfort level with the Army's weapons, few became marksmen in so short a time.[79] Sometimes men earned proficiency ratings on equipment that they could barely use. On the day of his tank driver's test, Vince Krepps could not get the tank out of first gear and ambled around aimlessly until the instructor asked a soldier sitting next to him how he had done. "Great," was the reply, and Krepps passed the exam.[80] In more than a few cases, men found themselves on a Korea-bound troop ship trying to make up for what they had not learned at basic training. Walter Ogasawara found out after sailing that he would become the gunner of a 57 mm recoilless rifle team. "I knew shit about firing a 57 mm recoilless rifle." So, while en route, he simulated firing it without ammunition. Similarly, Pedro Behasa worked on getting used to the 60 mm mortar while aboard ship, using eight rounds of ammunition for "live" practice.[81] No wonder, then, that a great many of those ordered to Korea felt like Merle Wysock that "I really wasn't ready to be an infantry-man even after . . . basic training."[82]

For men who entered service before the outbreak of the Korean War, another factor hindered the effectiveness of their basic training—the fact that they had completed it months or even years earlier. Lured into the military by recruitment posters that emphasized the benefits of military life, these troops joined an Army that in the post–World War II 1940s seemed to have forgotten that the principal business of soldiers remained to fight and if need be to die.[83] Convinced of the supremacy of nuclear weapons, the Army in these years used basic training to apply a thin layer of military socialization before ordering men to their first assignments.[84] Unfortunately, this system allowed men to learn a particular specialty without internalizing how to be a soldier.[85] Consequently, when hostilities began in Korea, Army cooks, lifeguards, drivers, teletype officers, and clerks suddenly found themselves headed to the battle zone as riflemen and infantrymen, jobs for which they never received adequate preparation.[86] Such was the experience of Milton Griffey, operator of a quartermaster laundry in Japan in 1950. Ordered to the Pusan Perimeter, Griffey on arrival asked where to find his laundry. To Griffey's horror, he received an M-1 rifle and the news that "[y]ou are an Infantry soldier. No laundry duty here!"[87] Griffey made a fast transition and performed well, but others proved less lucky. Men died, went home wounded, and became prisoners of war because their training had been incomplete or had occurred too long before the war to remember. Also, longtime soldiers often carried the additional weight of physical unfitness. Speaking of the Occupation forces sent to Korea from Japan in the early days of the war, one sergeant remarked, "Some of them are so goddam fat they can't hardly walk around. Most of them haven't had to put their pants on for years; always had a couple of geisha girls to do that for 'em."[88] Some, in fact, went to war so out of shape that when enemy forces broke the lines they just sat down and waited to be captured.[89]

While Army basic training had some grave limitations, it did prepare most men well enough that they survived their wartime tours of duty. Not every skill of soldiering could be imparted in a matter of weeks, but even the softest recruits and inductees who completed the course left it strengthened physically, conditioned to obey orders and perform duties despite fear, and more confident in themselves and their superiors. The sleepless conditions at basic became tutorials for battle, where exhausted men had no choice but to work and fight through days, nights, or even weeks.[90] Films and classes on hygiene translated into fewer deaths from disease and infection than in previous wars.[91] Hours and days spent at the firing range encouraged the bulk of the Army's trainees to shoot their weapons even if they did not feel completely comfortable with the idea of killing. The ratio of fire, or the percent of men firing their weapons in battle, increased significantly in the Korean War from World War II.[92] Especially after combat veterans returned from Korea to become instructors, basic training became more informative, more relevant to the war at hand, and trainees increasingly felt "physically and mentally conditioned to fight."[93] Observers from the press duly noted that Army basic training had taken clerks, factory hands, and schoolboys and given them the "weathered look of well-trained troops."[94] By December 1951, the Senate Preparedness Committee concurred, pronouncing Army training satisfactory.[95] Army basic training in the Korean War period had both strengths and weaknesses, but drill sergeants and cadre usually did the job they were called to do—they provided trainees with an introduction to warfare. And, then, as now, the old salts rested easy with the knowledge that the Army could teach men to march and give them the fundamental skills of soldiering, but that no amount of training or time could prepare soldiers for combat like combat itself.

Marine Boot Camp

"Sand fleas," "shit birds," boot camp "POWs"—you could call them anything but marines.[96] Recruits and inductees in the Korean War era could not be marines, could not even wear the Corps' emblem, until they successfully completed boot camp. Like the Army, the Marine Corps in the early 1950s had an obligation to train and produce combat-ready infantrymen in as short a time as possible, but the Marine Corps stood unparalleled among the armed forces in instilling esprit de corps in those who joined its ranks. Unlike Army trainees who could end up at any one of many basic training centers, all with their own strengths and specialties, all regular marines passed through either Parris Island or the San Diego Recruit Depot, boot camps dedicated to only one thing, the building of marines.

More challenging than the basic training offered by other branches of the military, Marine Corps boot camp began the moment trainees boarded the camp-bound shuttle. If enlistees or draftees entertained any notions that boot camp would not be as bad as the stories they had heard, the desolate landscape along the way gave them pause. Except for a few loblolly pines and a red cedar or two, Parris Island, tucked away in the sandy part of South Carolina, supported virtually no grass or shrubbery, and in the hot, sultry summer months the unshaded heat beat down on buses, buildings, and people relentlessly.[97] San Diego, of course, appeared less foreboding, but even there entering trainees would have been hard pressed not to realize the camp's utter isolation from civilian life.

Instead of providing reception battalions or a slow, easy in-processing phase, the Marine Corps immediately began to tear down and discipline trainees. Mean-tempered instructors boarded the buses cursing and shouting at their new charges, ready to enforce all the rules and make it clear that "our souls belonged to God, but our butts belonged to the United States Marine Corps."[98] Huston Wheelock recalls that on his arrival at the San Diego Recruit Depot, three guys lit up cigarettes in front of a "no smoking" sign. The Marine cadre threw "them up against the wall and beat the hell out of them right there."[99] Anyone still unconvinced that the Marine Corps meant business had a very long eight to fourteen weeks ahead of him.[100]

Marine boot camp followed the same general format as Army basic training and instilled many of the same skills. But, Marine Corps boot camp, for all its similarities, was not Army training. Determined not only to achieve the highest possible survival rate in battle but to be the premier branch of the armed forces, the Marine Corps pushed its trainees, especially male trainees, to the limit, both mentally and physically.[101] Drill instructors awakened Boots before dawn to begin days that lasted sixteen to twenty hours.[102] In those long days, Boots learned to perform with perfection or to suffer terrible consequences. Serious about stamping out individual identity and building marines, cadre unhesitatingly employed corporal punishment. Men caught smoking had to smoke an entire pack of cigarettes with a bucket over their heads.[103] Those who failed to shave at the ordered intervals found themselves dry shaving while marching and singing "The Marine Corps Hymn."[104] Messing up during a drill earned one a whack on the head with a "swagger stick." Freezing during grenade practice resulted in a good beating administered by the drill instructor. One trainee caught with three candy bars had to eat them on the spot, wrappers and all.[105] Another who coughed up phlegm and spit it out without permission had to lick it up off the ground. Not infrequently, an entire platoon paid for one man's mistake by missing out on recreational time or by having to drill longer.[106] From the standpoint of the cadre, one man's mistakes in battle could cost the lives or freedom of everyone.[107]

Technically, Marine Corps trainees had Sundays off, but the pressures of training rarely subsided even for a day. Unsatisfied and overzealous drill instructors took free time away in a flash, ordering platoons that had performed poorly during the week to drill on Sundays and organizing competitive and compulsory football games and boxing matches to fill the day for others.[108] Even treats, like a trip to the movies, could be used to teach lessons. Ralph Cutro remembers that once a week on very cold nights the cadre marched recruits to the drive-in to freeze "our tails off" in a sort of cold weather exercise.[109] While the experience was brutal, most marines who served in the Korean War and other wartime eras look back upon boot camp as instrumental to their survival. "They taught us everything we needed to keep us alive when we went into combat."[110] Some even credit it with "the most amazing transition I can ever imagine . . . much of that training helped all of us involved, both in Korea, and life long after."[111]

Even more than the Army, the Marine Corps regimented the life of its trainees. Almost from arrival, Boots did everything as a group and they did it in a uniform way.[112] They got up at the same time and made their bunks at the same time in the same way. When it came time to shower, the men lined up, marched to the showerhead as a group, pulled the ring to wet their bodies, applied soap in the prescribed order to their various body parts, rinsed, dried, and marched back to the bunks. Trainees went to chow together, trained together, and learned to do every task identically throughout their day until they all went to bed at the same appointed time. Boots even learned to communicate with one another using approved Marine Corps vocabulary. No longer did male or female trainees go upstairs or downstairs—they went topside or down below. They hit the deck, not the floor, and walls and windows became bulkheads and portholes while latrines became heads. Also, Boots learned that no matter where they were, the rules and procedures remained the same. Whether on base, at the pool, on a train, at the movies, stateside, or overseas, the Marine Corps expected marines and marine trainees to employ the lessons they had been taught and to recognize the chain of command.[113] In quick fashion, trainees learned to act and be alike and they also learned to respect and rely upon those who had internalized the same lessons as themselves. For many marines, this lesson stuck with them not only in the heat of battle, where they acted without ever doubting that their comrades would back them up, but in later life as well. They, like Norman Weibel, were certain that "I could always count on my buddies and they on me. Response would be instantaneous."[114]

Those who completed boot camp felt more than a deep sense of accomplishment. They had watched some of their number wash out, unable to handle the constant pressure, and seen others held back by an inability to perform satisfactorily on proficiency tests. But they had made it, and these new marines saw themselves in a new light. Strict drill instructors and cadre not only had prepared recruits well for whatever duty lay ahead; they had transformed them as individuals. "We arrived at boot camp as mere boys, but left there as men."[115] No prouder day could be imagined than graduation, when former trainees finally got to pin the Corps emblem on their uniforms and pass in review in front of the camp's big brass, a symbol that they had entered the exclusive world of the Marines.

Marines they might be, but for those destined for wartime duty in Korea, more training waited just around the corner. Unlike the Army, which sometimes shipped new soldiers straight from six or eight weeks of basic to the war zone, the Marine Corps decreed in September 1950 that all marines leaving for Korean duty had to have at least twelve weeks of training.[116] Also, by the end of the war, all war-bound soldiers had to pass through specially designed programs at Camp Pendleton, California before their embarkation to Korea. New boot camp graduates assigned to any of the supporting arms groups, such as artillery or tanks, first entered the Supporting Arms Regiment for an additional four weeks of training. All men at the rank of sergeant or below with less than six months in a military occupational specialty (MOS) passed through the Infantry Training

Regiment for four weeks of infantry training. All marines, regardless of length of service, joined the Staging Regiment for three weeks of processing, physical and combat conditioning, lectures and demonstrations, and intensive cold weather training.[117]

At the Staging Regiment, the final stop before heading to the Far East, marines received all of their combat equipment, from helmets and rifles to mess kits and canteens. They updated their administrative records, including pay allotments, insurance, wills, emergency data forms, and dog tags. Doctors and dentists performed thorough examinations, making sure cavities got filled, shots were up to date, and men met the minimum standards of physical fitness. "Nothing was left to chance, no body part left unexamined."[118] Trainees attended lectures and classes on a variety of subjects such as how to live in the field, laying and removing land mines and booby traps, and life aboard troop ships. Experts warned them once again of the dangers of venereal disease, producing photos and films that showed "scabbed,

"Taking up positions in the snow, Marine infantrymen act as 'aggressor troops' during winter and mountain warfare training in the Sierra Nevada Mountains at Pickel Meadows, California in the early 1950s." Photo, with accompanying caption, courtesy of the U.S. Marine Corps (Official Marine Corps photo number A-177834).

deformed, and oozing genitalia."[119] Officers emphasized the Universal Code of Military Justice, again and again cautioning marines not to do anything that might land them in a naval prison or worse. Men practiced for war by marching, completing obstacle courses, conducting close order drills, throwing live grenades, and firing pistols, carbines, and BARs.

Perhaps most importantly, especially for those leaving for Korea in winter, marines at the Staging Regiment underwent cold-weather training. At camp, they watched films demonstrating how to survive the cold and the consequences of improper preparation. James Brady recalls a color film clip in which the surgeon did not have to cut off the toes of a frostbite victim, "he simply bent them back and they broke off in his surgical glove, all five toes, bloody at the stump but otherwise black and dead." Brady also remembers the lesson—"Avoid this . . . keep your feet dry, change your socks, and don't get frostbite."[120] Then the men received the latest in military-issue winter clothing—long underwear, fur parkas, wool gloves, socks, hats, vests, and, by late 1952, rubber thermal boots—along with another demonstration on the use and care of their new items. After such preliminaries, the men were loaded onto Greyhound buses for a twelve-hour trip to Pickel Meadows, California, in the Sierra Nevadas, where they would spend six days and nights surviving the elements.

At Pickel Meadows, marines learned many things about surviving in the cold.[121] They built shelters, melted snow to make water, warmed frozen rations to an edible temperature, and saw how weapons performed differently at extreme temperatures. After the second day, marines spent their time hiking through the snow, breaking trails, crossing streams, and living out of their packs. Sufficiently beaten down by the weather, trainees learned that the Marine Corps had another lesson to teach them. Frostbite or hypothermia could kill, but so too could the enemy. Marines pretending to be Chinese soldiers took every opportunity to attack the hapless and exhausted trainees—they pounced in the dead of night after men had bedded down, at wayside lunch breaks, and as men stopped to catch their breath after miles of hiking through the thin air. Trainees unfortunate enough to be captured did not return to some safe, warm holding cell. Instead, their captors interrogated them all night in sign language and Chinese.[122] Eventually, the exercise ended and the trainees returned to Camp Pendleton, but the brutal and realistic experience left its mark on all. Back at camp, some men had to be treated for frostbite.[123] Only now did the Marine Corps deem its men ready, after a final parade and weekend of liberty, to ship out for the real war in Korea.[124]

Marine Corps boot camp differed from Army basic training in many ways, but perhaps most importantly in its thorough, lengthy, and continual training process. In explaining why marines in prisoner of war camps did not "crack" as often as Army soldiers, Colonel William Frash explained that the Marine Corps did not rely upon past training. "From the day a man enters the Marine Corps he is under training of some sort or another. . . . His officers are constantly under training."[125] And, the kind of training that marines received mirrored the situations they would face in combat as nearly as possible. Trainees underwent extreme physical and mental challenges with little rest or respite. Thus, the Corps rarely had occasion to commit "green" or undertrained troops to battle or to command positions within the war zone.[126] As a result, marines in Korea could fall back on what they had learned and represent well the Corps that sent them.

Navy and Air Force Boot Camp and Basic Training

Like all branches of the military, the Navy and Air Force used basic training and boot camp to indoctrinate recruits and prepare them for life within the service. Trainees learned military customs and courtesies, discipline, personal hygiene, pride in unit, rules of conduct, emergency first aid, and military insignia.[127] Most Boots also got the opportunity to drill and become familiar with weaponry, such as the M-1 rifle.[128] In general, however, both Navy and Air Force basic training focused less on the development of combat skills than on other things.

Navy boot camp, which lasted nine to eleven weeks during the Korean War and took place at either Great Lakes, Illinois, or San Diego, California, instructed recruits on naval history and traditions while familiarizing them with the skills they would need aboard ship or in future technical training.[129] The Navy provided trainees with a copy of the *Blue Jackets Manual*, or the "Sailor's Bible"—outlining the duties and requirements of becoming a seaman and containing information on ships—and expected them to know it. Both men and women studied naval exploits from John Paul Jones to the Battle of Midway and learned to recognize different types of ships and flags.[130] They learned about naval organization and the different rates and rankings of personnel. Classroom lectures explained compass directions, semaphore signaling, ship navigation, the types and uses of aircraft and weapons, and the contents of the Universal Code of Military Justice. Cadre conducted hands-on drills to familiarize trainees with firefighting techniques, damage control, anti-aircraft gunnery, and gas mask usage.[131] Male enlistees watched films on the prevention of venereal disease and underwent exercises designed to help them survive at sea. At some point during their training, men jumped into the water from twenty- or thirty-foot towers and then took off their trousers to use them as flotation devices.[132] Throughout the course, recruits took a number of quizzes and exams on the material thrown at them, but in the end, everything came down to whether or not one could swim. No matter how well a trainee had done on other things, he or she could not graduate Navy boot camp before passing a swimming proficiency exam, treading water for a set amount of time and swimming the length of the pool.[133]

Having separated from the Army, the Air Force revamped its eight- to thirteen-week basic training in the late 1940s and early 1950s.[134] Recruits continued to learn military drill and basic military subjects, but new elements became increasingly important. For women, formal studies replaced long marches, bivouacs, and combat training. Female trainees attended courses in advanced mathematics, citizenship, airplane recognition, map reading, first aid, personal hygiene, and survival in the tropics or the Arctic.[135] Men submitted to an Airman Classification Test Battery, where information on their educational background, occupation, hobbies, and aptitudes was collected and handed over to Career Guidance personnel who then assisted the trainee in selecting the best Air Force specialty for him. Army instruction did not completely go away, but it became so watered down that soon after the Korean War, while the Army tried to increase the length of its basic training, the Air Force reduced its basic training to four to six weeks for any recruit selected for technical training.[136]

Less physically and emotionally demanding than that offered by the Army or Marine Corps, Navy and Air Force boot camp and basic training were still basic training. Drill instructors and cadre told recruits when to eat, sleep, shave, shower, march, and write home. Those failing to conform or follow the rules faced punishment. Caught chewing gum, a substance banned because of the possible damage to ship decks, Glen Schroeder had to wear the offending piece on his nose.[137] Another naval recruit who refused to bathe regularly got ordered to the shower where three members of his squad bathed him, clothes and all.[138] As one veteran notes, the cadre may not have used corporal punishment, but "it doesn't mean that they did not inflict pain."[139]

Also, Navy and Air Force trainees lived in cramped and uncomfortable quarters. WAVE recruits slept in small cubicles with two double-deck bunks and four lockers while WAFs occupied two-bed cubicles in barracks of fifty or more women.[140] Male Navy trainees often stayed in more typical barracks, but had to stow all their belongings in sea and ditty bags that hung from the front of the bunk.[141] Air Force enlistees only dreamed of the luxuries enjoyed by those in other branches of the military. Lackland Air Force Base, the Air Force's primary basic training location, became so overcrowded during the war that rumors of suicides, epidemics, and deaths spread, prompting various investigations. With almost seventy thousand recruits crammed into the camp built for less than thirty thousand, the Air Force offered only tents for housing and the training program all but collapsed. Senator Lyndon Baines Johnson publicly censored the Air Force, prompting further studies of the crowded conditions. Red Cross, Air Force, and other reports eventually exonerated the Air Force, finding "no instance of actual hardship," but countless recruits suffered the cold winter rains or hot summer winds in their leaky, rickety tent city. The Air Force seemed an easy alternative to Army service, but training conditions at Lackland ranked among the worst in the military.[142]

In most cases, what happened at Navy or Air Force boot camp stayed at boot camp, but one offense in particular could haunt recruits for the rest of their lives. Throughout the 1950s, all branches of the military scrutinized trainees for evidence of homosexuality, but the Navy and Air Force enforced the military's antigay policy with special vigor. In a reversal of World War II practices, both began intense indoctrination programs designed to encourage revulsion toward homosexuals and impart a willingness to inform on those suspected of being gay.[143] At their physical exams, future female airmen had to answer a series of questions like, "Do you prefer going to parties with all boys or all girls?" and "Have you ever had any feelings for women that you think might not be acceptable to other women?" The Office of Special Investigations stalked possible lesbians, opening their mail, questioning them in the middle of the night, and interrogating their friends.[144] For its part, the Navy treated WAVES to a three-part series of lectures on the legal, medical, and moral consequences of homosexuality. Line officers explained that women who "branded and disgraced themselves" with homosexuality would receive less than honorable discharges and could be court-martialed. Medical officers debunked the idea that homosexuals "are born and not made" and affirmed that lesbians too contracted gonorrhea and syphilis. Chaplains warned against women alienating themselves from God and spirituality through even a single homosexual encounter.[145] For men, the antigay lectures became more graphic. Recruits received explicit advice on how to spot gays, reject their advances, and report them to officials. In 1948, the Navy made a startling connection between homicide and homosexuality. Instructors described "grisly murders" where "sometimes the bodies of these victims are horribly mutilated" and noted that the impulse that led to such events could usually "be linked to homosexuality."[146] For recruits careless or foolish enough to get "outed" at basic training or after, disastrous consequences awaited. General discharges under less than honorable conditions or dishonorable discharges carried with them more than shame. Even if a court-martial did not follow, the recipient of such discharges could lose the right to vote, the ability to work in any government or government affiliated agency, and veterans' benefits.[147]

The men and women who completed Navy or Air Force basic training, not unlike the trainees of other branches of the armed forces, welcomed graduation day. Not only did they possess more knowledge, skills, and physical fitness than when they enlisted, but they had survived the trials of military training. Now, these newly minted servicemen and servicewomen had only to be fitted into their respective services, to enter the professions in which they were needed. Many would attend advanced training, some would ship out to the war zone, but all would go where ordered by Uncle Sam.[148]

National Guard and Reserve Training

As early as the Revolutionary War, Americans dreamed of an Army of patriots, citizen-soldiers who would muster in during times of national crisis and then go back to their own lives when peace returned. The balance, though, proved tricky—men too wedded to civilian ways remained difficult to manage and unskilled in the art of war while those too well trained found themselves best suited for the regular military. Still, in the years after World War II, Army planners, scrambling to devise a system that would allow for a smaller regular Army as well as provide the country with adequate military protection, decided to lean heavily on the National Guard. Army Chief of Staff George C. Marshall and others gambled that Guard units, which answered to their respective states rather than to the Army except when federalized, could transform "weekend warriors" into a combat-ready force capable of augmenting the Army at a moment's notice.[149] The sudden and unexpected outbreak of the Korean War, however, revealed the training and preparation of the Guard unworthy of such a burden. The immediate deployment of Guard troops to Korea or anywhere else simply could not take place. Only months of additional training, including Army basic training, could prepare guardsmen for active duty.[150]

In the mid-1940s, the Army developed a six-year training program for National Guardsmen, but these plans never reached fruition. Confronted with the reality of three-year enlistments, the National Guard halved the length of its training in 1948. Theoretically, recruits would spend one year each on basic soldier skills, beginning specialist training, and advanced skills.[151] But, a year of National Guard training throughout the 1940s and 1950s consisted of only ninety-six hours of weekly or biweekly drills and a two-week summer camp, a very short time in which to produce qualified infantrymen or artillerymen.[152] Also, because guardsmen never completed basic training, NCOs and officers had not only to hone the skills of their recruits but also to somehow fit lessons on military customs and rules into their schedules.[153] Personnel turnover further intensified the time crunch by ensuring that the thinly stretched Guard had to offer separate classes for men of different skill levels.[154] Unsurprisingly, Guard recruits, who lived at home and trained in their own neighborhoods with friends and relatives, lacked the kind of indoctrination given regular Army draftees and enlistees and remained amazingly independent of military life and unprepared for the battlefield.[155] By early 1950, an Army Field Forces report lamented that "it is doubtful if the training and overall efficiency of the Guard will ever reach its desired standards."[156] The press agreed, stating that though guardsmen "were called soldiers, they were not soldiers, and, in the true meaning of the word, had never expected to be soldiers."[157]

National Guard training before activation for the Korean War might have been inadequate, but the fault usually lay with the system itself, with the lack of training time and equipment, and not with the NCOs and officers. By 1950, many of those in charge of educating recruits possessed wartime experience, having served in World War I or II.[158] They knew the demands of battle and tried to impart as many martial skills as possible to their men in the time allotted. On drill nights, guardsmen marched, trained on weapons ranging from rifles to .50 caliber machine guns, learned Army regulations and tactics, performed close order drills, and practiced the particular specialty of their company—artillery, maintenance, etc.[159] When summer came, they played soldier for a couple of weeks at camp. The men went on bivouacs where they lived in the field, learned to shave with cold water, and ate c-rations. Even here, though, discipline remained much more lax than in the regular Army. Frank Rowan remembers that after being denied a pass, he simply snuck his girlfriend into the camp to spend the weekend with him, an action that would not have gone unnoticed or unpunished in Army basic training or Marine Corps boot camp.[160] These experiences could not replace the basic training given to regulars.

Consequently, when news of war in Korea broke, few guardsmen had the preparation to fulfill even their traditional role—taking over the stateside training responsibilities left behind by deployed reservists—and many seemed surprised to be activated at all.[161] Ordered to prepare for active duty, National Guard units had much to do. The ranks had to be filled, no easy task given that the draft took its allotment of eligible men and that the Guard could no longer rely upon high school student enlistments to pump up the numbers.[162] Equipment had to be put in order and prepared for shipment to wherever the Army had decided to send the unit. And, as much training as possible had to be squeezed in around administrative paperwork and processing.[163] Then, the units gathered at the armories to be formally brought under Army orders, ready to ship out for further training.

Before they could be of use to the Army, either at home or in the war zone, newly activated guardsmen first had to complete basic training. Like other Army recruits, they left home for camps around the country, where they marched, fired weapons, passed through obstacle courses, and endured bivouacs. But, the nature of the National Guard made for a different kind of basic training experience. Guardsmen stationed at a camp near home could return to their families at night as long as they made it back to training by reveille. Officers and NCOs refrained from much of the usual harassment of trainees and allowed enough free time that the men could while away evenings at the PX or cruise the local bars in search of women.[164] More importantly, because the National Guard had to put together units and not just train individual replacements, it had to continue to offer basic training to "fillers" even after original members of the group had completed the course.[165] So, at any given time, a National Guard unit might be conducting training on all levels from individual basic to regimental drills. Command of all of this complicated training could fall to almost anyone because officers and NCOs continuously rotated in and out of the unit while attending various schools. Arthur Kelly, a second lieutenant, became battery commander by default, saddled with the responsibility of conducting basic training, qualifying men for individual weapons, and getting everything ready for overseas orders.[166] Similarly, only eighteen years old, George Hubbard, who had been in the Army for just six months, began leading men through basic training.[167]

Finally, after many months of individual, company, battalion, regimental, and division training and numerous proficiency tests, the Army deemed National Guard units ready for duty. Some remained stateside to function as training battalions, but the Army ordered many others to ship out to Japan or Korea.[168] Not surprisingly, guardsmen headed for the Far East felt great apprehension about their new assignment, a fear only

made deeper by the upheaval that their units faced on the eve of departure. Even while packing equipment and conducting last-minute drills,
some units had to find replacements to bring them up to strength. Levies
taken by the Army to sustain divisions already in Korea siphoned off hundreds of members while Army policies requiring fourteen weeks of basic
for overseas duty disqualified some of the men on hand.[169] Despite having
enlisted in part to go with the men they knew, many guardsmen found as
they boarded the troop ship that they instead would be going alone. Still,
many felt proud that the Army had chosen to send them.[170] When relatives
of men in the Oklahoma Thunderbird Division staged a protest against
the division's overseas assignment, bombarding state and federal Congress members with letters demanding that the 45th not be sent to Japan or
Korea, members home on leave discouraged such activities and put an end
to the movement.[171] Most guardsmen felt they would rather deal with the
communist problem at hand than leave it to become a larger problem for
their children to solve and echoed seventeen-year-old Private First Class
Joseph Popolo, who said, "What comes, will come. We are all ready to go if
called."[172]

For National Guard troops, training often did not end with arrival in the
war theater. Units in Japan and Korea continued to train, either completing
drills that had been left unfinished or applying lessons from the situation at
hand as they now understood it, before actually entering the conflict.[173] Even
so, regulars continued to eye guardsmen suspiciously and to believe them
inadequate and poorly trained.[174] Whether that was true in general or not,
guardsmen did possess varied and uneven levels of training, leading many
after the war to conclude that before entering the Guard men should have
to complete Army basic.[175] Much as their militia forebears had to do, Korean
War National Guardsmen all too often learned their new trade "the hard way
on the battlefield."[176]

Like National Guardsmen, members of the Reserves, especially the inactive Reserves, greeted the Korean War with gloomy unpreparedness.[177]
Although the post–World War II Navy conducted boot camp for its reserve
recruits, other branches of the military frequently allowed weekly meetings and summer camps to suffice for training.[178] As thirty-two men later
wrote from Korea, "Our training consisted, mainly, of reading Army manu-
als, engaging in close order drill and hearing ambitious brass tell us what
wonderful soldiers we were."[179] Worse still, some units, pressured to recruit
and retain enlistees, made even this trivial amount of training voluntary. In
Evansville, Indiana, where high school coaches recruited a number of teenage athletes for Marine Corps Reserve service, reservists did not have to

attend a single meeting or summer camp in order to maintain their reserve status.[180] Additionally, in times of peace, reservists could quit any time they chose.[181] As a result, training cadre could not afford to make training too strenuous or meetings too dull. Instead, Reserve get-togethers emphasized fun and games, leaving new recruits completely uninformed and unprepared for the possibility of actual combat. Veterans too suffered from this lack of vigorous training as any skills they had acquired during active duty faded away through years of tepid or nonexistent drilling.[182] Thus, on the eve of the Korean Conflict, the ready-to-go Reserves, like the National Guard, stood in dire need of time to train its members.

Unfortunately, reservists stood next in line behind the tattered and understrength regular military to enter the Korean battleground. All too quickly conditions grew grim along the Pusan Perimeter, and the military had no choice but to call on the Reserves to deploy as replacements regardless of whether or not they had received adequate training. Fresh-faced high school and weathered veteran reservists alike found their fates suddenly sealed.[183] In short order, they shuttled to military hubs, often located on the coast to allow for quicker deployment, for a couple of weeks of refresher training and then boarded Japan- or Korea-bound ships or airplanes.[184] Official policies called for underage or undertrained recruits to be removed from combat duty, but the drive for expediency sometimes meant that such rules got overlooked.[185] One commander promised his teenage charge "all the boot camp you want" after returning from Korea.[186] Pat Burris recalls that a couple members of his Marine Corps squad enlisted after the war began and had to be taught how to handle their weapons while on the troop ship.[187] The Air Force sent "qualified" pilots, but many had not flown since World War II, and a three-week refresher could not prepare them for all that had changed since then. Most reservists had been trained on propeller planes, not jets, and few had experience with the type of formation flying now deemed essential.[188] Reservists simply had to learn while on the job and in the war. No wonder that many felt unprepared for war and that regulars frowned upon having to serve with reservists.[189] But, as Martin Chamberlain, commander of the Seattle Organized Naval Reserves Number 1, declared, "Anyone who joins a reserve unit by that action has told Uncle Sam he's willing to go."[190]

In general, however grudgingly, most reservists during the Korean War accepted their assignments. Infantrymen, some of whom had held a gun for the first time on their way to Korea, humped from village to village and battle to battle. Seamen left their wives and children for months or years to ferry soldiers back and forth between the war and home or to cart supplies to the troops. Pilots qualified on propeller aircraft learned through trial and error to fly jets over the Asian hills. But, some backlash from reservists did occur during the war. Air Force pilots, frustrated that an inordinate number of reservists were being sent to Korea while regulars remained stateside, grumbled that "the regulars are policemen, so let them fight the police action."[191] Some attempted to evade duty by claiming a newly developed fear of flying or by trying to resign. Finally, in April 1952, six flying officers training at Randolph Air Force Base staged a "stay-down" strike in part to protest the use of reservists in the Korean War.[192] Well aware of both the inequities of the reserve call-up system and the problematic nature of reserve training, the House of Representatives introduced a new Armed Forces Reserve Bill in mid-1951. The bill provided for reservists to be classified either "ready" or "standby," depending upon how much time had passed since basic training and/or active duty.[193] The bill came too late, however, to be of any use to the thousands of reservists uprooted from civilian life and sent to Korea with little regard for the current status of their training. They would simply have to learn whatever else they needed to know when they arrived in the war zone or die trying.

Training Oversights and Distractions

As days of war spun into years in the Korean hills, pitting American troops against both North Koreans and Chinese "volunteers," all branches of the armed forces stepped up efforts to make troop training tougher and more realistic. The Army especially turned away from "spit and polish" to focus instead on the mechanics of combat.[194] These revamped programs managed to give recruits and draftees a more realistic foretaste of battle, but in a major training oversight the military failed to help trainees understand why they had been called to learn military skills at all and why they might have to fight in Korea. As a result, after arriving in the war zone, soldiers bitterly questioned their assignment.[195] By the time Matthew Ridgway took command of the Eighth Army in Korea in late December 1950, the new had completely worn off the war and he discovered that rallying the troops would have to wait until after he explained why their mission mattered and how it related to the homespun values of freedom and democracy.[196]

While the military rested easy in its authority to train men and order them to whatever post seemed most appropriate without explanation or apology, such cavalier treatment did nothing for the morale of those being sent to fight in a war far from home and in fact disregarded the very nature of the American fighting man. The crusadelike nature of World War II's total mobilization perhaps left the armed forces with amnesia, allowing them to forget that unlike the forces of many countries, American troops, pulled from the ranks of the citizenry, needed a cause in which to believe before making what could turn out to be a total sacrifice.[197] In the Revolutionary War, Baron von Steuben wrote, "You say to [a Prussian, French, or Austrian soldier], 'Do this,' and he doeth it. But I am obliged to say [to an American soldier], 'This is the reason why you ought to do that,' and then he does it."[198] In the intervening century and a half, not much had changed, and while Americans enlisted out of patriotism, vague notions of devotion to country gave only cold comfort to men caught in a "limited" but still very hot war. If they were to serve and fight effectively overseas, marines, Army infantrymen, pilots, and sailors needed something more concrete to sustain and encourage them or else their only focus would be on the day they could rotate home.[199]

A little under a year into the war, the Department of Defense introduced a new citizenship education program designed to impart to servicemen in the Army, Navy, and Air Force a better understanding of that for which they would be fighting. Developed by the Teachers College of Columbia, "Hours of Freedom" consisted of one-hour sessions, each dealing with a basic concept of democracy. Through lecture, discussion, debate, and dramatization, men would learn the value of an individual in a free society, the differences between democracy and communism, people's role in government, and presumably the importance of American involvement in a place as seemingly small and insignificant as Korea.[200] Unfortunately, the new program debuted at basic training, where young trainees crowded into classrooms too tired or bored to concentrate on the material at hand. Also, not infrequently, those in charge of educating the men had little knowledge or experience themselves and no time to prepare.[201] In the end, men continued to filter into Korea throughout the war with almost no information on why they had been sent, a poor recipe for combat effectiveness no matter how complete other training had been.[202]

GIs might have had few thoughts on democracy, but they often thought about home and family. The military attempted to make training all-consuming, but for many of those who served during the Korean War, financial hardship and the problems faced by their families as a result of their military service became distractions. During World War II, Congress created a system of family allowances to eliminate dependency as a cause for automatic exemption, but such legislation, deemed too costly, had lapsed by the Korean War.[203] As reservists and draftees mustered in, leaving civilian jobs and pay behind, they found it impossible to support themselves, much less their families, on the seventy-five or eighty-five dollars a month that the military paid them. Despite the 1940 Soldiers' and Sailors' Relief Act, which offered protection against the loss of a home should a man be called to active duty, servicemen watched helplessly as creditors foreclosed on their houses and repossessed their belongings, leaving wives and children to move in with relatives or fend for themselves.[204] Jim Kasler, an Air Force lieutenant, made so little money even with his flying allotment that his wife and daughter had to move in with his parents.[205] Donald Sipes's wife, left with a one-year-old and only twenty dollars in her pocket when her Marine Corps reservist husband left for active duty, struggled knowing that a sewing machine bought on time soon would be repossessed and that their home could no longer be afforded but was in no shape to rent or sell.[206] Similarly, Barbara Gates, mother of two small children, agonized that when her husband left, the family lost the home they were purchasing with a GI loan, and "they took the furniture, too."[207] How could servicemen focus on preparing to fight for their country when they were losing their own hearths and homes in the process?

By August 1950, the realization that America's men at arms desperately needed financial assistance had become widespread. Some states and localities responded quickly, offering cash or other benefits to the dependents of men sent to training or shipped overseas. Washington State began to provide assistance to military wives with minor children through welfare's Aid to Dependent Children program, convincing federal authorities to match funding.[208] On the national level, President Harry Truman appealed to Congress to make benefit payments to military dependents, and both the House and Senate debated various proposals.[209] Ultimately, federal payments from the government to families of the lowest ranks of enlisted men found approval, but servicemen had to chip in, sending money from their paychecks home.[210] These allowances relieved some of the pressure felt by servicemen, but as late as 1952 the Senate sought a 3 percent raise for enlisted men and junior officers, who continued to have difficulty supporting their families.[211]

Largely because of the social climate of the 1950s, which stressed the American male's role as provider, servicewomen rarely benefited from legislation designed to assist service families. Although paid more equitably in the military than in other sectors of the economy, female members of the armed forces found it almost impossible to qualify for the same allowances being handed out to the military dependents of men. The government automatically allotted support to the wives, children, and even parents of male service members, but gave nothing to the husbands or dependent parents of servicewomen.[212] In order to receive dependent benefits for their families, female service members had to prove they contributed at least half the support of their loved ones. Not until the 1970s would this discriminatory application of military allotments be challenged.[213]

Given quarters pay and other perks, officers usually had less cause to worry about money than the average GI, but those headed to the battlefront sometimes had good reason to wonder whether they remained too "green" for war. Many avenues existed for becoming a commissioned officer, not all of which provided a solid military education. The United States Military Academy at West Point and other service schools, as well as Officer Candidate School (OCS), proved rigorous and exacting, an excellent preparation for Korea or anywhere else a soldier might end up, but ROTC and other programs could be less so. Also, even if an ROTC program challenged its members, they might not enter the regular service until much later. One second lieutenant stationed in Japan by mid-1950 reflected that he had "experienced not a single day of active duty or training since the ROTC days at Purdue in 1948" and had been sworn in as a regular Army officer simply on the basis of having completed a graduate degree.[214] Such officers could only turn to their outfit's seasoned NCOs for help and hope that they learned fast enough to lead their men in war.

Doctors and other specialists got rank with even less military instruction. Hank Litvin enlisted in a Navy program for doctors that gave ensign's pay in return for two years of Navy service after residency. Before he could go through boot camp or receive any training at all, Litvin ended up at Inchon, where a supply clerk issued him a rifle and the unsought and unwelcome opportunity for on-the-job training.[215] More fortunate medical personnel did attend a short basic training before shipping overseas, but that did not mean that the military had prepared them for all of their new duties.[216] Many doctors and nurses arrived at MASH units or hospital ships with little knowledge of field medicine, surprised to find that their particular specialty mattered far less than the ability to learn fast and fill in where needed.[217] In Korea, general practitioners became anesthesiologists or VD officers, and surgeons operated literally by the book, performing procedures they had never even seen done.[218] Unfortunately for both the armed forces and the young soldiers counting on military doctors to piece them together again, the rotation system left doctors in the war zone for only about a year. By the time a doctor became useful, the military replaced him with an untrained and unskilled newcomer.[219]

Throughout the Korean War, all branches of the military did what the government expected by churning out enough servicemen and servicewomen to alleviate the manpower shortage and keep the war effort alive. To accomplish this, however, the armed forces all too often trained officers and enlisted men with haste, heedless of the fundamental needs of trainees. These shortcuts in training left many American troops less motivated and effective than they could have been. Asked to make their lives forfeit, to leave their families behind come what may, those sent to Korea deserved to be trained not adequately, but well, and their sacrifices warranted an explanation of why their mission mattered.

Beyond the Mechanics of Warfare: Training and Race

From the standpoint of the United States armed forces in the late 1940s and early 1950s, military training existed only to create competent service members, not to alter prevailing societal attitudes or to effect social change. Thus when President Truman issued Executive Order 9981 in 1948, requiring an end to racial discrimination in the military, most of the services responded glacially, refusing to integrate anything, much less their training camps. Led by Secretary of the Army Kenneth Royall and Army Chief of Staff Omar Bradley, the Army argued that segregation did not constitute discrimination and need not be ended.[220] Following suit, the Marine Corps and Navy refused to mix white and black troops.[221] Only the Air Force, led by Stuart Symington, accepted the order and quickly began to phase out all-black units and end racial preference as a factor in personnel policies.[222] But, by the end of 1950, domestic political pressures and then manpower needs in Korea eroded resistance to desegregation and all branches of the service started to integrate at least basic training.[223] Born primarily of military necessity, changes in the racial composition of troops at boot camp or other training sites had little effect on military infrastructure, but did greatly impact individual troops. Suddenly and intimately exposed to persons of other races, trainees learned lessons that went well beyond the mere mechanics of warfare.

For all its trappings of a modern industrial country—large cities, a proliferation of factories and businesses, a visible and active scientific community—America in 1950 remained astonishingly parochial. Individuals and families had moved around both during and after the Second World War, but most Americans still knew little about people and places beyond their own street corners and neighborhoods. Except perhaps in larger metropolitan areas where the fabled melting pot more closely resembled real life, people drew lines to keep themselves separate from those who looked or seemed different from themselves. In particular, and most especially in the South, racial separation maintained a not quite invisible and almost unbridgeable chasm between white citizens and others. Thus when men and women followed the beat of Uncle Sam's drum to newly integrating training centers during the

Korean War, they could only guess at what life would be like shared with people from the other side of the line.

Carefully packed among their toothbrushes, underwear, and other personal possessions, most recruits and trainees carried with them their own ideas about Americans of other colors. White troops often took for granted that African Americans would be dirty, foul-mouthed, lacking in self-control, and untrustworthy in combat.[224] And, the stereotypes did not end there. Asked in 1950 how he felt about integration, one twenty-year-old private replied that blacks were human but should not be mixed with white soldiers because "some of them, the bestest [sic] percent, are still like Head Hunters. They have bad blood, some of them are like animals."[225] A few whites did voice the opinion that the "Negro soldier has the right to rate the same as any other man no matter what," but a greater number resented the very idea of sharing sleeping quarters or a mess hall with blacks.[226] For their part, African Americans often entered service with the notion that no matter how well they performed, white comrades and superiors would never give them the credit they deserved. For others, especially those who had experienced Jim Crow first-hand, negative feelings ran even deeper.[227]

Entering the armed forces did not automatically erase trainees' personal biases on the issue of race, but in general boot camp and other training centers offered little opportunity for men or women to act upon such prejudices. Regardless of what one might have preferred, from the moment of swearing in, recruits and inductees had no alternative but to do things the military way—even if that meant bunking, eating, or sweating with someone of a different color. And, as the process of turning civilians into "Government Issue" continued, new habits and ideas began to supplant those so carefully brought along by trainees from home.[228] As black and white soldiers shared tents, meals, conversation, and the rigors of training, they discovered a multitude of similarities and often developed not only a new tolerance for one another but also interracial friendships.[229] White trainees, at first resentful of being placed in interracial outfits or barracks, came out of the experience averring that "now some of my best friends are of the Negro race. I can see no reason at all why colored and white cannot get along together in the Army."[230] Some concluded that it "is all in your mind. . . . If you can live with whites you can live with most colored."[231] Even National Guardsmen "changed [their] thinking . . . [blacks are] just the same as we are."[232] As Charles Moskos noted, "The thickness of a man's lips is not a factor if he offers you a drink from his canteen in the Texas desert."[233] African Americans underwent a similar transformation in racial attitudes. As one African American enlisted man noted after experiencing integrated basic training, "I think that mixed units are the best. I have several white friends. . . . We eat and sleep together. We train and work together. There ain't no difference."[234] Indeed, southerners marveled at "the amiability of the white and colored here [on the military reservation]."[235] As servicemen and servicewomen of different colors trained and spent time together, they became more accepting of individual comrades and more positive about desegregating the military as a whole.

Racially mixed training also produced troops more favorable toward integration in general.[236] Having spent a good deal of time at basic training getting used to the idea of associating freely with soldiers of many colors and nationalities, men and women, both black and white, who ended up at southern duty stations became indignant about the existing inequalities of Jim Crow communities. It seemed strange to them that bus stations, airports, movie theaters, and even municipal buildings had "white only" and "colored only" water fountains, restrooms, entrances, and sections. They resented the local customs and laws that prevented friends who dined and drank together on post from sitting together on the bus to town and from frequenting the same bars or restaurants once there. While the various services accepted the segregation and discrimination just outside their gates, troops who had learned to judge worth by character rather than color had trouble leading this double life. Some argued that the South, like the Army, should simply be integrated, that after a time people there "would accept the American Negro as an individual who is only reaping the benefits of those rights due him under the Constitution of the United States."[237] Others took a more active approach. In San Antonio, white servicemen ordered food for their black buddy who by prearrangement was to join them at a white restaurant.[238] Elsewhere, an all-white Airborne Ranger company walked out of a restaurant that refused service to the all-black 2nd Company.[239] Lieutenant Thomas Williams, a pilot in training at Craig Air Force Base, refused to sit in the colored section of a bus traveling from Florida to Alabama, stating that he did not feel obligated to obey laws that were unconstitutional.[240] In Columbus, Georgia, men headed to and returning from Korea rioted in response to police brutality toward black soldiers and the beating of a uniformed African American by white policemen at a nightclub.[241] Throughout the Korean War era, incidents like these proved few and insignificant—acts of civil disobedience belonging more to a later generation—but they clearly illustrate the changing viewpoints of men and women trained in integrated settings. Boot camp and basic training did not necessarily educate trainees to become social radicals, but the close contact it provided between the races did chip away at stereotypes and foster expectations of a more integrated world.

Not all of those who went through mixed training altered their original ideas about people of a different color. Moreover, even within the military integration faced difficulties. As late as 1951, at least one Army base, Fort Bragg, North Carolina, had yet to implement anything other than token integration, and at other locations tensions between black and white troops erupted in violence.[242] Additionally, even if trainees accepted a more racially diverse corps, officers and noncoms sometimes resisted the changes ordered from above. One Army division commander, when asked about integration, replied that "[i]t's God's law of the fish in the sea, the birds in the air, the animals on land. You don't mix them."[243] In Fort Jackson, South Carolina, two white sergeants brutally beat an eighteen-year-old black private, and at Camp Atterbury officials allowed the 31st Infantry (Dixie) Division Military Band to wear gray uniforms reminiscent of Confederate attire.[244] Sent to Fort Leonard Wood, Missouri, for boot camp, Stanley Stone wrote his mother that the Army discriminated against blacks by forbidding them to go into any of the nearby towns and that "we are being trained by some Negro hating white officers who are Southern bred . . . we are cursed at and berated and the Southern Negroes here are afraid to move."[245] Leadership and circumstance could make all the difference in the way men who trained together felt about each other.

To its credit, though, the military did try to prevent such racial incidents and uphold its commitment to institutional integration and equality of service. On posts throughout the country, PXs, movie theaters, and even swimming pools ceased to operate on a segregated basis. Men and women who worked together during the day found themselves able to socialize on their own time as well. Troops did not always take advantage of this opportunity. On some reservations, blacks and whites informally divided up recreational facilities or limited their use to service members, especially if the potential existed for men and women to come into close contact. Often clubs became segregated on dance nights or sponsors enforced the unwritten rule that men would dance only with partners of their own color.[246] Whatever impact integrated training had on the racial attitudes of trainees, it seldom prepared them for unbridled social integration. The most liberal might espouse equality yet still affirm, "I don't think they should marry one another . . . but that's all."[247]

For African Americans, mixed training in the 1950s sent mixed messages. On the one hand, from the moment of swearing in, black men and women could expect to be treated just like any other recruit or draftee. They would proceed to processing, be issued clothing, enter basic training, and eventually receive an assignment based on their skills and performance.[248] With few ratings now restricted, blacks could move into positions where they gave orders to whites—a situation deemed "nothing less than a miracle" by veteran Reuben Carter.[249] But, after being trained alongside whites, African Americans then could find themselves assigned to all-black units.[250] Throughout the Korean War, the Army maintained segregated units and even resegregated some units.[251] Also, African Americans learned that military protections ended the moment they stepped off the base. All branches of the military demanded that service members bow to sectional customs, including segregation, or face the consequences alone. Commanding officers in the South passed out maps of local communities showing black troops which neighborhoods, streets, and sections of town they could go to and warning that anyone breaking the rules would be at the mercy of the local police.[252] Townspeople in some places bragged that "[w]hen the colored [soldiers] come to town, they conform to the way we do things."[253] The military declined to intervene even when locals clearly mistreated soldiers off post. In Columbus, Georgia, police routinely terrorized black servicemen, beating them, taking their money, jailing and fining them, and warning them to stay out of town—and yet the Army did nothing.[254] White townspeople forced Sergeant Herbert Bradshaw from his car at gunpoint in Brownsville, Tennessee, dragged him to a building, and had a civilian beat him with a pop bottle as four police officers looked on. Tellingly, protests of Bradshaw's treatment came not from the military but from the NAACP.[255] Until after the Korean War, when local commanders forced business owners to integrate by making segregated recreational facilities off limits and the Department of Defense effected school integration by threatening to cut off federal subsidies, all guarantees of equality and fair treatment for nonwhite service members ended at the reservation gate.

The military had only one goal when conducting training: to produce more effective infantrymen, sailors, and airmen. But, the very nature of the process, tearing down civilian identities and rebuilding individuals, left men and women more open to new ideas and experiences. When boot camps and basic training centers integrated in the late 1940s and early 1950s, the armed forces merely saw the development as an easy way to boost efficiency, but for the tens of thousands of recruits of all colors who learned to live together it became a mild revolution. Perhaps unintentionally the Army, Air Force, Navy, and Marine Corps imparted a new attitude toward racial equality along with weapons training and close-order drills. Not all servicemen and

A young officer and his wife sit at the dock in San Diego staring at the waiting aircraft carrier before he leaves for Korea in 1950. Courtesy of the National Archives (photograph no. 306-PS-50-10828, War and Conflict Book no. 1381).

servicewomen took the lesson to heart, but, along with battlefield experiences, mixed training influenced many who returned to civilian life to envision a less monochromatic future for America.

Ready for Duty

The weeks or months of training may have seemed to last forever, but for every soldier, sailor, airman, and marine, the time eventually came to report for duty. Most hoped for a lucky break—stateside orders to keep them safe and sound or perhaps assignment to some European post where they could see the world and while away the time owed to Uncle Sam. War in Korea, though, meant that many of those completing training in the early 1950s began their military adventure aboard a crowded troop ship bound for the Far East.

Men destined for Japan or Korea usually had only days to prepare for departure and much to do.[256] All civilian clothing and personal effects except for hand-held musical instruments, radios, or cameras had to be sent home. Since cars could not be driven to the point of embarkation, they too had to be sold or stored.[257] Medical and dental records had to be updated, and farewells had to be said.[258] Some men hurried home for a few days with family or friends or to marry their sweethearts before shipping out.[259] A few attended parades given in their honor by hometown folks. Still others made the most of the freedom they had left by hitting bars and clubs and forgetting for a moment what lay ahead. Then, just as they had before basic training, men piled into buses, trains, ferries, and "cattle cars," this time on their way to the piers at San Diego, San Francisco, or Seattle.[260]

For the first time in a long time, the men could relax and reflect upon where they had come from and where they were headed. Thoughts of home, like freight cars hooked to an overnight express, sped through their minds, as did a million questions. Would home be as sweet when they returned in a year or two—if they returned at all? Would other neighborhood kids grow up and join the Army? Why had they been chosen to serve when many others had successfully defied the draft? What would it be like to live or maybe die so far away from remembered streets and familiar faces? Had the military already changed them? The answers could come only later, and for some they would not come at all.

Eventually those slated for overseas service reached the docks. As they waited in line to pick up their pay and board the ships, crowds cheered them and bands played in their honor.[261] Sometimes officers addressed the moving sea of olive drab. "God bless you, soldiers. You are the best-fed, best-equipped, and best informed army in the world. Complete your mission and we will be here to welcome you home."[262] Then, troop ships pulled out of the harbor with courses set for the land of morning calm and men standing on the decks waving goodbye and wondering if they would ever see home again.

Even for men accustomed to military life, troop ships offered some nasty surprises. Living quarters consisted of bunks stacked four or five deep floor to ceiling and about eighteen inches apart. The narrow aisles soon became cluttered with seabags, field packs, and weapons. Helmets, though, proved in short supply. Men unused to sailing soon became violently seasick, vomiting into whatever they had handy. For days, the latrines remained occupied with helplessly sick soldiers. At the mess hall, which consisted of rows of waist-high counters that men stood at while eating, the floor became a gross mixture of spilled food, water, trays, and vomit. Weather permitting, men stayed on deck to avoid the putrid smells and sights of the ship.[263]

Most men eventually developed sea legs on the two- to three-week journey, but they still looked forward to dry land, no matter if that put them closer to the war. Upon arriving in Japan or Korea, everyone rushed to the deck to catch a glimpse of the Asiatic landscape. Soldiers gaped in awe at the rugged beauty before them. "Its [Korea's] mountains and trees seemed to come right down to the water's edge. Of course, if we had any inkling the hell that was awaiting us there we might not have thought it so beautiful."[264] Soldiers prepared to disembark. The time had come to put their military training to the test.

A young marine finds a quiet moment just before the 1st Marine Division launches an offensive against the enemy c.1951. Courtesy of the National Archives (photograph no. 127-N-A156900, War and Conflict Book no. 1462).

4

In Country in Korea

A War Like Any Other?

Remembering World War II, newspaper reporters canvassed Korea through-out the war in search of human interest stories for hometown readers. They expected to find troops filled with the same patriotic spirit and singleness of purpose as in the last war, but the tired and ragged young soldiers they encountered could not supply the pithy anecdotes that would make for good reading back home. Arriving in country, servicemen and, in the case of military nurses assigned to the war theater, servicewomen, often took a dim view of the land Uncle Sam called them to defend. Few had ever seen such poverty. Here existed a place where to own a shovel made a person rich, where orphaned children survived by eating garbage, and where the stench of human waste permeated every breath.[1] Even those most sympathetic to the Korean cause wondered what such a place could be worth. Not surpris-ingly, then, when asked what they were fighting for, troops seldom mustered the bravado for the kinds of answers journalists wanted to hear. Instead they insisted, "I'll fight for my country, but damned if I see why I'm fighting to save this hell hole" or "I'm here because the goddam president of the United

States would put me in jail if I didn't report for duty."[2] They asked themselves over and over, "What the hell am I doing here? Why should I be fighting for this stinkin' rice paddy?"[3] And, like one nineteen-year-old corporal in Korea during the early months of the war, too many of those in the war zone discovered, "I can't answer my own question."[4]

Hastily pulled from civilian life or from the peacetime American military, the men and women stuck at ground view during the Korean War can be forgiven for not immediately understanding the reasons for their sacrifices or the forces that swept them to that remote corner of Asia. Americans today still grapple to make sense of this abbreviated, limited, half-won conflict that became the first hot war of the Cold War. Frequently, Korea ends up only in the footnotes of other, longer or more successful wars, and even scholars sometimes settle for citing the numbers: almost six million men and women served in the United States armed forces from June 1950 to July 1953, but only 1,789,000 went to the Korean theater. Of those, 36,940 died in country, 92,134 suffered nonfatal wounds, and 8,176 ended up missing in action.[5] But, beyond the statistics, it has become clearer in the last fifty years just how and why American troops ended up on the Korean Peninsula in 1950 and perhaps why they remain stationed there today.

Before World War II, America had little interest in Korea, the small, backward colony of Japan. It possessed a certain barren beauty in the form of rough, jagged ridgelines, but aside from a few dams built to produce hydroelectric power and some stretches of Japanese rail lines, Korea had little to offer monetarily or strategically to the United States.[6] After World War II, Korea was the same—a country of dirt roads and populations living on the edge, mired in poverty and illiteracy and susceptible to devastating waves of diseases—but now the world looked different to policymakers in Washington. The fall of the Nazis and Imperial Japan divided nations into polarized camps, those who believed in "free" government and those who adhered to the doctrines of communism. As the Allies dismantled Japan's Greater East Asia Co-Prosperity Sphere, the United States had to decide what to do about these territories, whether to move in and block Soviet influences or risk losing them to communism forever.

The choice seemed clear, even for places as seemingly remote and irrelevant as Korea. Thus, American units, like their Russian counterparts, moved into Korea even before World War II officially ended. In a sort of gentleman's agreement, the uneasy allies accepted a temporary split of Korea at the 38th Parallel, with the thought that the country eventually would be reunited. Until then, Russians would remain above the line and Americans below it. Unfortunately for the Koreans, time brought no resolution to the tensions between the United States and the Soviet Union, and what began as a temporary division hardened into a partitioned Korea. In North Korea, Kim Il Sung created a communist state while in South Korea Syngman Rhee leaned heavily on U.S. aid to fashion a pro-American country, if not exactly a democratic one.[7] Satisfied enough with the status quo and confident that it would last, the United States began withdrawing servicemen until the last seventy-five hundred troops left Korea in mid-1949, leaving only a token number of Americans to staff the Korean Military Advisory Group (KMAG).[8]

While Americans and Russians complacently accepted the arrangement in Korea, both North and South Korea dreamed of unifying the country. After years of border skirmishes, Kim Il Sung made his move, sending the North Korean People's Army, the Inmun Gun, over the border in the early morning hours of June 25, 1950. Composed of hardened veterans fresh from fighting in China and supplied with modern weaponry, including Russian-built T-34 tanks, the Inmun Gun quickly crushed the far inferior and underequipped South Korean forces it encountered and began a quick march south.[9] President Harry Truman found himself in much the same position he had occupied in 1945. Should he let South Korea fall into communist hands or should he gamble American lives and resources on the chance that the country was worth the cost of saving it?

Only a short while before, South Korea seemed not worth even the $110 million in promised American aid, only slightly more than half those funds being delivered by June 1950. And, when delivering a speech at the National Press Club in January 1950, Secretary of State Dean Acheson made no mention of Korea at all when outlining America's Asian defense perimeter.[10] But now, in the wake of China's recent fall to communism, Truman felt compelled to draw a line in the sand.[11] Within days Truman ordered American troops to the defense of South Korea in the name of "collective security" and called upon the United Nations to join the effort.[12] Whether soldiers at the time understood the forces at play in bringing them to Korea or not, American troops fought in Korea because of vague, if lofty American ideas about containing communism and because of Harry Truman's unwillingness to let South Korea become another China either in reality or in the minds of the American public. They fought because one half of a country invaded the other and to the president of the United States and to a good many other people that action appeared to threaten "human liberty" and "the free way of life."[13]

Throughout the war, it became almost as difficult for troops to discern what military plan directed operations in country as to decipher the reasons for U.S. involvement in Korea. Unlike World War II, where men served in different theaters of the war but had the same ultimate goal of total victory, the war in Korea unfolded in different and distinct phases, sometimes without benefit of clearly defined war aims. Unfortunately for those whose lives remained forfeit to the cause, the Korean War proved a haphazard affair. In the end, one's wartime experiences very much depended upon when and where a person served in the war zone.

American air and ground personnel committed to Korea in the early months of the war had no idea what to expect. Most of them had been stationed in Japan on easy duty as occupation troops, and they did not really understand that what President Truman persisted in calling a "police action" was in fact a war. Rounded up from lifeguard duty, mess halls, and both support and infantry units, the first men sent to Korea to hold off the North Korean advance and save South Korea from communism believed officers who reassured them that they would be back to the good life in Japan in thirty days after "handily whip[ping] the North Koreans' asses."[14] In reality, they would be gone quite a bit longer than that, many of them not returning for years, if at all.

In this first phase of the Korean War, Truman initially charged American troops with hanging on in the peninsula and not allowing themselves to be driven into the sea. Even this limited task proved difficult. In sharp contrast to the seasoned troops of the Inmun Gun, American soldiers often lacked the conditioning and training necessary for effectively waging war. Some of the men stationed in Japan or elsewhere and subsequently hurried to Korea in June or July 1950 had already cracked under the pressure of battle in World War II and been placed on "limited service," a bad omen for their potential combat performance in this war.[15] Others had become physically unfit for the rigors of battle. Huffing and puffing up the hills of Korea in August 1950, Sergeant Marcelo Vendiola noticed that "no one was in physical shape."[16] Entire units, such as the 29th Infantry, previously tasked with guarding airbases on Okinawa, had to enter battle with an assortment of new fillers and without the benefit of field training or time to zero their rifles.[17] Commanders did not help matters any when they plugged men into units wherever they were needed regardless of expertise. Truck drivers, ROTC graduates, and men who hadn't seen an M-1 since basic training had to become gunners, artillerymen, and infantrymen literally overnight.[18] Also, back in the States, base commanders required to find replacements for Korea took the opportunity to rid themselves of their worst soldiers, men with bad attitudes or questionable soldiering abilities.[19] As one colonel of the Eighth Army noted in the early weeks of the war, "They've had to learn in combat, in a matter of days, the basic things they should have known before they ever faced an enemy. And some of them don't learn fast enough."[20]

Regardless, for weeks upon weeks men entered Korea in what they perceived to be scattered bands along a fluid and ever-changing front. Casualties mounted, as did the number of Americans taken prisoner by the North Koreans. Maybe the generals had a plan, but on the ground it looked as though the war would last forever and the sacrifices would never lead to victory or peace. Still, by September 1950 these piecemeal groups managed to secure a perimeter, the Pusan Perimeter, around the southeast corner of Korea. While far short of anyone's definition of victory, this achievement did at last encourage President Truman and his officers in the field to begin planning the reclamation of South Korean territory held by the North Korean People's Army and the second phase of the Korean War.

The successful landing of marines and soldiers at Inchon Harbor on September 15, 1950, transformed the war in Korea. What had for Americans begun as a shaky defensive operation now metamorphosed into a tactical offensive. The war without end gave way to almost certain victory as United Nations and United States ground forces trapped and neutralized what units of the Inmun Gun remained between the Pusan Perimeter and roughly the 38th Parallel. South Korea had been saved and American GIs, ragged and worn down from their months in country, began to talk of going home for Christmas or even Thanksgiving.[21] If not for General Douglas MacArthur's determination to exploit North Korea's military setbacks and reunify Korea American-style, these hopes might have been realized and the war ended as early as October 1950, by which time UN forces had restored pre-invasion boundaries.[22] Instead, with heavy boots and heavy hearts, and quite possibly without President Truman's blessing, the full force of the Eighth Army, along with other UN troops, crossed the 38th Parallel on October 9, 1950, with a new objective, the conquest of North Korea.[23] After a week or so of hard fighting, the North Koreans retreated, leaving Americans to capture Pyongyang, the northern capital, and advance toward the Yalu River, the border between North Korea and Manchuria. Americans once again smelled victory and the sweet aroma of Christmas dinner that would welcome them home before long. The United States had achieved its original goals in Korea and much more.

Filled with hubris, General MacArthur, with President Truman in tow, failed to heed warnings from communist China that should United Nations forces cross the 38th Parallel, "the Chinese People's Republic will send troops to aid the People's Republic of Korea."[24] As American, United Nations, and Republic of Korea (ROK) forces dutifully gathered in North Korea in late October 1950 to mop up the remnants of war, a new and unexpected third phase of the Korean War erupted. Stationing about 180,000 "volunteers" in front of the Eighth Army and another 120,000 in the mountains around Cho-sin Reservoir, the Chinese made good on their threat.[25] By early November, ROK forces began reporting engagements with Chinese units, and before long all of the United Nations troops in the north learned to dread the haunt-ing whistles and bugle calls that accompanied attacks by Chinese Commu-nist Forces.[26] As in the early days of the Korean War, American troops had to pull back and try to find a line they could hold. Unlike in those early months, the enemy resisted even their retreat and men caught at Chosin Reservoir and elsewhere had to fight no matter which direction they went. Battle took a heavy toll on soldiers and marines, and the bitter Korean winter exacted a heavy price from those held in its grip. Surprised by both Chinese interven-tion and frigid temperatures, as much as thirty degrees below zero, the U.S. armed forces had yet to supply the troops with adequate cold weather gear.[27] Fighting day and night for weeks at a time against a determined and far more numerous foe as socks and guns froze to their feet and hands, infantrymen quickly became casualties of both enemy fire and frostbite. From their van-tage point, more than just real estate, taken so easily and quickly after the Inchon Landing, passed into Chinese hands. Fingers and toes and lives went missing, too, and these were lost forever.

Back in Washington and Japan, war planners had to reevaluate not only the strategies of the war but the entire war ethos. What should the United States, after Chinese intervention, now hope to accomplish in Korea? Largely unanswered throughout the rest of the war, this question still weighs heavily on the American conscience. But, by this stage in the game, men in the field did not really care anymore what politicians and generals wanted to gain from the war. They had already determined that "the only thing of value it [Korea] holds for the men here is a 6x6x6 plot of burial ground and what future is that to look forward to?"[28] Many of them had entered the conflict in its early days, prepared to spend a month or so in country. One month turned into six or seven and in that time they had pushed forward, pulled back, gained ground, given it up again, and sought refuge in the very same shelters going both directions.[29] After months of dirt and grime and count-less tragedies, they still could not see what, if anything, Korea could be worth.[30] "A lot of them were saying, 'Fuck this place, I want to go home.'"[31]

By July 1951, the war in Korea settled into its fourth and final phase, a deadly stalemate between Chinese volunteers and United Nations troops. All along the 38th Parallel both sides dug in, forming "a rambling messy ditch or series of ditches five to seven feet deep."[32] Men lived and fought for months from dusty, littered, fixed positions on a static line. Americans and Chinese alike initiated actions beyond the main line of resistance (MLR), as in the outpost war in the hills around the parallel, but by and large GIs had it right when they complained that "the Army wasn't going anywhere, and everyone knew it."[33] In some places demoralized Army troops established a temporary and informal truce with the enemy across the way, causing a few marines to wonder at the "blatant lack of aggressiveness on the part of our Army."[34] More than a year into the war, young men both in the war zone and stateside wanted to know, "How can the President have 'guts' enough to ask my fellows to sign up for the armed forces or draft them, after seeing what a heavy loss we've already had? . . . I still don't know what we are fighting for."[35]

National Security Council (NSC) 48/4 called for a unified, independent Korea, but with public opinion wavering on the Korean War and the costs of reunification of the peninsula mounting in terms of American lives and money, the United States decided the time had come to compromise. On June 29, 1951, General Matthew Ridgway, the United Nations commander, informed North Korea and China that the UN was prepared to negotiate an armistice. The first meeting of peace negotiators opened on July 10, 1951, in Kaesong, the ancient capital of Korea. The talks went nowhere, adjourning until October 1951, but the fact that the United States sought to resolve the conflict on the bargaining table set the tone for the last two years of the war.[36] Rather than pursuing total victory and a free and unified Korea, the United States had a new objective: to "inflict such losses on the communists that they would agree to a negotiated settlement" before Americans suffered too many casualties or had to use resources earmarked for the protection of Western Europe.[37] A war of attrition, measuring both success and failure in body counts, appealed to the brass charged with making the most of an already overstretched military, but held little appeal for men on the line. American fighting men wanted the opportunity to win something more than a partial victory. From their perspective, "The Chinese sat down at the peace tables of Panmunjom in July of 1951 because they were hard pressed. And instead of pushing harder, we sat on our asses for the rest of the war."[38]

The Army, Air Force, Marine Corps, and Navy continued to ship reluctant replacements into what remained a hot war, but negotiators in Panmunjom and tight-fisted officials back home compelled the armed forces to limit their efforts as they anticipated an armistice.[39] On the ground, troops suffered from ammunition shortages as well as from the feeling that their country had forgotten them and the frustration of accomplishing nothing.[40] Fighting within view of the balloons floating above Panmunjom, one nineteen-year-old sergeant complained, "We are doing nothing but holding on to what we already have and fighting to get back what we lose. Then, after getting it back we sit down and wait for them to try and take it away again. We should be pushing on and getting this war over and done with."[41] Another GI observed, "Most of us are pretty fed up with the peace talks over here. One guy said last night he wished we'd stop all the backing and filling and get on with the fighting."[42] Fighter pilots echoed these same sentiments, pointing out that they had "to watch the enemy strike at them from what General Douglas MacArthur has called their Manchurian sanctuary."[43] Washington ordered American aircraft to stay below the Yalu River, leaving them unable to knock out enemy anti-aircraft guns or pursue the enemy MiGs (jet fighters) that crossed the border between Manchuria and Korea at will to attack them.[44] Until the bitter end, however, the peace talks reigned supreme. United Nations commanders planned offensives in order to hasten China's acquiescence to terms at the table or to sweeten the pot for the UN member countries, not to bring a victory like the soldiers of World War II had won, and the men in Korea knew it. Eventually, they reassured themselves, negotiations would bring peace. All that many of the troops hoped for now was to live to see it. No one wanted to "be the last guy killed."[45]

At 10:00 p.m. on July 27, 1953, the guns finally fell silent in Korea. Twelve hours earlier the representatives of North Korea and the United Nations, Lieutenant General Nam Il and Lieutenant General William K. Harrison, met at Panmunjom to sign a ceasefire agreement.[46] Though only an armistice and not a treaty, the agreement meant that soldiers on both sides of the line could finally lay down their weapons. Newly elected, President Dwight D. Eisenhower informed the American public that this ended "the fighting between the United Nations forces and the Communist armies."[47] Perhaps breathing a sigh of relief, Americans returned to their business and all but forgot about the bitter little war in Korea that had claimed 36,940 American lives. But on the men and women who served and fought in country from June 1950 to July 1953, the Korean War left indelible marks.

Into the War Zone

On June 27, 1950, just two days after the Inmun Gun's attack on South Korea, President Truman ordered the first Americans, naval and air personnel stationed nearby, into the war zone to support ROK forces.[48] United States Navy destroyers, like the USS *Mansfield*, *De Haven*, *Collett*, and *Lyman K. Swenson*, and cruisers, like the USS *Juneau*, hurriedly answered the call, transporting men from peacetime patrols to firing positions along the Korean shoreline. There, American sailors entered the conflict, shelling land positions and establishing a blockade.[49] Similarly, airmen, recently enjoying life in their own little enclaves in occupied Japan, quickly became commuter warriors.[50]

For some pilots, Korea began as a commuter war. In 1950, Captain Johnnie Gosnell leaves Japan for another mission over Korea as his wife and children wave farewell. Courtesy of the National Archives (photograph no. 542207).

With airstrips all but nonexistent in Korea and the fluid nature of the war making air base construction impossible, pilots and their crews began flying missions out of Japan and over Korea, returning home to wives and kids, backyard barbecues, and officers' clubs at the end of the day.[51] With the American Navy and Air Force in place, the first deployment of U.S. ground forces landed in Korea on July 1, 1950, followed just days later by fifty-seven female Army nurses tasked with setting up a hospital at Pusan.[52]

Dispatched swiftly and unexpectedly, these first American arrivals in Korea, especially those on the ground, often dropped into the war zone with no preparation. Desperate in the early weeks of the war to stop the North Korean advance, the Army pulled men from all units and military occupational specialties in Japan to form a fighting force for Korea.[53] With no time to spare for additional training or the notification of families, the men of Task Force Smith and, later, other outfits of the 24th Infantry Division airlifted straight into Korea where the Army expected them to begin fighting almost immediately.[54] Even after the initial deployments, the process of entering the war zone remained frenetic. Sailing from Sasebo, Japan, to Korea in July 1950, Private First Class Susumu Shinagawa received an M-1 rifle and ammunition to go with it, but no poncho or combat boots. Possessing only dress shoes, he had to borrow boots and stuff them with toilet paper to make them fit.[55] Marty Nelson arrived in Japan only to be rushed off to Korea without a rifle.[56] This could not have been the introduction to war that most American servicemen expected.

Aside from a few dramatic landings, such as at Inchon Harbor in September 1950, American arrivals in country settled into predictable and systematic routines. Both Army and Marine replacements usually filtered to the front by way of Japan, docking in Kobe or Yokohama for a few hours or days. With any luck, men headed to Korea got enough liberty to enjoy the crowds at the pier, hire rickshaws for sightseeing, or head into town to shop or search out ladies for one last bit of female companionship.[57] Then, the time came to resume travel. Some returned to the troop ships, but most boarded trains bound for the interisland ferries at Sasebo.[58] Already tired, men found the train rides wearing. Not only did the trains take hours or days to reach their destinations, but smoke funneled into the cars through open windows and at best restroom facilities consisted of oblong holes in the floor of the car guarded by latrine orderlies who made sure that people disposed of their waste before exiting.[59] At the docks of Sasebo, the troops climbed aboard the flat-bottomed ferries with their weapons, packs, and c-rations and waved goodbye to the GIs and Japanese who had gathered below to throw rolls of confetti and shout "Sayonara" while the bands played. Leaving under blackout orders, after having seen the grim look on the faces of those returning from the combat zone, young replacements began to consider that "this is a one way passage for many of us" and to wonder "who will return in coffins."[60] Perhaps for the first time they realized that they were sailing out of one world and into another and that regardless of how many men went with them they would enter the war alone.

No matter what month or year men and women arrived in Korea during the war, getting settled in proved a real challenge. For some, the haunting, "ghostly shadow of Korea rising out of the mist" produced a certain awe, but for most the smells and sights of the land simply made them long for home.[61] While still miles out, those aboard ferries could smell the fecal odor emanating from Korean rice paddies and farms, and when they landed, the scents of charcoal, garlic, smoke, unfamiliar food, and gunpowder created a sickening combination.[62] As days of war lengthened into months and years, newcomers saw only devastation as they looked around them. Broken buildings, ripped-up roads, hungry refugees, ever-present clouds of dust and flies—these characterized Korea. But, however much they wished to turn back around to Japan or the United States, soldiers, marines, doctors, nurses, and, later, Air Force personnel had no choice but to dig in and stick it out in Korea for the remainder of their tours.

Harried and desperate in the first days of the war, the U.S. Army could do little to help personnel acclimate to their new surroundings or to improve living and fighting conditions in country. The need for soldiers at the front frequently outweighed protocol, which called for staging areas to orient soldiers before turning them loose in the combat zone. Men in the vanguard of the Eighth Army Far East Command docked at Pusan or elsewhere while South Korean bands played and then rushed off to the battle on trucks or on narrow gauge railroads built decades earlier by the Japanese. Reaching positions late at night or early in the morning, they furtively dug foxholes, sometimes while under fire by North Korean artillery.[63] Even when soldiers had the chance to pass through a staging area, communications could fail with unpleasant results. One soldier recalled that after arriving in Pusan his outfit marched to a warehouse "staging area." After spending the night there, the men realized that their staging area was actually a collection point for the human feces used by Korean farmers.[64]

Later in the war, both the Army and the Marine Corps established regular reception centers for their troops. Soldiers got unit and station assignments in Pusan while marines trucked into ASCOM City to await assignment and transport.[65] At ASCOM City, marines heading to the MLR turned in their seabags, which carried most of their personal possessions, and prepared to live out of field packs. After a couple of days marines moved out by train, with new replacements stopping at the battalion command post for four or five days of orientation. Here marines heard lectures about the Korean War in general and the units opposing them, made practice patrols at night in the paddies, and received additional equipment.[66] Unlike marines, soldiers sometimes shipped straight to the line from the reception center without any sort of explanation of what to do or what to expect.[67] As one Army draftee put it, "That's what scares you the most when you're new. Nobody tells you anything."[68]

Once at the front, all that men could do was wait for the war to come to them. Some, like Marine Corps Second Lieutenant John Nolan, felt prepared, perhaps even anxious for the fight to begin. "I thought that was what I had been trained to do, educated to do, I felt ready to do it."[69] But most found the anticipation of battle harrowing. Some examined the faces of those who had already experienced battle, taking note of the "thousand yard stare" and determining that "days of combat without sleep, water, and food and being close to being killed every day must have done that to them."[70] Others began to wonder how they would perform under fire and whether they would survive at all, realizing suddenly that "I will soon have to kill a man or be killed by him."[71] All in all, whether one arrived before the Inchon Landing or after the entrance of Chinese volunteers, the minutes, hours, or days before one's first experience in battle filled soldiers and marines alike with "a spooky feeling."[72] War might prove different altogether, but the experience of waiting for it was "all very strange and terrifying."[73]

Fighting in Korea

No matter their branch of service, a good many of the men serving in theater during the Korean War ended up in combat sooner or later. Precise figures remain elusive, but recent surveys of veterans suggest that upwards of 70 percent of those stationed in country saw action.[74] In this limited, conventional ground war, Army and Marine infantrymen had the greatest risk of finding their way onto the battlefield and suffered the most casualties and fatalities, but Navy and Air Force personnel also served and died on the front lines during the war.[75] Flying from aircraft carriers off the coast or from bases in Japan or Korea, pilots flew more than a million sorties over the Korean peninsula, dropping bombs, providing air cover to troops below, and engaging in deadly duels with enemy MiGs, all while trying to evade hostile fire.[76] Men aboard ships delivered soldiers and marines to the war zone, but also became combatants themselves. They cleared coastal waters in small minesweepers, manned the guns while "softening up" land targets with heavy and sometimes reciprocated bombardment, evacuated soldiers and civilians, and tendered protection and support to men on the battleground.[77] American servicemen in Korea endured combat and shared an uncomfortable intimacy with war.

For ground troops, the topography and climate of Korea hardly could have been worse for fighting. Marines and soldiers at every stage in the war had to hump up and down steep, craggy hills weighed down by M-1 rifles and packs stuffed with c-rations, extra socks, and ammunition.[78] Members of crew-served weapons added to their loads heavy, bulky pieces of equipment and even heavier large-caliber rounds. One 138-pound BAR man complained that he had eighty pounds of gear with which to keep up.[79] Before arriving at the battlefield, men grew weary. And, reaching the battlefield often meant attacking uphill with grenades and artillery raining down from the North Koreans or Chinese entrenched above. As Corporal Jay Hidano put it, "Braving enemy fire was one thing, but having to crawl up the steep slopes with bullets buzzing and striking all around us was just madness."[80] Generals, politicians, and reporters on the sidelines dreamed up romantic names like "Heartbreak Ridge" for the hills of Korea, but those doing the marching agreed with one wry soldier who retorted that it was "more like Ass-break Ridge."[81]

The hills of Korea became a nemesis to many a GI, but extreme temperatures made this war particularly miserable. Summertime in Korea brought monsoons and temperatures soaring well over one hundred degrees, with humidity reaching the 90 percent range. Winters dished out even harsher conditions on the peninsula as temperatures dipped to thirty or forty degrees below zero.[82] Men trying to live, much less fight under such conditions faced tremendous challenges. As at Chosin Reservoir when Chinese volunteers overran American positions, men succumbed not just to the enemy but to the freezing cold. A few froze to death in their foxholes and a great many more suffered from frostbite, losing toes or developing other problems that would plague them for life.[83] Weapons malfunctioned and socks and equipment froze to unprotected skin.[84] Pete Behasa remembers one man having to urinate on another man's hand to free his palm from the rifle muzzle where it had stuck.[85] Water had to be cut with alcohol, c-rations had to be chipped out of the cans and melted in one's mouth like ice cubes, and vials of morphine had to be kept warm in the mouths or armpits of medics and corpsmen.[86] The permafrostlike ground made digging foxholes and graves a misery if they could be shoveled out at all. Sometimes the dead just had to be strapped onto the running boards of vehicles, buried in holes blown out of the earth with TNT, or left until the spring thaw.[87] Hot and tired or cold and tired, the ground troops of Korea had to manage to survive the elements and find the resolve to pick up their guns and fight.[88]

Stowed away aboard ship or flying above the ridgelines, sailors and airmen had less cause to worry about the Korean landscape or climate when involved in engagements than their infantry counterparts. Still, especially for pilots, the weather and nature of the peninsula posed certain challenges. If forced to crash land or abandon the aircraft for any reason, pilots experienced the same problems as ground combatants as well as a few all their own. The rugged layout of the land, a series of slopes and valleys, made emergency landings risky. Even if a pilot could lay the craft down safely, how could he be rescued? Other pilots unfailingly did what they could to save a fallen comrade, risking their own lives to circle the crash site and hold off the enemy until rescue helicopters could arrive.[89] But, this wasn't always enough. Men burned to death after crashing into hillsides and froze to death after parachuting into Korea's icy cold waters. In winter, a downed airman could

In the cold winter of 1950, a wounded chaplain performs a memorial service over dead marines covered with snow in Korea. Courtesy of the National Archives (photograph no. 127-N-A5552, War and Conflict Book no. 1512).

expect to survive for only twenty minutes after landing in the sea—a very short time in which to mount and complete a rescue mission. After the first four minutes in the drink, a man's hands froze stiff, his face turned purple, and his feet became useless.[90] The Korean Peninsula itself killed airmen as handily as the North Koreans or Chinese.

Aside from extremes in weather and topography, the combat experiences of men in Korea proved largely reflective of the American war experience as a whole. No one knew how individuals or units would perform until after the first couple of battles or missions. Thinking of the competency of a BAR man almost tossed out of the military before the war, Uzal Ent noted that one "can't tell beforehand who's going to perform well in combat."[91] Similarly, an outgoing platoon leader warned new platoon leader John Nolan, "You really won't know what you have until you go through a fire fight with the members of your platoon."[92] Spit-and-polish servicemen sometimes washed out when it came to the business of killing and surviving while other, perhaps less conventional men discharged their duties heroically.

In the Air Force, the widespread lack of prewar training, especially early in the war, made it equally difficult to predict how men would fare under combat conditions. Pilots learned new formations through "trial and error" in the Korean skies and were certified combat-ready just hours before setting off on missions in aircraft they had seldom or never flown before.[93] Upon arriving at his outfit, "Boots" Blesse, an F-80 pilot, learned that he would have to fly a P-51 on his mission the following morning. Not yet certified to fly that aircraft, Blesse spent the rest of his day training in a "clean airplane," completing three hours of flight time and ten landings. The next day Blesse set out in a storm, his P-51 loaded down with napalm rockets and a .50 caliber machine gun.[94] Similarly, Bob Ennis, an Air Force pilot with no flying time in B-26s before the war, learned to fly them in Korea, and Robinson Risner was declared "combat ready" after seven hours and thirty minutes flying time in the F-86.[95] How Blesse, Ennis, Risner, or anyone else would do under enemy fire before they had gone through it remained a mystery.

What was combat like in Korea? Firefights, at least for infantrymen, began in a number of different ways. Early in the war, when they enjoyed numerical superiority, North Korean troops attacked en masse, rolling forward in a huge human wave. In instances where Americans had surrounded themselves with concertina wire, the first North Koreans to reach the barrier threw themselves onto it, allowing those behind to move ahead by stepping on them.[96] Regardless of the number of dead, soldiers of the Inmun Gun kept advancing until they reached enemy positions or died trying. With the possible exception of men who served in the Pacific during World War II or in the Philippines during the Spanish American War and Philippine Insurrection, few Americans had faced an enemy as determined as the North Koreans or one with a greater disregard for human life. As North Korean numbers dwindled and American forces grew on the peninsula, however, North Koreans husbanded their manpower resources more carefully, abandoning costly human wave assaults. Then, both sides usually initiated operations by pounding the enemy with artillery to soften targets. Before sending men

A gunner with his gun crew, part of the 31st RCT, fires a 75 mm recoilless rifle in support of infantry units across the valley near Oetlook-tong, Korea. Courtesy of the National Archives (photograph no. 111-SC-369801, War and Conflict Book no. 1435).

clambering up the hills, artillerymen from the attacking side shelled enemy strongholds until the land resembled a barren, pockmarked moonscape. As one soldier remembers, "At night I witnessed artillery fire so violent that it lit up the sky to an incredible degree. I still wonder how anyone survived such terrifying onslaughts."[97] Men did live through these barrages, but found them horrifying.

When the Chinese entered the conflict in October 1950, they brought few tactical innovations to bear against American troops. Like the North Koreans before them, Chinese volunteers "came straight at us, like a mob."[98] Even with mortars pouring down, the Chinese attacked in formation and "kept coming with absolutely no regard for their lives. It was like committing suicide."[99] And, short on technology, the Chinese seldom attacked quietly. The eerie wailings of bugles, sharp calls of whistles, rattling cans, and directional orders yelled in "sing-song" voices all alerted UN forces when an engagement was imminent.[100] In Korea, where the scrubby, barren hills provided little cover for would-be attackers, Chinese tactics might have proved the undoing of the People's Volunteer Army, but the Chinese minimized their losses by attacking after dark when possible, a fact that most Americans despised.[101] Nighttime operations not only hampered the support efforts of American airpower, but chipped away at American morale. One young soldier wrote home in 1951, "The Chinks never hit in the daytime, that's the hell of it. At night while I'm on watch . . . I shiver and shake whether it's cold or not."[102] After the war stalemated and both the Chinese and Americans holed up in bunkers along the line, Chinese troops often withdrew to their foxholes at dawn, coming out again at night to fight. With the "no man's land" between the bunkers denuded, making daytime patrols and raids suicidal, Americans had no choice but to operate in the dark as well. Ultimately, "It simply became a habit. We were quite comfortable in the dark."[103]

Engagements rarely lasted more than a few hours and almost never more than a few days, but once a battle got going, combatants had little time for such mundane things as eating, drinking, changing socks, sleeping, or relieving themselves.[104] In the best of circumstances, enemy fire had to be returned from afar and mortars and bullets had to be dodged. The skyline overhead filled with flares, tracer bullets, and searchlights in various shades of orange, red, and green. If American troops got lucky, further up planes whizzed by to strafe ridges and unload deadly cargoes of napalm in much-appreciated support.[105] Yet, even these anonymous, distant interactions with opposing forces made an impression on participants. If shells landed near enough, they sucked the breath right out of a man, leaving behind a blast of dust and gunpowder to remind him that at any moment his number might be up. When the enemy made it behind the lines or when Americans pressed into communist-held territory, the war had to be fought up close and personal. Soldiers, and even marines, who disliked the defensive nature of foxhole fighting, generally tried to shoot from the relative safety of their fortified shelters, but not infrequently in this war there were "so god damn many" of the enemy that they "just kept coming," forcing men to engage in hand-to-hand combat.[106] Men used bayonets, gun butts, knives, fists, and even helmets to stave off attackers. This close combat, coupled with smaller squads than in previous wars and the need to use teamwork to destroy targets, ensured that most Korean War infantrymen would fight and that a larger percentage of them would be willing to fire their weapons than in the last war.[107]

No matter how well-planned an engagement, close combat and the nature of warfare in Korea fostered confusion. At the Inchon Landing, one of the most carefully orchestrated actions of the Korean War, marines discovered too late that their Korean interpreters could not speak English, guide boats had not arrived to lead them in, and their own boats had no compasses.[108] In a later offensive, the brass ordered soldiers to ride in on a column of tanks, hopping off when the tanks stopped and back on when they started up again. This required men to pass their guns around and try to find them at appropriate intervals, sometimes while under fire from the enemy.[109] In the heat of battle, men received conflicting orders from different levels of the command structure and had to determine which to follow.[110] Some GIs simply made up their own orders, as when a number of infantrymen decided to remain in the safety of ditches along a road rather than coming out to protect a line of tanks.[111] Communications throughout the war rested upon equipment salvaged from World War II, and one location had to reach another by being patched through by other places on the line, an unreliable system at best.[112] In some units, men did not even speak the same language. Korean Augmentation to United States Army (KATUSA) replacements frequently knew no English, and the mixture of Koreans, Puerto Ricans, Hawaiians, and white or black Americans in the same platoons or companies meant that language classes had to be conducted when in reserve so that everyone could communicate on at least a basic level in battle.[113]

Also, hungry, thirsty, dirty, exhausted, and terrified, men in the thick of battle got lost in the moment, their attention "sharply focused on . . . [their] immediate surroundings, which nothing else gets into at all."[114] In such an atmosphere, things could and did happen. One new platoon leader confessed that in his first engagement he forgot his rank and began to function as a rifleman.[115] Similarly, Corporal Wall lobbed a hand grenade at an enemy machine gun position but forgot to pull the pin.[116] Another soldier recalls that when a North Korean tried to surrender, someone discharged a weapon causing everyone else to shoot in reaction.[117] In July 1950, at a small hamlet in South Korea called No Gun Ri, refugees allegedly first fell victim to misdirected American-conducted air strikes and then to the fire of soldiers of the U.S. 7th Cavalry who got spooked and mistook them for elements of the North Korean People's Army.[118] In other instances, ground troops went temporarily berserk. In the bayonet charge that won him the Congressional Medal of Honor, Lewis Millett "hit somebody in the throat with a bayonet, another one in the head" and killed a bunch of Chinese but later had "no memory of that at all."[119] During one firefight, a platoon mate of Vernon Warren determined he had to escape the war and stuck his hand out of the foxhole until he got shot.[120]

Seldom knowing "the reason behind what we were doing, what the objective was, or what was coming next," men on the front lines could hardly view battle as anything more than a personal, "everyday affair of survival" and react accordingly.[121] Desperate to survive, some men tried to run away from enemy fire. ROK troops and the all-black 24th Infantry Regiment developed such reputations for bugging out, perhaps undeserved, that American GIs joked that the acronym KMAG (Korean Military Advisory Group) stood for "Kiss My Ass Goodbye" and composed little ditties like "The Bug Out Boogie."[122] Meant as a derogatory comment on black soldiers and units, lines like the following as aptly described the behavior of many non–African Americans:

> When them Chinese mortars begin to thud
> The old Deuce-Four begin to bug.
> When they started falling 'round the CP tent
> Everybody wonder where the high brass went.
> They were buggin' out
> Just movin' on.[123]

Whether men broke ranks of their own accord or followed orders to retreat, their situation grew only more precarious upon leaving the field. Alone or in small groups, they lacked leadership and direction.[124] Throwing away weapons or canteens with no one to stop them, those fleeing argued among themselves over which direction to take or what to do, greatly increasing their chances of becoming casualties or prisoners of war.[125]

For men on the ground in Korea, combat could provide a source of exhilaration and pride unlike anything they had previously experienced. The adrenalin rush and self-confidence that came with performing well in firefights and escaping injury or death proved "enormously satisfying."[126] But, battles also engendered great fear and anxiety in those who fought them. In the heat of engagements with the enemy, participants "got the feeling that death was right around the corner and the next shell had my name written on it," and they were "scared as hell." "I almost wished I would get hit so I could be sent to the rear area to get away from the nightmare I found myself in," wrote one soldier.[127] Afterward, the lingering uncertainty of when the next attack would come caused some men to nearly crack. At night they did not sleep because "there's too much to worry about; such as . . . are those little yellow bastards going to hit us tonight." They got jumpy when they heard gunfire, no matter how distant, and shook uncontrollably, cold with the fear that their luck might finally have run out.[128] With time enough to think, many GIs also became consumed with guilt, saddened because they had taken another life, given orders that got men killed, or survived while someone close to them perished in battle.[129]

"Everyone has a limit," and in Korea some soldiers and marines reached theirs, succumbing to combat fatigue.[130] In their foxholes, along the line, and even in reserve, men broke down. With teeth chattering, they sobbed uncontrollably, shivered, sweated, called repeatedly for their mothers, and refused to take comfort. As Addison Terry says of one who cracked, "The war had gotten into his guts and he could not get it out."[131] Over the course of the Korean War some 12 percent of American troops suffered combat stress reactions requiring treatment.[132] Acting on research begun in World War I, which suggested that evacuating a person from the war zone intensified shell shock, doctors in Korea generally treated mental health casualties just behind the lines with a few days rest, simple psychotherapy, and/or a supply of barbiturates. As a result, a majority of patients returned to duty, sometimes in a matter of days, ready again to face the rigors of living in a war zone.[133] This is not to say that they went back the same men they had been before their breakdowns. War, in which "things happen that are worse than anything you've ever seen and maybe anything that you could imagine," left scars even on those well enough to rejoin their units.[134]

The shared experience of battle served to draw men involved in the Korean ground war closer together. As one veteran put it, "These were my friends from combat, and no other activity or environment forges stronger relationships."[135] In part, they realized that their own survival depended upon the willingness of those around them to fight, risking their own lives on behalf of the group.[136] When the bullets began to fly, a man could no longer count on anything or anyone except for himself and his buddies. "You're depending on them, and they're depending on you."[137] But, the connection ran deeper than this. Men who fought together developed familial feelings for one other with the result that they struggled not just for their own survival but with a willingness to die and suffer wounds for their comrades. Of a mortally wounded radio operator in his unit, Martin Stephens remembers, "He did that for his pals. He did that for us."[138] Similarly, Douglas Humphrey, twice hit and finally killed by a grenade, refused to leave an attack because "he wanted to stay and help his friends as much as he could."[139] Such ties compelled men to remain in position during combat and made leaving the war zone a difficult task for more than a few men when they rotated out.[140] Instinctively, they knew that "there is something you get in battle that you get nowhere else. There is a camaraderie that is unique."[141] In the years after the war, many battle buddies would remain in close contact with one another, sharing an unbreakable bond forged decades earlier in the hills of Korea.

Just as combat in Korea cemented friendships among those who fought together, it fostered a deep loathing among Americans for the North Koreans,

A soldier comforts another infantryman in August 1950. U.S. Army, courtesy of the Harry S. Truman Library (photograph no. 2007-443).

for the Chinese, and sometimes for Koreans in general. Saddened by their losses and terrified by the experience of battle, GIs blamed the enemy for their misery. If the North Koreans had not invaded South Korea or if the Chinese had stayed home, American soldiers would not be fighting and dying over Korea's worthless, barren hills. Americans greatly resented the atrocities perpetrated by North Koreans early in the war when they brutally murdered

Americans who by rights should have been treated as prisoners of war.[142] They concluded, "Those Gooks! They're not even part human!"[143] Unsurprisingly, "many men fought with a visceral hatred of the enemy."[144] Sometimes that hatred transferred to all Koreans. South Korean civilians looked so much like North Korean adversaries that it could be difficult to tell the difference. How many times had a cloud of South Korean refugees shielded approaching North Korean soldiers disguised as peasants? And, with a culture they deemed so perceptibly inferior to the American way of life, many soldiers wondered what made any of them worth saving anyway, especially if the price might be one's own life.[145] A few Americans, however, found a measure of compassion for their Asian adversaries. Fred Lawson felt sorry for Chinese soldiers sent in tennis shoes to fight in the cold of North Korea, and Uzal Ent acknowledged that the enemy "was serving his country and following orders, just as I was doing for my country."[146] But, such instances proved rare. Like most men in war, the soldiers and marines in Korea contentedly and perhaps necessarily vilified those whom they had to kill.

Generally stationed well away from the front lines and flying above much of the pandemonium, men involved in the air war experienced combat differently than their infantry counterparts. They had flight schedules telling them when they would fly missions and engage in combat, giving them the luxury of preparing both mentally and physically for the challenge ahead.[147] Many pilots, especially those dueling in the skies with MIGs, looked forward to facing the enemy. They had "no thought of getting shot down yourself. It's always the other guy who runs out of luck."[148] Also, while American pilots realized that other humans operated hostile aircraft and lived in the hillsides being bombed out, aerial warfare seemed impersonal to them. In general they did not see the blood spilling or the bones shattering.[149] They saw only puffs of smoke and flames on the ground and hunks of metal falling from the sky. Machines, not people, engaged in combat and suffered casualties.[150] Like a real-life video game, Korea afforded airmen the opportunity to score points by shooting down enemy planes or destroying targets, and those points translated into rank and medals for those lucky or skillful enough to collect them.[151] "Wrapped inside the cocoon of a high-tech fighting machine," one's experience of aerial warfare in Korea definitely differed from that of "crawling through the mud, gun or knife in hand" on the front lines.[152] And, at the end of the day, pilots flew back to the base or aircraft carrier where they could cozy up with a nice shot of whiskey while being debriefed and then hang out at the "O Club" until time for bed.[153]

All of this is not to say that pilots and their crews escaped the horrors of battle. Airmen, regardless of branch of service, risked their lives every time they went on a mission. Many died in the line of duty, "blown to bits as their shot-up planes exploded before they were able to reach the runway or crushed to death because a parachute didn't open when they bailed out," many more became prisoners of war, and some developed debilitating mental illnesses or the fear of flying.[154] Despite their belief in luck, almost none left Korea without a close call to remind them of their own mortality. Like Bud Biteman, they had scars or bullets as mementos, reminding them "how thin and fragile is the thread of 'luck' and just how close I came to using my entire allotment."[155] Also, pulling the trigger on targets sometimes proved anything but impersonal. After shooting a MiG, Harold Fischer pulled up alongside the burning, dying aircraft. Inside, the trapped pilot had no power, no place to land, and no way out of the insufferable heat. All Fischer could do was fire a few rounds behind the plane to try to shorten the pilot's misery while reflecting that the enemy consisted only of flesh and blood after all.[156] Other pilots had orders to fly low and strafe enemy troops, drop napalm in areas where both North Korean or Chinese and American forces would be hit, and stop waves of refugees by shooting into the crowd. They discovered that talking about such missions in the "detached atmosphere of the Operations Office" differed considerably from actually implementing the plans and seeing people killed from a lower altitude.[157] Still, unlike most infantrymen who could not wait to get out of the war zone, many pilots lived for the thrill of missions. They extended their tours of duty, flew on holidays, used sexual language to describe their aircraft and their kills, and feared any injury that might keep them from flying again. "That's all we wanted to do, all of us. To be able to get up the next morning and fly an airplane."[158]

In Korea, as in every war, whether one served on the line, in the cockpit, or aboard ship, death lay at the heart of battle. For some American servicemen, the transformation from civilian to combatant happened effortlessly. "It's like killing a rabbit if you're a hunter. . . . You look at the enemy in abstract terms . . . as a cobra snake . . . it's something that needs to be destroyed."[159] For a few the changes became too complete. "All we wanted to do was kill gooks. Kill gooks this minute, kill gooks by the thousand, kill them with hot lead, cold steel, or ripping explosives—but kill gooks."[160] But for most Americans, killing did not come naturally and the suffering and deaths they caused or witnessed affected them profoundly. Half a century after the war, Walter Benton still remembers with regret the ancient Korean woman he met on Christmas Eve, 1950, while awaiting evacuation from Hungnam, North Korea. Bringing her to the warmth of the fire where he fed her tomato soup, the eighteen-year-old listened to the old woman's tale of exhaustion and lost family and then tried to convince her to leave for a safer place. While "White Christmas" played in the background, Benton watched from the deck of the ship as charges set off to destroy abandoned munitions eviscerated the old woman.[161] Similarly, the memory of a Korean child hit with napalm still haunts Jessie Forrest, whose captain forbade him to shoot the boy and end his pain.[162] Killing North Korean or Chinese soldiers should have been easier, and at the time they usually were, but pulling the trigger left men with loads of emotional baggage to carry long after the end of the war. James Appleton writes,

> It is hard for a veteran to explain . . . what it is like to line up an enemy soldier in the cross hairs of your sniper rifle, as this unassuming individual walks along not knowing that in the next instance you are going to squeeze the trigger of your rifle and take the top of his head off, and his mother will have lost a son and he will never have children of his own.[163]

Not all men in country or even in battle killed someone, but scarcely a combat survivor rotated out of Korea without first tasting the bitter harvest of death that war produced in abundance. Early in the war, North Korean troops often beat and killed enemy soldiers rather than taking prisoners. Consequently, as UN troops recovered land in the last few months of 1950, they found numerous American bodies with hands lashed behind their backs and skulls smashed in or bullets in their heads.[164] Aside from these atrocities, plenty of other deaths played out in Korea. Reluctantly leaving the safety of his foxhole to repair communications wires, Bennie Gordon returned to find his mate dead and for three days had to work around the body. In the aftermath of the Chinese offensive in the winter of 1950, Vernon Warren discovered a friend with his entire backside blown off. Helpless, Warren bandaged the dying man and tried to calm him with reassurances that "you're going to make it."[165] Jim Dick radioed the field to inform Lieutenant Griffin that his wife had given birth to a baby boy only to learn that Griffin's head had just been blown off by a mortar round.[166] Jessie Forrest watched his buddy jump on a grenade. The man saved ten or twelve lives but lost his own.[167] After chasing a MiG all the way to China, Major Robinson Risner and pal Joe Logan ran out of fuel. Risner made it to safety, but Logan's neck became entangled in his parachute and he drowned.[168] Ships hit mines or took fire from shore batteries and sailors died in the line of duty.[169] Policymakers counted costs in terms of rounds of ammunition or dollars spent, but on the line men paid for the war with blood. They understood what it was like "to see your buddy, with whom you were talking . . . about girlfriends or home cooking, suddenly lying there in the trail with blood gushing out every orifice and he is trying to hold his guts in from spilling out on the ground."[170] For them, this "loss of close friends is indescribable."[171]

For most servicemen, the tally of American war dead and wounded grew longer and more personal than they had imagined it would. As they watched comrades die, stumbled across bloodied GIs, and experienced close calls themselves, men became reminded of their own mortality and vulnerability. Not only were they not bulletproof, but their lives and those of the men with whom they shared foxholes or cockpits and stories could be snuffed out unexpectedly in an instant. Some, like Rolly Miller, responded to such realizations by drawing closer to comrades, remarking, "It's funny how a severe action kind of makes you feel like a family."[172] Others distanced themselves from those around them. Like Doug Michaud, they "no longer wanted any buddies." They stopped asking new men their names and kept to their own company as much as possible. That way, "If you get killed, I don't know you and I don't care. You're just another number, another rifle."[173]

Battle changed men emotionally. In order to survive, soldiers and airmen had to put their emotions aside and "get on with what had to be done."[174] "One could not, must not, be upset by death."[175] Thus, instead of crying over fallen comrades, men in Korea learned to greet the deaths around them calmly, matter-of-factly, perhaps even callously. In his diary, Raymond Myers recorded that he "[d]rove the jeep all day. We had chicken for supper. Draper got killed. A round hit right in his hole. All I could find was a piece of meat. Nothing else."[176] Similarly, reporter Marguerite Higgins noticed that "[w]hen someone was killed they [the marines] would wearily, matter of factly, pick up the body and throw it in the nearest truck."[177] Upon seeing a dead friend, Private First Class Guy Robinson fixed his eyes on the man ahead and kept walking.[178] In the war zone, on the battlefield, a man could only take note of the losses, attend a makeshift funeral if time allowed, and move on. Only later, when a man left the war, could he begin to deal with the guilt, regret, and emptiness saved up from the tragedies of Korea and ask, "Could I have done better? If I'd done a better job, would fewer men have died?"[179] And only then could a man know if when he left the war, the war left him. Combat did not stop for such questions, and, if one looked away for too long, he might run out of time for answers. In battle, men necessarily had to focus their attention sharply on survival, and if they succeeded in surviving, they somehow had to learn to live within the war.

Living within War

Undoubtedly, combat produced the most poignant memories for those who fought and made for some of the best stories later, but battles seldom lasted more than a week and never for any person's entire tour of duty. In reality, most, if not all, Americans spent far more time living in Korea than fighting there. Their war was "one of long periods of great boredom with a few flashes of intense terror."[180] As Thomas McLain wrote his parents in the spring of 1951, "Combat sure is different than I figured. I thought you fought day and night but sometimes it's days before I even hear a shot fired. . . . We seldom even see the Chinks."[181] Still, "nothing ever came easy in Korea."[182]

For men and women accustomed to luxuries like home-cooked meals, telephone service, electricity, clean clothing and bedding, furnaces, and running water, the primitive living conditions in country made them long for home. Except in places like Seoul, where modern buildings existed, American military personnel lived in crude and simple dwellings. In some cases, such as at airfields or mobile hospital sites behind the lines, tents surrounded by sandbags became temporary or permanent shelters. These had the distinct advantage of being above ground, but often they lacked electricity, running water, adequate heating and ventilation, flooring other than dirt, and any semblance of privacy.[183] Pilots, who below the rank of major shared "hootch" space with six to twelve other men, piled up packing crates and debris inside their tents to carve out private cubicles for themselves. Standard furnishings included small oil-burning stoves for heat, candles for light, and cots, but not much else.[184]

Intended for common use, showers and latrines were located outside, an unpleasant fact given the extreme winter temperatures in Korea, with no privacy at all. At the "40-seater thunderbox" at one airbase, pilots sat shoulder to shoulder on a long wooden bench with holes in it to do their business.[185] Elsewhere troops straddled shallow ditches, called slit trench latrines, or sat back to back when relieving themselves.[186] For all of their privations, however, those who lived in Korea's tent cities had many benefits unavailable to the men holed up in the country's hills, including ready access to cheap labor. Pilots and others often employed native laborers to clean the barracks and latrines, do their laundry, shine their shoes, keep stoves burning all night, serve them in the mess hall, and make life in country more pleasing and comfortable.[187]

In the field and at the front, accommodations afforded far fewer luxuries to occupants than did the tents. There, men lived in dusty, moist holes shoveled into the ground or hillsides in an attempt to protect themselves from enemy fire and attack. For months they slept on "nothing better than the ground with some straw on it."[188] As the war stalemated, forcing men to live in the same positions for many months, trenches eroded and some shelters collapsed in landslides or from the weight of wet sandbags, causing men to have to dig deeper.[189] Over time, conditions in these permanent bunkers grew increasingly grim. When men rotated out, they left behind piles of garbage and, in some cases, towers of human waste. Not only did the number of men outstrip the available space at latrines, but the potential danger of traversing the ground between foxholes and bathrooms discouraged some from making any unnecessary trips to the pit toilets. As a result, four-inch "piss tubes" appeared outside of many dugouts, creating stalagmites of frozen urine in the winter and puddles of filth in warmer weather.[190] Unlike with latrines, nobody bothered to burn these makeshift urinals or police the mess men made using them. Attracted by all the refuse, rats infested almost all living quarters, providing a constant source of irritation and illness for the men inside.[191]

Field conditions left many GIs with virtually no access to showers or laundry facilities. When on the move, men might happen across places to bathe or wash, but they had little time to spare for personal hygiene and could end up regretting any such efforts on their part. Trying to keep clean, Harry Van Zandt washed his only two pairs of socks just before being ordered to march. For six days he wore wet socks inside of his rubber shoe packs with the result that his skin came off with the socks once he removed them, and he developed a chronic case of athlete's foot.[192] When troops parked somewhere along the front, showers were far enough behind the lines to discourage men from frequenting them. Along the main line of resistance and on outposts, water had to be carried in, sometimes across "no-man's land" in full view of the enemy.[193] As a result, men made the most of every drop of water they had. On outposts, men boiled coffee, drank some of it, and washed their faces and brushed their teeth with the residue.[194] Everywhere, soldiers and marines got filthy quick and stayed that way.[195] GIs worked, dug holes, sweated, bled, fought, and slept in the same pair of fatigues until relieved by another unit or sent into reserve. After three weeks in Korea, Harrison Lee realized, "I still had on the same set of fatigues that I was wearing when I landed at Pusan."[196] He was fortunate. Elgen Fujimoto spent sixty-three days on the line before he finally got to take a hot shower and change clothes.[197] In wintertime, wearing the same uniforms could prove especially problematic. Though warm, the bulk of winter garments made using the bathroom a real challenge and some men could not get out of them fast enough.[198] Men smelled like the holes they lived in or worse, suffered from dysentery and lice, and developed hacking coughs that never seemed to go away.[199]

As an added burden, throughout the war troops had difficulty obtaining all of the supplies and equipment they needed or wanted. Early in the war, soldiers had trouble getting such necessities as ammunition and antitank weapons. Caught in North Korea in the winter of 1950 when the Chinese entered the conflict, soldiers and marines still complained that they had to deal with ammunition shortages, but they could add depleted provisions of food and an inadequate supply of cold weather gear to their list.[200] By February 1951, servicemen fighting near Seoul began writing home asking for food and canned goods to supplement the "gook rice" on which they had to survive.[201] Once the war stalemated, it became more difficult to fill requisitions as politicians and bureaucrats tried to limit war costs while waiting for some kind of peace agreement. Fighting on an outpost, John Sullivan complained that he had flamethrowers but couldn't get the two-dollar disks to ignite them. He, probably accurately, placed the blame on a battalion commander who was "screwing around with some idiotic cost-reduction program."[202]

Men in the outposts and along the main line of resistance could seldom get little luxuries like candles or paper and pencils through the regular channels. Unfortunately, as in most wars, troops in the rear echelons took many of these items out of supply shipments long before they could reach the fighting war up front. If a soldier were determined or clever enough, however, he might be able to get some things on his own, much like Radar O'Reilly in the television sitcom *M*A*S*H*. In Korea, possession often depended less upon official authorization than upon one's ingenuity. Men secured the things they wanted or needed by bargaining with other individuals or units. Arthur Kelly remembers his unit swapping lumber to the Marines for the use of a bulldozer so that they did not have to hand-dig their artillery bunker.[203] All too often, though, not even a good trade could produce the necessary items. Ralph Parr, a pilot, had a pair of flying gloves and a flight suit only because he brought them with him to Korea. Other pilots did without these essential pieces of equipment early in the war. And, Parr had to wear a broken jet helmet held together by masking tape while other men donned plastic football helmets for flying because the Air Force had not yet issued jet helmets to those in Korea.[204] In all wars, supplying the troops presents logistical, financial, and other problems, but the limited nature of the Korean War intensified these issues, straining the resolve and the commitment of people on the home front to the conflict and to the men fighting it.

Despite occasional shortages, however, the military usually managed to provide troops with regular rations of food. Behind the lines, mess tents offered at least one hot meal a day, a luxury that troops in reserve appreciated.[205] Most combat soldiers, though, even once the war turned static, found walking to the mess tent both dangerous and impractical, and so they subsisted on the food delivered to their positions. When possible, Korean laborers brought warm meals in containers to soldiers, but more often these GIs ate cold "c-rats" straight from the cans.[206] During the Korean War, "c-rats," or combat rations, consisted of several little cans of food, including entrees like spaghetti and meatballs, chicken stew, beans and franks (a favorite dish), ham and lima beans (an unpopular selection known widely as "ham and motherfuckers"), and beef stew, as well as items like canned fruit, tinned biscuits, candy bars or chocolate, coffee, and beverage powders. Meant to supply a man for an entire day, "c-rat" boxes, about the size of shoeboxes, also contained toilet paper, soap, cigarettes, gum, and small can openers.[207] As long as men stayed put at their holes, most of the ration might be consumed, but not uncommonly young Americans ended up pocketing and eating only the sweets—canned peaches or candy—and either abandoning the remainder when they moved out or trading it for local produce or someone else's fruit or cigarettes. Not surprisingly, soldiers and marines lost weight while living on the line and many got cavities.[208]

A host of other things made life in Korea unpalatable for Americans. For those living in the foxholes and trenches across from the North Koreans or Chinese, enemy propaganda made life miserable. In its most innocuous form, such efforts consisted of scattered leaflets admonishing the Americans to stop trying to grab Korea for themselves.[209] But, the communists found other, more effective techniques to demoralize and terrorize American troops before the war's end. Sometimes they beat drums or blew "Taps" at dark to remind their captive audience in the opposite trench line that Korea might offer them nothing but death.[210] At other times they played American music in an attempt to make soldiers homesick or produced eerie sounds to frighten them.[211] The North Koreans and Chinese also made nightly broadcasts over loudspeakers or on the radio. These ranged from almost laughable attempts to convince GIs of the righteousness of the communist cause to more haunting presentations given in flawless English. At least one American woman, Anne Walker Suhr, dubbed "Seoul City Sue" by soldiers in Korea, lent her voice to the communist propaganda effort. Suhr, a one-time Methodist missionary to Korea who married a Korean national and adopted his communist beliefs, aired a radio program during the war in which she read aloud the names of dead Americans while jangling dog tags in the background.[212] Frequently, North Koreans and Chinese called out the names of the men and units across from them, making soldiers aware that the enemy knew who they were, and encouraging them to surrender or go home. Black soldiers particularly found themselves targets of psychological warfare. Grant Hauskins, an African American veteran, remembers hearing, "Hey black soldier, what are you doing here, your war is not here but on the streets of America, where they treat you like pigs and dogs."[213] Regardless of color, patriotism, or corps, enemy propaganda had the effect of making young Americans living a world away from home more lonely, frightened, homesick, and tired of war. And, in an environment where sleep came only with difficulty anyway, these chilling messages from the enemy further ensured a lack of rest for Americans on the front lines.[214]

Along with physical discomfort, troops living in the war zone faced mental challenges. Even during periods of calm, the landscape of Korea provided ample reminder that "the business of war is to kill."[215] At church services, men received communion with "rifles slung from their shoulders" and wondered if they would be "forgiven for breaking the commandment, 'Thou shall not kill.'"[216] More conspicuously, American GIs frequently used enemy bodies as protective barricades or simply left them where they had fallen. In winter, these froze solid, but in warmer weather they rotted on the concertina wire below the trenches.[217] Arthur Kelly remembers walking past a leg sticking up out of the ground and wondering who the man was and if his family knew he was dead. For him, this symbolized "the reality of war . . . an inhumane, sad thing."[218] Others felt a keen sense of tragedy or guilt when confronted with the presence of refugees or orphans. Having lost everything, including family, South Koreans survived by begging or living off American waste. Major Dean Hess, who founded the first Air Force–sponsored orphanage in Korea, noted, "It was both heartbreaking and nauseating to see these ragged children lean over and dip their swill with tin cans, trying to scoop up choice morsels from our garbage."[219] Many Americans did what they could to alleviate the suffering around them. GIs shared their food, donated time and money to relief projects, and provided medical assistance to civilians. Some even advertised in stateside newspapers for shoes, clothing, candy, soap, and other things to be distributed to needy Koreans on Christmas Day.[220] In the end, though, most could not help but feel haunted by the shattered lives and sad images all around them.

American troops might have coped better emotionally with the devastation they witnessed if they believed the war had some larger purpose, but "very few of us involved in the war understood why we were there."[221] Of course, everyone heard the rhetoric, that the United States had undertaken the defense of South Korea to protect the world against the spread of communism and preserve democracy in however small a place. Many even accepted this as worthwhile. "I was going to fight for a country against the aggression of North Korea and the arms and weapons support from Red China as well as the USSR. . . . [A]t the time and even today the fight was worth it!"[222] In a similar vein, before he was killed in action, Rolly Miller wrote home, "We are fighting a godless thought . . . we're combating this ideology. If we accomplish nothing more than proving to the world we'll fight with the little guy to

In August 1951, Chaplain Kenny Lynch conducts a church service north of Hwachon, Korea, for men of the 31st Regiment. Courtesy of the National Archives (photograph no. 111-SC-378917, War and Conflict Book no. 1463).

protect his dignity as a human being, I feel we have done enough to justify the sacrifices we have made."[223] Stirred by patriotism, others asserted, "I love America and always will, and I'm ready to give everything for her—even life itself if that's what God wants."[224]

In light of ugly realities like bombed-out villages and American casualties, vague generalizations tended to ring hollow. As one GI put it, "We heard all the bullshit about fighting the spread of communism to protect our land of liberty. What the hell did we know about communism? Not a motherfuckin' thing."[225] Reflecting upon democracy back in the States and the segregation that it tolerated, black soldiers wondered, "What the hell am I doing over here?" and "What had the commies ever done to us black people (that is, before we came to Korea)?"[226] Furthermore, as the war dragged on, Americans in Korea sensed that there existed no viable means of winning the war and no way of measuring victory anyway.[227] They might fight forever and still not make a dent in the Chinese army, much less drive it off the Korean Peninsula. Eventually, some men found their own rationales for fighting the war—to provide a more hopeful future for the children of South Korea, to ensure that communists would never again try to subdue a free nation, to prove their loyalty to the Constitution and the United States—and now, more than half a century later, most agree that their service meaningfully contributed to American national security and endowed South Koreans with the freedoms they presently enjoy. But at the time, a lot of American servicemen thought of Korea as nothing more than "a miserable war . . . and a useless war," and their only goal was to survive it one day at a time.[228] In 1951 David Duncan, a photographer for *Life,* asked a marine in Korea, "If I were God and could give you anything you wanted, what would you ask for?" The marine didn't ask for peace or freedom or even the chance to go home. He simply said, "Gimme tomorrow."[229]

Whether or not they believed in their mission or in American involvement in Korea, Americans living in country struggled with their feelings toward the home front. Certainly, almost everyone suffered from homesickness and tried to keep in touch with what was happening in the States. Millions of letters passed back and forth between men and women in Korea and their loved ones back home. Newspapers printed servicemen's advertisements imploring people to "Please Write This Lonely GI" or send homemade goodies like cakes and cookies to those serving overseas.[230] And people responded to such pleas. In towns and cities all across America, women formed circles to buy and ship familiar sundries like paper, soap, shaving cream, razors, and candy to the war zone.[231] A few women even became romantically invested in their pen pals, bringing men closer to home in mind if not in body.[232] Men also pumped new replacements for any sort of stateside news.[233] They wanted to know what bands or songs were being played back home, what hometown newspapers were saying about the war, and who looked good for the World Series. Like Edgar Miller, they tuned in to "Voice of America" on the radio. "Even though it wasn't my hometown, it was America, and the station brought 'home' to me as I listened."[234] Americans held tight to their memories and pictures and from their tents and dugouts they dreamed about returning to hot ham and egg breakfasts, clean sheets, cold beer, new cars, Sunday dinners, and all the other things about home and country that they "so completely took for granted before I left."[235]

While GIs often longed to rotate back to the States and worked to maintain connections with the home front, interactions from the war zone could prove disheartening and disappointing. On a personal level, many men found their relationships with girlfriends, wives, family, and friends strained by the long separation. Letters might keep them in touch, but mail was at best a "poor substitute for conversation" and "woefully inadequate" at maintaining feelings of closeness. Couples like Charles Bussey and his wife, Thelma, moved "further and further apart" with each passing month, and many men's marriages unraveled while they remained stuck in Korea.[236] Not uncommonly, men discovered that their spouses, unable to cope with the lengthy deployment, had sought comfort with someone else back home.[237] Others, like Frank Bifulk, received "Dear John" letters, unexpectedly informing them that one less person was awaiting their return from the war.[238] With no way to lobby for themselves in person, servicemen could do little but try to put the sadness behind them and focus on surviving. Even when things seemed fine, soldiers and marines worried about being forgotten or forsaken by the ones they had left behind, and letters home reflected a deep need for reassurance. As Thomas McLain wrote, "I'm not worried about myself hon, I'm worried about you. I want to be sure and have your love when I get back."[239] Songs like "Dear John Letter" and "Korea Blues" revealed and perhaps deepened these fears of losing lovers or friends because of duty in Korea.[240]

Under the best of circumstances, marriages and other relationships weathered the challenges of distance and time, giving men the feeling that they had someone to live for and something to tie them to their old lives. These connections, however, did not always result in complete satisfaction on the part of those who participated in the war. Men in country needed to believe that they could rotate back to the States and be the husbands, brothers, sons, and friends that they had been before this conflict. But, a great many feared that the things they had done or seen in Korea had worked too many changes on them, changes that people back home would not be able to accept.[241] Combat veterans especially felt that "there was no way the folks at home could understand any part of my life."[242] And, to a large extent, they were probably right. Back on Main Street, old notions of appropriateness still ruled the day, but in the topsy-turvy world of the war, where very little made sense anyway, different standards applied. Here, profanity became the preferred, habitual means of expression, and irreverence dominated the humor and outlook of the average GI.[243] In medical units, doctors rushed to the bedsides of critical patients who turned out to be skeletons outfitted with fake medical tags and diagnoses like diarrhea or fractured skull.[244] Infantrymen sang ballads with verses such as these:

> F*** 'em all, f*** 'em all,
> The Commies, the U.N. and all;
> Those slant-eyed Chink Soldiers
> Struck Hagaru-ri
> And now we know the meaning of USMC.[245]

Men sewed stars on their fatigues and declared themselves generals, with the rationale that "[n]obody in this chicken shit outfit promoted me, so I promoted myself."[246] And soldiers composed poems like "Appropriateness," which demonstrated that in Korea few topics proved off-limits for entertainment. "Mortar shrapnel ripped his canteen from its web belt. / We all laughed. / Had it been his head / We would not have laughed 'til later."[247] These behaviors could not be explained easily by a son to his mother or a boyfriend to his sweetheart. Consequently, letters from Korea remained guarded.[248] Instead of talking about the brutal realities of battle, the loneliness and fear that permeated everyday life on the front, or their somewhat unconventional ways of dealing with the stress, men (and women) conveyed funny stories or dwelt on the mundane, generic topics that would find ready approval among their friends and families.[249] Unfortunately, while censoring and sanitizing their correspondence helped GIs salvage their marriages and protect home ties, it also left them with the uneasy feeling that perhaps when they returned home these relationships might yet become casualties of the war and of the real, if unspoken, gulf that separated Korea from the home front.

Depressingly aware that they were paying the costs of the Korean War with divorces, deaths, uncomfortable living conditions, moments of terror, and personal tragedies, many Americans in country came to resent both the United States government and the American public. As Private First Class James Cardinal put it, "The troops over here are mad, mad at America, Americans and America's leaders. We all feel we've been let down by our incompetent and blundering leadership, from the White House down."[250] Old enough to remember the respect and gratitude accorded to World War II veterans and too young to recollect their country's treatment of veterans of earlier wars, service members in Korea felt entitled to something more than they were receiving for their troubles. On a basic level, men and women serving in the war zone wanted recognition that Korea was as much of a war as any that the United States had fought in the past, not merely a "police action," as President Truman and the press persisted in calling it. They complained bitterly that "[t]hey may call this a police action, but men are loseing [sic] their lives the same as in the last war" and "they should make that comment to the parents or wives whose sons or husbands were killed in action."[251] They also felt that their country owed them the same benefits that it had seen fit to grant to the veterans of World War II. From the hillsides and battlefronts of Korea, servicemen angrily demanded a comparable GI Bill. Asserting, "I would like to go to college if I live thru this damn police action," they asked "what is the government doing about us over here?"[252] And, when the answers failed to satisfy them, they persisted. "Why, sir," one man wrote Senator Robert Taft, "are we excluded from the rights, the hostilities were over for 2 years and fellows who enlisted for a peacetime army for 18 months receive the benefits of the Bill of Rights, but those who are now in Korea, even if only for a year are forgotten or seem to be by our government?"[253] Eventually such lobbying paid off and Congress passed a Korean GI Bill of Rights, but for many veterans the seeming reluctance and slowness with which this was done served only to reinforce notions that America somehow regarded them differently than its sons and daughters of the Second World War.

Aside from a lack of political recognition, the troops in Korea had other reasons to feel like the home front had abandoned and forgotten them. Every day Americans laid down their lives in service to country on the Korean Peninsula, but back in the States people seemed completely disinterested in the war. Front-page headlines advertised "a growing shortage of beef, graft scandals in the Government, strikes as usual, [and] prospects of a new-car scarcity."[254] The war just did not seem all that newsworthy after the early months and especially once it stalemated. As editorial cartoonist Bill Mauldin noted of the Korean War infantryman, "He fights a battle in which his best friends get killed and if an account of the action gets printed at all in his home town paper, it appears on page 17 under a Lux ad."[255] And, more than not paying attention to the war, people on the home front actually compromised the ability of men and women to carry out their duties in Korea—at least from the perspective of those in the war zone. Strikes and the attention paid them not only distracted Americans but also deprived men in the field of the supplies they needed. Shortages at home meant the rationing of things like ammunition and equipment in the war zone.[256] Of one strike a frustrated GI in theater wrote, "We felt it very definitely in the shortage of supplies and especially of equipment for several days. It woke me up to how closely connected all the fronts we battle on are. You begin to wonder if the old country realizes there's a war going on over here."[257] Similarly, returning from Korea, another serviceman asserted, "Strikes at home make the GI feel . . . that people are so preoccupied with their own self-interests that they seem to have forgotten that we are fighting a war. The shortages due to the shipping strike in New York last autumn could be felt in Korea within two weeks."[258]

Soldiers in country repeatedly complained that their country and fellow citizens left them to fight the war with secondhand weapons, trucks, jeeps, and artillery.[259] With a Marine Corps platoon somewhere in Korea, Richard Bevier pondered the fact that the warranty on his unit's howitzers had expired as the manufacturer only guaranteed them for three years or ten thousand rounds of ammunition, whichever came first. Wryly he concluded that the guns were still more dependable than the ammunition, much of which was dated 1940. "It had probably been to the Pacific and back a couple of times."[260] More succinctly, James Boden complained of "[g]uns that would not work, ammo that would not fire."[261] All too often that proved to be the case. Caught in battle, First Lieutenant Eismann threw four grenades before one exploded properly and then, when attempting to fire on two enemy machine gun operators, discovered that his M1 rifle would not fire.[262] Men fighting in Korea wanted people in the United States to "know and give a damn," but believed that "they don't know and don't care. Because it doesn't touch them."[263] No wonder then that when they talked "about the old home country," their conversations contained both "sadness and even a little bit of bitterness."[264]

If men or women felt unhappy about their situation in Korea, they could complain in letters or to members of the press, but seldom could they express themselves at the ballot box. With catchphrases like "If they are old enough to fight they are old enough to vote," some senators and congressmen in 1951 pushed to lower the minimum voting age from twenty-one to eighteen. They did not want men to "feel they are being shanghaied into the Armed Forces without having a voice in their own government."[265] A year later, President Truman called on Congress to pass a new GI voting bill, saying, "When we have soldiers overseas defending the cause of freedom, it is unthinkable that we should go backward instead of forward in enabling them to exercise the rights that all citizens possess."[266] Throughout the war, however, such efforts invariably failed, leaving thousands of young draftees eligible to fight in Korea but ineligible to vote in state or national elections.[267] In the 1950s, color also excluded some of those in Korea from voting. More than a decade before President Lyndon Johnson's Voting Rights Act, many southern blacks could not participate in the political process, and some Native Americans did not get the right to vote until the late 1950s.[268] Even if service members met all the requirements for voting, they might not be able to vote from

Korea. Some states banned absentee voting outright while others required all voters to register in person, rejected the federal postcard as application for an absentee ballot, or refused to allow enough time for the voting process to be completed by soldiers. Restrictive voting laws barred as many as a million GIs around the world from voting in elections like the presidential race of 1952.[269] Also, the complicated process discouraged service members from casting absentee ballots. In the 1952 presidential election, for instance, GIs had to apply for a federal postcard from a voting officer, fill it out, and mail it to his/her home state. When the ballot came, the GI had to go before the voting officer, mark the ballot, seal it in an envelope, sign it, get it notarized, and then take it to the registered mail window at the post office.[270]

As a result, a few men settled for writing letters to their congressmen or hometown newspapers, but with mixed results. In 1951 letters sent from an engineer detachment in Korea to stateside papers questioning the purpose of the war prompted a discussion in the House of Representatives as to whether or not the men should be investigated by the Army as possible participants in a communist plot. Ultimately, Representative S. J. Crumpacker Jr. from Indiana defended the soldiers, saying, "We cannot expect to draft men and send them to fight and possibly die for us in Korea and then refuse to tell them why we are doing so and what our purpose is in fighting such a war."[271] But, in the deepening Cold War climate and in the middle of an unpopular and stalemated war, the situation could have turned out far differently. Congressmen and Americans might easily have viewed tired and confused soldiers as communists or collaborators, and these men might have faced courts-martial for misconduct or worse, as happened to returning POWs after the conflict.

Perhaps GIs could not influence the government or public opinion back home, but a few managed to work the system and find a safe and legal way to leave Korea before their tours of duty ended. In the early 1950s Army policy allowed soldiers, even those in the war zone, to apply to Officer Candidate School. If chosen, an applicant returned to the United States as soon as OCS could make room for him. Army regulations then barred those men from reassignment overseas until they completed a minimum stateside tour. Sensing the possibilities, infantrymen and artillerymen in Korea applied for OCS, shipped back to the States, and then resigned from their respective programs after only a couple of weeks. They still had to finish their twenty-one or twenty-four months with the Army, but, by then, most had so little time left that they "sweated out" the remainder in America rather than in the deadly hills of Korea. By the spring of 1952, the Army closed off this avenue of escape with new policies eliminating the waiting period for voluntary withdrawals, but by then scores of men already had slipped out of the war zone to the safety of home.[272]

While in Korea, marines, sailors, airmen, soldiers, doctors, and nurses found ways to entertain and distract themselves. Behind the lines, service personnel played chess and checkers, set up volleyball and basketball courts, had barbecues and beer busts, and formed poker clubs.[273] They attended USO events when possible and indulged in drinking alcohol rations or black

Undoubtedly a welcome sight in the Korean heat of July 1951, a load of beer donated for marines is carried by Corporal R. L. Quisenberry. Courtesy of the National Archives (photograph no. 127-N-A156550, War and Conflict Book no. 1474).

market booze.[274] Early in the war, the military supplied enlisted troops with two cans of beer a day and officers with a bottle of whiskey a month, just enough to fend off boredom and help one temporarily forget about the war.[275] Even teetotalers sometimes began drinking in Korea, but perhaps nobody in country enjoyed liquor more than airmen. Alcohol flowed freely in the various "O Clubs," and this fact, coupled with the availability of cheap liquor at base exchanges, helped make drinking the "primary recreational activity" of many of those stationed at or around airfields. So common was overdrinking among pilots that they learned to adjust the oxygen levels in their planes to cure hangovers.[276] On the front lines and in the outposts, where drinking was usually prohibited, men made their own home brew, called "apple jack," secured liquor from foreign troops or the black market, and brought back beer or whiskey when they returned from R & R.[277] Still, combat soldiers had little time for drinking and more commonly used cigarettes to fill their hours and days. Stuffed into combat rations, cigarettes came cheap and easy in the war zone, a ready-made and nearly irresistible destressor. Like the soldiers of World War II, many veterans of the Korean War remember first smoking when in the Army or in the war.[278]

In addition to cigarettes and liquor, some men in the war theater found love or something like it.[279] Especially for gay men, who faced persecution and suspicion back in the States, Korea and Japan provided the opportunity for both openness and fulfillment.[280] Occupied with the business of war and survival and concerned primarily about the competence of their crews, commanders had little time to waste ferreting out the sexual orientations of those under their commands, regardless of regulations. Indeed, most homosexuals found commanders more than willing to look the other way so long as they performed well on the job.[281] In the zone, one "could be as open as you wanted to be" and there existed little pressure to act straight.[282] Gay men stationed in Japan frequented gay bars there, but willing partners turned up elsewhere as well. Straight men in Korea, Japan, and aboard ship courted homosexuals when women were in short supply or likely to be infected with venereal diseases and when they needed sex but could not endure the thought of being unfaithful to their wives with another woman.[283] In general, gays found serving overseas a refreshing experience, free of some of the fear and repression they suffered at home. Even so, homosexual acts still violated the military's code of conduct, and one who engaged in them could be punished accordingly. Just one week before his three-year commitment ended, the Navy brought Tony Lankford up on charges of homosexuality. With "no representation, no rights, no nothing," Lankford ended his tour of duty with a dishonorable discharge.[284]

For straight men, local girls in both Korea and Japan could be had as prostitutes or long-term "girlfriends" for a low price and, despite the admonitions of the military, many Americans hired them. Concerned about the spread of venereal disease, at least one air base instituted "pussy patrols" to prevent airmen from having sex with Korean women, but undoubtedly clandestine relationships and the transmission of diseases continued in country. Additionally, men in all branches of the military found opportunities with Japanese partners while on leave or R & R in Japan.[285] Such liaisons had consequences, both physical and emotional, for those who engaged in them.

Many men contracted sexually transmitted diseases. By January 1952, the VD rate of the 51st Wing soared to 8.12 percent, and in the summer of 1953 a wave of gonorrhea and genital warts in the 45th Infantry Division forced many to undergo treatment before returning home.[286] Infection caused tremendous hardship in the field, where men had trouble getting penicillin. Richard Bevier remembers a man in his platoon having to treat his "affected area" by soaking it for two hours twice a day in a solution of potassium permangate mixed up in a sawed off beer can. Seeking privacy, the man sat in one of the tractors, at least until the time when his crew got orders to fire while he was soaking and the unexpected recoil from the gun "not only splattered our friend from head to toe with purple stuff," but "almost circumcised him in the process."[287]

Japanese and Korean women sometimes became pregnant, forcing GIs to either abandon their children when they rotated out or to begin the long, wrenching, and often unsuccessful process of trying to get their families to the United States. Inevitably, even without the pressure of fatherhood, more than a few men either mistook their "business deals for real relationships" or fell in love with the women they employed, leading them to try to marry their Asian paramours.[288] The U.S. military did not ban such unions, but did discourage them with plenty of red tape.[289] Many Japanese and Korean women did become war brides, but many others found their relationships a dead end. Given the nature of the war zone and the slowness of the process, soldiers and marines not infrequently died, rotated back to the States, or simply lost interest before they could obtain approval to marry their girlfriends.[290] Aside from one-time lovers, American servicemen left behind thousands of illegitimate sons and daughters, unrecognized by the United States and shunned by the Japanese and Koreans.[291] Love affairs blossoming in the war zone all too often ended disastrously for everyone.

The military treated men and women who remained in Korea long enough to a turn at Rest and Recuperation, or R & R. Early in the war this might be nothing more than a day or two of rest somewhere behind the lines where a front-line soldier or marine could eat a hot breakfast and lunch, shower, get clean clothes, and maybe see a movie.[292] By the spring of 1951, though, R & R had become a formal program in which men left the war zone for a five-day rest in Japan.[293] Men so looked forward to R & R that they were willing to take considerable risks in order to get it. Harold DeVries remembers that when his turn came to go to Japan, his unit was pinned down by the enemy, but rather than lose the opportunity, he left by crawling "down a road ditch with artillery hitting all around me."[294] Another GI allegedly sold everything he had on the Korean black market, bought whiskey with the proceeds, and used the whiskey as a bribe to buy himself five days in Tokyo.[295] Designed as a way to give men a break from the constant danger and stress of the battle-field, R & R proved a mixed blessing for participants. Men coming from hard fighting needed the time to rest and relax, but not all of them could do this away from their units and buddies. They worried about friends in the war zone and felt guilty every time they "took a hot bath, ate a hot meal, and slept on a nice bed."[296] Many also realized that after months of remaining on guard their bodies simply would not accept the sleep that they craved.[297] Later in the war R & R took on a different flavor. Men still tried to catch up on some much-needed rest, but they also spent a good portion of their time drinking and chasing women, thus earning R & R the unenviable nickname "I & I" or "intercourse and intoxication."[298] One female veteran stationed at a hospital on Okinawa during the war recalls, "I felt very disappointed in our guys' actions away from home" and "to this day feel disgust at things I know of and have seen."[299]

Eventually, if one lived within the war long enough, his or her time to return home came. Doctors, nurses, and sailors ticked off the months and completed their tours of duty. Pilots finished the requisite number of missions. Infantrymen and support personnel in Korea earned enough points to rotate out. In an effort to be equitable, to allow service members who had risked the most or spent the most time in Korea to leave first, the military set up a rotation system for individual soldiers and marines.[300] For each month spent in theater, American troops received a certain number of points, ranging from four awarded to men stationed on the front lines to two given to men in the rear echelon. Once a person accumulated thirty-six points, he became eligible to rotate out of the war zone.[301]

On the one hand, rotation, or the "Big R," boosted the morale of those serving in country. Regardless of whether or not the war ended, "every man would ship out of Korea for discharge or other duty station" when his time was up.[302] But, rotation created many problems for American service members in theater as well. With the military "mobilizing, demobilizing, and fighting a war, all at the same time," troop commanders reflected that "we were creating real units until rotation."[303] For those trying to survive combat, it became increasingly clear that the loss of seasoned infantrymen and artillerymen and resulting influx of inexperienced replacements broke down unit effectiveness and integrity.[304] Some career officers careened into the war zone just long enough to get their tickets punched, put combat on their records, and then move on to something more lucrative and less dangerous, leaving units in Korea without adequate or consistent leadership.[305] Veterans in the ranks only reluctantly and slowly accepted replacements, adopting a "wait and see" attitude until new men proved their worth.[306] Noncommissioned officers sweated bullets before engagements, knowing half of their troops were green, fresh from basic training.[307] Replacements had to make buddies and learn the ropes fast or risk finding themselves even more alone in the unfamiliar and unforgiving terrain of the war. Unfortunately, many of these replacements became casualties within hours or days of their arrival.

Men with little time left before rotation developed "short-timers syndrome." Worried about dying only weeks or days before their tours of duty ended, short-timers became increasingly reluctant to volunteer for dangerous duty, fight, or even stray far from their foxholes. Some took to wearing their flak jackets and helmets around the clock, and at least a few determined to "never, ever leave his bunker again" until time to go home.[308] Generally soldiers tried to help short-timers out, but this meant the early loss of seasoned and competent soldiers from the field.[309] Rotation did not provide a real end to the conflict, and it hindered the war effort in almost as many ways as it helped, but for those lucky enough to sail back to the States before July 1953 it provided a most welcome exit from the war.

Leaving the War

Begun June 25, 1950, the Korean War lasted until the ceasefire went into effect at 2200 hours on July 27, 1953. Until that appointed time the shooting continued. Then, men on both sides of the line celebrated, setting off live ammunition and waving at each other across the hills, "happy the war was over and we would be going home." But, except for prisoners of war (some nine hundred of whom the Chinese would be unable to account for at the prisoner exchange), eighty-one hundred Americans missing in action, twenty-four or so Navy and Air Force pilots detained by China as political prisoners, and those Americans still on duty in theater at the time of the armistice, the conflict had ended days, months, or even years earlier.[310] In Korea, the American armed forces waged a new kind of limited war, one designed to prevent a direct confrontation between the Soviet Union and the United States, preserve manpower resources in case of a wider conflict, and avoid overly taxing the patience of the American public. Consequently, Americans rotated out of the war zone individually after completing a certain length of service there rather than staying with their units and coming back as a group after hostilities ceased.

Strangely enough, the United States during the Korean War shipped not only survivors back home but also the remains of GIs who had given their lives in duty to country.[311] In both World Wars I and II, Americans killed in action were buried in temporary gravesites until after the fighting stopped, sometimes long after, when the wishes of the next of kin determined whether the bodies would be interred in permanent overseas cemeteries or returned to the States.[312] At first, Korean War dead were treated the same way. Around the Pusan Perimeter, members of Graves Registration companies, part of the Quartermaster Corps, collected bodies, identified them by comparing teeth to dental charts, cleaned out pockets, repinned any live grenades they happened across, shipped personal effects (except for pornographic pictures, which by orders were to be thrown away) to family members back home, and arranged for a proper burial complete with a memorial service if time allowed.[313] As early as mid-July 1950 a temporary cemetery existed at Taejon, and soon others sprang up at places like Kwan-ui, Sindong, Kum-chon, Miryang, Masan, and Taegu.[314]

As the war progressed, however, American troops retreated, losing control of many of these cemeteries. Perhaps uncertain that any territory in Korea could be permanently held by United Nations forces, Major General K. L. Hastings, the quartermaster of the Far East Command, recommended the evacuation of all remains from temporary gravesites.[315] Acting on this, the United States made the unprecedented decision to return deceased Americans to their homeland while still engaged in combat in Korea. Graves Registration companies in country now had the double task of disinterring previously buried bodies for shipment and preparing casualties fresh from the battlefield for the trip home.[316] Most American dead passed through the Zone Headquarters of the American Graves Registration Unit at Camp Kokura, Japan, for final identification. There, staff members collected fingerprints and recorded information about "hair color, skin pigmentation, height, shoe size, . . . tattoos, scars, physical abnormalities, . . . bone malformations and peculiar tooth and cranial formations" and prepared reports and case histories to establish "beyond all doubt the identity of each individual."[317] Remains then passed through the mortuary to be embalmed, placed in caskets, and finally processed out. At the mausoleum area, chaplains held

Following the break-out from Chosin Reservoir in December 1950, men of the First Marine Division pay their respects to fallen comrades in Hamhung, Korea. Courtesy of the National Archives (photograph no. 127-N-A5426, War and Conflict Book 1514).

weekly memorial services in which a symbolic flag-draped casket escorted by an Honor Guard was placed by the flagpole and treated to religious rites, the firing of three volleys, the sounding of "Taps," and the lowering of colors. From March 22, 1951, to September 1953, most American war dead—except for a few unidentified soldiers buried as token representatives of the United States at the permanent United Nations cemetery and bodies unrecovered from both North and South Korea—were loaded onto ships to begin their final journey back to the country for which they had given their lives.[318] This at least gave some small measure of comfort and solace to men like the young sergeant who wrote home in July 1950, "I have one request. If I don't survive, please don't leave me to rot in Korea. When the Army permits, let me come home to rest."[319]

Receiving permission to rotate out, survivors left the war zone with far less ceremony than their fallen comrades. If they served in a unit short of men, the Army or Marine Corps might offer them promotions in exchange for a few extra months of Korean duty, but other than that they simply said their farewells and left with little more than their well-worn fatigues and combat boots.[320] Most men and women, after initial processing at battalion, regimental, or divisional headquarters and perhaps a delousing, once again passed through Japan to await the troop ship that would ferry them home.[321] Some went wild, buying clothing or trinkets with the money saved up from unspent paychecks, reveling in dozens of pairs of clean, white underwear and tailor-fitted dress uniforms.[322] Others thought about America, "where people are free to vote and just plain old free. Where the sound of guns and the sight of blood are in the past, where you get hot dogs, hamburgers, banana splits, and hot rods, where American women don't bend over and kiss your ass . . . and damn a thousand other things that I left behind."[323] They looked forward to "getting home to the wife I had married two days before shipping out to Korea" or to the children growing up in their absence.[324] Men who had served on the line wondered "whether I was more homesick for Decatur or for Love Company" and "couldn't stop thinking about my buddies. I loved them so."[325] Feeling a great loss, they asked, "Sure, I was out of it, but what about all my friends who were still fighting?" Still, those exiting the war theater "knew how a man on death row must feel when he gets a reprieve."[326] Eventually, it came their turn to board the homebound ships and after just a few more weeks of military food, fire or guard duty, gambling, and waiting, they would be home, "back to the greatest country on the earth."[327]

Although crowded together aboard transport vessels or planes, men and women leaving the Korean theater left the war alone.[328] Instead of unit members shipping in and out together, most individuals moved into outfits where needed and left at different times as their tours of duty expired or as they accumulated enough points to earn a final rotation back to the States. Instead of making the long trip home with men made close through the shared experience of combat or service, Korean War veterans had only the hard good-byes "with guys you've shared so much with" and then close quarters with unfamiliar faces, "all strangers, / like me, on their way home."[329] En route, men talked about the war, "the only subject we could discuss intelligently," and thought about the Americans still fighting.[330] "Remembering was one way of keeping people alive, and the least I could do."[331] They also tried to prepare themselves for the transition from war to the safer, slower life they would soon enjoy. Reminiscing with others who had experienced the same things or "endured situations which made my own seem like a picnic," some men found that "by the time we reached the United States after three weeks at sea, most of us had been drained of any meaningful hang-ups."[332] "Thirty-three days from Inchon to San Francisco. The transformation is / complete. By the time we re-enter / society, society has re-entered us."[333] Some, though, had more difficulty putting the war behind them as they passed from one life to another. This time around they traveled "with baggage I can't just check through."[334] They "had adjusted to being in the war zone and could not figure out how they were going to react when they got out of the . . . combat zone and back into civilian life."[335]

To those leaving, rotation meant "it wasn't my war anymore; it belonged to other men," but it also "wasn't a real end to the war."[336] And because the calendar rather than victory brought them home, veterans of the Korean War had no meaningful way to measure what they had accomplished during their time in country. The losses, of course, seemed evident. The tug-of-war over real estate left the Korean countryside broken and cities devastated. A 1951 *Time Magazine* article declared, "Peace if it comes will find Korea's cities dead. In Seoul the gutted, white-domed capitol of the Republic of Korea stands like a skeleton among the city's ruins. Suwon's huge, half-destroyed gate, once a monument to Korea's kings, guards only rubble now."[337] By the end of the conflict, virtually every village and city on the peninsula had been damaged, which in human terms translated into many millions of Koreans killed or rendered homeless.[338] The United States pumped billions of dollars into the effort, but casualties skyrocketed, numbering almost thirty-seven thousand dead by the end of the war.[339]

And what had they won? When peace finally came, "no land had been occupied, no grand goals had been reached, no clear victory had established a winner, no surrender received to mark the end of the war."[340] American troops held the same line they might have had in the fall of 1950. An October 1953 Gallup poll revealed what the American public thought about this achievement; they would not support renewed hostilities even to hold the territory already purchased at so dear a price.[341] As they rotated out, men "didn't feel like you accomplished a hell of a lot," and they "carried around a feeling that somehow we hadn't given it [Korea] the same effort [as in World War II]."[342] "I remember coming back from Korea . . . I was almost embarrassed being in Korea because we didn't win. We cut a deal. We got a draw. We failed where our older brothers had won."[343] They contemplated that "[w]e should have used our arms the way they were intended to be used. . . . Because you hold and cradle guys in your arms that die right there talking about their wives and wishing they could see their kids again."[344]

In light of the Vietnam War, the end of the Cold War, and the rise of North Korea as a potential nuclear threat, most veterans of the war in Korea now, fifty years later, recognize that their victory lay in preventing North Korea and China from imposing communism on the Republic of South Korea, as well as possibly deterring communist efforts elsewhere.[345] They agree that "[o]ne forgotten war may eventually turn out to have been the decisive conflict that started the collapse of communism."[346] But, at the time, men and women often felt that success had to be gauged in smaller, more personal terms. "I'd made mistakes. But I'd done things that had merit. . . . I hadn't lost any men through stupidity or from fear. If you summed it up, that was the real achievement, what you had to keep with you. I was going home whole, that was something pretty important too."[347] In surviving, they had learned lessons like "it's okay to cry . . . [and] there are no winners in war and . . . we must learn to live in harmony with this world."[348] And, dropped into the war zone and left to experience fear, compassion, and the sting of death, the men and women serving in the Korean theater grew up. Leaving "youth and immaturity behind," they "returned, still young but no longer innocent."[349]

POWs being interviewed by the press at Freedom Village, Korea, in September 1953. Among them are (*left to right*) Corporal Edward F. Beck, Sergeant Frederick C. Brock-mays, Corporal James H. Sweeny, Private First Class Joseph Junear, and Corporal Rodney C. Scott. Courtesy of the National Archives (photograph no. 542274).

5

Behind Enemy Lines

In April 1951, Bob Ward's luck nearly ran out. A United States Air Force P-80 captain, Ward found himself downed somewhere in enemy territory with broken legs and little hope of survival. Thinking he would die, Ward made a cross and waited. But, Ward's captor, indicating that he too was a Christian, did the unthinkable. He grabbed a flashlight and directed American planes to Ward's position so that he could be rescued. After falling "from one kind of war to another," Ward had been redeemed after only a brief and tolerable interlude behind enemy lines.[1]

Ward's tale is not the only one of its kind. Other American prisoners of war (POWs) in Korea also managed to escape captivity after only a few hours, days, or weeks and with a minimum of hardship.[2] But, for most of the 7,190 Americans taken prisoner by the North Koreans and Chinese during the Korean War, release took months or even years, if it came at all.[3] No prisoner exchanges took place until April 1953, when the UN Command and the communists traded "sick and wounded" prisoners in the operation known as "Little Switch." At that time, 149 Americans began their long-anticipated trek home.[4] A few months later, after the signing of the armistice, "Big Switch" returned another forty-three hundred American POWs to the custody of the United States. For nearly three thousand Americans, though, the exchanges came too late. Wounded, malnourished, exposed to the elements, or simply put to death, they had already perished, their bones whitening in the cold Korean sun.[5] Also, despite Chinese assurances at the peace table that all willing POWs would be repatriated, some 3,404 United Nations POWs, including 944 Americans, came up missing after the final count.[6] The Chinese admitted to holding some of these—they claimed, for instance, that airmen had flown over the Yalu River and thus were not prisoners of war but rather spies and war criminals subject to Chinese justice—a few of whom they eventually freed to return to the States. Yet, after all the repatriations and a flurry of research and investigations, 450 known American POWs presumed to be alive remained missing.[7]

Understandably, Americans felt angry that so many GIs would not be marching home as expected. Speaking with the secretary of the Army in late 1953, President Eisenhower noted that "if he had fully appreciated the situation [in April 1953]," he might have "insisted on their [the missing POWs'] return as a precondition to the [peace] conference."[8] Upon learning the facts, the American public vocally agreed with Eisenhower's sentiment and flooded the Oval Office and newspapers around the country with telegrams and letters demanding action. Retired Navy Lieutenant Charlie Duerson insisted, "If military men are being imprisoned or executed by any foreign power without reason we should be prepared to defend our position immediately and with the utmost power at our command." Similarly, retired Army Captain Eugene Guild asked the president, "Do . . . you think Americans prefer to abandon their own GIs and live as jackals rather than run the risk of fighting for those boys who lost their freedom fighting for ours?"[9] However, while the Eisenhower administration expressed concern for the men retained by China and did what it could to negotiate the release of about eighteen airmen, it did little else to bring the boys home.[10]

Americans did not forget the missing of the Korean War, but public attention naturally shifted to the survivors who shipped back to the home front in the spring and summer of 1953. Newspapers eagerly covered the return of local sons and, as it became clear just how heavy a price U.S. servicemen had paid for their capture, both regional and national publications featured detailed and lengthy stories describing the horrors of captivity endured by Korean War POWs. Initially, these articles emphasized the brutality suffered by American prisoners in communist hands—the death marches, starvation diets, exposure to cold, lack of medical care, and general mistreatment that had resulted in the "haggard faces and emaciated bodies" of the men passing through Freedom Village.[11] But, almost immediately after Little Switch, a bigger scoop worked its way into the headlines and into the public imagination. Rumors began to circulate that through indoctrination or "brainwashing" the Chinese had successfully "turned" many Americans in their care, if not favorably disposing them toward communism, at least leading them to commit various acts of treason or collaboration such as signing false confessions or denouncing America and its leaders. In fact, Army psychiatrist William Mayer, present at Little Switch, when many so-called progressives who had openly collaborated with the enemy were repatriated, claimed that one-third of American POWs had "yielded to brainwashing" in North Korea.[12] Operating on this premise, the Army began investigating and interrogating former prisoners of war nearly as quickly as they were released.[13]

Ultimately, the Army concluded that most American POWs had collaborated at least nominally with the enemy. Determined to hold former prisoners of war accountable for their actions, the Army initiated fourteen courts-martial in the mid-1950s, charging thirteen men with collaboration.[14] Though only a few faced formal charges, suspicion fell on all, particularly after twenty-one Americans declined repatriation and chose to stay with the Chinese. This prompted a number of POWs to proclaim their innocence. Sick and wounded returnees at Valley Forge Hospital in Pennsylvania noted publicly that they were "burned up" over the idea that they "might have succumbed to Communist propaganda in Korean prison camps."[15] Similarly, Major David MacGhee wrote a piece for *Collier's* entitled "In Korea's Hell Camps: Some of Us Didn't Crack," in which he asserted that he had held out against communist pressure.[16] But, while many Americans stood ready to forgive former prisoners of war for their crimes and any lapses in judgment given the ordeal they had just endured, the public overwhelmingly found the chilling novelty of brainwashing and tales of collaboration infinitely more interesting than POW denials that Chinese indoctrination had succeeded.

Filmmakers, journalists, and psychiatrists in the 1950s proved all too happy to feed the fascination with "brainwashed" prisoners of war, producing a number of motion pictures and articles devoted to the topic. Movies like *The Rack* (1956), *Manchurian Candidate* (1959), and *Time Limit* (1957) all dramatically depicted Americans giving in to communist coercion.[17] Meanwhile, Dr. Benjamin Spock, Betty Friedan, Eugene Kinkead, and a host of others offered up theories as to why so many Americans presumably collaborated with the enemy.[18] Some charged that this latest generation of American POWs, unlike the men captured in World War I or World War II, simply lacked the "right stuff." They argued that coddling mothers, a broken educational system, weak characters, and an even weaker sense of national pride all made Korean War POWs overly susceptible to Chinese indoctrination. Concerned with the apparent danger of bringing brainwashed POWs back to the United States, other authors pondered whether or not brains could be "rewashed," how the country should fight the new "war for the P.O.W.'s mind," and whether the country should extend clemency to returning collaborators or instead demand punishment of them.[19] Despite this flurry of opinions, theories, and expert assessments, the entire POW story did not unfold in the pages of American newspapers or magazines. Everyone wanted to know what made this generation of soldiers behave differently in captivity than Americans captured in previous wars—few people questioned whether or not POWs actually had acted less patriotically or heroically—but virtually nobody bothered to investigate or write about what made the Korean War POW experience unique.[20] To understand why so many communist-held POWs signed false confessions, made propaganda broadcasts, attended lectures on communism, failed to mount successful escapes, or came home less jubilant than the public thought they should be, Americans needed details about what life had been like under the North Koreans and Chinese. What had gone so terribly wrong for American prisoners of war in Korea?

North Korean Captors and American Prisoners of War

Signed in 1929, the Third Geneva Convention established guidelines for the acceptable treatment of prisoners of war. Under its terms, a detaining power could compel POWs to give their name, rank, date of birth, and serial number, but nothing more. Furthermore, the various articles of the agreement required captors to adequately feed, clothe, and house their prisoners as well as protect them "against acts of violence or intimidation or against insults and public curiosity." In short, "prisoners of war must at all times be humanely treated."[21]

Of course, North Korea had not signed the Third Geneva Convention in 1929, nor had it ratified the larger Geneva Conventions in 1949.[22] But, at least initially, some hope existed that the North Koreans would abide by them during the Korean War. Making contact with Pyongyang soon after the start of hostilities on the peninsula, representatives of the International Red Cross inquired whether or not North Korea intended to follow the Geneva Conventions. No doubt everyone breathed a sigh of relief when Pak Hen Yen, North Korea's minister of foreign affairs, replied that the People's Republic of North Korea "is strictly abiding by the principles of the Geneva Convention in respect to prisoners of war."[23] For a while, no one had reason to doubt North Korean sincerity in the matter. After all, even Nazi Germany, barbaric by other standards, for the most part had complied with the terms set forth in Geneva, at least with regard to American and British prisoners.[24]

Weeks passed before the outside world discovered Pak Hen Yen's lie, but to United Nations soldiers captured by North Korean troops it quickly and painfully became clear that this enemy had no intention of treating prisoners of war humanely. North Koreans routinely shot, bayoneted, or beat to death those Americans unlucky enough to be caught within their grasp. In mid-August 1950, in what came to be called the Hill 303 Massacre, North Korean troops gathered together forty-five POWs whom they stripped of boots and other possessions before leading them to a ravine where they were shot. Only four survived, including Roy Paul Manning Jr., who later testified, "I looked around and I saw my buddies was falling, getting murdered with their hands tied behind their backs." About two weeks later, North Koreans forced four American soldiers to carry their ammunition for them before taking their fatigues, boots, rings, and dog tags and handing them a paper saying, "You are about to die the most horrible kind of death." In September 1950, North Koreans in Taejon forced some sixty American prisoners to sit in ditches and then shot them at point blank range. One man, seriously wounded, survived by playing dead and allowing his would-be killers to bury him alive. At Kaesong in November 1950, North Koreans shot another thirteen American prisoners without warning after forcing them to march for about two miles. A month later, North Koreans tortured five captured airmen, puncturing their flesh with sharpened, heated bamboo sticks before allowing the men to bleed to death.[25] Massacres such as these tend to stick in the minds of historians and the public alike, but countless other Americans, alone and afraid, suffered similar fates at the hands of the North Koreans.

If one happened to be spared, more brutality would follow. A member of Task Force Smith, the understrength battalion charged with slowing the North Korean advance in early July 1950, Ambrose Nugent got caught behind enemy lines, where he observed North Korean soldiers murdering wounded GIs in an aid station. Soon after, Nugent became a prisoner himself. Nugent's captors stripped him of all but his most basic clothing, tied his hands behind his back, and "just beat the hell out of me" with their fists, rifle butts, and feet.[26] Similarly, after first trying to shoot Lloyd Kreider in the head, despite the fact that as a medical aid man he wore a Red Cross arm band, the North Koreans confiscated all of Kreider's clothes except for his pants, leaving him barefoot and miserable. Then, before leaving the front, the North Koreans forced Kreider, wounded and nearly naked, to carry their packs, water, and rice for them and tried to make him fire a rifle at the American lines.[27] For no discernible objective other than to torture another human being, Corporal

One of four American soldiers of the 21st Infantry Regiment, 24th Division found between the forward observation post and the front line in July 1950. Most of these men, who were probably captured and then shot, were shot through the head with their arms tied behind their backs. U.S. Army, courtesy of the Harry S. Truman Library (photograph no. 2007-435).

Charles Kinard's captors tied his hands behind his back, beat him with rifle butts, and forced him to march double quick time with pebbles in his shoes. After he collapsed from pain and exhaustion, the North Koreans stuck a can opener into his open shoulder wound and burned his feet with cigarettes.[28]

Any American POW holding out hope that treatment would improve after his initial capture soon faced grave disappointment. Becoming a prisoner merely marked "the beginning of what can only be described as . . . living hell."[29] Particularly early in the war, when the front shifted from hour to hour and day to day, North Koreans walked their prisoners north as quickly as possible, away from the lure of friendly forces and the possibility of escape. Traveling at night so as to avoid attack by American airplanes, North Korean guards pushed their prisoners relentlessly for days through both soaring temperatures and snowstorms toward collection points, often denying them food, water, and medical treatment.[30] The condition of the men, especially the wounded, deteriorated considerably, making it difficult for them to keep up. However, the North Koreans discouraged their wards from slowing up or falling down by clubbing them on the head or in the back with rifle butts.[31] If anyone became too ill or weak to continue walking or began to straggle too much, the North Koreans had a remedy for that, too. A quick twist of the bayonet in the belly or shot to the head immediately prevented an individual from holding the entire group back. Sometimes GIs could only imagine what happened. Akira Chikami remembers how after the North Koreans left several men behind he heard shots from a burp gun and "knew the North Koreans had shot them." At other times, the North Koreans made the rest of their captives watch as they murdered those unable to march.[32]

When POWs finally reached the temporary camps set up for them by the North Koreans, they found conditions no better.[33] Housed in caves, Korean huts, or whatever other structures happened to be available, prisoners, still clad only in what remained of the fatigues they wore when captured, suffered acutely once the weather turned cold. To keep warm, and because they had little choice given the small amount of space allotted them, GIs slept close to one another, covering up with rice sacks or anything else they could find. Sleeping this way did not always provide as much warmth as anyone liked, but it did give the resident lice an opportunity to infect one and all.[34] Desperately in need of a healthy diet and medical care, prisoners received neither. The North Koreans fed Americans any combination of millet, sorghum, soybeans, and rice, which, along with the contaminated water consumed by Americans on the marches and in the camps, caused chronic diarrhea and dysentery, leading to further malnutrition and yet more deaths. American medics and doctors did what they could to ease the suffering and curb the death toll, but without proper medications, access to sanitary facilities, or even fresh bandages, in many cases the most they could offer to their fellow POWs were words of encouragement.

Undoubtedly, the ragged GIs stuck in these dingy, dilapidated, overcrowded, unsanitary quarters looked forward to moving to a new location, but the next phase of their POW experience often proved worse. After keeping their prisoners in temporary camps for anywhere from a few days to a few months, the North Koreans prepared to march them to permanent camps along the Yalu River or to other holding facilities further out of the reach of UN forces. These marches turned fatal for Americans worn down by dysentery, disease, hunger, exposure, and mental stress. Any march could become a "death march" for the weak and weary.

On Halloween night 1950, more than eight hundred prisoners, including American servicemen as well as civilians and political prisoners ranging in age from infants to senior citizens, began the infamous "Tiger Death

March."[35] Shuttled from Pyongyang to Manpo by the North Korean Army after the UN's successful Inchon Landing, these prisoners suddenly found themselves under the authority of the North Korean Security Police and a "homicidal maniac" known to Americans only as "the Tiger."[36] Dividing the group into fourteen companies, the Tiger announced that "[w]e are going on a long march. I am in command, and I have the authority to make you obey."[37] Then, after ordering pacesetters to maintain good speed, the Tiger started his prisoners on the journey that would lead them through North Korea's rugged mountains and wide valleys all the way to the Yalu River. No matter how fast the group walked, "it was never fast enough for him," and the Tiger soon demonstrated the consequences for straggling.[38] Though it was obvious that the sick and wounded could scarcely walk, much less keep up the blistering pace required, the Tiger halted the column on November 1 to demand that the officers serving as company leaders explain why people had fallen behind. Insisting, "I'll kill you all," the Tiger made an example out of Lieutenant Cordus Thornton, shooting him in the head while the other prisoners looked on.[39] From that point forward, the guards committed similar acts of brutality, beating those who stumbled or fell and killing anyone who broke ranks for any reason. "We knew we just had to keep up. If you dropped out, you were a dead man."[40] To survive, prisoners thought, ate, and defecated while walking. "Better dirty than dead, we said."[41]

Such conditions transformed ordinary men into heroes. Numerous POWs shouldered their wounded and weakened buddies, carrying them as far as their own strength would allow. Many more encouraged and prodded men to "keep going." Pop Wilson warned a fellow prisoner that he had better keep walking because "[I'll] stick my boot up your ass if you don't."[42] Nevertheless, the inhumanity of the march took its toll, reducing some GIs to a less than noble state. Private First Class Susumu Shinagawa remembers that, suffering from the cold, a soldier stole an airman's crutch for firewood, causing the airman to fall behind and get shot.[43] Similarly, one young, barefoot soldier ran back to a friend who had fallen by the wayside to remove his shoes and run off with them.[44]

In the end, neither sacrifice nor selfishness guaranteed one's survival. By the time the Tiger Death March concluded at Chunggang on November 8, nearly a hundred prisoners had died. To the gaunt and hollow-eyed survivors, the Tiger proclaimed, "You have made this march to repent for your sins of coming to Korea."[45] But, the Tiger had not yet finished exacting penance. Almost immediately he instituted an exercise program sure to finish off many of those who, despite suffering the ill effects of malnutrition, exposure, pneumonia, and frostbite, had willed themselves to complete the long pilgrimage to Chunggang. After dark or before dawn, prisoners gathered outside in the frigid winter weather to perform calisthenics.[46] Unsurprisingly, within a year of the march, fewer than half of those who had begun it remained alive.[47]

Unfortunately, the Tiger Death March did not represent a departure from the treatment characteristically given POWs by the North Koreans. In October 1950, when it seemed clear that UN forces were going to capture Pyongyang, the North Koreans herded about 180 survivors of a Scoul-to-Pyongyang death march into open railroad cars and headed them further north. After weathering exposure to the cold wind and raw temperatures for days, the POWs finally reached a tunnel near Sunchon. There, fearful that the Americans might be able to liberate the prisoners, the North Koreans first tried to suffocate them with engine smoke, but, failing in that, settled for leading successive groups of forty or so men out of the tunnel to be shot. A few men managed to survive the slaughter by lying under those who had been killed, thus protecting themselves against North Korean bayonets as the enemy tried to make certain no one lived through the Sunchon Tunnel Massacre. Rescued by American soldiers, every survivor looked, after only a few months in North Korean custody, "like a walking dead man."[48] And, the emaciated, mutilated remains of the dead hardly looked human at all. Part of a graves registration company, Bill Chambers never minded his job of identifying and burying the dead, "but following the trail of that death march, seeing what the North Koreans had done to those people, I never got over that."[49]

Eventually, for those men who lived long enough, the marches ended at either a temporary or permanent prison camp in North Korea where North Koreans continued their abuse of American POWs. Fed a meager diet lacking the appropriate caloric and nutritional content, prisoners dropped as much as half their body weight.[50] One survivor remembers, "A head of cabbage and a pint of beans would make five hundred gallons of soup without a bit of trouble."[51] Unaccustomed to dining on soybeans or millet and already weakened, many in the camps contracted dysentery, further compounding cases of malnutrition and adding to the unpleasantness of captivity. With latrine lines long and facilities often in short supply, not every man could hold out, the wretched result being that they defecated in the only pants they owned.[52] Guards witnessing such incidents tended to react with brutality rather than sympathy, smearing with their own feces the faces of those unfortunate enough to be caught in the act.[53] The North Koreans punished men for other perceived offenses even more harshly. POWs found themselves stripped and forced to kneel in the snow, sometimes while guards poured cold water over them.[54] And, all the while, the North Koreans deprived their wards of warm clothing and housing, proper medical care, and most of the basic necessities crucial to preserving and saving lives.[55] As a result, disease and death became constant companions in the camps, so constant that those experiencing the losses became inured to the pain. As one repatriate noted, "At first, when a buddy died, I'd get very upset and not talk to anyone for days. But after it happened so many times, I didn't seem to care—and I wouldn't feel anything."[56]

Given the hopelessness of their situation, prisoners fantasized about escaping from the North Koreans and, though this was extraordinarily rare, a few Americans broke free. After marching for weeks, Private Paul Smith's group moved into a camp where the North Koreans expected the POWs to work the fields of a farm. By then, Smith had lost sixty pounds and had dysentery, beriberi, and pneumonia, but, seeing his chance at freedom, he stole a truck and drove south until he ran out of gasoline. Then he walked all night until he reached the American lines.[57] Most American captives, however, had neither the opportunity nor the strength to mount an escape attempt. Even if they did, breaking out of camp and temporarily shaking the guards did not ensure success. Without food or water, escapees necessarily had to live off the land, cautious of being seen since their skin color, features, and even gait marked them as American. Also, POWs could not expect either sympathy or assistance from North Korean civilians, who maintained a healthy hostility toward them.[58] Indeed, the vast majority of American POWs had to wait until the end of the war to regain their freedom. Long before then, though, American POWs met another master in Korea: the Chinese.[59]

The Chinese and American POWs

In late fall 1950 the Chinese People's Volunteer Army began crossing into North Korea in order to push back encroaching UN forces. For the average American infantryman in country, this signified the end of one war—the one in which they could mop up the remnants of the North Korean Army and still make it home for Christmas dinner—and the beginning of another, longer and perhaps more deadly conflict involving a fresh and seemingly inexhaustible adversary. Caught off guard by both the existence of a new enemy and the sheer number of Chinese troops facing them, UN units quickly began what turned into a slow and difficult retreat. Before reaching safety, however, many Americans died and many others became prisoners of the Chinese. The newly captured found captivity an unwelcome turn of events, but those already languishing in North Korean prison camps felt even more disheartened as they realized that the Chinese presence portended a longer wait for peace and repatriation.[60]

In either case, American POWs could scarcely imagine what life would be like under the watchful eyes of the Chinese communists.

In sharp contrast to the North Koreans, the Chinese often welcomed new prisoners with kind words and friendly gestures. As Captain Bert Cumby testified after the war, Chinese soldiers gave POWs pats on the back, shook their hands, and insisted, "We are friends. We are not enemies."[61] Captured in October 1951, Richard Bassett recalls that, instead of tying him up, the Chinese handed him a slip of paper stating that "we were now safely in the hands of the Chinese People's Volunteers and that we would be treated well and had nothing to fear." Indeed, Bassett's captors "were all smiles, and many of them wanted to shake hands."[62] In other instances, Chinese soldiers offered prisoners reassurance that "[w]e are not mad at you. We are mad at Wall Street."[63] And, on numerous occasions they rescued Americans from almost certain death. Trying to escape from a group of hostile North Korean soldiers, William Shadish ended up the hostage of a Manchurian unit. As he wrote in his memoir, "I figured this time we were surely finished." Instead, the Chinese ran off the pursuing North Koreans, untied Shadish, and offered him water and cigarettes. One captor "even gave me a swig of liquor from his canteen."[64] Similarly, Chinese troops ordered the North Koreans who had captured Sergeant Clarence Young to quit killing prisoners and saved Donald Elliott's life by seizing his North Korean guard's gun and sending him away.[65] More astonishingly, the Chinese in charge of Jay Hidano's group of POWs had a doctor inspect the wounded and afterward left those who could not walk in a shack by the side of the road where American tanks later picked them up.[66] To be sure, the Chinese did not always resist the urge to punish POWs with blows from their rifle butts or to steal whatever valuables prisoners possessed, but neither did they routinely engage in the wholesale murder or mistreatment of GIs at the time of capture.

Once under the control of the Chinese, however, POWs suffered nearly as much as under the North Koreans. Wounded or not, captured GIs had miles of walking ahead of them. First, the Chinese prodded prisoners along to assembly points. Marching at night to avoid strafing by American aircraft, POWs rarely received any food, water, or medical treatment, and the guards refused to halt even when temperatures dipped below zero and ice covered the pathways. As a result, men dropped out of the ranks either to die on their own or to be shot by the Chinese, their bodies left to litter the roadsides. Others, however, like Lawrence Bailey, who trudged forward despite having frozen feet that "felt like pieces of wood," were determined to survive the trip no matter what, but when they reached the collection points, things did not get much better.[67]

On arrival, English-speaking Chinese officers admonished Americans for interloping in the "civil war between North Koreans and South Koreans" and advised them, "You are not prisoners. You are students, and as students we are going to educate you." The Chinese continued, "We could have executed you, but we spared you in order for you to learn the good points of Communism. If you cooperate with us, we will be very lenient, but if not, we will treat you as war criminals."[68] At the collection points, as at the temporary and permanent camps later, the Chinese failed to live up to their words. Cooperative or not, POWs received only an inadequate ration of food, so little in fact that stories abound of men picking through other POWs' vomit or diarrhea for undigested kernels of corn or other sustenance.[69] The communists also regularly denied the men in their care even the most rudimentary medical supplies. Afflicted with a foot wound, Bill Funchess showed a Chinese doctor his foot. The doctor looked away, refusing to treat Funchess, and when further pressed merely pointed to a used and bloody bandage on the floor and then went about his business.[70] After treating their prisoners with such callousness and indifference, the Chinese then expected these same POWs to march again, this time toward temporary or permanent prison camps, or to die trying.[71]

Despite Chinese assurances that conditions would be better once POWs reached the camps, things seldom were. Temporary camps like the Valley, Death Valley, Mining Camp, and Bean Camp had extraordinarily high death rates and as many as 50 percent of all POWs passing through them died.[72] There, men struggled to survive the same "savage and barbaric handling . . . which existed on all the marches" and "in the worst camps, the prisoners existed by the skin of their teeth and raw courage."[73] Missing jackets or boots—these often having been lost, confiscated, or not received by the time of capture—and housed in unheated Korean huts without blankets, POWs tried to stave off the bitter cold.[74] Despite their efforts to keep warm, they experienced frostbite and in places like Death Valley men passed the time pulling off frozen toes, fingertips, and ears.[75] They also fought starvation by consuming the soybeans or sorghum meted out to them by the Chinese. Unfortunately, eating out of common bowls with filthy hands only served to make some men even more ill, as did the type of meals provided them. Feeding POWs twice a day, the Chinese sometimes proved careless in their preparation. When improperly cooked soybeans hit prisoners' digestive tracts, they passed through rapidly, causing damage, discomfort, and dysentery.[76] Some prisoners preserved their sanity in the temporary camps by helping others. They fed their comrades, tended to their wounds, and picked lice off them. Challenged both physically and mentally, other POWs could not help but give up, filling the long nights with their sobbing and agony.[77] Not infrequently, discipline disappeared altogether in the temporary camps, leaving prisoners yet more vulnerable to the pressures of captivity.[78] As one veteran notes about Death Valley, the stunning thing about the temporary camps, whether supervised by the North Koreans or the Chinese, "is not how many men died there but that anyone survived."[79]

Ultimately, most American POWs ended up at one of the numbered permanent camps along the Yalu River.[80] At first crude and primitive, these continued the privations of the temporary camps with the same result: American dead began to pile up. Thrown atop the frozen earth or buried a foot deep somewhere on the surrounding hillsides, the bodies made for a "dreadful scene," one that caused POWs to wonder, "Would I be the next to die?"[81] Over time, however, the Chinese instituted changes that improved both the general living conditions in the permanent camps and one's chances of survival. Following the resumption of the peace talks at Panmunjom in October 1951, the Chinese adopted a "lenient policy" that translated into better treatment for POWs.[82] After all, what might the outside world think of China if POWs continued to die in such alarming numbers? The Chinese most assuredly understood that the outcome not only of the Korean War but of the larger struggle between communism and the free world rested as much on propaganda as on military superiority.

That winter, POWs in the permanent camps received allotments of blankets, padded uniforms, and new shoes.[83] Food also became more plentiful and sometimes more palatable as rations of rice and flour worked their way onto the menu.[84] At times, the Chinese accommodated prisoner requests as when one camp asked for vegetables and ended up with 101 meals of boiled turnips.[85] In general, men still lacked meat and vegetables in their diet and consequently continued to suffer night blindness and a host of other ailments caused by malnutrition, but they less frequently felt the old, unbearable hunger pangs that had accompanied starvation. Conditions varied somewhat according to how well or poorly the talks seemed to be going, but by the following spring men could look forward to things like getting new uniforms for the season, washing their clothes, ridding themselves of lice infestations, reading mail, and writing home. Also, if healthy enough, they could participate in athletics. Making their own equipment, men in the camps played basketball, softball, and volleyball. In November 1952, eager to show the world how well they treated POWs, the North Koreans and Chinese held the POW Olympics and more than five hundred prisoners from various countries competed. Some prisoners took advantage of the new mood to establish churches and hold religious services. The Chinese still disapproved of prisoners gathering to worship, but they began to tolerate such meetings, pretending they did not know what the POWs were doing. Also, medical care, nearly nonexistent in the early months, improved so much that men began to seek rather than avoid treatment for illness and injury. That is not to say that the medicine practiced in the camps ever reached Western standards—plenty of incompetent practitioners remained the only available option and commonly communist doctors offered a cure-all to patients, sewing a chicken or pig liver under the skin—but at least POWs no longer had to say a final goodbye to friends entering the hospital as a matter of routine.[86] In short, men who had survived to 1952 more than likely would live to return home when the war finally ended.[87]

Despite the "lenient policy" and all that came with it, life in North Korea's prison camps remained dangerous and unpleasant. The Chinese could not control the weather or the persistence of pests like lice, bedbugs, rats, and flies. At one point, flies became such a nuisance in Camp 5 that the Chinese offered POWs one cigarette for every one hundred flies they killed.[88] What the Chinese could regulate, however, they did with brutal efficiency. From the outset the Chinese attempted to break down the morale of those whom they captured. Prison camps had separate areas for officers, enlisted men, and African Americans, presumably to create chaos and mistrust in the ranks, dividing the men and making them more manageable. Also, while giving prisoners new uniforms might be viewed as charity, substituting blue "student" uniforms and canvas shoes for United States military uniforms and boots had the effect, no doubt intended, of robbing POWs of their identity as American GIs.[89] Successful enough, these tactics and others, including the Chinese educational program, worked to turn some prisoners into collaborators willing to inform on others, pose for propaganda photos, sign confessions, or do nearly anything else for more food or a ration of wine or cigarettes.[90] Never knowing just who might rat them out to the Chinese, men necessarily became cautious about forming friendships or doing anything that might get them into trouble. Thus the Chinese succeeded in destroying whatever reserves of military order, discipline, and unity the POWs had left. Instead of joining together to thwart their common enemy, most POWs settled for "playing it cool," trying to stay under the Chinese radar.[91]

Prisoners had good reason to fear the wrath of the Chinese. In the permanent camps, guards dispensed quick and often terrible justice for any number of offenses. In addition to overt physical torture and deprivation, the Chinese punished POWs by making them write and publicly read self-criticisms, stand barefoot in the snow, keep their bodies in unnatural and uncomfortable positions for hours, or spend time in solitary confinement.

All of the camps had places called "the hole" or "the icebox," an enclosed, isolated cell little bigger than a coffin built partially underground or sealed off to prevent light from filtering in. The men sentenced to spend time there could scarcely sit up, straighten out, fend off bugs or other pests, or keep warm. Depending on the guards, prisoners in solitary might not be let out for any reason, even to defecate or urinate, and thus had to live, lie, eat, sleep, and endure being poked and prodded by the Chinese all while surrounded by their own waste. Indeed, such conditions could make a man wish he were dead, and in many cases punishment directly led to a man's demise.[92]

For relatively minor crimes, such as getting caught stealing a chicken, a POW might have to spend a few days in solitary confinement and then offer a "confession" to the group. Willing to risk this comparatively mild punishment, POWs regularly attempted to pilfer from the Chinese and some stole into town to raid villagers' vegetable gardens or animal pens. Some strove to have a little fun with their self-recrimination. Forced to confess, Hector Cadero promised, "I will not be caught stealing chickens again."[93] Perhaps because they never got very far, the Chinese tended to let would-be escapees off rather lightly as well, generally assigning them a tolerable number of days in solitary confinement.[94] The Chinese, however, reacted less charitably to men who refused to cooperate by absenting themselves from educational sessions, leading other prisoners in open resistance to the Chinese, or embarrassing the guards in some way. Believing that Donald Elliott had participated in burning down a camp recreational room and throwing rocks through the window at the Chinese headquarters, the guards forced Elliott to consider his "crimes against the common people's republic" while standing at attention for thirty-four hours and then required him to write a confession.[95] The Chinese repeatedly punished one so-called reactionary who did not attend classes, study communist materials, or sing propaganda songs by beating him, hanging him by his arms and thumbs, forcing him to balance with his knees on a stick, keeping him in the hole for sixteen months, and staging mock executions.[96] He survived to tell about it, but Major Hume did not. Because he asserted that a Chinese lecture was "not worth the paper it is written on and the paper is not worth a damn," the communists tossed Hume into a partially underground structure at Camp 5 where he soon died, "a direct result of the barbaric treatment by the Chinese."[97] With chances of success so slim and consequences so potentially deadly, it can be no wonder that more American POWs did not challenge the Chinese or refuse to comply with their orders.

Under both the North Koreans and Chinese, one had to muster all his strength to bear the physical strain of captivity, but the Chinese added another dimension to the survival experience—a deliberate and coordinated attack on the minds of POWs. Initially, the Chinese confined their psychological warfare to interrogation. After briefing prisoners on their situation, the Chinese began asking questions. Taking prisoners one at a time to speak with an officer or giving them forms to fill out, the Chinese expected POWs to reveal everything they knew about military matters such as the composition, number of men, and weapons possessed by various military units.[98] They also demanded that POWs tell them about their lives back home. What kind of work had a prisoner done before entering the military? What sort of job did his father or mother have? What kind of car did the prisoner's family drive? What religion was he?[99] Men resisted answering—and most knew little of military significance anyway—but the Chinese had ways of making POWs talk. In some instances, the Chinese used a show of force to try to elicit responses. Meung Ho Kim, a Korean American, recalls that after he was held in an uncomfortably hot room, a Chinese officer came in with his pistol cocked to tell Kim, "If you don't tell me the truth, we might as well end things here." When Kim said nothing, the officer pulled the trigger. The chamber held no bullet, but that did not lessen the terror.[100] The Chinese also played "good cop–bad cop" or took prisoners on "walking conferences," where a Chinese officer invited an individual POW to walk away from the squalor of the camp and talk about why he seemed so sad or worried.[101] Whatever the method, POWs found it difficult to avoid giving up something.[102] As one veteran asserts, "I never would have made it past that first interrogation point had I continued to follow those guidelines [of the Geneva Conventions] of giving my name, rank, serial number, and where I was born."[103] And, interrogation "was a never-ending process." Many prisoners faced examination at least twice, and 18 percent were interrogated five or more times, with resisters or reactionaries suffering a hundred or more sessions.[104] Perhaps the Chinese hoped to gather significant intelligence, but interrogation proved equally useful as a tool to break down prisoner resistance and to prepare POWs to do their captors' bidding.[105]

Shepherding about 250 soldiers and marines captured at the Chosin Reservoir to Kanggye, a small valley in central Korea, in December 1950, the Chinese moved forward from interrogation to debut what would blossom into a full-fledged education and indoctrination program by the summer of 1951.[106] The details differed from camp to camp, but the pattern followed a predictable course. The Chinese first softened their prisoners, conditioning them to accept the lessons that would follow. While keeping POWs cold, hungry, and confused, the Chinese forced them to attend hours of lectures a day devoted to topics like, "Who is the aggressor in Korea?"; "Why do the

Chinese love peace?"; and "Why is the U.S. the aggressor?"[107] Well trained, dedicated, and skillful, the Chinese in charge of tutoring POWs tailored the content of meetings to fit the audience. African Americans, for instance, relearned American history and politics with an emphasis on racism and the way their country had wronged and failed them.[108] With these speeches, the Chinese hoped to hammer home to POWs that "[y]our government lies to you. The rich people don't care about you, that's why they sent you here to die. Your government makes war to oppress the Korean people."[109] If Americans only could be made to believe that they had been misled by "our 'aggressive, capitalist, warmongering leaders,'" then their minds would be ripened to accept instruction in communism.[110]

Once students made satisfactory progress, the Chinese moved on to the next phase of indoctrination, the "suction phase."[111] Frequently while fattening prisoners up on better rations, the Chinese now provided men with a contrast to the depiction of America they had just completed. Idealizing life in "new democracies" like China and the Soviet Union, the Chinese touted the merits of communism.[112] Called "brainwashing" by the popular media after the war, this stage in the program required POWs to read and memorize communist doctrine and propaganda.[113] Day after day, week after week, month after month, POWs attended classes, studied publications like the *Shanghai News* and *Peiping Daily*, gathered in small groups to discuss the material, and took notes in books provided by the Chinese.[114] Few Americans became converts, but these methods did have an effect. "He [the Chinese teacher] relentlessly pounded this Communist theory down, around, and through our skulls. Repetition, repetition, repetition, until whether we wanted it or not, unconsciously a little of this poison began to seep into our brain cells, although in our hearts we knew it wasn't true."[115] Of course, Chinese tactics also had an impact, and many POWs walked away from their experiences more convinced than ever of the necessity of combating communism.[116]

To ensure proper participation and compliance, the Chinese employed a number of techniques, including harassment, humiliation, threats, and promises of leniency. On the one hand, Chinese officers reminded prisoners,

> You are the aggressors and if you don't accept the lenient policy and change your views, we have dug a hole which we are going to throw you in. . . . A person who does not accept our doctrine is not a human being because he is not for the masses. . . . You will learn the truth. . . . We don't care if you die here because we will bury you and bury you so deep that you won't stink.[117]

To prove their point, they made resistance unpleasant. For example, after one POW challenged the assertion that the United States had initiated the Korean War, the instructor forced the entire class to remain standing until he recanted.[118] Also, as noted above, reactionaries, those who refused to cooperate with the Chinese, suffered severe penalties such as being thrown in the hole for weeks or months at a time. Those who cooperated, however, especially those who agreed to serve as monitors or who taught lessons, wrote for the camp newspaper, sang songs praising Mao, or made propaganda broadcasts, received extra food or cigarettes as well as the hope of something better. Some believed that cooperation ultimately would lead to freedom and, in rare cases, it did. In May 1951 the Chinese dropped nineteen newly enlightened POWs off near the American lines to make their way back to the other side of the war.[119]

After about twelve months of compulsory lessons and intense indoctrination, the Chinese ended mandatory attendance and study.[120] Most prisoners "viewed that as a victory for us."[121] Progressives, though, continued to hold and even lead meetings. After the war, critics used this fact to show that "[t]he behavior of too many of our soldiers in prison fell far short of the historical standards of honor, character, loyalty, courage, and personal integrity," casting doubt on the loyalty of all those Americans held captive in Korea.[122] While some progressives did serve as "the willing tools of the Chinese," informing on their fellow prisoners and willingly signing off on peace petitions or other propaganda, many continued to participate for other reasons, such as boredom or the belief that they could benefit either themselves or POWs as a whole by doing so.[123] At any rate, less than 12 percent of American prisoners of war joined special or voluntary study groups, and when the war ended only a tiny fraction of those decided to remain with the communists.[124] Other prisoners and later the public reviled progressives, but given the circumstances, their weakness is understandable. In the camps, the pressure exerted by the Chinese, who also held all the power, made it impossible for one to remain truly neutral.[125] As one POW notes, "There are no heroes in POW camps—the heroes died fighting."[126]

Behind enemy lines, men realized that in addition to staying out of trouble and avoiding the ire of the enemy, "you have to adjust to prison life or you're finished" and "you can't lose hope or you can't make it."[127] Those wishing to survive had to find ways to sustain not only their bodies but also their spirits. For some, the knowledge that "someone always had it worse than us" kept them going. When things got bad, Walter Adelmann thought of a Bataan Death March survivor whom he met in a Korean prison camp.[128] Similarly, watching a blind Korean woman with a naked baby digging through the camp trash, another POW found "it was a heartbreaking sight, but one that helped me because I actually realized that even though I was a prisoner of war I was lucky compared with her."[129] In Camp 1, prisoners whiled away the days playing chess, telling dirty jokes, and listening to stories.[130] Men in Camp 2 took turns teaching classes on subjects like algebra in order to keep their minds sharp.[131] All over, prisoners delighted in playing pranks on the guards. Navy Captain Johnny Thornton drove the Chinese crazy by riding an imaginary motorcycle around the camp. Thinking Thornton had mental problems, the Chinese ultimately "confiscated" his chopper, citing rules and regulations.[132] At other times, when guards appeared for bed check, they found that a POW had hanged himself. When the hapless guards brought officers to investigate, the body, not really dead, had vanished.[133] Many Americans renewed their religious faith, reading Bibles if they had them or attending makeshift churches.[134] Some GIs went another direction, coping by smoking marijuana. With marijuana growing wild all around the camps, most prisoners tried it at least once. After all, when high, "you didn't give a damn whether anything happened that day . . . everybody would lie there laughing and hollering. You'd never know we were in a POW camp."[135] Whatever they did, survivors tried to avoid dwelling too much on home because "if you thought too much about home, you were going to make yourself sick and . . . if you got too homesick, it would kill you."[136]

Still, until the day of their release, most POWs dreamed of escaping. Contrary to American perceptions after the war, popularized in the writings of Eugene Kinkead, William Mayer, and others who wanted to demonstrate that Korean POWs exhibited less courage and fortitude than those of previous wars, Americans did attempt to free themselves from the permanent camps.[137] When Camp 5's General Deng offered to have the guards pack a lunch and give a two-hour head start to any POW wanting to try and escape, men signed up. Of course, the Chinese had no intention of releasing their hostages, and those who tried to accept the offer faced interrogation, but their willingness to risk it shows the greatness of their desire to be free.[138] Ethnically Chinese, Clarence Young twice tried to get away. The first time he pretended to be a Chinese guard marching prisoners and the second time he and seven others attempted to swim across the Yalu River. Both times the Chinese apprehended Young, punishing him with solitary confinement.[139] Out for twenty-eight days, another POW made it all the way to the ocean before being apprehended.[140] In nearly all of the permanent camps, men risked their lives to get out, but none of them made it. While the camps themselves frequently had no fences to enclose the POWs, once a prisoner ventured beyond the confines of the prison, there was no food or water, no easy path south, and no way for men who did not look Korean to avoid notice if someone happened to see them. As one veteran notes, "Your faces are the barbed wire."[141]

The Road Back to Civilization

Once it became clear that the talks at Panmunjom likely would result in peace, the Chinese began preparing their prisoners for repatriation. In all of the camps men noticed the larger quantities of food apportioned them in order to help plump up their puny bodies. In some places, the Chinese held farewell parties and offered to return to prisoners anything that had been stolen from them—watches, money, and other personal items—and, for once, they made good on their word.[142] Nevertheless, the Chinese could not restore to those whom they had bullied, tortured, and terrorized the wasted years, their health, memories free from the taint of prison, or any semblance of certainty about the world in which they had once lived and that they would rejoin after making their way across the "Bridge of No Return" to Freedom Village at Munsan-ni.

Assisted by the International Red Cross, the communists shuttled men to Little Switch and Big Switch in trucks. In some instances they tried to retain reactionaries or "war criminals," but at the insistence of the Red Cross and the United Nations, most men eventually ended up camped in tents at the site of the prisoner exchange to await their turn to cross over the five hundred yards of "no man's land" to Freedom Village.[143] On the other side, an officer stood ready to greet returnees with salutes and handshakes. Marines received new utility caps with the Marine Corps emblem on them.[144] Seeing the "flag waving in the breeze" for the first time in years, many prisoners broke down in tears of joy and relief.[145] Then they moved on to shower, delouse, receive medical attention, and eat. Offered virtually anything they wanted to dine on, prisoners heartily consumed milkshakes, steaks, mashed potatoes, gravy, pie, bread, and other long-missed items only to find that their bodies could no longer tolerate such rich fare, forcing them to vomit nearly as soon as they finished eating.[146] Grown accustomed to the unassuming existence of captivity, one former prisoner recalled, "These things reminded me of another life. It seemed so unreal, yet it was real."[147]

Americans observing the repatriation proceedings noticed that returning POWs lacked something. A few hopped off the trucks roaring with glee, but most seemed "a little confused, and surprisingly unenthusiastic about being back."[148] Some observers felt confident that "in a few days they will be much more normal and alert," but with allegations of brainwashing floating around, others were less convinced.[149] Maybe there was "nothing to this brainwashing that a good steak and an ice cream cone won't cure," but then again perhaps the matter would prove more serious than that.[150] After all, the Air Force would not even release the names of some of its returning men, deemed "victims of Communist propaganda," because the service did not want to mark them publicly for life as communists.[151] Conjecture whizzed all around the men passing through Freedom Village, and before long many began to "think we were all classified as communists until proven innocent."[152] To a large extent, they had it right.

Boarding homebound vessels, POWs left behind the nightmare of North Korea's prison camps but sailed right into an equally unsettling reality. Noting the "emotional isolation and apathy present in most of the returnees" at Little Switch, the Army decided to assign psychiatrists to the ships to help reorient POWs before returning them to civilian society.[153] Perhaps partially altruistic, therapy sessions also elicited information about what had taken place in the camps, and to more than a few POWs they seemed reminiscent of the interrogations they had so recently endured. They had to wonder, "Why were they asking so many questions about how other prisoners behaved during the captivity. I was getting annoyed, or perhaps angry is the right word."[154] Indeed, the military, specifically the Army, since both the Marine Corps and the Air Force declined to pursue the prosecution of their own, seemed more intent on ferreting out collaborators and, anyway, what could anyone who had not been through the terrible months in North Korea understand about the experience?[155] Aboard ship, POWs stuck together, except in cases where nonprogressives made it their business to "try" progressives or "rats," handing out justice in the form of beatings.[156] What POWs wanted was for people to let them be and "forget you ever knew / That I was ever a prisoner, for I want to forget it too."[157] That did not happen. The questions kept coming, sometimes years after POWs docked at their home ports, and even decades later men discovered the degree of blight their POW status cast upon their reputations.[158] Unbeknownst to them at the time, the Army continued investigations long after the end of the war, denoting some POWs as collaborators in their records and secretly issuing less than honorable discharges to others, costing Korean War POWs both benefits and respect.[159] After twelve or fourteen days on the ocean, men reached the familiar coast of San Francisco, but, clearly, they were still a long, long way from home.

An integrated unit in Korea. Sergeant First Class Major Cleveland, weapons squad leader, points out the North Korean position to his machine gun crew in November 1950. Courtesy of the National Archives (photograph no. 111-SC-353469, War and Conflict Book no. 1426).

6

Our Fight?

Gender, Race, and the War Zone

When the Korean War broke out in June 1950, an American service-woman, not a United States marine or soldier, first answered the country's call to duty. Stationed in Korea, Captain Viola McConnell, an Army nurse, abruptly found herself charged with evacuating the wives and children of Americans assigned to KMAG as well as other foreigners desperately trying to flee the country. This would have been a difficult task under the best of circumstances, but Ambassador John J. Muccio made it even more onerous by hindering McConnell's efforts. Certain that if the North Koreans captured Seoul they would grant Americans diplomatic immunity and fearful of the international incident that would occur if the communists shot down a plane full of refugees, Muccio opposed evacuation altogether and refused to allow air transportation. Undeterred, McConnell proceeded to shepherd 643 people, including babies, pregnant women, alcoholics suffering withdrawal, and at least one senile woman onto a Norwegian fertilizer ship built to hold twelve passengers. Aided by an Army wife, several missionary nurses, and one female missionary doctor, McConnell earned a Bronze Star and Oak

Leaf Cluster by seeing to it that the nearly three hundred infants on board received adequate rations of formula, sick people got proper care, and all passengers made it safely to Japan in two days only a little worse for the wear.[1]

Even as McConnell's ordeal came to an end in Fukuoka, Japan, Major Mildred I. Clark's responsibilities in the Far East began to mushroom. Having relinquished the position of director of nurses for XXIV Corps in Korea to become chief nurse and director of nurses for the Far East Command in Tokyo, Clark had spent several years overseas and by mid-1950 planned to rotate to a duty station nearer home. As luck would have it, General Douglas MacArthur called upon Clark to complete one more task before her departure. Realizing that America's role in the struggle on the Korean Peninsula would involve U.S. casualties, MacArthur asked Clark to join the Far East Command surgeon in putting together two Mobile Army Surgical Hospitals (MASH) for deployment to Korea. This Clark willingly did, readying volunteer nurses, physicians, and enlisted personnel to field the 8054th and 8055th. Major Genevieve Smith, accompanying an advance party of these MASH

Some of the personnel and equipment of the 8225th Mobile Army Surgical Hospital assembled in Korea in October 1951. Courtesy of the National Archives (photograph number 111-SC-382662, War and Conflict Book no. 1457).

volunteers to Korea, where she was to become chief nurse for the Eighth Army, became one of the first American casualties of the war when the aircraft transporting the group exploded.[2]

From the onset of hostilities in Korea, servicewomen expected to serve in the war theater and experience the same kinds of risks and challenges faced by military women in World War II. However, as the Korean War unfolded in the months and years after the heroic efforts of McConnell and Clark, it became evident that while the military needed females in the ranks, it seldom had a place for them in Korea or the surrounding areas. Early in the war, all branches of the service most needed men—soldiers, sailors, marines, and airmen—for combat and used women primarily as stateside replacements. Later, when manpower levels stabilized and the limited nature of the war crystallized, even less reason existed to send servicewomen into harm's way. Thus, far fewer female military personnel served overseas during the Korean War than during the Second World War. Still, nurses and other women completed tours of duty in the war zone, many of them close to the action in MASH units near the front lines, on hospital ships, and on evacuation planes carrying wounded infantrymen. Like their male counterparts, these servicewomen came to recognize their value to the war effort and few rotated home from Japan or Korea without feeling that this fight belonged as much to them as to any American. But, did nurses and other servicewomen experience the Korean War the same as the men in the foxholes? And would their participation in this war change them or transform their lives?

Allowed into the military in greater numbers than ever before, African Americans harbored similar questions about what the war would mean to them, but they also had a few of their own. Not every African American called the South home, but all knew about segregation and its injustices, and even in the North one still encountered pockets of Jim Crowism. How could a country allow this discriminatory system to remain intact and then ask its victims to lay down their lives on the battlefield in the name of liberty? Why should African Americans fight in Korea when promised nothing more than second-class citizenship at home? Was Korea the black soldier's fight?

Women in the War

Despite the efforts of General Mark Clark and others to pressure the various armed forces into sending more women, especially nurses, to the war zone, relatively few women served in Korea or even in the Far East during the Korean War.[3] Stateside, the military suffered from the shortage of nurses that began with World War II, and female recruitment remained difficult.[4]

Moreover, all branches of the military primarily used women as replacements in the United States or Europe so that servicemen could be sent to Korea as soldiers, corpsmen, sailors, or support personnel.[5] Units on the line, especially in the early months of the war, needed men to replace casualties more than they needed nurses to help save them. Thus servicewomen available for duty in the Far East tended to be in short supply, and assigning women there remained a low priority for all the services. Still, hundreds of servicewomen completed tours of duty in Korea and thousands more supported the troops in theater.[6]

In early July 1950, Army nurse volunteers sent to establish a hospital at Pusan became the first servicewomen to enter the Korean War. Within a month, almost fifty more nurses joined them, bringing the total number of military women in Korea to nearly a hundred.[7] By the spring of 1951, more than three hundred Army nurses were scattered across the peninsula "at field, station, evacuation, and MASH hospitals."[8] Army nurses traveled with the troops, waited for them behind the lines, and staffed hospital trains.[9] Air Force and Navy nurses became flight nurses with air evacuation units and

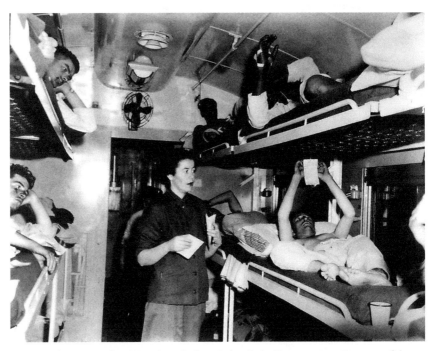

A nurse taking care of patients aboard a hospital train in Korea c. 1950. Courtesy of the Harry S. Truman Library (photograph no. 2007-732).

worked on hospital ships.[10] Countless other servicewomen lived and worked at hospitals or installations in Japan, Okinawa, Iwo Jima, and the Philippines in direct support of the Americans fighting in Korea.[11] In addition to nursing, women staffed commands throughout Japan, including the Far East Command Headquarters, performing administrative, communications, intelligence, and other duties.[12]

Because of the fluid nature of the war and the desperate need for medical personnel, most women in theater were nurses.[13] Like stateside nurses, these got patients cleaned up and settled in, making them as comfortable as possible wherever they happened to be.[14] Nurses also managed supplies and ordered replacements when necessary.[15] But, particularly in the war zone where the number of casualties quickly became overwhelming, nurses took on greatly increased responsibilities. They learned to triage patients, begin blood transfusions, suture wounds, and initiate courses of antibiotics, frequently performing these tasks and more without the direct supervision of a doctor. At MASH units, nurses worked with male corpsmen, teaching them the procedures necessary in combat medicine.[16] As doctors could seldom be spared for a long trip, nurses generally ran the show as the highest ranking officers aboard hospital trains, doing everything from disinfecting the cars with DDT to managing medical aid men and treating patients.[17] Similarly, flight nurses aboard the unpressurized cargo planes used to transport wounded soldiers from Japan to Hawaii routinely tended to thirty or forty critically wounded men at a time with only the assistance of a medical technician.[18] Even in Japan WACs rose to be ward masters, a position traditionally held by male NCOs.[19] A member of the U.S. Navy, Captain Katherine Keating became the first woman officer to relieve a man at sea when ordered to the USS *Haven* as a pharmacist.[20] In contrast to stateside service, which offered little room for advancement as women were herded into "pink collar" jobs, duty in theater tendered military women many more opportunities to learn new skills and to act in supervisory roles.[21]

Though never stationed right on the front lines like corpsmen and medics, servicewomen in the Far East served under difficult and stressful conditions. In Korea, nurses with field and MASH hospitals followed the troops, living and working in "tents, barns, schoolhouses, rice mills, churches," or whatever other structures seemed practical under the circumstances. Close to the lines, they sometimes found themselves in the thick of the action. Nurses on their way to Pusan in October 1950 had to take cover in ditches for fourteen hours while an engagement unfolded around them. Later that year, servicewomen in North Korea had to evacuate to ASCOM City when Chinese volunteers overran American positions.[22] In country, women suffered many of the same deprivations as men. They traveled in "flea-ridden conveyances," went to the bathroom in slit trench latrines, showered outdoors, washed their clothes in tin pans and hung them to dry in the corners of their tents or Quonset huts, and suffered from shortages in supplies and gear. Uniforms, if they could be procured despite their scarcity, made summers even more unbearably hot yet provided little comfort from the cold. Catherine Neville remembers sending boots to a friend hastily shipped over to Korea without warm enough clothing for the frigid winter temperatures.[23] Life for women in Korea came with many hardships.[24]

Even in outlying parts of the theater of operations, servicewomen ran into unexpected, life-altering difficulties. Recalling her wartime service, Audrey Reid recounted that while overseas she was attacked twice by male members of the U.S. armed forces. On Okinawa a soldier Reid knew sexually assaulted her, and in Japan an Air Force enlisted man who offered her a ride from the airport after a delayed flight attacked her. Fearing she would be blamed, Reid did not report either incident. Only twenty years later did Reid resolve to file a claim with the Veterans Administration, receiving a disability pension for post-traumatic stress disorder.[25]

Whether in Korea or elsewhere in the Far East, servicewomen faced long days and heavy workloads. To accommodate the huge numbers of casualties, hospitals expanded beyond their capacities. Hospital ships with room for a hundred patients stacked bunk beds two and three tiers high to make room for 5,000 patients and 60-bed MASH units somehow managed to service two hundred wounded and sick persons when the necessity arose.[26] GIs from the battlefield came by ship, train, helicopter, bus, and ambulance, and "they just kept coming."[27] In some places, the civilians came too, infected with worms and tuberculosis or injured as a result of the war.[28] Without rest and sometimes without nourishment, nurses stayed on duty for shifts lasting twelve, eighteen, or even more hours—however many it took to care for those depending upon them.[29] No matter how much time women put in, though, they found it "just isn't possible to get everything done."[30] When nurses finally laid down to rest, they slept in their long johns, half ready for another wave of casualties or an early flight into the zone to pick up medical evacuees. They hoped that the ambulances rumbling in or the artillery in the background would rock them "to sleep in my Army cot from the reverberations."[31]

Caring for wounded and dying American GIs had a profound effect on servicewomen. In the field and in operating rooms and wards they witnessed scenes that would haunt them for life. Commander Emery of the USS *Repose* wrote a letter home describing her patients, "eyes shot, legs shot off. And others half dead with abdominal wounds."[32] Commander Haire took note of

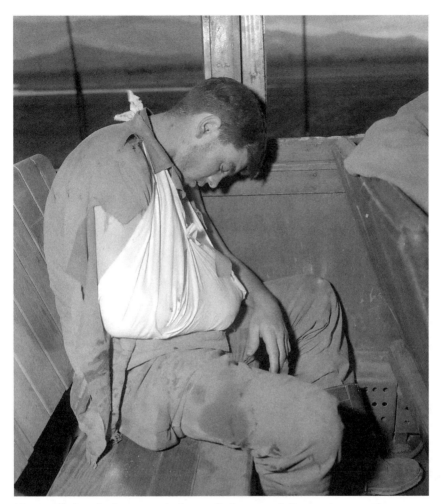

The wounded reached nurses and other medical personnel dirty, unshaven, and exhausted. Private First Class Orvin L. Morris of the 27th Regiment on a hospital train headed to Pusan, Korea, in July 1950. Courtesy of the National Archives (photograph no. 111-SC-345322, War and Conflict Book no. 1454).

the appearance of Marine casualties brought out of combat. "They came in unshaven, dirty, looking about forty years old. And most of them are still in their teens."[33] For Anita Bean, the image of "burnt bodies" would be the one she could not shake and carried with her out of Korea.[34] At the time, most nurses felt like they could "just sit down and cry for them [American GIs], if I had the time."[35] Many women, like Julia Baxter, did allow themselves a few tears. "When I first went to Korea, each soldier that came in the operating room seemed like my brother. It took a little while to get over that. We did a little crying, then got back to work."[36] Witnesses to the carnage of the battlefield and the "vivid inhumanity of war," servicewomen stationed in the Far East wondered "what people in America would do if they had to go through some of the things that you would see in the war."[37] Time might dull some of the feelings of fear and remorse, but "the smell and sights do not leave you."[38]

Despite the hardships of working and living in the war zone, American servicewomen frequently ended their tours of duty with a great sense of personal satisfaction.[39] In country they met successfully the challenges set before them, saved lives, learned new skills, and fulfilled their duty to country. They discovered "where some of my weaknesses were, where some of my strengths were . . . and grew from that experience, both as a nurse and as a person."[40] Also, just like men who forged deep bonds in the midst of battle, women in Korea formed lasting and binding friendships unlike any they would "have again in . . . life." As war veterans, they became aware that "you can never fully share these things with civilians as they can't possibly understand where you've been or what you have done or what it all feels like." They joined an exclusive and special sisterhood of veterans in which others unequivocally "know how you feel and who you are."[41]

Race and the War

For the most part, the United States Armed Forces began the Korean War just as they had begun every war since the Civil War, racially segregated.[42] Despite Truman's 1948 Executive Order 9981 mandating an end to discrimination in the military, segregation remained rampant. Prior to the Korean War, the Air Force began phasing out segregated units, the Marine Corps and Army flirted with integrating some types of training, and the Army eliminated racial restrictions barring African Americans from certain jobs and technical schools.[43] But, especially in the Marine Corps and Army, racial prejudices in both the upper echelons and lower ranks resulted in the continuance of all-black or, in some instances, all–Puerto Rican units. Thus, at the outset of the war, black men, whether or not they had trained in mixed outfits, often served in segregated units overseas.[44]

In theater, as at home, life in all-black units proved anything but "separate but equal" for the men stuck in them. First, there existed the matter of reputation. The American military and press generally accepted the belief that blacks could not perform as well in combat as whites, writing them off as unreliable and cowardly. Early reports of the all-black 24th Infantry Regiment in Korea reinforced these stereotypes, alleging that black soldiers "melt into the night" only to return the next day with tales of getting lost.[45] White troops fighting alongside the regiment disgustedly recounted how "blacks bugged out and left their artillery in place" and "made the black soldiers targets of racist remarks and actions."[46] Poor behavior characterized both black and white units deployed in July or August of 1950, before they were adequately prepared and equipped, but derision fell disproportionately upon African Americans.[47] Keenly aware of this, many blacks in Korea tried "to prove ourselves as equal to—or better than—the white soldiers." They decided that "[w]e could not let ourselves down. . . . We couldn't let our race down. We couldn't afford to fail."[48] Many believed that they succeeded. They "had gone into combat and had fought well," and "given an even chance, we could out-soldier and out-fight any white soldier."[49] Occasionally, as in May 1951 when a white captain brought the men under his command to see an all-black Ranger unit, telling them, "This is what happens when men don't panic," black troops received the praise they craved.[50] But, even long after Yechon, the earliest victory of the war and one for which courageous black troops deserved most of the credit, blacks had reason to complain that "Whitey would never acknowledge all our deeds of honor" and to point out their discouragement "that no other papers outside of our own have been willing to give them [black troops] credit."[51]

Given prevailing prejudices, few whites relished the idea of commanding all-black troops. Not only did they assume that African American soldiers or marines were less competent than white ones, but they viewed such an assignment as "the worst thing that can happen to [an officer] in the military," a "dead end" for their careers.[52] Consequently, segregated units often became a "dumping ground" for officers not wanted in white units but uncommitted to their new black ones.[53] Also, despite Samuel Stouffer's landmark study on American soldiers in World War II, which showed that blacks unequivocally preferred to serve under northern rather than southern whites, the Korean War military continued to assign white southerners to leadership positions in units like the 24th Infantry Regiment with the idea that they had more experience dealing with people of color.[54] Southern-born or not, many of the white officers assigned to black units served diligently and faithfully, but more than a few went into the job with a "patronizing expectation of failure," and others were simply "outright racist sons of bitches."[55] One commander in the 24th decided to make the men "mad enough to fight" by telling them how bad they were, and other officers in the regiment routinely ridiculed the men in their charge rather than encouraging them.[56] Similarly, when Colonel Chester B. DeGavre, a white West Point graduate, took over as regimental commander of the all–Puerto Rican 65th Infantry Regiment, he ordered all the men under him to "shave their moustaches 'until such a time as they gave proof of their manhood'" and made some of them wear signs reading, "I am a coward."[57] It certainly crossed the minds of black soldiers that the same officer leading them in Korea "could be the very one that put a rope around one of our necks next year someplace in the States" or might be "the very one to deny us the very rights that we are here fighting for the South Koreans to enjoy." At least among themselves, black troops asked, "How can they wonder why we don't trust them? Would they trust us if they were in our place?"[58]

Making matters worse, African Americans found it difficult to rise in rank. In segregated units, the armed forces tended to appoint white officers and pass over blacks when it came time for promotions, giving men the impression, "If you were black, to occupy the position of platoon sergeant or first sergeant . . . was mission impossible."[59] After integration, the problem persisted. "While Blacks and whites fought, slept, and ate together in Korea

General Douglas MacArthur inspecting troops of the 24th Infantry at Kimpo airfield in February 1951. Courtesy of the National Archives (photograph no. 306-PS-51-10432, War and Conflict Book no. 1375).

there was not a corresponding sharing of parity in terms of promotions and quality of MOS's."[60] Despite some breakthroughs, most blacks found themselves trapped on the lower rungs of the military ladder in infantry, service, or supply outfits rather than climbing up in personnel services, intelligence, or the officer corps. Now willing to allow African Americans to fight, the military exposed a slightly higher percentage of them to combat than their white counterparts.[61] Blacks drew the worst assignments and found little redress despite complaints.[62] And, entering the officer corps did not guarantee equal treatment. In Dan Grimes's platoon, the first lieutenant was a black medical doctor whom the Army had assigned as an infantry platoon leader.[63] Still, when African Americans managed to secure promotions, they felt that they had beaten the odds and rejoiced that they had won "a battle in the continuing war against Jim Crow."[64]

Hindered by ineffective leadership, a lack of trust between officers and enlisted men, poor morale, and the general unpreparedness typical of all American units in the early months of the war, black troops perhaps did not perform as well in combat as they might otherwise have done, and many individuals suffered grave consequences because of it. By the end of 1950, officers of the 24th had made complaints against 118 GIs in their care. Of the eighty-two that led to courts-martial, fifty-four accused African Americans of displaying misbehavior before the enemy, namely, cowardice. With only eight white soldiers charged with the same offense, African Americans concluded that "the Army's policy was to punish Negroes more harshly than white soldiers. . . . It was common knowledge that Negroes went to trial for offenses that were only winked about when perpetrated by white soldiers."[65] The findings of the all-white investigating officers and the all-white Inspector-General Judge Advocate's Office staff seemed to bear out these suspicions. Thirty-two blacks were convicted and sentenced to death, life, or five to fifty years' hard labor. At the same time, courts-martial found only two of the eight whites guilty as charged. Convinced that they had been railroaded, several of the accused appealed to the NAACP for assistance with their defense. As chief legal counsel of the NAACP, Thurgood Marshall arrived in Tokyo to conduct his own investigation and represent the men on appeal. Initially denied entrance by General MacArthur's office, Marshall ultimately concluded that "the condemned men had been the victims of deep-seated racial prejudice."[66] Eventually the NAACP succeeded in getting "reduced sentences or reversed convictions for most of the men it defended, but these cases illuminated the discrepancies between ideals and practice in a society plagued by racism."[67]

In theater, the perception that African Americans were being unfairly targeted by officers for courts-martial merely added to the discontent of black servicemen, which continued to fester throughout the conflict. Serving America overseas, blacks reflected that "colored Americans are dying in Korea today for less than a square deal."[68] Back home, especially in the South, the same country that now expected them to make grave sacrifices for it relegated them to second-class citizenship. William Weathersbee recalled that "[w]e were 'boys.' No one ever referred to us as 'men.'" And when his all-black Airborne Ranger company, the 2nd, left for Korea, they had to enter through the back door of the Columbus, Georgia, train depot while the all-white 4th strolled through the front. "We were going to Korea together, but we couldn't go through the train station together. . . . We couldn't travel together in the civilian world."[69] Similarly, a Kansas restaurant refused service to Air Force officer John Smith, who had orders for Korea in his pocket, telling him, "We'll fix you some sandwiches and you can pick them up in a brown bag at the back door."[70]

News from home confirmed that nothing had changed since they had left.[71] Along with a clipping about his meritorious service in Korea, Charles Dryden's wife included a letter detailing how their four-year-old daughter had been separated from other children and given different food at nursery school because of her color.[72] Wives and mothers of men fighting in Korea had to band together in Milwaukee, Wisconsin, to overcome discrimination in hiring at factories and businesses, their advocates pointing out that blacks "are doing a good job of fighting for democracy, but these women are denied a chance to work."[73] In Carthage, North Carolina, three men who raped a soldier's nineteen-year-old wife while he fought in Korea got off with a sentence of 16-24 months in what the black press termed "Dixie justice."[74] And, as always, African Americans continued to be lynched back in the States, a sharp and painful reminder to men on the battlefield of "the racist attitudes of some of our fellow Americans back home." As one veteran pointed out, "It always left a bitter taste in my mouth, especially after viewing the torn bodies of comrades who maybe an hour or so earlier had been fighting at my side but now lay dead all around me."[75]

Even in the military and in the war zone, plenty of things reminded black soldiers and marines of their status. In a 1951 scandal involving Confederate flags hanging from Army tanks, Hunt Clement Jr., the spokesman for the secretary of defense, ignored U.S. Army regulations forbidding the private use of "official, personal, or organizational flags" and asserted that "there is no policy on the display of that particular flag."[76] Almost a year later the Army gave permission to the 31st Infantry Division band to wear Confederate uniforms because the rebel gray "represents the regional origin of the division which enjoys all the heritage of the 'Deep South' from which the division comes."[77] Worse yet, rebel flags fluttered in abundance in Korea, and the Red Cross continued to label blood by race until faced with protests by United Nations employees.[78] In Japan, General Douglas MacArthur's headquarters sported a plethora of Jim Crow signs and "the 'great man' did absolutely nothing to clean up his command."[79] In the zone of operations, black men, regardless of training and expertise, often ended up unloading munitions in Pusan or working at some other "job beneath my training and intelligence."[80] Symbolic of the low esteem in which the American military and society held "tan soldiers," the all-black 24th Infantry Regiment and the all–Puerto Rican 65th Infantry Regiment became the first and only units to be disbanded and have their colors rolled while members continued to fight on the battleground.

Confronted with such harsh realities, black troops suffered from low morale and questioned their role in America's latest fight for democracy. On a personal level they wondered, "Why should the black man fight when he's not free?"[81] They "felt they were stupid to risk their lives unduly because when they got home they didn't have the rewards citizenship should have provided."[82] They were "supposedly fighting to protect the freedom of American society, even as that freedom was denied us in our own country."[83] About the war, African Americans in uniform asked, "Can we as leaders of the 'free world' tell anyone about democracy when we have organizations like the Ku Klux Klan running people out of certain places because of their color?"[84] Undoubtedly a few agreed with activists back home who suggested that Korea "is not the Negro war" and that the Army integrated only so it could continue to use African Americans in its "fight to reduce other colored people to the same status as Negroes."[85] Contrasting the enemy with fellow Americans, black soldiers asked, "Have the communists ever enslaved our people? Have they ever raped our women? Have they ever castrated our fathers, grandfathers, uncles, or cousins?"[86] Blacks had "had to fight for the right to fight," but now many pondered just where and against whom that struggle should be—in Korea against the North Koreans and Chinese or back in the United States against Jim Crow and second-class citizenship.[87]

Meanwhile, manpower needs on the Korean front pushed the military to integrate units in country. Commanders of all-white units on the line, in dire need of replacements, began to fill their ranks without regard to race. By August 1950, the 9th Infantry of the 2nd Infantry Division had two black officers and eighty-nine black enlisted men, and by Christmastime African Americans composed roughly 11 percent of the division.[88] Convinced of the practicality of this ad hoc, unauthorized integration, other outfits followed suit so that when General Matthew Ridgway replaced Douglas MacArthur as supreme commander, he could see first-hand the smooth transition to mixed units in the field and the underlying potential for greater efficiency in the use of manpower. On May 14, 1951, Ridgway requested permission to abolish segregation in the Far East Command, and shortly thereafter it became policy to assign men individually to understrength units based on nothing more than military occupational specialty.[89]

Within a few months, changes became apparent. Not only did the Army deactivate the 24th, but the Marine Corps canceled its last all-black unit designation. Almost 20 percent of blacks in the war zone were serving in units experiencing integration, and a fair number of whites had been assigned to predominantly black units with black officers and NCOs.[90] National Guard units like the Oklahoma 45th, initially exempted from integration, began accepting African American replacements while in theater.[91] With desegregation proving a great success on the battleground, raising morale among black troops and streamlining the channels delivering men to the field, officials in the armed forces began to lean toward full integration worldwide.[92] This took some time, however. Not until September 1953 could the Army announce that 90 percent of its black strength was serving in integrated units, and the secretary of defense had to wait until October 30, 1954, to proclaim the abolition of the last segregated unit of the armed forces. As late as 1955, the Navy continued to shuttle more than half of its African Americans into the Stewards' Branch, prompting Representative Adam Clayton Powell Jr. of the Committee on Education and Labor to inform Assistant Secretary to the Navy for Air John Floberg, "No one is interested in today's world in fighting communism with a frying pan or shoe polish."[93] Though the Korean War did not turn out to be a fully integrated war, as did Vietnam later, it provided a testing ground for integration, bringing thousands of Americans of different colors and ethnicities into close contact with one another for the first time.

Both hope and apprehension surrounded the decision to integrate the military. Officials optimistically recalled the end of World War II when black and white infantrymen fought side by side in Germany.[94] Soldiers had accepted the situation quickly. As one white platoon sergeant from South Carolina admitted, "When I heard about it, I said I'd be damned if I'd wear the same shoulder patch they did. After that first day when we saw how they fought, I changed my mind. They're just like any of the other boys to us."[95] It had not mattered then who was "firing next to you when you're both killing Krauts," and the military had every expectation that the same would prove true for Americans fighting the communists in this war.[96] Many African Americans viewed desegregation in country as a stepping stone on the path to respect and equality. If they fought well and whites saw them fight well then there would be "no way they could justify their racist attitudes toward their fellow American comrades in war or peace."[97] Blacks expected that "[w]hen the white boys get back and tell of their experience with the colored over here . . . that will help some."[98] Then, "our struggles and sacrifices for freedom in Korea would result correspondingly in a larger measure of freedom, dignity, and opportunity for our loved ones at home."[99] On the line in Korea, weary soldiers and marines were ready to welcome more men and "didn't care who, what, or where they came from— we needed help."[100] "We could use all the men we could get. The overriding thought was that, white or Negro, a Marine was a Marine."[101]

Still, members of both races had misgivings. General Mark Clark believed that all-white units were the most effective and accepted desegregation only because "Negroes . . . demonstrably, cannot or will not fight effectively as all-Negro units, [so] there is really no choice . . . except to insert small percentages of them into white units."[102] Similarly, many white soldiers presumed that "black soldiers were not reliable and [in] many cases [were] a liability," and they "did not trust them to stay and fight."[103] For their part, African Americans sometimes feared joining white units where they might suffer from discrimination or lose the comfortable positions they held in segregated units.[104] As one enlisted man said, "I would rather be in a colored unit for the simple reason I don't like them (white people). I would rather be with colored people all the time. You can't always trust a white man."[105] And, many African Americans thought that even if integration functioned smoothly in the war zone, the gains in race relations would not last. "It might work in Korea. White man is your friend as long as you're protecting his ass. In the States and over here it's different. When the white man think he out of danger then he will act different."[106] In the end, it did not matter how men felt about the idea of serving in a mixed outfit. Like most decisions since they had mustered into the service, the military would make this one for them.

Once a unit integrated, things could be tense for a while. Raised on opposite sides of the color line, African American and white troops found that real differences existed between them, and both possessed deep-seated prejudices. In general, whites objected to the way blacks used the word "motherfucker" in a "freewheeling manner," noticed uncomfortable dissimilarities "like the way they think about women, like their education and bringing up," and had little regard for black culture or capability.[107] Influenced by the reputation of all-black units in Korea, they shunned the idea of incorporating nonwhite elements into their ranks. Who wanted to be saddled with men who would simply bug out at the first hint of trouble?[108]

Furthermore, many whites strongly objected to serving under black offi-cers, declaring, "We ain't letting those niggers run us!"[109] In instances where white southerners made up a large percentage of an outfit, officers had to be particularly careful in making command and bunker assignments because "the distrust between the Southerner and the black man was still evident."[110] African Americans put into previously all-white units understandably often felt uncomfortable at first. Beverly Scott remembers the cool recep-tion he received when transferring from the 24th. Although he was a com-munications officer, badly needed everywhere along the line, each unit he came to claimed to have no vacancies for his specialty. Finally accepted by a primarily Hispanic outfit, Scott found other officers unfriendly and was passed over for the position of company executive officer although he out-ranked the other lieutenants.[111] The first black in his unit, Ronald Johnson recalls, "I caught hell. Constant fights, verbal abuse and did not feel that I belonged."[112] Others observed that "a few of the regulars were still a little too 'cracker.'"[113] Put into mostly black units, whites did not fare much bet-ter. They "had a sort of funny feeling, kind of out of place," and got "trouble from a few belligerent people."[114] Occasionally when blacks and whites were shuffled together, riots erupted, such as in Tokyo in 1953 where a scuffle between different colored soldiers "over the merits of their respective com-bat units" led to a brawl in which several men were injured.[115] Such inci-dents proved rare, however. On balance most integrating units in country could claim, "We had not one racial difficulty."[116]

Given time, men in mixed units usually grew to look beyond race when judging comrades. In civilian life, people of a different color "were an unknown equation."[117] But, jumbled together aboard ship or in foxholes, men (and women) "got to know each other" as individuals and their attitudes changed.[118] Whites "found that the more time I spent with them [blacks] the less prejudice I had" and discovered "that a colored man is just as good as a white."[119] Blacks saw that "these 'fay [white] boys ain't so bad to get along with. I find them no different from other folks."[120] Even men with more deeply rooted racial biases came to respect those with whom they served. One white infantryman declared, "I didn't like niggers nohow, but now I think there are some exceptions who are good as white men." Similarly, a black enlisted man noted, "I hate white people. Now if all white people were like the boys in this company, it wouldn't take long before everybody would get along swell."[121] The familiarity with persons of different races fostered by military service in the Korean War helped many Americans understand that a person's worth and character depended more upon "what their background is" than on the pigmentation of their skin, and they came to believe, "If men

The war zone, like training, helped forge friendships and unbreakable bonds between soldiers of different races. Stan Jones's three tent mates, Sergeant First Class Goodman, Sergeant First Class Albright, and Staff Sergeant Strong, pose for the camera. Courtesy of Stan Jones.

would get used to each other as we do here, there'd be no trouble anywhere about race."[122]

On the fighting front, transformations happened even more quickly and completely than behind the lines. With a real enemy just across no-man's land or over the next ridge, men "were too busy . . . to entertain race problems."[123] "When you jumped into a foxhole for cover, you weren't thinking about the color of the fellow next to you. That was the least of your concerns."[124] Also, combat forced men to depend upon one another for survival, ensuring that "one's main concern [with another man] was how well he could do the job assigned. . . . Whether a guy was black or white was way down on any list, if at all."[125] Whites might have harbored fears that blacks would perform poorly when it mattered most, but they proved "no better—or worse—than the rest of us," and most men in integrated units decided, "I don't think there is any difference between white and colored in combat."[126] As veteran Gilbert Pfleger noted, "Black man shot Chinese who was about to shoot me in back. Need I say more?"[127] Sharing the experience of the battlefield, African Americans and whites formed the same kinds of unbreakable bonds that men of the same color did. "We were like real brothers."[128] As such, they wrote letters to each other's mothers, stood up for each other when outsiders seemed to be dishing out unfair or unequal treatment, and risked their own lives to protect each other.[129] In perhaps the most famous example of inter-racial camaraderie during the Korean War, Lieutenant Thomas J. Hudner Jr., a white pilot, deliberately crashed his own plane in an effort to rescue Ensign Jesse L. Brown, the first African American to fly a carrier combat mission. Brown died where he landed, but the men of the USS *Leyte* did not forget him. They donated three thousand dollars of their own money to a trust to provide Brown's infant daughter Pamela with an education.[130] Such friend-ships promised a new future not just for the men involved but for the coun-try that sent them together into the furnace of war.

Whether in integrated detachments or not, service in the Korean War theater provided many African Americans with their first taste of life untainted by Jim Crow laws and customs. Segregation existed in some places in Japan, but, particularly in Korea, GIs of every color "were free to utilize all public facilities and accommodations."[131] They socialized with white friends, knocking back a few beers, killing time playing poker, or sit-ting down and shooting "the shit . . . for three or four hours."[132] At Yokota Air Base, blacks and whites not only flew and worked together, but they fre-quented the same "O Clubs" and visited socially in one another's homes.[133] In Gifu, Japan, blacks readily mixed with a willing local population without arousing racial tensions.[134] With such liberties available to them, blacks "felt freer in a foreign land than in the land of our birth."[135] Some felt so free, in fact, that they did not want to leave when it came their turn. A few passed up rotation because "we are not sure . . . that we want to be reassigned to the United States."[136] And, in the exchange of prisoners of war, several black Americans chose to stay with the Chinese, at least until such time as condi-tions improved for African Americans back home.[137] More often, though, African American troops, like their white counterparts, eagerly returned to the United States, many with a newfound determination to secure changes back home.

After the war, James C. Evans, the assistant on racial matters to the secre-tary of the Army, pronounced, "The greatest victory we had in Korea was the integrated use of our manpower."[138] Militarily, Evans was right. Desegrega-tion deepened the pool of replacements from which battered front-line units could draw men and resulted in "significant improvements in the perfor-mance of Negro soldiers."[139] In integrated units, blacks often had better lead-ership, more supplies, and the feeling that their service to the United States might result in something more than disappointment when they returned

home. Consequently, they fought better. Also, African American participation proved something of a psychological coup in a war that the enemy
would have liked to have cast in racial terms.[140]

Socially, however, Korean War efforts at integration produced a mixed
legacy. Certainly, close contact led individuals to develop intimate relationships with people of different skin tones, and the memory of wartime inter-
racial friendships translated into a shared willingness to tolerate or support
attempts at achieving racial equality back in the States.[141] Passing through
the Dallas, Texas, airport on his way back from Korea, Sidney Berry, who
had a close African American buddy in Korea, noticed the separate water
fountains for blacks and whites. "That dramatically brought home to me
that I was going back to my native South with its goddamned injustice . . .
[and that experience] solidified my resentment of racial injustice."[142] For
others, the transformation applied more selectively. Asked if he would take
a black man home, one white enlisted soldier replied that he would not,
except for his friend in the tent. "Oh, that's different. He's just like any of
the other boys. I'd take him home. I wouldn't think of treating him any different. He's a buddy of mine." Similarly, a white infantryman resisted the
idea that he would hang out with blacks back home because "[n]o girl'd
go out with me if I hung around with the black boys." But, he clarified that
with regard to his African American friends from Korea, "That's different. I owe them something for sticking with me. They're swell guys and I
wouldn't let them down. I'd do anything for them. . . . But even so, maybe,
I'd have to be careful."[143]

Despite shifts in attitudes, the camaraderie among men of different races
fell far short of a revolution in American race relations. Sometimes men
went back to their old ways even before reaching America's shores. On the
ship home, one African American came across a white GI whom he had carried injured off the battlefield. When he tried to remind the man of their
encounter, the soldier insultingly cut him short, saying, "I know who you
are boy."[144] When GIs returned to Georgia or Mississippi, they found that old
habits remained the accepted ones among friends and family who continued
to see the world in the same terms as before the war, in black and white. And,
returning after a long and emotionally exhausting tour of duty in the war
zone, many Americans just wanted to fit back into their old lives somehow,
even if that meant leaving the fight for social justice in America for another
time or another generation. The Korean War softened men and women to
the notion of racial equality, making them more likely to accept the goals of
the coming civil rights movement, but it did not bring that movement into
being.

Long after 1953, military service continued to offer African Americans their best shot at equality. Unlike American society at large, the armed forces during and after the war began a steady process of desegregating various aspects of life, including housing and schools. Perhaps that became the most enduring legacy of the Korean War era. The rewarding nature of military service encouraged blacks to make the Army, Air Force, Navy, or Marine Corps a career, and as they did so their expectations and the expectations of those with whom they worked changed.[145] Accustomed to working together, soldiers of different races or nationalities found that it became difficult to envision living in a segregated world. As veterans rejoined the ranks of civilians, they brought with them a new vision of what America could and should become.

While integration of black and white troops in Korea consumes most of the literature on race, it should be noted that the same sorts of interactions took place between white and black Americans and Hawaiians, Chinese Americans, Native Americans, Puerto Ricans, South Koreans, Turks, Japanese, and many other peoples throughout the war. Sometimes these interactions went well and sometimes they did not. For example, American GIs generally considered South Korean troops undependable and tended to show little respect for them, putting KATUSA (Korean Augmentation to the United States Army) replacements to work carrying heavy loads of ammunition or supplies, doing laundry, polishing boots, or cleaning rifles.[146] This lack of regard sometimes caused problems for anyone who appeared Korean. The American driver of a truck, mistaking Bertram Sebresos for a South Korean, refused to give him a ride until told, "I'm a GI too," and a white soldier tried to make Harrison Lee, a GI from Hawaii, do his laundry. Back at his unit after being treated at a battalion aid station where a doctor thought he was a "yobo," an ROK soldier, and made him wait six hours for assistance, two GIs assaulted Sergeant Clarence Young, trying to steal his jacket until he fired his M-1 in their direction and the captain set them straight on his status as an American soldier.[147]

Just as white and black men had grown familiar with one another, however, so too did they learn to live among these other peoples. Those who served with KATUSA units came to appreciate their diligence and dedication.[148] Men in outfits with different nationalities came to look beyond the features of one's skin or face. As Ben Nighthorse Campbell, a Native American senator from Colorado, remarked long after his Korean War service, "There was a camaraderie [in the Air Force] that transcends ethnicity when you serve your country overseas in wartime."[149] In Korea, men learned "to understand people who are different from you. . . . By working and fighting alongside these peoples of different colors, creeds, and backgrounds we are, at the same time I hope, beginning to learn how we may better live with them."[150] Imbued with the ability to generate such feelings in participants, the Korean War became for all Americans, black or white, male or female, their fight after all.

GREETINGS POP—Pfc. Thomas Lorden, of Berkeley, a Korean veteran returning home yesterday aboard the transport General Pope, is greeted by his 20 months old daughter, Carollane. Right is Mrs. Lorden.   —San Francisco Examiner Photo.

Veteran Tom Lorden returns home to his wife and twenty-month-old daughter in January 1953 after a tour of duty in Korea. Originally featured in the San Francisco *Examiner* (12 January 1953) and printed here courtesy of The Bancroft Library, University of California, Berkeley.

7

Coming Home

When Second Lieutenant Edmund Krekorian returned home from Korea, the city of Seattle welcomed him and others on the troop ship in grand style. Marine Corsairs escorted the ship to the harbor, flying off in victory rolls as a happy chorus of boat horns and whistles joined the shouts of hundreds of people gathered on the pier. There, Miss Seattle waited with a bouquet of flowers to meet the men as a band played "The Star Spangled Banner."[1] Also returning by way of Seattle, Russell Rodda vividly remembers the beautiful girls in bathing suits, one of whom stopped him on the gangplank to kiss him and thank him for doing his duty.[2] Treated to "dancing girls, in net stockings and 12-inch skirts," 185 Thunderbirds of the Oklahoma 45th scarcely could turn their attention to the crowds tossing confetti and streamers and shouting, "They're home, they're home, they're home!"[3] In San Francisco, Anthony De Angelis enjoyed a similar reception. Tug boats greeted the men with water salutes and, once they docked, civilians tossed beer up to them while WACs boarded to carry their duffle bags off the ship.[4] Welcomed home in grand style, these Korean War veterans "felt good for the first time in a year!"[5] "You just can't imagine how excited and how happy, and the tears and the laughter and the, you know, you're home! H-O-M-E, home!"[6]

Unfortunately, as the war in Korea lengthened and troop ships returned men and women more regularly, the nation's interest waned and homecomings became a matter of routine rather than cause for celebration.[7] Instead of sailing home to the gratitude and heroes' welcomes bestowed upon World War II veterans, most Korean War veterans passed under the Golden Gate Bridge or pulled into the harbor to find "no bands, no cheering crowds, and no tickertape parade."[8] Like Floyd Baxter, they wondered, "Where are all the people?"[9] Similarly, on the hospital ship *Haven,* those "who could wear shoes were shining them up to a brightness that dazzled the eyes" in anticipation of impressing the crowd of onlookers. Lined up in stretchers for the landing, though, they saw that "only a handful of apprehensive relatives and somber ambulances" had turned out to see them home after their "many long, pain-ridden months" away.[10] Thousands of men suffered the same disappointment. Roy Gray notes, "When we arrived, after all we had been through, all we had seen, all we had done in the line of duty, we were met only by the Red Cross. They gave us donuts and coffee. And, that was our homecoming."[11]

Regardless, one relative unfailingly awaited returnees as they disembarked—Uncle Sam. Men and women who completed their tours of duty overseas usually still owed the military days or months of service before they could officially muster out of the ranks.[12] In any event, they had to process out before heading home to family or friends on a thirty-day furlough.[13] Like in-processing, out-processing required much patience on the part of servicemen and servicewomen. Sent by train, bus, or convertible car convoy to places like Treasure Island, Camp Stoneman, and Camp Kilmer, "everyone was forced to stand in long lines." Moving from station to station over three or four days, they received physical examinations, blood and urine tests, "short arm" inspections, and shots and completed all the necessary paperwork.[14] Still, processing out often proved little more than a formality, prompting complaints that "I was just turned loose. . . . I didn't even know how to act around other people" and "the doctors did not give us real examinations."[15] One POW asserted, "Those Americans interviewing us after we were liberated never seemed to be that interested in our wounds or diseases. They really weren't interested in a damn thing except did we collaborate?"[16]

Some processors, however, took the job very seriously. Concerned that men who refused to speak about their wartime experiences would develop mental problems, the staff at Treasure Island pulled "about every twentieth man . . . out of the line and told [him] to go to the talking doctor." They instructed veterans, "When we got home we should not be afraid to talk.

If someone asked us what happened overseas, we should go ahead and tell him."[17] Thomas Shay attended classes for two weeks "just to know how to act, how to talk to people . . . [and] the words to say. . . . They told you . . . how to pass the potatoes [and] how to treat a lady."[18] The military made available to former prisoners of war booklets like "Welcome Back!" and "What Has Happened since 1950" to explain their responsibilities upon returning and to catch them up on events they missed while in captivity.[19] Aside from this, the military offered little by way of debriefing or therapy to men rotating out of the war zone, instead filling their hours with red tape, physical exams, and reminders that they still belonged to the service. Men and women once again began policing the area, serving on KP duty, picking up trash, and drilling.[20] Eventually, unless doctors determined that they needed further evaluation at a hospital or rehabilitation center, these new war veterans received their discharge or leave, pay, and a ticket home.[21]

Once released, most returnees could not wait to celebrate the end of their war. On the way to the train station or airport, they stopped off at bars and restaurants, ready to treat themselves to a first-class meal or cocktail. If they got lucky, some civilian would slap them on the back and say, "We're glad you're back" and "Let me buy you a drink." Ordering steak, martinis, ice cream, and whatever else they fancied, veterans lived it up until time to depart for home.[22] A few continued the festivities along the way. Changing trains in Chicago, Frank Almy and a few pals stopped by a bar where the owner told the servicemen "our money wasn't any good there. We had all we could eat and drink on the house."[23] Men aboard a seven-car troop train headed for Ft. Sill began drinking heavily at the outset and stopped the train en route to purchase more liquor.[24] For a while, excited returnees just wanted to say, "Hey, here I am. Come on America, here I am, ready or not." They didn't "think about the incidentals" that came with being back in the States because "for right now I'm home! . . . There is no place like home."[25]

Very quickly, however, it became apparent just how little thought civilians had given the war. At a restaurant near Camp Carson, Colorado, Robert Baken told the waitress he had been in Korea. Bewildered, she asked, "Korea, where's that at?" He realized then that "half the civilians in the United States didn't know [where] Korea was at, and the other half didn't care where it was at."[26] Rotating out of a MASH in Korea, Catherine Neville found resonance in the words of a friend stationed stateside: "The saddest part of this for you is nobody knows you've been away or where you've been. You'll know that when you get home. Nobody will notice it." Upon her return, Neville "just went back to duty someplace," as if the war never happened.[27] Indeed, a surprising number of Americans seemed apathetic about the conflict and about those who did their patriotic duty and served in it. As one veteran reflects, "You expect that the people would be more concerned about your service in Korea, but people showed indifference and were more concerned about their own interests."[28] Not surprisingly, a few returnees came to think "that all the true Americans were in the service—that the outside was loaded with draft dodgers . . . [and] politicians who didn't give a damn about the people."[29]

Recently removed from the war zone, men and women also discovered some unsettling things about themselves before reaching their destinations. While entering the straits of Seattle, one veteran had a "wave of uncontrolled grief and depression" wash over him as he "felt overwhelming guilt that I had survived."[30] Thinking of Korea, another noted that he had lost his best friend and nearly his life and "I know I lost myself, but no one cares. I am not the same person who left here."[31] Cursing excessively in an interview, Jack Wright realized, "My language wasn't the type you spoke around your mom, but I forgot where I was."[32] Jack Davis knew exactly how Wright felt. He was scared "to open my mouth for fear of what foul language might come out." In fact, Davis felt uncomfortable around "polite and civil" people altogether and he made them uncomfortable—a problem that continued for quite some time.[33] On an airplane with other soldiers, Edmund Krekorian felt fine, but once civilians filled the seats around him, he suddenly noticed that "I had so very little in common with these people whose primary conversation was limited to baseball and the movies. They seemed to know very little about the war and cared less. . . . I was no longer secure or comfortable. I fell asleep trying to imagine what my wife looked like."[34] Hoping for the best, some veterans reassured themselves, "I was still myself and when I got home would fall back into patterns of behavior, maybe even be civilized again. War changed you but you remained the same person."[35] Less certain, others wondered about their lives and thought, "I survived, I'm alive. What more could I want?"[36] Only time would tell.

Home

Returning to their hometowns from the war zone, many service members, especially servicemen, would have agreed with Dorothy in *The Wizard of Oz* that "[t]here's no place like home." Small towns in particular warmly welcomed their native sons and daughters. Even if they did not host parades for the veterans, who often trickled home one or two at a time, there might be welcome-home dinners, invitations to speak at the local high school, press coverage, an honorary police escort from the airport, the presentation of the key to the city by the mayor, or something more tangible like a state bonus to mark their completion of duty.[37] Some, like Thomas Gaylets of Old Forge, Pennsylvania, relished the attention. "It was a great feeling to be home."[38] Others felt uncomfortable with all the fuss. Having seen too many comrades die and too much misery, men who served in combat often did not feel like conquering heroes, and POWs most assuredly felt out of place around hometown folk.[39] A few men fled when friends or neighbors stopped by to see them or made it known they did not want any big to-dos to be given in their honor.[40]

In many places, though, especially larger communities and metropolitan areas, returnees did not have to worry about unwanted attention. "It was kind of like glad you're home. That was it. . . . I felt lonely."[41] All too often nobody other than wives or parents had even taken note of their departures. As Harlee Lassiter put it, "No one else seemed to have missed me very much."[42] Seeing them again on the street or at the store, old acquaintances asked, "Where've you been? I haven't seen you around."[43] Girlfriends quite plainly had moved on, getting engaged or married. Finding his old flame, Elaine, now married and pregnant, Barnett Wilson concluded, "Not only didn't she want to wait for me, she didn't miss me, either!"[44] The same could be said of some spouses. As contemporary newspaper accounts reveal, more than a few men discovered that in their absence wives sought comfort elsewhere.[45] Believing their husbands dead, the wives of some POWs remarried, creating a sticky and unpleasant situation for men who had spent their captivity dreaming of nothing but home. Daniel Schmidt's wife, now married to Alfred Fine, suggested through a magazine reporter that Schmidt and Fine both woo her again so she could decide between them. Astonishingly, she insisted that Schmidt was lucky since "[i]t's better to come home and find your wife happily married than running around with everybody."[46] Some veterans also found relatives little interested in their return. Floyd Baxter's brother briefly met him at the train station but then quickly announced that he and his girlfriend had "some place else to go."[47] Even if they had not desired parades or parties, this was hardly the homecoming that most veterans expected or wanted.

Except in a few cases, such as Baxter's, those returning from the war at least could count on members of their immediate family to provide a measure of reassurance that they had not been forgotten. Mothers, fathers, wives, sons, daughters, sisters, and brothers all turned out at train and bus depots to lovingly greet their own. Met at the station in Springfield by his wife and kids, Arthur Kelly decided, "That's all I needed. I didn't need anybody else."[48] Once they reached home, veterans found the signs that they had been missed unmistakable. Walking past all the neighbors lined up on their front porches to stare and smile at him, former POW William Allen finally reached his house, finding it unchanged. His mother had kept his room exactly as he had left it. She also went to great lengths to make all of his favorite meals and, along with his father, worked hard to not "say something wrong."[49] Jack Wright's stepfather offered him unlimited use of the family's new Studebaker, saying nothing though Wright nearly tore it apart.[50] Numerous wives, having kept the faith for almost two years, cried real tears of joy upon seeing their husbands again for the first time and did everything in their power to provide solace and warmth.

Although most family members tried hard to make their husbands or sons and daughters feel comfortable at home again, it quickly became apparent to almost everyone that adjustments needed to be made. At first, fathers and mothers had difficulty accepting that the men before them could no longer be viewed or treated as "their 'high school boys' who left home."[51] Though their children might still appear young, their experiences had made them no longer youthful. With his mind "drift[ing] back to my buddies still in Korea," one veteran "broke down and cried," angrily rejecting his mother's attempts at comfort by saying, "No! You, or anyone else who was not there, can never understand what it was like."[52]

Married just before soldiers shipped out for training or the war zone, some wives had to learn to handle the problems and moodiness of unfamiliar husbands, uncertain whether this was the man they married or the man the war made. Such was the case of one wife who expressed horror when her soldier-husband used a new gun to kill a porcupine without reason. Unable to feel guilt, he asked her, "What in the hell did you think I was doing for the last nine months?" The incident marked the beginning of failure for the marriage.[53] Relations also became strained between husbands and wives married longer. When John Pitre came home, he noticed, "Life at home had changed. My wife was different."[54] Like couples who hardly knew each other at all before a soldier's deployment, they had to find ways to reconnect after months or years of separation.[55] Many couples failed to piece their marriages back together, eventually divorcing. Korean War veterans, in fact, divorced at about twice the rate of men who served in World War II and were 26 percent more likely to divorce than men of their generation who did not serve.[56] Some, like Gilbert Towner, a marine who saw heavy combat in Korea, divorced more than once, finding marital bliss only decades after the war or not at all.[57]

Men might have envisioned coming home and picking up their lives right where they had left off, but that was seldom possible. Women, so recently expected to take care of the home and make all the important decisions, found it difficult to relinquish control to a returning spouse.[58] Even wives who wished for a return to the way things had been before the war could not always make that happen. This proved especially true with regard to the care and discipline of children. For a wife, two years was not a short while, but to children it was an eternity, and many initially refused to accept their fathers. Arthur Kelly's three-year-old daughter ran and jumped into his arms almost immediately, but his son ran halfway down the sidewalk toward him and then doubled back to the house. Later, after being chided by his father for flipping soup onto the table, Kelly's son slammed the door in his face, saying, "I told you to go back to Korea."[59] Only eight months old when her father left, Charles Bussey's two-year-old daughter "didn't know me" when he came back, referring to him as "that man."[60] Frightened of the father she had not seen since she was six weeks old, Lee Philmon's two-year-old daughter did not stop crying until he bought her a Coke.[61] Before men could reestablish their position within the family, they had to mend relationships with spouses or children who barely knew them or with aging parents, a daunting task requiring a more subtle and patient approach than some of those who had survived the war zone could muster.[62]

Even if home no longer felt quite like home anymore, men and women returning from the war theater tried to make the best of things and get on with their lives. As after World War II, many got married almost immediately. Ronald Ransom did not even wait for his thirty-day leave to end before tying the knot, and James Becker got hitched just two months after his return. Harvey Moore, carried home from the war with only one leg, went AWOL from Walter Reed Hospital to wed the sixteen-year-old sister of his overseas service buddy in Camden, New Jersey.[63] Others worked on starting or enlarging their families. In addition to accomplishing this in the old-fashioned way, a few remembered promises made in Korea or Japan and adopted orphaned children that they had known and grown fond of there.[64]

Buying their way into the consumerism of the 1950s, returnees also made major purchases after their return. Younger than the veterans who marched home from the Second World War, and perhaps not yet ready to commit to anything as significant as a spouse, a multitude of Korean War veterans spent savings and back pay on new cars. And, thanks to the 1952 Veterans' Readjustment Act, which guaranteed loans to veterans for real estate, about one-third of Korean War–era veterans had somewhere to park their wheels as they purchased their first home before program benefits expired in the 1960s.[65] Others used the funds to buy businesses or farms. Like many government programs, this one was laden with red tape and GIs complained of the difficulty of finding willing lenders and of the loan-origination and other fees attached once they did.[66] Black veterans in particular had difficulty getting loans, being refused "for the most irrelevant reasons," such as speaking "to the wrong individual."[67] African Americans found it difficult to find places to buy as well. Neighborhoods geared toward GI Bill customers, such as the postwar-era Levittowns, often enforced segregation, pushing nonwhite home buyers to consider less desirable areas.[68] However, a common practice of the VA and FHA called redlining frequently resulted in the government's refusal to guarantee loans on properties located in the places where nonwhites could buy.[69] For those who managed to obtain loans, the government financed 60 percent of a home up to seventy-five hundred dollars and 50 percent of a business up to two thousand dollars and sometimes offered incentives.[70] Before September 1, 1953, veterans could qualify for a gratuity payment of 4 percent of the guaranteed portion of their loan up to $160.[71] As after World War II, the housing market took off once Korean War veterans returned and started snatching up real estate.[72] In some places, lenders and sellers even "newly discovered" a "Negro market."[73]

Ultimately, as back and mustering-out pay ran out, returnees had to find a way to support themselves. Some GIs turned their wartime skills or contacts into careers. Robert Wilkins, a salesman at Hanson Chevrolet in Detroit before Korea, took down the names and addresses of other POWs while in captivity and after his release sent out letters offering them a three-hundred-dollar "Wilkins Discount." With five hundred replies and twenty-one sales in just a few months, Wilkins "did not have to worry about getting his old job back."[74] But, other veterans had less luck. With jobs in rather short supply, many veterans had to turn to benevolent organizations or to their Uncle Sam for help. Groups like "The 52 Association," first formed during World War II, offered a job placement program for wounded veterans.[75] Meanwhile, the government resurrected initiatives such as job reinstatement and veterans' preference.

Reemployment rights, begun with the 1940 Selective Service Act and revived in 1951, dictated that employers give returning veterans their old jobs back so long as circumstances had not changed to make that impossible.[76] To be entitled to their former positions, though, veterans, both male and female, had to apply for reinstatement within ninety days of their discharge and have a certificate of satisfactory military service. And, employers were under no obligation to pay returnees any more than they had been receiving when they left. Like Samuel Woodham and Barnett Wilson, veterans did go back to their former employers, but, regardless of the law, others discovered that old bosses would not rehire them or decided they wanted to do something else.[77]

In addition to using the Veteran's Employment Service (USES) to obtain job counseling, vocational guidance, and assistance in locating a suitable position, those returning from Korea could invoke veterans' preference laws to better their chances of finding employment.[78] Under veterans' preference laws, honorably discharged veterans who served active duty with any branch of the armed forces got points added onto federal competitive exam scores, moved to the top of certification lists, had preference in appointment to federal government and civilian positions, received waivers of age/height/weight requirements, had certain jobs like elevator operator reserved for them, and secured retention rights protecting them from reductions in the work force.[79] No small amount of public resentment and resistance developed in response to veterans' preference laws in the years after the Korean War, but the courts consistently upheld the statutes, giving Korean War veterans the same veterans' preference benefits enjoyed by other veterans before them.[80]

Despite assistance, not all veterans of the Korean War landed a desirable job or, in some cases, any job. As after World War II, these less fortunate veterans qualified for unemployment if they could not find work after separating from the military. Less generous than World War II's 52-20 Club (fifty-two weeks of twenty-dollar unemployment checks), the Korean War unemployment program allowed unemployed veterans twenty-six dollars a week for twenty-six weeks.[81] Also in contrast to World War II provisions, men first collected unemployment from their home state and then applied for federal unemployment compensation to make up any differences in benefits.[82] Although Korean War veterans usually had a waiting period of several months before they could collect, the money, when it finally came, certainly made a huge difference to the 20 percent unable to find a position in the slowing economy.[83] In all, about one million veterans of Korea took advantage of the unemployment offered them, but, according to government reports, they did not "milk" the system.[84] Over half of the Korean War veterans getting unemployment received no more than three hundred dollars total, and only 15 percent collected six hundred dollars or more.[85]

Whether actively seeking work or not, some veterans ultimately decided to delay their reentry into the civilian work force. Especially after the passage of the Korean GI Bill in 1952, many marched to school to earn a degree or learn a new trade. Others, despite the low esteem in which the public held military service as a career, decided to re-up or enlist in a different branch of the armed forces.[86] Perhaps because so many had already accumulated years of service in World War II or in the Reserves or National Guard, Korean War veterans were more likely than veterans of other twentieth-century American wars to choose a military career. Only 6 percent of World War II veterans and 12 percent of Vietnam veterans compared to nearly 17 percent of Korean War veterans earned discharge with a military retirement after twenty or more years of service.[87] Signing up for regular duty, many Korean War veterans "never looked back and never gave it a second thought."[88] This is all the more remarkable given that between the Korean and Vietnam wars the Army flushed hundreds of thousands of "marginal soldiers" from the ranks, Korean War veterans included.[89]

Over time, as veterans discharged the last of their wartime obligations, such as visiting the relatives of dead comrades or working off the last days of active duty, they tried to settle into their new cars, houses, marriages, and jobs. Many hoped that memories of the war and of military service in general would soon recede, to be replaced in their minds with the normalcy of Sunday sermons, weekend matinees, regular work schedules, clean linens, and family. But, looking around them, veterans, especially those who separated from the military, could not help but sense that maybe they had not so much left the Land of Oz as ended up in some other corner of it. Two years or more of military service had carried men and women further from home than they had ever traveled before and changed their outlook on a great many things. In their absence, the world kept turning, too, but somehow it had revolved in different directions.

Returnees, Race, and America

By the time Korean War–era veterans began filtering back into civilian society, the American military had far surpassed the home front in desegregation efforts. Manpower pressures in Korea breathed new life into Harry Truman's Executive Order 9981, breaking down segregation in the war zone and prompting changes on bases in the United States. Under President Dwight Eisenhower, the Department of Defense enacted an initiative to integrate schools on military installations, this before the 1954 Supreme Court ruling in *Brown v. Board of Education*.[90] Despite local resistance, especially in southern schools with long-term leases and in states with laws forbidding educational integration, by August 1955 only schools at Pine Bluff Army Arsenal in Arkansas, where there were no school-aged black children, and Fort Meade, Maryland, had not complied.[91] The VA also integrated its hospitals and homes in the mid-1950s. In response to critics who questioned the rationale of integrating other facets of military life while expecting African Americans soldiers rotating home to wait for hospital beds in segregated wards, Harvey Higley, administrator of Veterans Affairs, announced his agency's commitment to "wiping out segregation."[92] So quickly did veterans' hospitals accomplish this task that in 1956 a white patient complained that the Shreveport Veterans Hospital refused to treat him "unless he agreed to submit to integration with Negro patients." This incident triggered a resolution by American Legion Red River Post No. 118 against the infringement of the "cherished rights of those who were disabled in the service of their country," but to no avail.[93] On post, the military worked to abolish even the appearance of discrimination. When a black dentist at Chanute Air Base complained about separate barber shops for blacks and whites, the Air Force moved quickly to consolidate the shops.[94] On installations around the country, service clubs, swimming pools, movie theaters, athletics, and other recreational venues widely opened to all regardless of color during and immediately after the Korean War.[95]

This is not to say that integration always happened smoothly. Jumping into the Officers' Club pool at Maxwell Airbase, Charles Dryden, an African American veteran of World War II and Korea, "was amazed how quickly I became the sole occupant."[96] Overseas, a note left on the mess hall door of the 61st Artillery Battalion of the 1st Cavalry Division warned, "No n——s and dogs allowed, white only."[97] At Camp McCoy, Wisconsin, the Army fired Juanita Lewis, a black hostess, after she made it clear she would no longer officiate at dances with Jim Crow rules forcing African American troops to "sit in the corners and the rear and look on [while whites dance], or trudge slinkingly over to the line for refreshments."[98] At Fort Benning, Georgia, Grant Hauskin's commander told him that he would never be promoted as long as he stayed married to his white wife.[99] And, throughout the 1950s the military encouraged everyone from privates to generals to accommodate the discriminatory practices of local communities, even refusing to interfere when soldiers got into trouble with civilian law enforcement officials over segregation issues. The Air Force reprimanded one black pilot for refusing to move to the rear of a city bus in Alabama, noting, "Your open violation of the segregation policy is indicative of poor judgment on your part and reflects unfavorably on your qualifications as a commissioned officer."[100]

Still, the U.S. military establishment in the 1950s and 1960s far surpassed civilian society in racial progressivism, leading many within the military and government to push for an end to discrimination in cities and towns dependent upon bases for economic support. To improve the lives of those under their command, commanders in the South pressured movie theaters, restaurants, and stores off post to accommodate all GIs regardless of race by making all segregated establishments off-limits to military personnel, thus cutting off potential revenues.[101] Similarly, in an effort to deal with the inadequacy of off-base housing available to nonwhite servicemen, the Department of Defense in 1968 forbade military personnel from living in segregated housing. Not surprisingly, with their livelihoods in jeopardy, locals soon integrated recreational facilities and rental properties.[102] The Department of Defense also targeted for integration public schools attended by military dependents, threatening to either suspend public funding or use eminent domain as a justification for seizing them. Many schools built off post but with federal funds integrated as a direct result of this pressure.[103]

Those who separated from the military during or soon after the Korean War did not experience the full impact of military integration, but reentry into civilian life nonetheless proved a rude awakening. While homefront attitudes had shifted some with regard to race, leading more than half of Americans polled in 1958 to agree that at some point in the future blacks and whites would share schools, restaurants, and public accommodations, the realities of life had changed little.[104] As one black lieutenant put it, "When you get into town, it is the same old pattern that most know about. We have complete mixing on the post, but when you go into the city, it's just the same old story."[105]

In the South especially, time seemed to have stood still. Nearly a decade after the racial violence that accompanied African American soldiers home from World War II, southern towns remained relatively unsafe for blacks in uniform and in general. Just trying to vote, arguing over racial epithets, driving a car, or walking down the street made blacks the targets of police and civilian brutality in places like Alabama and Mississippi.[106] In Rupert, Georgia, Private Macy Yost Snipes defied the local white establishment by casting his vote in 1956 and paid with his life. Whites in the county then prevented Snipes's body from being buried in the family plot and underscored their resistance to black voting by running Snipes's family out of town.[107] As late as 1960, the Marine Corps refrained from assigning black marines to certain duty stations because of concerns for their welfare or the unavailability of off-post housing.[108]

Widespread discrimination in employment continued to limit opportunities for black veterans. Southern communities, for example, restricted blacks, even veterans, to certain occupations. In one Mississippi city, black ex-GIs could only use veterans' preference to become letter carriers, and the Montgomery, Alabama, VA office would only employ them as custodians. At Maxwell Air Base in Montgomery, every black worker started in the mess hall regardless of individual skills or qualifications.[109] After the war Vernon Warren went to school and became a certified public accountant, but when searching for work, "found the doors shut tight. . . . He was still a black man. The war had changed him, but it had not changed that."[110]

Outside of the South inequalities existed as well. Motels and eateries across the country routinely refused service to black patrons, making it necessary for African American servicemen and servicewomen traveling to either obtain a copy of the "Green Book," a guide listing places where blacks could stay, or risk having to sleep in the train station, in their car, or on the street.[111] Neighborhoods in several California cities refused to admit nonwhite home-owners or occupants. Elsewhere, whites formed mobs, planted crosses in the yards of blacks, and threw stones at the homes of people they wanted out. In Phoenix, Arizona, the veterans' cemetery allowed whites killed in action to be buried without clearance, but African American Thomas Reed's body was kept on ice after shipment from Korea because rules stipulated that blacks could only be buried after receipt of three notarized letters from veterans' organizations.[112] Similarly, a Sioux City, Iowa, cemetery refused to allow the burial of John Rice, a Winnebago veteran of World War II killed in Korea, because he was not of the "Caucasian race."[113]

Confronted with Jim Crow segregation and bigotry, the unsavory hall-marks of American life outside of the U.S. military, many nonwhite returnees felt confused, even angry. They had marched to war armed with the belief that their wartime service would result in a "larger measure of freedom,

Denied burial in Sioux City, Iowa, because of his Winnebago ancestry, fallen Sergeant First Class John Rice is laid to rest at Arlington National Cemetery with full military honors. Rice's mother, Mrs. Samie Davis, can be seen in the wheelchair in the front row. U.S. Signal Corps, courtesy of the Harry S. Truman Library (photograph no. 2005-12).

dignity, and opportunity for our loved ones at home." That had not happened and, like the wife of an Army veteran denied service at several California restaurants, they wondered why they had fought at all and "[w]here is the country that he fought for?"[114] Others asked, "Who was my worst enemy, really?"[115] Were communists abroad as bad as racists at home? White veterans, possessing intimate friendships across the color line from their service in the Army or Marine Corps, also felt "deeply perplexed about the racial discrimination" leveled against their comrades.[116] But what would they do about it?

In light of the activism and controversy stirred up by the Vietnam War and veterans of that conflict, historians have tended to view Korean War veterans as passive, easily accepting the status quo and peacefully melting back into society after returning from the war. Indeed, raised during the Great Depression and World War II, most veterans of Korea early learned and internalized the lesson that no matter the circumstances, one had no other choice but to uncomplainingly forget personal preferences and get on with the tasks at hand. The culture of conformity that rose with the Soviet threat in the years after World War II reinforced the inclination to subvert one's own desires for the security of the country. Consequently, Korean War veterans, whatever their ideas on the matter, did not launch any great crusades to win equal civil rights for Americans of all colors.

However, Korean War veterans individually protested Jim Crowism and contributed to the quest for social justice in invaluable ways. One black noncommissioned officer, frustrated at having to move to the back of the bus when it left the base, made a point while on post of sitting "right behind the driver, just to watch the cracker burn up."[117] Delbert White, faced with discrimination while looking for work, decided to do something about it and filed a complaint with a government agency.[118] During the Vietnam War, Clarence Adams, one of the American Korean War POWs who originally refused repatriation and went to the People's Republic of China, made radio broadcasts telling African Americans, "If you are going to fight, you need to go home and fight for your own cause. You're being wasted for a cause that isn't even yours."[119] Others joined the NAACP and contributed to its "Freedom Fund" to "help improve our democracy."[120] So many blacks at some American Legion posts joined the NAACP that two white posts unsuccessfully tried to get these kicked out of the organization on grounds that they were "dabbling in partisan politics."[121] Additionally, black veterans risked their lives to register to vote and turned out at the polls.[122]

Korean War veterans also joined activist veterans' organizations such as the American Veterans Committee (AVC). This socially progressive veterans' organization fought against Orville Faubus in Little Rock, Arkansas, demanded an end to racial segregation at the federally funded and supervised Columbia Institution for the Deaf in Washington, DC, called on the District of Columbia to pass and enforce a law banning discrimination in public recreational places, petitioned President Eisenhower to intervene in Prince Edward County, Virginia, where the Board of Supervisors decided to cut off all funding to public schools after it was required to integrate them, and worked tirelessly to tear down the walls of segregation.[123] Representatives of the Jewish War Veterans of the United States of America presented the Platform Committees of the Democratic and Republican National Conventions with a call for further "programs of education and legislation to wipe out racial and religious discrimination."[124]

More aggressively, some Korean War veterans, especially African Americans, "contributed to the increasing use of armed self-defense in the postwar decades."[125] In 1964, World War II and Korean War veterans founded the Deacons for Defense and Justice to protect people involved in the burgeoning civil rights movement, deter white violence in the South, and fight the Ku Klux Klan.[126] Veterans brought to the table not only a new sort of militancy but also technical expertise and the kind of courage learned on the battlefield. Protected by the Deacons of Defense, civil rights worker Robert Lewis notes, "We had veterans that have been to Korea and places like that [who] knew how to make stuff, just like the Molotov Cocktails. So we knew how to make the time bombs, too."[127] Similarly, Albert Turner, thinking back to the summer of 1965 when he worked in Crenshaw County, Alabama, registering voters, remembers that the local leader accompanying and watching over them was a Korean War veteran.[128] Generally working within the system, Korean War veteran activists did not seek or achieve the sort of visibility that their sons and daughters of the next war would, but in many small ways they did make lasting contributions to the movements that reshaped American life with regard to race. In part because of the vision instilled in servicemen and servicewomen by the military in the 1950s and 1960s, Americans of all races and nationalities came to live together in an integrated, if not yet color-blind, society.

Old Wounds and New Lives

Whether they knew it or not, many veterans of the Korean War "had more problems than anyone realized when I first came home."[129] They might have exited the war, but it most certainly had not yet left them. Accustomed to living in a prisoner of war camp, William Allen left burning cigarettes all over the house, throwing them on the floor without realizing it.[130] Another veteran, eating breakfast with his parents, unconsciously asked them to "pass the f——king sugar."[131] Irwin Crockett dove for cover when a truck back-fired.[132] Kenneth Dixon trembled and shook until he could not hold a cup of coffee.[133] Some veterans slept on the ground just as they had in Korea, and others showered multiple times a day or soaked in the tub for hours. After months spent in cold and filth, they could not get enough hot water, and they wanted to be clean again. "The dirt and grime of Korea was still in my pores and embedded under my fingernails. I had to soak it away."[134] Used to having to remain on guard in the foxholes, David Van Leeuwen almost killed his brother when he came to wake him up and Arthur Smith narrowly missed hitting his mother when she entered the room while he was sleeping.[135] Charles Bussey awoke frequently to "check security" and Jack Wright took to roaming the streets at night.[136] Some slept with guns under their pillows, making for close calls when someone inadvertently startled them.[137] More astoundingly, some veterans lashed out with tremendous violence. Ander-son Williams, a combat veteran, prowled around at night throwing rocks at women drivers, a habit that ultimately cost him three thousand dollars in fines and his driver's license.[138] Samuel Fikes choked his wife to death in a "jilted lover's quarrel" and Thomas Howell allegedly beat a ten-year-old boy he did not know.[139] To varying degrees, returnees had trouble acting normal. "After all, who or what did I have to compare normal living with?"[140]

From the trenches or hospitals in Korea and Japan, it had seemed that all would be well if only a person could return safely to family and friends, but for a great many veterans the war would not go away. When awake, they worried about friends still caught on the battleground and "could not stop thinking about all the buddies I'd lost in Korea. . . . Like me, they'd been look-ing forward to a future; one that would never happen for them."[141] They felt guilty "because I had survived and all my friends didn't" or because after they left friends died or got wounded and "I still felt responsible."[142] Sleep brought little respite from feelings of guilt or memories of the war as nightmares made everything real again. In Charles Bussey's dreams, "Chinese soldiers trampled over my shallow grave and double-timed over me," and in Leonard Korgie's he begged an officer not to send him back to Korea despite orders.[143] Hoppy Harris dreamed that "the decomposed bodies of the enemies I have killed come rising from their graves, and I rush madly about trying to push them back into their graves, but they will not stay there. They keep popping back as if trying to get at me, seeking revenge for my having sent them to an early grave."[144] As months and years passed, some men found their lives less frequently interrupted by sad or intrusive thoughts or frightening night-mares, but for many these never completely went away. As one veteran wrote, "My long ago war, so hauntingly remote / Still rings in my ears like an exploding shell, / Shattering this cozy peace surrounding me /And shouting old memories."[145] Over half a century after the conflict ended, Gilbert Towner continued to "grieve for the men that are still in the ground around Chosin Reservoir," and William Dannenmaier wondered if the dreams that troubled his sleep would end when he died or, "as I have sometimes thought, I died as a young soldier. Then, those dreams are my eternity."[146]

After participating in the great life-and-death drama of the war, no matter how terrible, many veterans found civilian life boring and inconsequential and had great trouble settling down and becoming civilians again. Returning from Korea, Jack Wright was "restless as hell." To take the edge off, he "spent every dime I made," including his back pay.[147] Others developed a "crazy longing to return to the front."[148] Of more significance, many felt "like an alien when I came home" and developed negative attitudes toward regular life or toward themselves.[149] To Seymour Bernstein, "all seemed temporal and unreal" and, after he had witnessed so many tragedies in Korea, the worries of the people around him seemed petty.[150] Similarly, William Dannenmaier believed, "Life was transient, ludicrous, and I was meaningless in it." Seeing people gathered to talk and laugh, he wanted to scream, "Why are you laughing? They didn't know what the world was like. They had no knowledge of the pain and anguish in the world."[151] Numb to the new realities around them, returnees had difficulty talking to nonveterans, "enjoying the things I once did," trusting people, making the most basic decisions, and expressing emotions.[152] Believing they "could kill anyone, stranger or friend, and walk away without concern," and frightened by their "tendency to look at those who annoyed me and consider the best way to get rid of them," they had reason to question whether they would ever really live again.[153] Unmistakably, the war aged and transformed those who experienced it. As one veteran put it, "I lost something in Korea."[154]

Eventually, veterans tried to come to terms with what they had experienced in the Far East and find ways to readjust to life at home. Initially, many sought out old friends in hopes of fitting in again. Frequently, these encounters proved counterproductive. Not only did high school or college chums know little about the war; they expected returnees to "be again the person I was before I went overseas," but "it was too late for that."[155] Elmer Payne nearly got into a fistfight when his old high school classmates insisted that he was "'lucky' not having to face the draft." Deciding he had better stay away from them in the future, Payne avoided them even at his fifty-year reunion in 1998.[156] To veterans, those who had not served during the war seemed so inexperienced and naive compared to themselves. "Somehow I felt I had nothing in common anymore with these guys; I couldn't relate to them. We were the same age, but they seemed younger than me."[157] Veterans had "experiences that they could never relate to, whereas they had had life experiences that I would someday be able to relate to, but did not yet have. Theirs was college, mine combat, face to face with the chance of death, all day, every day for over a year."[158] Worse yet, "time had moved on for them whereas it was just starting for me."[159] At home, people had married and started families, gone to college, gotten good jobs, and purchased homes. Veterans could not help feeling that they "had a time gap in my life that could never be filled" and considered themselves "hopelessly behind everyone else."[160] Thus, efforts to reconnect sometimes ended in bitterness and anger for veterans who resented the fact that peers at home had lived comfortable, undisturbed lives while they had suffered the pain and sadness of Korea.[161]

Realizing that "no one wanted to hear about where I had been, what I had done, and what I had seen," many veterans tried to repress their memories and "forget most of the bad experiences."[162] They seldom talked about the demons haunting them, the "killing, maiming, frostbite, barbed wire, fear, trembling, doubt, arson, exhaustion, death, or blood" that had entered their psyches in Korea and remained after they came home.[163] POWs especially kept quiet and guarded about their experiences. Almost as soon as they had been freed, the military warned them not to speak about what had happened in the camps and not to reveal any secrets.[164] Also, by the time POWs finally reached the States, the U.S. Army and others had begun a witch hunt, looking for "collaborators" and making the public suspicious of anyone who had been captured by the Koreans or Chinese.[165] At a parade hosted for returning POW Jack Flanary in Benham, Kentucky, officials from the VFW barged in to announce "'rumors' that the sergeant had been 'responsive to communist indoctrination.'"[166] The FBI and CIA badgered and investigated almost all POWs for years after their return.[167] Caught in the repressive social climate of the deepening Cold War, many veterans, whether POW or not, decided, "This is not good. I'd better just keep my mouth shut."[168]

Men or women who did talk about their experiences right after the war found most Americans ill equipped or unwilling to help them. As Paula Schnurr, an official at the Veterans Administration's National Center for Post-Traumatic Stress Disorder in 2000, admitted, both government and research scientists ignored the postcombat emotional problems of Korean War veterans.[169] Even when returnees reached places like mental care facilities that should have been able to help them, the staff and personnel proved uninformed. After visiting physicians and psychiatrists, Charles Bussey concluded they "had no idea of appropriate treatment for my problems," forcing him to try to cope on his own. Similarly, as a patient at a veterans' hospital, Walter Adelmann received the diagnosis of battle fatigue but was released without any effective treatment.[170] Furthermore, government budget cuts in the mid-1950s resulted in the curtailment of psychiatric services for veterans, even those already approved for and engaged in treatment, making the likelihood of finding a professional to talk to about wartime experiences still more unlikely.[171]

Sharing with other veterans might have helped men deal with their problems, but not all veterans' groups welcomed Korean War veterans. Congress did not designate Korea as a war until the late 1950s, giving war veterans' organizations ample excuse to turn away men who served in Korea.[172] Both the American Legion and the VFW, created and controlled by World War I and World War II veterans, refused to allow Verlin Rogers to join until years later, claiming that the "Korean War was 'not a war' and I did not qualify."[173] Some veterans claim that the American Legion took rejection a step further. In *To Acknowledge a War* Paul Edwards asserts that the American Legion blamed American servicemen for the stalemate in Korea and "supported a smear campaign," depicting these new veterans as both soft on communism and morally weaker than the veterans of other wars.[174]

"Screwed up mentally and . . . not ready for our world," returnees, especially men, commonly turned to alcohol or drugs to drown their troubles.[175] Walter Adelmann drank for two months after his return, and for Jack Orth "drinking became the order of the day, and that became more and more of a problem."[176] For many veterans of the Korean War, trying to do "the best I could" and unable to put the conflict behind them, early months of drinking spiraled into years or lifetimes of alcoholism or substance abuse.[177] Ted Hofsiss drank heavily through part of another reenlistment and Vernon Warren came home drunk nearly every day throughout his career as a postal carrier because "there was nothing he could do to push the war out of his mind." Bennie Gordon used alcohol to "numb the pain, and keep the nightmares away" for decades until put on medication and now "tries not to leave his house, unless he has to."[178] Alcoholism particularly plagued Korean War veterans who participated in combat, at rates somewhat elevated above those of their contemporaries. And, because these returnees were trying to cover one problem—the inability to forget the past and get on with their lives—with another—substance abuse—they often failed to recognize the "severity of their problems and . . . [did] not avail themselves of the opportunity for treatment."[179] As a result, many Korean War veterans still struggle with alcoholism, failed marriages, lost careers, and other issues.[180]

In retrospect, many veterans realize that post-traumatic stress disorder (PTSD) lay at the heart of their difficulty readjusting when they rotated home, but at the time they knew nothing "about post combat stress or anything like it."[181] Born into a generation reared to show the same can-do spirit exhibited by Americans during the Great Depression and the Second World War, most internalized the lesson that they were "to solve our own problems."[182] To do otherwise demonstrated a lack of resolve and revealed unacceptable and embarrassing personal and moral weaknesses.[183] Thus, veterans failing to readjust tended to believe that their problems "were my fault, some weakness in me."[184] This, coupled with a lack of programs to assist veterans in resuming a normal life, resulted in few Korean War veterans finding their way to specialists who could explain to them what was wrong.[185] And, when they did, Korean War veterans stubbornly resisted regular psychotherapy until "satisfied that their problems will not be solved through their own resources, such as by an educational or occupational adjustment; working with non-psychiatric physicians[;] . . . or utilization of some other external means."[186] Consequently, veterans suffered silently and alone. Severe headaches crippled returnees, as did flashbacks, irritability, nerve problems, restlessness, depression, nightmares, feelings of insufficiency, fatigue, post-anxiety-reaction hives, and difficulties in concentration.[187] Men afflicted with PTSD tried to forget the war, but "the memories of that horrifying time" persisted.[188]

POWs and men who experienced heavy combat tended to suffer more than other veterans.[189] As a result of the extreme conditions under which they had been held, POWs became mistrustful of people, uncomfortable in crowds or social settings, emotionally detached from loved ones, and unable to focus.[190] As Charley Davis noted, "I still size people up as soon as I meet them. I listen to the way they talk, and I watch how they act and react. I want to see if they are real or pretending to be something they are not. . . . In the camps you had to make sure someone wasn't going to get you in trouble over something you said."[191] Robert Maclean could not even take advantage of the GI Bill to go to college because being in the classroom "felt like I was back in prison camp again. I couldn't concentrate on anything they were trying to teach me."[192] As ex-POW Shorty Estabrook wrote, "Life has been cruel for many of us and we are time bombs ticking. We never did adjust properly."[193] Without professional help, many remained mired in mental illness caused by the war.[194]

Not until some twenty or thirty years after the armistice did therapy become readily available to Korean War veterans afflicted with PTSD, and then only by accident. Responding to the problems of Vietnam War veterans, the VA began to train therapists and offer and advertise counseling for men and women adversely affected by wartime service.[195] At about the same time, public awareness increased and Korean War veterans saw advertisements for therapy sessions on billboards at veterans' hospitals, read about PTSD in newspapers and magazines, and watched television programs on the topic.[196] Following the lead of the Vietnam generation, Korean War veterans began to attend meetings and to attempt to address their own problems. Suddenly, doctors and researchers as well as the government took notice and began to fund and conduct studies of Korean War veterans and the incidence of PTSD. These efforts demonstrated that contrary to previous assumptions, not only did Korean War veterans exhibit symptoms of PTSD right after the war but older veterans were still suffering the effects.[197]

By the late 1980s, VA hospitals in Tampa, Florida, and elsewhere were accepting Korean War veterans into PTSD clinics and actively searching out others in need of medical help or assistance with getting compensation. Many of the Korean War veterans who received letters or phone calls had not dealt with the VA for years, if ever, and knew nothing about the services and benefits available to them. "They are angry with the VA to begin with, and they're angry with the public. A lot of them have drinking problems, and they have a hell of a divorce rate. There's lots bottled up inside us because of what we went through, but nobody cares but us." So they thought.[198] Thirty, forty, even fifty years after the battles that scarred them, Korean War veterans suffering from PTSD finally began to reclaim their lives as civilians and begin the healing process.[199] Visiting the VA hospital in Fresno and attending sessions with a VA psychiatrist and PTSD counselor, Tony Velasquez wrote, "The nightmares, the flashbacks, the anger, depression and the guilt about the people I killed in Korea will never go away, but I am learning to control and to cope with my memories of the Forgotten War and my survival guilt."[200] Another veteran notes, "The more you talk about it, the more you get rid of it."[201] Unfortunately, some men did not live to see the improvement that counseling or other assistance might have worked on their lives. In addition to the thousands who died of natural causes in the intervening decades, some veterans committed suicide, often soon after coming home, or engaged in risky behaviors that ended with their untimely deaths.[202] Parents and friends were left to explain that their son "had returned from the war much the worse for his experience" or that "he had been highly nervous since he was discharged from the Army more than a year ago."[203]

Many veterans languished after coming home, but others ultimately found effective strategies for melting back into regular life and overcoming the trauma of war. Jack Jackson took a job driving a dump truck, where his language and mannerisms would not offend anyone and where coworkers helped him acclimate to his new, old life. Within about a year he felt comfortable around others, unafraid that he would embarrass himself or someone else.[204] Gilbert Towner eventually re-immersed himself "in my culture, sweathouse, religion (Indian) and cultural events." Though still plagued with nightmares, Towner managed to create a lasting marriage and quit drinking.[205] Harold Mulhausen became a workaholic, a habit that created some other problems but kept his mind off the war.[206] Clyde Queen enlisted the help of others, joined various veterans' organizations, began a career in law enforcement, and "got my life back and . . . turned out to be a good, and productive citizen."[207] Drinking heavily after his return, Douglas Anderson went to work for a year on a remote ranch, where he began to heal, losing much of his bitterness.[208]

Perhaps no one activity helped as many veterans recover from their wartime experiences as continuing to serve in the armed forces. Men who mustered out soon found themselves adrift in an unfamiliar and unwelcoming world of strangers. They no longer enjoyed "the security of belonging to a known society of like persons" and discovered "everything had changed including myself. . . . [I] no longer fit in."[209] Also, no matter how much one hated the rigor and discipline imposed on them, military life proved a hard habit to break and discharged veterans scarcely could organize their own lives. Raymond Delcambre remembers, "At first it seemed I couldn't make a decision for myself. I missed having some one tell me what to do."[210] Returnees who re-upped or had time left on their enlistments generally readjusted more easily. They "went to a new duty station and continued my career," reentering a community where "we didn't need to say much to each other. Didn't need to, we both understood."[211] Like Jack Wright, they found that "when I got back with other Marines I settled down and began to feel comfortable around people again."[212] Ralph Cutro agreed, "It was nice to get back among Marines. We helped one another to adjust."[213] This sense of belonging, the unspoken acceptance of their peers, and the structure that continued military service provided all greatly aided Korean War veterans in the successful transition from war to "normal" life.[214]

Aside from emotional trauma, many Korean War veterans struggled with physical impairments and injuries. New medical techniques and modes of transportation pioneered in Korea ensured that men returned from this war with wounds that would have proven fatal in World War I or even World War II.[215] Doctors in the field perfected the use of type O blood and plasma, experimented with antibiotics, and began substituting arterial repair for amputation when treating severed arteries.[216] The military moved medical detachments closer to the front lines for fast treatment and began using helicopters to transport the wounded more quickly.[217] As a result, only 2.5

percent of men wounded in Korea died compared to 4.5 percent in World War II.[218] Ironically, the lower mortality rate meant that rather than dying, some of Korea's wounded survived with more serious and unusual injuries than in previous wars. Regardless, many of those who survived the war returned with medical conditions that would affect their health and well-being for life.[219]

Among other things, returning Korean War veterans suffered from amputated limbs, shrapnel buried in their body tissue, lost eyesight, diminished hearing, ruined teeth, paralysis, tuberculosis, bleeding ulcers, and the loss of fingers or toes from frostbite. After arriving home, many more experienced bouts of malaria or other diseases, discovered they had intestinal parasites, or simply realized they physically were not the people they had been before going to Korea.[220] Veterans in the worst condition went immediately to Army or Navy hospitals where military staff members generally provided competent and compassionate care. In some places, nurses welcomed wounded

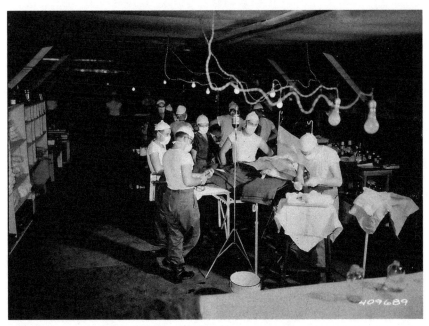

Improvements in field medicine and transportation during the Korean War helped save lives but also insured that men who might have perished in World War II would survive this one with more serious and unusual injuries than anticipated. Here, an operation is performed at the 8209th Mobile Army Surgical Hospital just twenty miles from the front line. Courtesy of the National Archives (photograph no. 080-SC-409689, War and Conflict Book no. 1458).

veterans with joyful, if unauthorized parties, and, after 1953, the Red Cross provided one-day cruises on the Potomac River in the newly deactivated USS *Williamsburg* for those well enough to go.[221] Nonetheless, the spirits of wounded men swung low, and some found their "will to live was down to about zero."[222] They faced more hardship when they discovered what other veterans already knew—that the American public and government had little

Wounded soldiers use crutches and wheelchairs at a hospital before learning to walk with synthetic limbs. Private First Class Charles Woody, wounded near Taegu, Korea, can be seen on crutches through the wheels of another injured soldier's wheelchair at Walter Reed Military Hospital in December 1950. Courtesy of the National Archives (photograph no. 306-PS-50-16899, War and Conflict Book no. 1461).

interest in the Korean War or in those who fought it. Frank Muetzel found a Silver Star on his hospital bed with nothing but a cover letter attached saying that it had been "delivered with appropriate ceremony" and, at the Bank of America, a loan officer who noticed Muetzel hobble in on crutches wearing his uniform and ribbons denied him a new car loan, saying, "I see you want to go back to school. You won't need a car there, anyway."[223]

For veterans healthy enough to process out without directly entering a hospital or rehabilitation facility, healing could take longer and come at far greater cost. Developed during World War I and later expanded to care for veterans with service-related medical problems, the veterans' hospital system that was administered by the VA proved woefully inadequate at ministering to the needs of veterans in the 1950s.[224] Cost-cutting measures and administrative wrangling during and after Korea led to the closure of various hospitals and the resignations of many VA doctors just as more of both were needed to handle the influx of casualties coming out of the Far East.[225] As a result, would-be patients had to wait for service.[226] Arriving home in September, former POW Shorty Estabrook, who came to consider himself "medically dumped," did not get dewormed until November.[227] Richard Curtis, a veteran of both World War II and the Korean War, could not get a hospital bed for the treatment of alcoholism and mental illness until his brother secured the intervention of James C. Hagerty, President Eisenhower's press secretary, in 1959.[228] Edward McAllister's wait finally ended when he collapsed and died at a construction site where he was working during a two-week delay in admittance by the Veterans Administration for service-connected hypertension and heart disease.[229]

Other veterans of Korea waited far longer for VA treatment. Recruiters promised many volunteers "free medical care for the rest of our lives," but these guarantees went unfulfilled after the war.[230] Initially, VA hospitals required men and women, unless service-disabled or impoverished, to give proof that the condition they were seeking treatment for was service connected. Not infrequently that proved an impossible task. Thousands of men suffered cold injuries at Chosin Reservoir, but at the time there were too many casualties of a more immediate nature for doctors or corpsmen to document frostbite cases.[231] Similarly, by the end of a battle in which one sustained injuries, there might be no one left able to verify the combat-related nature of their wounds. The VA x-rayed Gilbert Towner, finding shrapnel residue where he was wounded, but without four people to sign an affidavit attesting that he sustained the injuries in the war, Towner had no recourse but to fight the VA for the next twenty-seven years to "get almost what I think I deserve."[232] Frostbite victims fared worse. Men whose toes or fingers peeled off with their boots or gloves as a result of exposure to the bitter cold of Korea received medical care at the time, but the VA declined to help men who came forward later as aging veterans with throbbing feet, phlebitis, skin cancer, tingling fingers and toes, peeling skin, fungal infections, night pains, arthritis, misshapen toenails, joint deterioration, and other long-term conditions stemming from frostbite.

Ultimately, the VA made hospitals and doctors available to more Korean War veterans. In May 1951, the VA hospital in Tucson, Arizona, refused to treat David Arellano, a former marine who served five months in combat in Korea as a bazooka-squad gunner, for a throat ailment because it was not service connected. The hospital manager noted that, while sympathetic, he could not help because the United States is "not at war in Korea, so these men are not eligible for treatment" as war veterans.[233] Widely circulated, Arellano's story outraged the public and prompted President Truman to call a press conference and urge Congress to remedy the technicality in the law. Within a week, a new bill signed by Truman guaranteed Korean War veterans "all benefits of hospital and domiciliary care, compensation or pensions, and burial benefits for themselves and their dependents as provided for persons who served during the period of World War II."[234] Much later, those who sustained frostbite in Korea finally got satisfaction. After intense lobbying on the part of the veterans themselves, the government conceded the long-term health effects of cold exposure and in the late 1990s began to offer free medical care and monthly checks to veterans of both World War II and Korea who served in frigid conditions. Of Chosin Reservoir in the winter of 1950, VA sources admitted, "I don't know how anyone could have been there and not had frostbite given the conditions: the bitter cold, the lack of protective gear, the constant combat. Half the casualties were due to the cold. Frozen Chosen is right."[235] Furthermore, these needed no further evidence that their problems were service connected.[236] Such changes opened up VA medical services to thousands of Korean War veterans, but not everyone benefited. Some died before becoming eligible for treatment, the VA continued to deny the claims of others, and still more elected not to use VA resources.[237] In fact, perhaps as a result of early difficulties obtaining VA assistance or internalized lessons of shouldering problems themselves, Korean War veterans, unique among American war veterans, did not flock to use VA care.[238]

Whether or not one received medical care, arms, legs, fingers, or toes lost in the war could not be replaced and a host of other wounds and injuries could not be repaired, leaving veterans to cope with altered bodies and altered lives. Officials at the processing-out center advised Arthur Smith to list all his ailments and "we'll take care of it," but, three years later, at age twenty-two, Smith continued to suffer from a back problem, frostbitten feet, shrapnel working its way through his skin, false teeth, and facial wounds preventing him from shaving. Nobody could make Smith like he had been before the war or stop the grief these changes caused on a daily basis.[239] His feet blasted off by a mortar in Korea, Ted Hofsiss, still a teenager, would never run again, instead enduring pain for the rest of his life whenever he tried to walk.[240] Developing bleeding ulcers in Korea, another veteran nearly died and eventually had to quit working as a result of his service-related ailment.[241] William Dannenmaier never entirely recovered his hearing and fifty years after the war noted that he still had problems with his teeth.[242] Unaware of the extent of their injuries when they returned home, other veterans fell victim later to cancer caused by the DDT used to delouse them, smoking-related cancers rooted in tobacco addictions that formed while in service, and illnesses and disabilities stemming from wartime exposure and frostbite.[243] In 1985, participants in the first meeting of the Chosin Few, an organization for Army and Marine Corps veterans who survived the Chinese attack at Chosin Reservoir, noticed that in addition to difficulty walking, many of them shared symptoms like excessive sweating, infected tissue, skin cancer, oddly shaped toenails, sore legs, swollen feet, and sensitivity to cold.[244] The VA denied late-onset cold-injury symptoms as service related, but these men "had their lives compromised by this injury."[245] With no help available before the 1990s, these veterans managed by filling the cracks in their feet with Krazy Glue and stuffing maxi-pads in their shoes to absorb the weeping fluid.[246] Similarly, POWs, who survived unimaginable privations in the camps, never fully recovered from the effects of malnutrition, diseases like beriberi and pellagra, cold injury, long marches, and primitive wound care. Follow-up studies show that as long as twelve years after their release Korean POWs exhibited excess morbidity, disability, and adjustment problems when compared to civilians, non-POW veterans, and the POWs of other wars.[247] Undeniably and irreversibly, the Korean War etched its mark on the minds, bodies, and lives of those who participated in it.

Public Law 550, Compensation, and the Korean War Veteran

Living with the after-effects of war and enjoying little by way of acknowledgment for their sacrifices, many Korean War veterans wanted some sort of compensation for what they had lost performing their duty to country.[248] Remembering World War II's GI Bill, 81 percent of those who served overseas felt entitled to the same educational opportunities afforded earlier veterans, and another 78 percent believed the government should offer their generation low-cost home loans.[249] Even veterans who thought Uncle Sam owed nothing to the able-bodied or able-minded believed service-disabled veterans should receive compensation as well as medical care.

On Capitol Hill, legislators tended to agree that Korean War veterans, like their World War II predecessors, deserved something in gratitude for their service. However, though efforts to pass GI Bill–type legislation started in the first months of the war, disagreements in both Congress and the public arena over just who should receive benefits and what benefits should be granted hampered action for years.[250] Nearly everyone conceded that "adequate benefits should be provided for those who have disabilities which are related to their military service" and that men and women choosing to remain in the armed forces beyond the Korean War era should not be eligible for "readjustment" programs. [251] Beyond that, a wide range of opinions existed. Some people pointed out the unfairness of giving assistance to veterans not possessed of any special physical or financial hardship since this created a favored class of citizens who would be better off in their old age than other Americans.[252] Others suggested that only men or women who "bled and suffered in Korea, in the waters around it, or in the air over it" should receive government aid. Still more pointed out that servicemen and women are "subject to orders" and insisted that all Korean War–era veterans be the beneficiaries of legislation related to veteran readjustment no matter where they completed their tours of duty.[253] As congressman Thomas J. Lane of Massachusetts noted, "They fought for us and are coming home to us. Only a year and a half has been taken from their lives according to the calendar . . . however, we can not reckon the extent of their displacement, or the rehabilitation that may be required."[254]

On August 19, 1950, well before consensus on the issue of which veterans would receive benefits, the House of Representatives established a Select Committee to Investigate the Educational Program under the GI Bill to better inform their debate on what these new veterans should receive.[255] Known as the Teague Committee, after its chairman, Congressman Olin E. Teague of Texas, this group found that while "legions of veterans availed themselves of the educational and training benefits under the GI Bill," the program had been "marked by errors, abuses, waste, managerial inefficiency, and in some instances, corruption and larceny."[256] The Teague Committee recommended that a new GI Bill be written for veterans of the Korean Conflict and that it include safeguards to protect against the problems encountered in the administration of the World War II GI Bill.[257]

On July 14, 1952, the Korean GI Bill emerged as Public Law 550 "to provide vocational readjustment and to restore lost educational opportunities to" men and women who served in the armed forces after June 27, 1950, and separated from the military under other than dishonorable conditions after at least ninety days' active service.[258] Less generous in terms of time and money than the World War II GI Bill, Public Law 550 did make available to Korean War veterans educational and training benefits, unemployment compensation, mustering-out pay, and free assistance in finding jobs. With regard to education, Korean War veterans earned 1.5 months of assistance for each month spent on active duty, not to exceed thirty-six months. Rather than splitting monthly payments between schools and veterans, as it had for World War II veterans, the government directly paid this new wave of GI students monthly stipends, making them responsible for covering both tuition and living expenses. Those returning to school full-time received between $110 and $160 a month depending upon the number of their dependents, and on-the-job and farm trainees got from $70 to $130 a month. Regulations allowed veterans to use Korean GI Bill funds to pursue college or high school degrees or to obtain farm or other institutional or on-the-job training, but not to pay for bartending, dancing, photography, music, athletic, or public speaking courses except as part of an approved degree program. Forced to declare an educational goal to the VA before embarking on any sort of training through the GI Bill, Korean War veterans could only change their course of study once and could only enroll at schools that had been in operation at least two years and had no more than 85 percent of students receiving GI Bill money.[259] Under these new restrictions, the Korean War veteran found that the "field [was] narrower than his brother had after World War II."[260]

Americans anticipated that Korean War veterans would flock to college campuses and schools after the passage of their GI Bill just as those returning from the Second World War had done. But, despite predictions in the summer of 1953 that veteran "numbers will swell before the approaching fall semester," the expected deluge of Korean War GI students did not materialize.[261] When the fall semester of 1953 opened, journalists marveled that "Korean War veterans are not taking advantage of the Korean GI Bill of Rights with nearly the alacrity that veterans of World War II showed in respect to the original GI bill of rights."[262] Returning to school, thinking that "Korean War veterans would soon flood college campuses and that we would reprise roles played in 1946-50 by returning World War II veterans," veterans discovered the same thing. Throughout their training or schooling, Korean War veterans found that they did not attend "in large enough numbers to know and recognize each other" and did not get "the same feeling of respect from students or faculty accorded to the World War II veteran."[263]

Certainly, the 5.7 million Korean War veterans eligible for GI Bill benefits could not have the numerical impact on schools that 15.6 million World War

II veterans had had simply because there were fewer of them.[264] Less easy to explain, though, is why, when 7.8 million, or about 50 percent, of World War II veterans took advantage of training and educational benefits, only 2.4 million, or about 42 percent, of Korean War veterans did.[265] In the 1950s, reporters and others posited a number of reasonable explanations for this apparent failure of Korean War veterans to use the educational benefits granted them. *New York Times* columnist Howard Rusk suggested that these younger veterans of Korea did not receive the same type of indoctrination in their rights and benefits upon separation from the military that the older and perhaps more worldly World War II veterans got and thus did not even know about the various programs funded by the government.[266] This makes some degree of sense, as the law prohibited the VA from approaching veterans to "inform them of their personal status in the veterans' benefit program," limiting officials to responding only to individuals who sought them out first.[267] Private groups, like Veterans Benefit Inc. of Memphis, Tennessee, formed to help veterans learn about and apply for benefits, but undoubtedly many Korean War veterans never knew any of the entitlements bestowed on them by Congress.[268] Also, as journalist Benjamin Fine pointed out, a number of Korean War veterans did not need Korean War GI Bill–funded training. The post–Korean War economic climate, while slowed some by the war, still had enough health to make it relatively "easy for the veterans to get jobs." Furthermore, about a million veterans of the Korean War had served in World War II, enabling them to use the first GI Bill, and thousands of others had taken deferments and completed their educations before entering the military.[269]

The stipulations of the Korean GI Bill also made educational and training benefits less attractive to veterans than if Congress had tailored this piece of legislation to more closely resemble the original GI Bill. Attempting to curb corruption and waste, Congress inadvertently made it more difficult for Korean War veterans to take advantage of government-subsidized GI schooling. While paying veterans directly seemed the perfect remedy for bloated tuition bills, since schools would have to compete for the dollars of frugal GIs, the direct-pay method made it nearly impossible for veterans to pay their entire tuition bill upon registration or before beginning classes, as required by most schools and universities. Also, stipends seldom kept pace with inflation. Writing his parents in 1952, one marine bemoaned the fact that while he had thirty-six months of college coming to him, the $110 dollars a month allotted by the government fell far short of his current $450 a month salary.[270] Female veterans had greater reason to complain. Male veterans automatically received extra monthly pay for their wives and children, but female veterans, even those with dependent spouses, did not qualify under the law for any addition to their allowances.[271] Facing budget crunches, Korean War veterans regularly petitioned lawmakers for more money, charging that rising school fees and increased costs of living made it impossible to live on GI allowances. By and large such pleas fell on deaf ears, putting degrees and certificates out of reach for some financially strapped veterans.[272]

Additionally, Congress's attempt to exclude fly-by-night operations by limiting GIs to institutions with student bodies composed of no more than 85 percent GI Bill students hampered their enrollment. With so many men and women taking advantage of the two GI Bills and so few other students willing or able to pay their own tuition and expenses, many colleges as well as other types of schools had difficulty maintaining the mandated ratio of 15 percent tuition-paying students. This had devastating consequences. Like other institutions, a popular tailoring school in Jacksonville, Florida, had no choice but to relegate many Korean War GI applicants to a waiting list that in some instances moved their entrance date beyond the termination of their eligibility for benefits. Thus blocked from pursuing their chosen fields of training, Korean War veterans could do little else but decide upon another course of study, using up their one-time change of objective, or write their congressmen and senators that:

> I answered the call of my Country to protect it and all of its civilians and I do not feel that it is fair and right for me to be denied the privilege of better preparing myself to be a more useful citizen because of the fact that a sufficient number of the citizens I fought to protect do not care to go to school.[273]

In particular, African American veterans suffered under this restriction. Unable to enroll in segregated schools and subjected to discriminatory quota systems at other insitutions, black veterans often had to try to gain entrance into black colleges or trade schools and programs. But, even more than Americans in general, the black nonveteran population could not afford to pay their own fees, and many segregated institutions could not attract enough tuition-paying students to make their programs viable options for those wishing to use the Korean GI Bill, making it even more difficult for black GIs to find eligible institutions to attend.[274] This, coupled with the fact that many employers excluded African Americans from on-the-job training programs, made it extremely challenging for black veterans to use their benefits, whether living in the South or elsewhere.[275]

Time limitations attached to the Korean GI Bill's educational benefits also prevented some veterans from using them. Viewing Public Law 550 as a measure to help veterans readjust economically and educationally to regular life after leaving military service and not wishing to create a permanent class of privileged citizens, Congress mandated that veterans initiate their courses of training by August 20, 1954, or within two years of their release from the military, not to exceed the Korean War service period by more than seven years.[276] Most of those who mustered out after their wartime tours of duty had no trouble meeting these deadlines, but men and women who remained on active duty did. Barred from using the GI Bill while still in service, these found that time ran out before they could enter school. Any significant break in service started the clock ticking. Reenlisting in the Army in February 1955 after less than ninety days of freedom, Donald Dippe had both his application for GI Bill educational benefits and his appeal rejected by the Veterans Administration, which calculated his time of eligibility from his first discharge. Frustrated, he reflected, "I did not realize when I reenlisted . . . that at that moment I had thrown away a College Education."[277] And, once commenced, schooling could not be stopped for longer than twelve months without a veteran risking the loss of his or her entitlement. When the outbreak of the Vietnam War necessitated the recall of men to active duty, Congress had to pass legislation to prevent those who had not yet begun their studies under the GI Bill and those who had started but would now be interrupted from losing their benefits.[278] Enacting a GI Bill for peacetime veterans might have solved some of these bureaucratic nightmares and put an end to some of the injustices caused by time limits, but most Americans, including officials at the VA, opposed such measures in principle and proved not yet inclined to pay for the provision of "education and training benefits to peacetime veterans who had not been disabled as the result of their service."[279]

Aside from the challenges posed by Public Law 550, Korean War veterans had reasons of their own for not using the GI Bill. Many felt they did not deserve the same benefits as World War II veterans because they had not satisfactorily finished the job overseas. They thought Chesty Puller, a Marine Corps hero, said it right when he declared, "Stalemate, hell! We lost the first war in our history, and it's time someone told the American people the truth about it. The Reds whipped the devil out of us, pure and simple."[280] Public and media opinion reinforced this idea, focusing not on battlefield heroics but on the question of why this war had not been won like the last one. To be sure, the government handed out medals to those who fought in Korea, fifty thousand of them, but, perhaps for the first time in history, some of the relatives of posthumous Medal of Honor recipients refused to accept those tokens of the nation's esteem.[281] Korean War veterans concluded they had not earned the entitlements awarded them by Congress and, like Verlin Rogers, they declined to use GI Bill programs because "others deserved the money and help more than I did."[282] Furthermore, born into a generation raised to take responsibility and to earn respect by displaying independence, Korean War veterans frequently persisted in trying to carve their own paths through life without any assistance, especially from the government. Everett McFarland, who refused to use the GI Bill, later noted, "This cost me in terms of money but I was beholden to no one."[283]

In the end, though, enough Korean War veterans availed themselves of educational benefits under the Korean War GI Bill that the federal government spent nearly $4.6 billion on their schooling and training alone.[284] In general, this investment paid off handsomely for both veterans and the United States. Like their World War II counterparts, Korean War veterans proved to be good students.[285] At first stigmatized as a "silent generation," one without spirit or interests, Korean War veterans displayed concentration, resiliency, and determination in their studies and careers.[286] This was especially true of female veterans who, in spite of often beginning their training later than men, used a greater percentage of their entitlements than male veterans.[287] And, unlike World War II GIs, of whom only 25 percent of GI Bill participants worked toward college degrees, more than half of Korean War veterans who used government allowances attended universities and colleges, and many shifted into higher-paying occupations.[288] Of Korean War veterans who later went on to use VA educational assistance, only 24.9 percent had attended college before separating from the military. After they used the GI Bill, that rate increased to 57.4 percent, and the percentage of veterans possessing the equivalent of a college degree jumped from 8 percent to nearly 37 percent.[289] Unsurprisingly, Korean War veterans credit their GI Bill with "providing me with opportunities that would not have been available" and moving them from modest backgrounds into professions like law and teaching and up into the middle class.[290] However, through education or job training, Korean War veterans also gave back to their country by providing it with a new generation of doctors, engineers, scientists, businessmen, and teachers and by raising the national educational level.[291] Additionally, with more complete educations and employed in higher-paying fields, many Korean War veterans repaid the entire cost of their GI Bill benefits in taxes within fifteen years of reentering the work force.[292]

In addition to the Korean GI Bill, the federal government offered many other entitlements to worthy candidates.[293] Disabled veterans could select from a number of programs and benefits designed to "restore every disabled veteran to a useful place in our economy and society," including medical and dental care, vocational rehabilitation, insurance, pensions or other monetary compensation, automobiles, housing for paraplegics, and loan guarantees.[294] Soldiers who served on the front lines in Korea could apply for special combat pay through their local Veterans Administration.[295] POWs could file claims for about $2.50 a day for every day they were held as a POW, $1 for each day that they received food or care below the standard outlined by the Geneva Convention, and $1.50 for each day held in inhumane conditions.[296] Wounded veterans became eligible for disability ratings resulting in compensation and pensions.[297] Legislators, veterans' organizations, and individuals proposed other measures as well, such as a minimum compensation rating of 30 percent for ex–prisoners of war, paid transportation for POWs to motels in Florida for free vacations, and recognition of cancer or psychosis developing within two years of service as being service connected.[298] Not all of these ideas bore fruit, but returnees tried, with varying degrees of success, to take advantage of the VA and government offerings that became available.[299] By June 30, 1972, the government had paid Korean War veterans and their dependents over $5 billion in compensation, $740 million in pensions, $6 million for automobiles and special devices, and $14 million for homes for paraplegics. Adding in loan guarantees, burial allowances, various educational and training programs, health care, and administrative costs, the government's expenditure on veterans of the Korean War added up to nearly $17 billion.[300]

Nonetheless, competing with World War II veterans for public sympathy and government funds and returning to a social climate tainted by Cold War fears and malaise about the war in Korea, Korean War veterans did not always get that to which they were entitled. Four months after filing a claim for combat pay, Alfred Mishos wrote Senator Robert Taft in frustration, "I served 9 months with a front line unit . . . I have not received one dime or an explanation why."[301] The government did respond to Arthur Smith's claim, but only to inform him that neither his frostbitten feet nor his ruined teeth qualified as a disability and thus he would receive nothing.[302] In 1995 Gilbert Towner finally got a rating of 60 percent disability from a doctor for his frostbitten hands and feet only to have the VA counter with a rating of 10 percent.[303] It took Fernando Gandara fifty years to get a 40 percent disability rating for his damaged ears.[304] Perhaps POWs fared the worst. The Army held hearings to determine whether or not POWs had collaborated and, without producing any tangible proof of guilt, the VA denied men benefits and the $2.50 per day compensation due them for hardship.[305] A VA commission turned down the $2,507 claim of Joseph Hammond, a Bronze Star recipient rated at 40 percent disability for gunshot wounds, on the basis of vague accusations. When he asked to see the evidence against him, the chair replied that it was "classified." Because examiners stalled until the deadline passed, Hammond's appeal was dismissed.[306] Similarly, Louis Kutner, an ex-POW initially given an honorable discharge and allowed to reenlist, lost his POW compensation and right to GI Bill benefits after the Army presented secret charges against him at a special board of inquiry at Fort Sheridan.[307] Eventually, the government removed the stigma from Korean War POWs and the VA began to offer services through an outreach program, but when these veterans received their checks, pensions, or government-funded schooling, many found that these scarcely compensated for what they had endured.[308]

Regardless of whether or not veterans qualified for any special compensation or took advantage of the educational opportunities guaranteed by Public Law 550, they usually did not come out of Korea or out of the military empty-handed. In addition to any back pay accrued, veterans out-processing got mustering-out pay. Under Title V of the Veterans' Readjustment Assistance Act of 1952, the Korean GI Bill, service members who served sixty or more days outside the continental United States got three hundred dollars—one hundred dollars at discharge and one hundred dollars a month for two months thereafter. Those who served less than sixty days got a one-time payment of one hundred dollars.[309] Returning from the war zone, John Hatcher boasted that he had twelve hundred dollars in his bank account and, with a year of accumulated back pay and a reenlistment bonus in hand, Anthony DeAngelis had "more than I ever had in my whole life!"[310]

The men and women who served in the Far East during the Korean War marched to their duty stations with the imprint of World War II's tickertape parades and national unity embedded in their memories. But, instead of returning to the grateful nation they remembered, veterans of Korea came home to a civilian society marked by indifference to the war, racism, and sexism. Turning to the government for which they had offered up a year or more of their lives, veterans found not only insensitivity to their physical and psychological suffering but also a reluctance on the part of lawmakers to compensate and reward them for their services in the same way that men and women of the Second World War had been compensated and rewarded. In response, some Korean War veterans "quietly resumed their civilian lives . . . and set out to forget Korea," determining that "if we thought that we would receive any lasting public reward for our service, we were mistaken."[311] But, a great many others determined to make the most of their lackluster benefits and, like Robert Chappell and Elmer Payne, could claim years later that "today I'm reaping the benefits from it [military service] and I'm glad I did it" and "I actually benefited from military service which opened the door to a very rewarding career and pleasant retirement."[312]

In 2011, president of the Oklahoma chapter of the Korean War Veterans Association Harold Mulhausen stands in front of a sign demonstrating that Korean War veterans have taken their place among veterans of other American wars. Courtesy of Harold Mulhausen.

8

More Than Ever a Veteran

As men and women trickled back to the States from the Far East during and after the Korean War, a few Americans and groups did seek to honor them and memorialize their sacrifices. The United Nations dedicated a plaque to the Korean War dead at its headquarters on June 21, 1956, and on November 11, 1954, Armistice Day officially became Veterans Day in the United States, in part to recognize these new veterans.[1] But, with public support for such efforts as tepid in the 1950s as attitudes toward the war had been, early attempts to construct lasting monuments in remembrance of either the Korean War or veterans of that conflict often failed. As with the American Battle Monuments Commission's proposal to build a memorial in South Korea, neither enough interest nor enough money could be generated to sustain projects.[2] Tired of arguing that America "hadn't 'lost' in Korea" and quieted by the country's apathy, many Korean War veterans made their "earliest contribution to our generation of silence leading to our forgotten war" by trying to put the war behind them and forget that they were veterans at all.[3] All the same, Korean War service shaped the lives of the men and women who completed tours of duty in theater, and, later, sometimes years or decades later, members of the "silent generation" found their voice as American war veterans.

Most veterans of the Korean War see connections between their days in service and the way their lives unfolded after the conflict. Injured physically or mentally, some recognize that they have yet to recover from wounds "so deep that they scarred my very soul."[4] Others continue to wrestle with the unpleasant lessons they learned in the war, such as that "children and innocent people suffer."[5] A few note that service adversely affected their careers. "The guy who stayed home and went to college got the better job. I operated a machine. He was probably up in the office."[6] Most, however, acknowledge that they "learned many things during my stay in Korea, and . . . also grew as a person" and that they "learned a lot about myself" and "can give part of the credit for my good fortune to the Corps. My experience as a Marine was a very positive thing. As an enlisted man I learned self-discipline."[7] Like Edgar Miller, who became a business owner and mayor of a small town, veterans credit both the military and their wartime experiences with instilling the skills and character traits in them that enabled their success in the civilian world after mustering out.[8]

Financially, Korean War veterans seem to have profited from or at least not been impeded by their military service. In general, veterans of modern wars, including World War II, "suffer an earnings penalty in the civilian economy."[9] Removed from the regular work force for years, out of the loop for promotions and job-related training, and perhaps hindered by physical or emotional impairments caused by the war, veterans have a difficult time catching up to their nonveteran peers in terms of salary and occupational status. For veterans of wars other than the Korean War, it took as many as ten years for the disparity in earnings to even out, if it ever did.[10] But, maybe because they reentered a comparatively stable economy or because they were younger than veterans of some wars when they returned, Korean War veterans fared better than both other veteran cohorts and civilian contemporaries.[11] By 1979, studies indicated that Korean War veterans, rather than earning less than peers who had not entered the armed forces, had considerably more income, as much as 17 percent more. In fact, in that same year Korean War veterans had the highest median income of all groups of wartime veterans as well as the highest rate of home ownership.[12] More likely than veterans of World War II, Vietnam, and the Persian Gulf War to have earned a college degree, Korean War veterans in the work force managed to get the "highest rate of return for years of education."[13]

White veterans of the Korean War, especially those with less than a high school diploma, proved adept at converting military experience into civilian earnings, but minority veterans showed themselves most capable of making their service pay off.[14] Whether because a record of military service encouraged employers to hire them, because veterans' readjustment programs helped neutralize discrimination and other barriers to employment, or because service gave them more confidence and higher expectations, African American and Hispanic veterans of Korea far surpassed their nonveteran counterparts economically. For at least a decade after joining the work force, nonwhite Korean War veterans pulled in 10 percent more income than their civilian equals.[15] Minority veterans of other wars also found this to be true, but black veterans of the Korean War exhibited a greater resiliency to unemployment. In 1979, when more than 10 percent of black World War II veterans were out of work, the rate of unemployment among black Korean War veterans remained about half that.[16] In addition, some Mexican veterans received more than increased income as a result of their service. Responding in part to the 1952 deportation of Alberto Gonzales, a 21-year-old Mexican Purple Heart recipient wounded in Korea after crossing the border and enlisting in the U.S. Army, congressmen pushed to allow all Mexicans "who bore arms for this country to apply for United States citizenship and to remain here until they got it."[17]

While remunerated in some ways for participating in the Korean War, most veterans struggled after separation with the feeling that Americans had forgotten not just their personal sacrifices and the very memory of those who lost their lives on the Korean Peninsula but the conflict itself. In the 1950s and 1960s, World War II veterans dominated Memorial Day and Veterans Day events and parades as well as most veterans' organizations. By the 1970s, veterans of the Vietnam War began demanding their share of public attention. Where, in between World War II, the "Good War," with its victorious veterans, and Vietnam, the "Bad War," with its vocal veterans, did Korea, the "forgotten war," with its silent veterans, belong? Slowly, especially after the dedication of the Vietnam Veterans Memorial in Washington, DC, in November 1982, Korean War veterans, who had not yet been honored with a national memorial, began to reflect upon their own war and wonder, "We did what our country called us to do. Is it too much to ask that we be recognized for what we did?"[18]

After many years of silence about their wartime experiences, Korean War veterans found their identity as veterans rekindled.[19] Many for the first time began joining existing veterans' organizations like the VFW and the American Legion or pledged membership in newer groups like the Chosin Few (formed in 1983 for veterans of the action at Chosin Reservoir in the winter of 1950), the Korean War Veterans Association (incorporated in 1985), and Korean War Veterans International (formed in 1986). Attending meetings and reunions, they met up with old buddies and made new friends "among men who could understand what it means to have been in combat."[20] Here, Korean War veterans finally found some of the understanding and camaraderie that had characterized the post-Korea lives of men and women who stayed in the military after the war and that had been missing from their own. They felt that "I fit right in and I like that."[21] Although they were separated from each other for many years and only saw each other occasionally, "when we reunited it was as if time had stood still. The unspoken words, emotion, and common destiny are perhaps the glue that hold[s] our sprinkled . . . parts together for ever after."[22]

Reconnecting with other veterans had a healing effect on those who served in Korea, but it also provided the impetus for them to push for more outward recognition of their needs and rights as veterans and of the "forgotten" war they had fought so long ago.[23] As one veteran noted, "after 40 years of being quiet, we're ready to rattle our sabers."[24] By the late 1970s, and especially after the construction and unveiling of the Vietnam Veterans Memorial, veterans of Korea began to lobby for a national memorial of their own.[25] Eli Belil, deputy mayor of Marlboro, New Jersey, took it upon himself to correspond with various government agencies, the American Battle Monuments Commission, and veterans' organizations to draw attention to the fact that Korean War veterans had nothing to show for their duty to country except "a few fading pictures amongst themselves and scars that neither time nor the Government's apathy will heal."[26] In 1985, just three years after the dedication of the Vietnam War Memorial, forty veterans followed Balil's lead, forming the Korean War Veterans Association (KWVA) to, among other things, "establish war and other memorials commemorative of any person or persons who served in the Korean War."[27] Largely in response to the push by Korean War veterans and the KWVA, Congress in October 1986 authorized the erection of a Korean War memorial, but only allocated $1 million to the project, making veterans responsible for raising the other $5 million on their own.[28] On June 14, 1992, Korean War veterans finally broke ground on the Korean War Memorial in Washington, DC, and on July 27, 1995, President William Jefferson Clinton and Kim Dae-jung dedicated the completed memorial.[29] Forty-two years after their war in Korea ended with an armistice, veterans of the Korean War won "one of the biggest battles we had to fight," getting their memorial, a tangible reminder of the country's gratitude.[30]

In addition to struggling for a national memorial, some Korean War veterans fought for other things related to their veteran status. In the 1990s, black veterans launched a campaign to force historians and the military to reevaluate the official record and produce an unbiased account of African American troops in Korea. Though they failed to halt the 1996 publication of William T. Bowers's *Black Soldier, White Army: The 24th Infantry Regiment in Korea,* and though later works reaffirmed that all-black units performed poorly, these veterans did manage to force the reexamination of the facts that resulted in blame for poor performance shifting to the Jim Crow Army and away from individual soldiers.[31] Other veterans strove for rights to government-funded medical care. In 2002, Korean War veterans sued the government for the free lifetime medical benefits promised them by recruiters fifty years ago, and in 2005 some joined in a lawsuit over cuts in medical benefits.[32]

Perhaps most successfully, the survivors of the action at Chosin Reservoir in the winter of 1950 worked toward VA recognition of their frostbite-related maladies as service connected. After the several hundred men gathered for the first meeting of the Chosin Few in 1985 discovered they all suffered from diseases and conditions related to the frigid weather they had endured in North Korea, they began to mobilize. Marine Gunnery Sergeant Ernie Pappenheimer, who lost his toes and part of a foot to the cold, began researching frostbite complications. Along with Dr. Stanley Wolf, also a veteran of the early months of the Korean War, Pappenheimer formed the Cold Injury Committee of the Chosin Few. In addition to informing both veterans and doctors "about the latent effects of frostbite and cold injury," this group "sent delegations to Washington, lobbying" for government recognition and medical assistance.[33] Eventually, persistence paid off and the Department of Veterans Affairs agreed to "broadly recognize the long-term effects of frostbite as service-related injuries."[34] In 1997, veterans of the Korean War began getting compensation for their cold injuries, and in 2004 the Senate put forth a bill to require the VA to "carry out a program of outreach to veterans of World War II and the Korean Conflict on the nature and availability of benefits."[35] In the first year alone, as many as four thousand Korean War veterans benefited from these changes in the VA stance on frostbite.[36] It did, however, take VA doctors a little while to catch up to VA rulings and develop sensitivity to the needs of these older veterans. Visiting VA doctors for the first time with regard to the later effects of frostbite, Korean War veterans noticed that "[w]hen they view frostbite patients they ask 'Why didn't you put on more clothes.'"[37]

As Korean War veterans began to lay claim to veterans' rights, the American public responded with increased attention.[38] On July 27, 1988, church bells across America rang out at 10:00 a.m. to mark the thirty-fifth anniversary of the armistice.[39] In 2000, Bruce Salisbury, an Aztec, New Mexico, resident, suggested putting one Purple Heart for every American who died in combat in Korea along designated highways, saying, "It would be hard to ignore or overlook Purple Hearts stretching for 37 miles along a highway."[40] New York held a "belated official homecoming" complete with a parade from Broadway to Battery Park for Korean War veterans in June 1991.[41] As evidenced by the onlooker who asked if the festivities celebrated Desert Storm, to which one veteran replied "Do me a favor, walk the other way. We've waited 40 years. Desert Storm can wait a couple of months," not everyone knew exactly what the parade marked, but still 250,000 people showed up.[42] Denied the Republic of Korea War Service Medal in the 1950s because of rules forbidding American military personnel from wearing medals issued by foreign governments, Korean War veterans got another chance to apply for one in the 1990s.[43] Since the late 1980s, numerous communities have designed and constructed state and local Korean War memorials or added the Korean War to existing war monuments.[44] Korean War veterans, no longer silent or forgotten, not infrequently took charge of these efforts to memorialize them. When Camden County, New Jersey, officials planned to build their Korean War memorial on a traffic island on the highway, veterans successfully pressured them into changing the location.[45]

Reestablishing their identity as veterans, many of those who served in Korea during the war decided to return once more to the "Land of the Morning Calm." Remembering the bullet-riddled buildings, the hungry peasants "in a land ravaged by war," and the shelters made of "corrugated tin, cardboard, and anything else that could be used," veterans could scarcely imagine that the Korea before them had once been the site of their war.[46] They marveled at the "hillsides covered with trees . . . [and that] Seoul was a huge modern city . . . with numerous skyscrapers, including the tallest building in the Orient . . . rebuilt . . . by men and women whose grandparents knew only oxen and the rice paddy."[47] Of course, not everything had changed. With North Korean troops still patrolling the 38th Parallel, searchlights illuminated the DMZ and soldiers continued to stand guard along the border between North and South Korea. As one veteran said, "It was eerie to stand in a concrete-lined South Korean observation post located on the same spot where I had dug a foxhole."[48] For some, the trip reawakened old sadness and they "felt like a burn victim whose raw nerve ends are suddenly exposed to air."[49] But, after all, though they visited Korea, "it was not *my* Korea."[50] The war zone had metamorphosed into a land of happy, industrious people who "appreciate what we did and the sacrifices those men made."[51]

Sixty years after the war that turned them into veterans, and in light of South Korea's progress and the greater willingness of Americans to recognize the sacrifices of those who served in the Far East in early the 1950s, what do Korean War veterans now think of the Korean War? Unsurprisingly, most "look back and think we did a good thing."[52] From their perspective, not only did the United States help "the Korean people gain something," but soldiers in Korea "accomplished what the troops in Viet Nam were denied: We drove the enemy back across the border and denied them the victory they so desperately sought."[53] Some veterans wish that "the Korean War had slammed the door harder on communism, for we had to sail the same ideological boat in the Vietnam War just a few years later, and the Cold War did not end for a decade and a half," but they still acknowledge, "Had we not taken a stand on the Korean Peninsula when we did the Cold War would not be past history."[54] They also challenge Americans "who regard the defense of South Korea as worthless . . . [to] imagine what a unified Korea today under a communist dictatorship would be like."[55] Arned Hinshaw goes one step further, positing that by draining Red China of resources, the Korean War possibly saved Formosa from Chinese aggression.[56] In the final analysis, most veterans of Korea agree with Jack Orth, "I don't think I thought it worthwhile in 1953—but I do now!"[57] And, they "look back with pride in our work and what we did," believing, "If I had to do it all over again, I would do it."[58]

For a few veterans, however, bitterness still lingers over America's involvement in "a stagnant war that was not meant to be won."[59] They remain angry about the "waste of beautiful young lives" and want to know, "Who ordered this ridiculous poke at the enemy? Was it a politician sitting on his fat duff in Washington?"[60] Some argue that "[t]he Korean War was a mistake as a limited war. The Korean War should have been fought all out" or lament, "If we had been allowed to finish the job maybe North Korea would be an ally and free instead of an opponent and not free."[61] Like Burdette Thomsen, they believe the United States "should have finished the job. . . . When you play the game you play to win"; or, like Walter Klein, they contend, "We could have done it in a good old American style and finish[ed] that thing off for a long, long time with the Chinese never again saying 'Paper Tiger' to the Americans."[62] Because of their experiences or because they blame the Vietnam War on failures in Korea, some of these veterans have decided, "Korea, like most wars, settled nothing. There were few gains and many, many losses" or even that "war is futile. No one ever wins except perhaps for the politicians and the people who manufacture combat equipment."[63] James Campbell, who at the time thought the war a worthy cause, now keeps a bumper sticker on his car, "Veterans for Peace."[64]

Nearly two million servicemen and servicewomen returned home alive from the Korean War in the 1950s after paying a hefty price for the defense of South Korea. Like veterans of the American Revolution, the War of 1812, the Mexican War, the Civil War, the Spanish-American War, the Vietnam War, Desert Storm, the war in Afghanistan, and the Iraq War, Korean War veterans lost their innocence along with fallen comrades, felt connections to the home front loosen or sometimes snap, and suffered physical and psychological wounds on the battleground. Reentering society, they fared sometimes worse and sometimes better than those who marched back from other wars. But, Korean War veterans hold a unique place in the pantheon of American war veterans. Reared during the Great Depression and World War II to place country above self, the men and women of Korea unhesitatingly "did what was my duty, my obligation" when Uncle Sam asked.[65] They served in the shadow of the glorified soldiers of World War II, receiving little recognition for their own sacrifices and accomplishments. When it became clear that the country preferred to forget not only the Korean War but also those who fought it, Korean War veterans carried their burden of war quietly, almost imperceptibly. But, given that they request VA headstones at a rate only slightly lower than World War II veterans and account for 18 percent of all internments in national cemeteries, it seems clear that Korean War veterans remember their war and in the twilight of their lives choose to define themselves by it.[66]

NOTES

Bradley Commission	U.S. President's Commission on Veterans' Pensions
Carlisle Barracks	U.S. Army Military History Institute, Carlisle Barracks, Pennsylvania
CFSOKW	Center for the Study of the Korean War, Graceland University, Independence, Missouri
DDE Library	Dwight David Eisenhower Library, Abilene, Kansas
KWE	Korean War Educator website at http://www.koreanwar-educator.org
MOHP	Mississippi Oral History Program, University of Southern Mississippi, Hattiesburg, Mississippi
NA	National Archives, Washington, DC, and College Park, Maryland
Taft Papers, LOC	Papers of Robert A. Taft Sr., Library of Congress
VHPC, AFC, LOC	Veterans History Project Collection, American Folklife Center, Library of Congress
WVHP, OHC, UNCG	Women Veterans Historical Project, Oral History Collection, University of North Carolina at Greensboro

PREFACE

1. *M*A*S*H* aired from 17 September 1972 to 28 February 1983 on CBS.
2. *M*A*S*H*, "Der Tag," written by Everett Greenbaum and Jim Fritzell and directed by Gene Reynolds, first broadcast 6 January 1975.
3. Max Klinger in *M*A*S*H*, "The Interview," written and directed by Larry Gelbart, first broadcast 24 February 1976.

INTRODUCTION

1. There are 6.8 million Korean War–era veterans, but only 1,789,000 of those served in theater. Tom Heuertz, "The Korean War + 50: No Longer Forgotten, Teaching Resources," Box FF "A.0957-A.0986," Folder A. 0974, Center for the Study of the Korean War, Graceland University, Independence, MO (hereafter CFSOKW) and "Section XI: Mortality and Combat Service," "Section 11," 1, U.S. President's Commission on Veterans' Pensions (Bradley Commission): Records, 1954-58, A 69-22 and 79-6, Box 61, Dwight David Eisenhower Library, Abilene, Kansas (hereafter Bradley Commission and DDE Library).
2. John E. Wiltze, "The Korean War and American Society," *Wilson Quarterly* 2 (Summer 1978): 131.
3. Robert Henderson, *Korean War Veteran Survey*, 9, CFSOKW.
4. Two demonstrate the discrepancy in number and quality between movies about World War II and movies about the Korean War. Larry Langman and Ed Borg's exhaustive compilation of films produced from the 1940s through the late 1980s devotes ten times as

much space to World War II films as to Korean War films, and movies about World War I, the Civil War, and Vietnam individually fill more lines than those about Korea. Lawrence Suid explains that the nature of the Korean Conflict made it less appealing to filmmakers than World War II. Langman and Borg, *Encyclopedia of American War Films* (New York: Garland, 1989) and Suid, *Guts and Glory: The Making of the American Military Image in Film*, revised and expanded edition (Lexington: University Press of Kentucky, 2002).

5. Some noteworthy exceptions exist. Lisle Rose's *Cold War Comes to Main Street: America in 1950* (Lawrence: University Press of Kansas, 1999) investigates the impact of the Korean War on domestic attitudes, and David Halberstam's *The Fifties* (New York: Villard Books, 1993) frequently refers to both the war and returning veterans.

6. Elaine Tyler May, *Homeward Bound: American Families in the Cold War Era* (New York: Basic Books, 1999).

7. Rudy Tomedi, *No Bugles, No Drums: An Oral History of the Korean War* (New York: Wiley, 1993); Donald Knox, *The Korean War: Pusan to Chosin; An Oral History* (New York: Harcourt, Brace, Jovanovich, 1985); Donald Knox, with additional text by Alfred Coppel, *The Korean War: An Oral History*. Vol. 2, *Uncertain Victory* (New York: Harcourt, Brace, Jovanovich, 1988); and Linda Granfield, *I Remember Korea: Veterans Tell Their Stories of the Korean War, 1950-1953* (New York: Clarion Books, 2003).

8. Recently, new works have become available, but these also tend to withdraw from meaningful analysis of the veteran experience. For example, Patrick Dowdey, Donald Goldstein, and Harry Maihafer produced poignant photographic histories of the Korean War, but the authors generally leave the photos to speak for themselves. Patrick Dowdey, ed., *Living through the Forgotten War: Portrait of Korea* (Seattle: University of Washington Press, 2004) and Donald M. Goldstein and Harry J. Maihafer, *The Korean War: The Story and Photographs* (Dulles, VA: Potomac Books, 2001).

9. U.S. Department of Veterans Affairs, Assistant Secretary for Planning and Analysis, Office of Program and Data Analyses, *Data on Veterans of the Korean War, June 2000* (online publication at www.va.gov/vetdata/demographics/KW2000.doc).

CHAPTER 1

1. William D. Dannenmaier, *We Were Innocents: An Infantryman in Korea* (Chicago: University of Illinois Press, 1999), 10.

2. Robert E. Baken (AFC 2001/001/1443), Folder 2, Interview by Matthew Baken, 23 November 2001, 2, Veterans History Project Collection, American Folklife Center, Library of Congress (hereafter VHPC, AFC, LOC); Lynn Harold Hahn, Memoir (Korean War Educator website at http://www.koreanwar-educator.org/) (hereafter KWE), 2; Rudolph W. Stephens, *Old Ugly Hill: A GI's Fourteen Months in the Korean Trenches, 1952-1953* (Jefferson, NC: McFarland, 1995), 14; Howard Matthias, *The Korean War: Reflections of a Young Combat Platoon Leader*, revised edition (Tallahassee, FL: Father & Son Publishing, 1995), 1-2; William E. Anderson, Memoir (KWE), 2; and Frances Omori, *Quiet Heroes: Navy Nurses of the Korean War, 1950-1953; Far East Command* (St. Paul, MN: Smith House Press, 2000), 69-70.

3. Dannenmaier, *We Were Innocents*, 2.

4. Robert E. Baken, Interview by Baken and Baken, 2, VHPC, AFC, LOC; Stephens, *Old Ugly Hill*, 14; O Lynn Harold Hahn, Memoir (KWE), 1-2; Matthias, *The Korean War*, 176; William E. Anderson, Memoir (KWE), 2; and Omori, *Quiet Heroes*, 15.

5. The projected average age for Korean War veterans in 2010 according to the U.S. Department of Veterans Affairs is 78.5, making 1931 the median birth year. U.S. Department of Veterans Affairs, Assistant Secretary for Planning and Analysis Office of Program and Data Analyses, *Data on Veterans of the Korean War, June 2000*.

6. Lisle Rose makes a compelling case for the idea that the Great Depression and the New Deal changed Americans' way of thinking about the government. Rose, *The Cold War*

Comes to Main Street: America in 1950 (Lawrence: University Press of Kansas, 1999), chapter 1.

7. In their memoirs and interviews, Korean War veterans commonly mention their own efforts during World War II. See Richard Bevier, "Nearly Everyone Should Write a Book," account attached by the author to *Korean War Veteran Survey*, 3, CFSOKW; Professor Charles Marx, Oral History by Dr. Orley B. Caudill, 28 October 1976, Volume 185 (1981), transcript, Mississippi Oral History Program, University of Southern Mississippi, Hattiesburg, Mississippi (hereafter MOHP), 3; Glen Schroeder, Memoir (KWE), 1; and Ralph David Fly, Memoir (KWE), 2.

8. See Martin Markley, Memoir (KWE), 2.

9. Writing about children from 1932 to 1945, William M. Tuttle Jr. emphasizes that a major effect of the Second World War on kids was increased burdens falling on them due to the absence of fathers and older siblings. Tuttle, *"Daddy's Gone to War": The Second World War in the Lives of America's Children* (New York: Oxford University Press, 1993), 241.

10. Jack Orth in Henry Berry, *Hey, Mac, Where Ya Been? Living Memories of the U.S. Marines in the Korean War* (New York: St. Martin's Press, 1988), 282.

11. James Ryan, "The Chit," 1, an unpublished piece included by the author with *Korean War Veteran Survey*, CFSOKW.

12. Public Relations Coordinator, Defense Advisory Committee on Women in the Services, Office of the Assistant Secretary of Defense, "Policy Guide for Women in the Armed Services Information Program 1953 U.S. Army, U.S. Navy, U.S. Air Force, U.S. Marine Corps," 8, Staff Files, Files of the Special Assistant Relating to the Office of Coordinator of Government Public Service Advertising, Women in the Services—Correspondence 1952-53, Box 9, folder "Women in the Service (Policy Material)," DDE Library.

13. Grace S. Alexander, Interview by Hermann J. Trojanowski, 20 January 1999, Women Veterans Historical Project, Oral History Collection, University of North Carolina at Greensboro, 10-11 (hereafter WVHP, OHC, UNCG).

14. Margaret S. Jacob, *Korean War Veteran Survey*, 3, CFSOKW.

15. Charles F. Cole, *Korea Remembered: Enough of a War; The USS Ozbourn's First Korean Tour, 1950-1951* (Las Cruces, NM: Yucca Tree Press, 1995), 20.

16. George Q. Flynn, *The Draft, 1940-1973* (Lawrence: University Press of Kansas, 1993), 7.

17. Black leaders like A. Philip Randolph refused to support Universal Military Training because it would require African Americans to serve in a segregated Army. Paul T. Murray, "Blacks and the Draft: A History of Institutional Racism," *Journal of Black Studies* 2.1 (September 1971): 66-69.

18. On the transformation of American attitudes toward nuclear weapons, see Paul Boyer, *By the Bomb's Early Light: American Thought and Culture at the Dawn of the Atomic Age* (New York: Pantheon Books, 1985).

19. Flynn, *The Draft*, 109.

20. This thought appears in Cole, *Korea Remembered*, 20.

21. Rose, *Cold War Comes to Main Street*, 291-301.

22. On the homogenization of Americans in the 1930s, see Lizabeth Cohen, *Making a New Deal: Industrial Workers in Chicago, 1919-1939,* 2nd edition (New York: Cambridge University Press, 1990).

23. Flynn, *The Draft*, 127-28.

24. Jimmie L. Clark, Memoir (KWE), 1.

25. Elaine Tyler May, *Homeward Bound: American Families in the Cold War Era* (New York: Basic Books, 1999).

CHAPTER 2

1. At the San Diego Naval Training Center men completing their training yelled "You'll be sooorry" at new trainees. Glenn Schroeder, Memoir (KWE), 3.

2. "100 Volunteer for Army, Air Force in Single Day," *Baltimore Afro-American*, 5 August 1950, 7.

3. Veterans often mention this. James Coulos and Donald M. Byers, Army Service (Korean War) Questionnaire, page 1 for both surveys, 2nd Division, 23rd Regiment, Alphabetical Box 1, Department of the Army, U.S. Army Military History Institute, Carlisle Barracks, Pennsylvania (hereafter Carlisle Barracks).

4. The age of acceptance varied by branch of service. The Marine Corps took men aged 17-28, but the Air Force usually required one to be nineteen or twenty. "Report on Conditions of Military Service for the President's Commission on Veterans Pensions," 15-17, Bradley Commission: Records, 1954-58, A 69-22 and 79-6, Box 58, DDE Library. Enlistees rarely had to provide proof of age, however, and approximately two hundred thousand veterans of World War II and the Korean Conflict enlisted while underage kids. Don Green, whose father died leaving eleven kids on a family farm in Nevada, saw military service as his only escape from poverty and enlisted at age fourteen. He turned sixteen while fighting in Korea. "Military Veterans Say They Were Underage," *New York Times*, 29 October 2003, Article 0654, CFSOKW. Similarly, thirteen-year-old Richard Cecil Jones entered the Army and served at two different camps before writing his mother to get him released. See "Lad, 13, 'Jives' Army, Does 145 Days . . . Bubble Bursts," *Pittsburgh Courier*, 2 February 1952, 13. Also, "Soldier, 14, Coming Home," *New York Times*, 11 April 1951, 31.

5. On the AFQT, see Bernard D. Karpinos, "Mental Test Failures," in Sol Tax, ed., *The Draft: A Handbook of Facts and Alternatives* (Chicago: University of Chicago Press, 1967), 35-53.

6. Harold Wool, "Military Manpower Procurement and Supply," in Roger W. Little, ed., *Social Research and Military Management: A Survey of Military Institutions* (Inter-University Seminar on Armed Forces, Inc., September 1969, AFOSR 70-0661TR), 41 and 44. Just prior to the Korean War, 62% of blacks scored in the lower percentile ranges of the AFQT compared with 33% of whites. Leo Bogart, ed., *Project Clear: Social Research and the Desegregation of the United States Army* (New Brunswick, NJ: Transaction Publishers, 1992), xxiii. During the war 69% of white accessions scored above mental group IV, but only 21% of other groups did. About 4.3% of whites and 31.3% of other registrants entered the military via administrative acceptances. "Section 1: Selection Process," 20, Bradley Commission: Records, 1954-58, A 69-22 and 79-6, Box 58, DDE Library.

7. "Report on Conditions of Military Service for the President's Commission on Veterans Pensions," TAB AF-1, Bradley Commission: Records, 1954-58, A 69-22 and 79-6, Box 58, DDE Library.

8. "Processing Procedures, 1950-1953 (Reproduced from 'Medical Statistics of the United States Army,' 1953; in press)," 48, Bradley Commission: Records, 1954-58, A 69-22 and 79-6, Box 58, DDE Library.

9. The military frequently lowers standards for service in order to fill the ranks rapidly in wartime. In the Iraq War, borderline troops qualified for positions beyond their capabilities and ended up on the front. See Dan Ephron, "He Should Never Have Gone to Iraq," *Newsweek*, 30 June 2008, 33-34.

10. From March 1947 to September 1949, when manpower needs were low, the minimum acceptable score on the AFQT increased from 31% to 49%. Manpower shortages in Korea drove acceptable scores for high school graduates back down to 31% by July 1950, and after Chinese intervention in November 1950, all male applicants scoring 21% or better were accepted. Standards continued to drop until July 1951, at which point men achieving only 10% on the AFQT were considered fit for service. "Report on Conditions of Military Service for the President's Commission on Veterans Pensions," TAB AF-1, Bradley Commission: Records, 1954-58, A 69-22 and 79-6, Box 58, DDE Library. Lower standards beefed up the numerical strength of the military but hindered its effectiveness as these lower-quality men had the potential to drag the overall quality down. William M. Donnelley, "'The Best Army That Can Be Put in the Field in the Circumstances': The U.S. Army,

July 1951–July 1953," *Journal of Military History* 71 (July 2007): 822-29, and William M. Donnelley, "A Damn Hard Job: James A. Van Fleet and the Combat Effectiveness of the Eighth Army, July 1951–February 1953," paper presented at the Society for Military History Conference, "Warfare and Culture," Murfreesboro, Tennessee, 2-5 April 2009.

11. The order of events after the mental qualification test varied somewhat.

12. W. D. McGlasson, "Manpower for the Korean War," *VFW*, June/July 1990, 23, Article 0057, CFSOKW, and William T. Bowers, William M. Hammond, and George L. MacGarrigle, *Black Soldier, White Army: The 24th Infantry Regiment in Korea* (Washington, DC: Center of Military History, United States Army, 1996), 29.

13. National Security Council (NSC) 68, produced in April 1950, acknowledged the inadequacy of the U.S. armed forces. Flynn, *The Draft*, 110. On the armed forces on the eve of the Korean War, see James L. Stokesbury, *A Short History of the Korean War* (New York: Morrow, 1988), chapter 2, and David Halberstam, *The Fifties* (New York: Villard Books, 1993), 67.

14. Many men stationed in Japan and subsequently sent to Korea at one time had been classified "limited service" for mental or physical reasons and sent to places like Japan after being moved to "general duty." Many of these became psychiatric casualties after only a few days of combat in Korea, further weakening the U.S. presence there. Albert J. Glass, "Psychiatry in the Korean Campaign," *U.S. Armed Forces Medical Journal* 4.10 (October 1953): 1392-93.

15. Flynn, *The Draft*, 113.

16. Chinese Premier Chou En-lai informed Indian Ambassador K. M. Pannikar that China would intervene in Korea if troops other than South Koreans crossed the 38th Parallel. The Indians warned the British, who in turn warned the Americans, but the CIA, President Truman, and Secretary of State Dean Acheson did not take the threat seriously and thus did not anticipate Chinese intervention. Stokesbury, *A Short History of the Korean War*, 83.

17. Although the armistice was signed in July 1953, the Korean War era includes June 25, 1950, to January 31, 1955. In these years, 6,807,000 men and women served in the U.S. military. "Cost of War," Central/Official files, OF 152-H, Box 819, DDE Library.

18. Flynn, *The Draft*, 119. This is consistent with the Vietnam War, when draftees, draft-motivated enlistees, and true volunteers each accounted for about one-third of those serving. Christian G. Appy, *Working-Class War: American Combat Soldiers and Vietnam* (Chapel Hill: University of North Carolina Press, 1993), 128. B. G. Burkett, *Stolen Valor: How the Vietnam Generation Was Robbed of Its Heroes and Its History* (Dallas, TX: Verity Press, 1998), 52. During World War II, however, over half of those who served were draftees. "National Survey of Veterans, 1987," National Archives, Record Group 015, Box 1 (hereafter NA).

19. By July 18, 1950, the Air Force extended all enlistments set to expire before July 18, 1951, by twelve months. The Extension of Enlistment Act of 1950 authorized the president to extend the enlistments of members of the armed services by twelve months.

20. The Universal Military Training and Service Act of June 1951 lowered the age of induction to 18.5 and lengthened the term of service to twenty-four months. This partly explains the relative youthfulness of Korean enlisted men in comparison with earlier wars. In World War I, men eighteen to forty, inclusive, and in both World War II and the Spanish American War men eighteen to forty-five, inclusive, were required to register for Selective Service. "Report on Conditions of Military Service for the President's Commission on Veterans' Pensions," table 2a, and "Section 11," 8, Bradley Commission: Records, 1954-58, A 69-22 and 79-6, Box 58 and 61, respectively, DDE Library.

21. By 1951, Congress imposed draft liability on all permanent residents and other male aliens who had been in the country a year or more. James B. Jacobs and Leslie Anne Hayes, "Aliens in the U.S. Armed Forces: A Historico-Legal Analysis," *Armed Forces and Society* 7

(1981): 193. Some men, even naturalized citizens, returned to their native countries rather than be drafted. See "Two Delinquents Now Abroad," *Seattle Post-Intelligencer,* 9 August 1950, 18.

22. Glen Schroeder, Memoir (KWE), 2.

23. James Brady, "Leaving for Korea," *American Heritage,* February–March 1997, 72.

24. Dawn Scher Thomae, "Wisconsin Warriors: Interviews with Native American Veterans," *LORE* 43.3 (September 1993): 9-18 (online at www.mpm.edu/collect/vet.html).

25. Donald A. Bohlmann, Army Service (Korean War) Questionnaire, 1, 1st Cavalry Division, Surnames A-L, Carlisle Barracks.

26. Frank Rowan, "History of the 161st Ordnance Depot Company and the 502nd Ordnance Depot Platoon 1948/1952," updated 9 October 2001, 1-5, included with *Korean War Veteran Survey,* CFSOKW.

27. G. Richard McKelvey, *The Bounce: Baseball Teams' Great Falls and Comebacks* (Jefferson, NC: McFarland, 2001), 92.

28. Franklin Kenneth Manzar (AFC 2001/001/16128), Folder 3, Interview by Alexa Kapilow, 1 February 2003), 1, VHPC, AFC, LOC.

29. In the absence of the draft in 1947, only nine to fourteen thousand men enlisted per month as compared to twenty thousand after Truman requested a new draft in March 1948. Forty percent of enlistees who were polled admitted that they enlisted in order to avoid the draft. For the Korean War years, as many as 60% of male enlistments were draft-motivated. See Flynn, *The Draft,* 118.

30. Commander Fred Ewing Smith in Frances Omori, *Quiet Heroes: Navy Nurses of the Korean War, 1950-1953; Far East Command* (St. Paul, MN: Smith House Press, 2000), 84.

31. Arthur Smith, Memoir (KWE), 1.

32. Warren Grossman, Army Service (Korean War) Questionnaire, 1, 1st Cavalry Division, Surnames A-L, Carlisle Barracks.

33. Clyde H. Queen Sr. (AFC 2001/001/10115), Folder 2, Transcript, 1, VHPC, AFC, LOC.

34. Shirley Brantley, Interview by Eric Elliot, 2 May 2001, WVHP, OHC, UNCG, 15.

35. Dr. Frank E. Becker to Harry S. Truman, 15 September 1950, Box 35, CFSOKW.

36. Gilbert Towner, *Korean War Veteran Survey,* 3, CFSOKW. Towner was mistaken; Native Americans became subject to the draft in 1940. Alison R. Bernstein, *American Indians and World War II* (Norman: University of Oklahoma Press, 1991), 21-26. Also, Tom Holm, *Strong Hearts, Wounded Souls: Native American Veterans of the Vietnam War* (Austin: University of Texas, 1996), chapter 4.

37. John Edward Nolan, Interview by J. Cantwell, 29 December 1999, American Century Project, St. Andrews Episcopal School Library Archive (online at www.doingoralhistory. org/), 1-2.

38. Anthony B. Herbert, *Herbert: The Making of a Soldier* (New York: Hippocrene Books, 1982), 12.

39. Henry Berry, *Hey, Mac, Where Ya Been? Living Memories of the U.S. Marines in the Korean War* (New York: St. Martin's Press, 1988), 229 and 282.

40. John Kamperschroer, *Korean War Veteran Survey,* 4, CFSOKW.

41. Sergeant Wadie Moore in Mackey Murdock, *The Forgotten War: Texas Veterans Remember Korea* (Plano: Republic of Texas Press, 2002), 109.

42. Gilbert Towner, *Korean War Veteran Survey,* 1, CFSOKW.

43. Thomae, "Wisconsin Warriors," 9-18; George Hopkins and Joseph Morey, Army Service (Korean War) Questionnaire, 1 (on both surveys), 1st Cavalry Division, Surnames A-L; Richard L. Ballenger, Army Service (Korean War) Questionnaire, 1, 2nd Division, 23rd Regiment, Alphabetical Box 1, Carlisle Barracks.

44. Henry Litvin, phone conversation with Melinda Pash, 30 September 2004, notes in author's possession. Hank finished his internship in July 1950 and accompanied the Marines as they landed at Inchon—without any training at all.

45. Douglas G. Anderson, Army Service (Korean War) Questionnaire, 1, 2nd Division, 23rd Regiment, Alphabetical Box 1, and Charles H. Smith, Army Service (Korean War) Questionnaire, 1, 1st Cavalry Division, Surnames M-Z, Carlisle Barracks.

46. Shirley Brantley, Interview by Eric Elliot, 2 May 2001, WVHP, OHC, UNCG, 15.

47. Robert Chappell (AFC 2001/001/188), Folder 2, Interview Robert Chappell by Laura M. Clifton, 23 November 2001, 1, VHPC, AFC, LOC.

48. Harold Mulhausen for the first time after joining the Marine Corps Reserve had "3 pairs of shoes at one time." Harold L. Mulhausen and James Edwin Alexander, *Korea: Memories of a U.S. Marine* (Oklahoma City, OK: Macedon, 1995), 5.

49. Cecil L. Cavender (AFC 2001/001/1226), Folder 5, Interview Cecil L. Cavender by Kasey Quackenbush, 8 November 2001, 2, VHPC, AFC, LOC.

50. Elmer Palmer Payne, *Korean War Veteran Survey*, 4, CFSOKW.

51. Johnson Slivers, *Native American Korean War Veteran Survey*, 2, CFSOKW.

52. Melvin D. Rookstool in Lewis H. Carlson, *Remembered Prisoners of a Forgotten War: An Oral History of Korean War POWs* (New York: St. Martin's Press, 2000), 99.

53. Curtis James Morrow, *What's a Commie Ever Done to Black People? A Korean War Memoir of Fighting in the U.S. Army's Last All-Negro Unit* (Jefferson, NC: McFarland, 1977), 26.

54. James L. Murphy, *Korean War Veteran Survey*, 4, CFSOKW.

55. Harry S. Truman, Executive Order 3000, 24 December 1952 (www.envirotext.eh.doc.gov/data). Veterans mention that Truman released prisoners from Army stockades, promising exoneration if they fought well in Korea. George Zonge in Rudy Tomedi, *No Bugles, No Drums: An Oral History of the Korean War* (New York: Wiley, 1993), 98. David Halberstam relates that men headed to the stockade "were reprieved and marched, still in handcuffs, to Yokohama" so they could fight in Korea and clear their records. Handcuffs were removed on the planes and ships on the way to Korea. Halberstam, *The Fifties*, 70-71.

56. *Sands of Iwo Jima*, Republic Pictures, 1994 (originally released 1949).

57. Linda Granfield, *I Remember Korea: Veterans Tell Their Stories of the Korean War, 1950-1953* (New York: Clarion Books, 2003), 65-67.

58. Charles M. Bussey, *Firefight at Yechon: Courage and Racism in the Korean War* (Lincoln: University of Nebraska Press, 2002), 3.

59. Gilbert Towner, *Korean War Veteran Survey*, 3, CFSOKW.

60. Peter A. Soderbergh, *Women Marines in the Korean War Era* (Westport, CT: Praeger, 1994), 29.

61. Jane Heins Escher, Interview by Eric Elliot, 20 May 1999, WVHP, OHC, UNCG, 9-10.

62. Valeria F. Hilgart, Interview by Eric Elliot, 1 March 2000, WVHP, OHC, UNCG, 6-11.

63. Military heritage is a constant refrain throughout memoirs, interviews, and surveys. Of almost two hundred respondents to the *Korean War Veteran Survey* (CFSOKW), over 80% had a close relative in service.

64. "Status of Alien Veterans," *New York Times*, 2 December 1952, 30.

65. *United States Statutes at Large*, 64, part I, 316 (1952) and Senate, Report No. 2366, 85th Congress, 2d sess., *Senate Reports*, volume 5 (Washington, DC: U.S. Government Printing Office, 1958) (Seriel Set 12065), 3-4, and "Eisenhower Signs Citizenship Bill for Alien Korea GI's," *New York Times*, 1 July 1953, 22. United States policy regarding naturalization in exchange for service had a checkered record before Korea. For an example, see Allan R. Millett, *The War for Korea, 1945-1950: A House Burning* (Lawrence: University Press of Kansas, 2005), 6-9.

66. *United States Statutes at Large*, 64, part I, 316 (1952) and Senate, Report No. 2366, 85th Congress, 2d sess., *Senate Reports*, volume 5 (Washington, DC: U.S. Government Printing Office, 1958) (Seriel Set 12065), 3-4.

67. Richard G. Chappell and Gerald E. Chappell, *Corpsmen: Letters from Korea* (Kent, OH: Kent State University Press, 2000).

68. Arthur Smith, Memoir (KWE), 2.

69. Robert A. Maclean in Carlson, *Remembered Prisoners of a Forgotten War*, 123, and Harold L. Keith, "Sarge Volunteers for Korea Duty: Wants to See His Pals," *Pittsburgh Courier*, 7 February 1953, 2.

70. Franklin D. Hodge in Keith, "Sarge Volunteers for Korea Duty: Wants to See His Pals," 2.

71. Captain Helen Louise Brooks in Frances Omori, *Quiet Heroes*, 82.

72. Thomas T. Howard, "Sees Young Marine's Revenge Idea 'Wrong,'" *Pittsburgh Courier*, 30 August 1952, 11. Joseph Timanaro, Army Service (Korean War) Questionnaire, 1, 1st Cavalry Division, Surnames M-Z, Carlisle Barracks.

73. George Pakkala, *Korean War Veteran Survey*, 5, CFSOKW.

74. Many women comment on the allure of military uniforms in their memoirs and interviews. See Jane Heins Escher, Interview by Eric Elliot, 20 May 1999, 10, and Shirley Brantley, Interview by Eric Elliot, 2 May 2001, 7, WVHP, OHC, UNCG.

75. Soderbergh, *Women Marines in the Korean War Era*, 30.

76. Jeanne Holm, *Women in the Military: An Unfinished Revolution* (Novato, CA: Presidio, 1982), 113-22.

77. Judith Bellafaire, "Volunteering for Risk: Black Military Women Overseas during the Wars in Korea and Vietnam," Women in Military Service for America Memorial (http://www.womensmemorial.org/ Education/BWOHistory.html). Also, Cynthia Kellogg, "Door Is Open for Women in the Forces," *New York Times,* 25 November 1955, 35.

78. Marie Bennett Alsmeyer, *The Way of the WAVES: Women in the Navy* (Conway, AR: Hamba Books, 1981), 71, and Mary V. Stremlow, *A History of the Women Marines, 1946-1977* (Washington, DC: History and Museums Division Headquarters, U.S. Marine Corps., 1986), 45.

79. Office of the Assistant Secretary of Defense, Memorandum for the Advertising Council, "Information about Women in the Armed Services," 8 December 1952, 5, Staff Files, Files of the Special Assistant Relating to the Office of Coordinator of Government Public Service Advertising (James M. Lambie Jr.), Women in the Services: Correspondence, 1952-1953, Box 9, folder "Women in the Service (Policy Material)," DDE Library. Personal accounts support this view. See Anita Bean, *Korean War Veteran Survey*, 5, and Marie Alberti Rogers, *Korean War Veteran Survey*, 3, CFSOKW.

80. Katherine Towle quoted in Soderbergh, *Women Marines in the Korean War Era*, 21.

81. "Report on Conditions of Military Service for the President's Commission on Veteran's Pensions: Section 2," 17, Bradley Commission: Records, 1954-58, A 69-22 and 79-6, Box 58, DDE Library.

82. Philip A. Klinkner with Rogers M. Smith, *The Unsteady March: The Rise and Decline of Racial Equality in America* (Chicago: University of Chicago Press, 1999), 203-13, and Walter White, *A Man Called White: The Autobiography of Walter White* (Athens: University of Georgia Press, 1995), 330-31. Also Bernard Nalty, *Strength for the Fight: A History of Black Americans in the Military* (New York: Free Press, 1986), chapter 13A, on the violent treatment of returning black World War II veterans.

83. John Egerton, *Speak Now against the Day: The Generation before the Civil Rights Movement in the South* (Chapel Hill: University of North Carolina Press, 1994), 361-62.

84. The years 1952-1954 were the first lynching-free years after World War II. On postwar lynching and discrimination, see the introduction to Gail Williams O'Brien, *The Color of the Law: Race, Violence, and Justice in the Post–World War II South* (Chapel Hill: University of North Carolina Press, 1999).

85. "Smearing Negro GI's in Korea," *Crisis*, December 1950, 715. Alex M. Rivera Jr., "Dixie Justice," *Pittsburgh Courier*, 2 February 1952, 1 and 4.

86. Roy C. Wright, editorial, *Pittsburgh Courier*, 27 January 1951, 11. John E. Rousseau, "'War with Korea Not Cure' Patterson Tells La. Negroes," *Pittsburgh Courier*, 3 March 1951, 2.

87. Morris J. MacGregor Jr., *Integration of the Armed Forces, 1940-1965* (Washington, DC: Center of Military History, U.S. Army, 1981), 312.

88. Bussey, *Firefight at Yechon*, 37-39.

89. James W. Allen (AFC 2001/001/13391), Folder 3, Interview by Judith Kent, 20 December 2002, 1, VHPC, AFC, LOC.

90. Beverly Scott in Tomedi, *No Bugles, No Drums*, 182.

91. Quoted in Chuck Haga, "Legacy of the Korean War: Blending of Black and White," *Minneapolis Star Tribune*, 7 July 2003, 1B.

92. "Unity, Duty, and Rights," editorial, *Pittsburgh Courier*, 20 January 1951, 6.

93. Under the quota system, qualified African Americans were turned away while other, poorly educated candidates remained in service because after World War II, blacks, who served primarily in support units and thus had less combat time and eligibility for discharge, remained in uniform, reducing the number of new recruits who could muster in. When quotas were lifted, some of those rejected earlier were notified they could now enlist. W. H. Frost, Interview by Melinda Pash, 26 October 2004, CFSOKW. Also Bowers, Hammond, and MacGarrigle, *Black Soldier, White Army*, 29. After the quota system ended, black enlistment rose steadily. In April 1950, African Americans accounted for only 10.2% of enlisted personnel, but by December of 1952 they comprised 13.2%. MacGregor, *Integration of the Armed Forces*, 430. By mid-1951, nearly one in four of the Army's new recruits was black. James E. Westheider, *Fighting on Two Fronts: African Americans and the Vietnam War* (New York: New York University Press, 1997), 22.

94. "Coronet Films Announces, 'Are You Ready for Service?'" (October 1951), NA, Record Group 330, Box 697.

95. National Council against Conscription, "This Concerns You" (no date), NA, Record Group 330, Box 697.

96. On Army and Navy programs, see Henry C. Herge, et al., *Wartime College Training Programs of the Armed Services* (Washington, DC: American Council on Education, 1948). Martin A. Markley also mentions these. See Memoir (KWE), 1-2.

97. The Morrill Act required land grant universities to offer courses in military tactics, but as late as 1949 some black schools were not in compliance. Perhaps this steered educated African Americans away from military service or prevented them from entering as officers when their time came. Office of the General Counsel, Memo to Commissioner of Education, "Land-Grant College Acts-Military Training in Land-Grant Colleges for Negroes—Your Memorandum," 9 June 1949, Central/Official Files, OF 142-A, "Negro Matters—Colored Question (1)," Box 731, DDE Library.

98. Richard C. Bevier, "Nearly Everyone Should Write a Book," 4-7, account attached by the author to *Korean War Veteran Survey*, CFSOKW.

99. The government provided free health care benefits for World War II– and Korean War– era veterans for almost a half-century, but cut them off in 1995, saying that recruiters had no legal authority to make such promises. Curt Anderson, "Vets Not Eligible for Lifetime Care," Associated Press News Service, 20 November 2002.

100. People questioned Marshall's expenditure on recruitment when the draft was in place, but Marshall claimed that without such efforts, draft calls would have to be raised and deferments ended. See Flynn, *The Draft*, 119.

101. Soderbergh, *Women Marines in the Korean War Era*, 21.

102. Jean Ebbert and Marie-Beth Hall, *Crossed Currents: Navy Women from World War I to Tail Hook* (Washington, DC: Brassey's, 1993), 132. Also "Army Readies Call for Nurses," *Daily Oklahoman*, 12 July 1950, 11. Even the Reserves competed for female enlistments. "Hey Girls! There's Still the Reserves," *Daily Oklahoman*, 2 July 1950, A13.

103. Public Relations Coordinator, Defense Advisory Committee on Women in the Services, Office of the Assistant Secretary of Defense (M&P), "Policy Guide for Women in the Armed Services Information Program, 1953, U.S. Army, U.S. Navy, U.S. Air Force, U.S. Marine Corps," 9 February 1953, 3, Staff Files, Files of the Special Assistant Relating to the

Office of Coordinator of Government Public Service Advertising (James M. Lambie Jr.), Box 9, DDE Library.

104. Ebbert and Hall, *Crossed Currents*, 129.

105. Holm, *Women in the Military*, 150-51.

106. See Marie Rogers, *Korean War Veteran Survey*, 1, CFSOKW.

107. Office of the Assistant Secretary of Defense, Memorandum for the Advertising Council, "Information about Women in the Armed Services," 8 December 1952, 7, Staff Files, Files of Special Assistant Relating to the Office of Coordinator of Government Public Service Advertising (James M. Lambie Jr.), Box 9, DDE Library.

108. Holm, *Women in the Military*, 151-52, and Soderbergh, *Women Marines in the Korean War Era*, 49-50.

109. The committee specifically did not want women with family or weight problems or emotional instability, or who had violated moral or legal codes. Public Relations Coordinator, Defense Advisory Committee of Women in the Services, Office of the Assistant Secretary of Defense (M&P), "Policy Guide for Women in the Armed Services Information Program, 1953, U.S. Army, U.S. Navy, U.S. Air Force, U.S. Marine Corps," 9 February 1953, 3-5, Staff Files, Files of the Special Assistant Relating to the Office of Coordinator of Government Public Service Advertising (James M. Lambie Jr.), Box 9, DDE Library. Also, there were fears about enlisting lesbians. In the Marine Corps, "athletic" women were interrogated, some with lie detectors. Soderbergh, *Women Marines in the Korean War Era*, 61-62.

110. Raymond Delcambre, Army Service (Korean War) Questionnaire, 1, 2nd Division, 23rd Regiment, Alphabetical Box 1, Carlisle Barracks.

111. Martin A. Markley, Memoir (KWE), 1.

112. Joe DeMarco quoted in Berry, *Hey, Mac, Where Ya Been?* 133.

113. Roger W. Little, "Procurement of Manpower," in Roger W. Little, ed., *Selective Service and American Society* (New York: Russell Sage Foundation, 1969), 27; Wool, "Military Manpower Procurement and Supply" in Little, ed., *Social Research and Military Management*, 70; and Flynn, *The Draft*, 119.

114. Bussey, *Firefight at Yechon*, 9. William Price quoted in Harold L. Keith, "Sarge Volunteers for Korea Duty: Wants to See His Pals," *Pittsburgh Courier*, 7 February 1953, 2.

115. Flynn, *The Draft*, 119. This is consistent with Vietnam, when the number of voluntary enlistments declined as the war continued. Appy, *Working-Class War*, 28.

116. Samuel H. Anderman to Mr. Truman, 29 June 1950, Box "(43) Korean War: North Korea's Invasion of South Korea, 1 of 2," folder 11, CFSOKW. In 1950, Woody Guthrie put out "I've Got to Know," an antiwar song with stanzas like "Why do these war ships ride on my waters? Why do these bombs fall down from the skies? Why do you burn my towns and cities?" Doris Schmidt, "Americans Change Their Tune: The Korean War in Country and Folk Music, as Represented in *Billboard* and *Sing Out!* Magazines," 55, Box "A.0776 to A.0806," folder 0784, CFSOKW. See also Brenda Gayle Plummer, *Rising Wind: Black Americans and U.S. Foreign Affairs, 1935-1960* (Chapel Hill: University of North Carolina Press, 1996), 207.

117. George Gallup Jr., *The Gallup Poll: Public Opinion 2000* (Wilmington, DE: Scholarly Resources, 2000), 194.

118. Lawrence S. Wittner, *Rebels against War: The American Peace Movement, 1933-1983* (Philadelphia: Temple University Press, 1984), 202.

119. Gallup, *The Gallup Poll: Public Opinion 2000*, 194.

120. John E. Wiltze, "The Korean War and American Society," *Wilson Quarterly* 2 (Summer 1978): 131.

121. LaVergne Novak in Soderbergh, *Women Marines in the Korean War Era*, 69.

122. "Korea: The Forgotten War," *U.S. News and World Report*, 5 October 1951, 21. Gallup, *The Gallup Poll*, 1019.

123. Maurice Isserman, *The Other American: The Life of Michael Harrington* (New York: Public Affairs, 2000), 95-96.

124. Schmidt, "Americans Change Their Tune" 52-54, Box "A.0776 to A.0806," folder 0784, CFSOKW.

125. Rowan, "History of the 161st Ordnance Depot Company and the 502nd Ordnance Depot Platoon 1948/1952," 4.

126. The length of service was extended to twenty-four months in June 1951. William Berebitsky, *A Very Long Weekend: The Army National Guard in Korea, 1950-1953* (Shippensburg, PA: White Mane, 1996), 5, and "Folder X: Duration of Service," 9-11, Bradley Commission: Records 1954-58, A 69-22 and 79-6, Box 61, DDE Library.

127. Flynn, *The Draft*, 112-14. Also Wiltze, "The Korean War and American Society," 131.

128. As the war continued, some branches of the service revised their policies on what factors disqualified a woman for service. The Navy, for instance, by the end of the war no longer allowed women to leave simply because they were married or even because their husbands were wounded or discharged. Ebbert and Hall, *Crossed Currents*, 129. See also Soderbergh, *Women Marines in the Korean War Era*, 45 and 112, and Stremlow, *A History of the Women Marines*, 44.

129. This total represented 37% of the National Guard forces available. Berebitsky, *A Very Long Weekend*, 4-5.

130. Many guardsmen and reservists shipped out to Korea as individual replacements instead of as units because many units were in poor condition and unprepared to fight effectively. Flynn, *The Draft*, 114. This effort to reinforce units in Korea "gutted the General Reserve in the ZI [United States]" and resulted in troops being shipped to the war zone with little by way of "refresher training." Donnelley, "The Best Army That Can Be Put in the Field in the Circumstances," 814-17.

131. Lawrence M. Baskir and William A. Strauss, *Chance and Circumstance: The Draft, the War, and the Vietnam Generation* (New York: Knopf, 1978), 50; Flynn, *The Draft*, 119; and McGlasson, "Manpower for the Korean War," 25.

132. Hank Buelow in Granfield, *I Remember Korea*, 18-19.

133. John Michael Kendall, "An Inflexible Response: United States Army Manpower Mobilization Policies, 1945-1957" (Ph.D. diss., Duke University, 1982), 221, note 1.

134. Martin A. Markley, Memoir (KWE), 2. Also, Arthur L. Kelly, Interview by Birdwhistell, 16 April 1985, 4 (Kentuckiana Digital Library at http://kdl.kyvl.org).

135. Quoted in McGlasson, "Manpower for the Korean War," 25.

136. Kendall, "An Inflexible Response," 206; Flynn, *The Draft*, 123; and Wiltz, "The Korean War and American Society," 132.

137. A letter written in 1951 by thirty-two men, quoted by congressman Williams in *Congressional Record* (House), 82d Congress, 1st sess., 97:4, 5285, and Carl Vinson in "New Deal for Reserves," *Newsweek*, 30 October 1950, 28.

138. About six hundred thousand of the reserve personnel called to duty during the Korean Conflict were World War II veterans. McGlasson, "Manpower for the Korean War," 25.

139. Wallace R. Donaldson (AFC 2001/001/8350), Folder 2, Interview by Anne Woodward and Carmella Santos, 12 February 2003, 2-3, VHPC, AFC, LOC.

140. Thomas W. McLain (AFC 2001/001/256), Folder 1, "Remembering Korea, 28 June 1950 to 3 December 1951," 1, VHPC, AFC, LOC.

141. Scott L. Defebaugh in Granfield, *I Remember Korea*, 50-53.

142. Quoted in Joseph C. Goulden, *Korea: The Untold Story of the War* (New York: Times Books, 1982), 135.

143. "New Deal for Reserves," *Newsweek*, 30 October 1950, 28.

144. *Ibid.*, and McGlasson, "Manpower for the Korean War," 25.

145. "New Plan Affects Reserve Officers," *New York Times*, 7 April 1951, 27.

146. Kendall, "An Inflexible Response," 207; "Reservists: Forgotten Men," *U.S. News and World Report,* 20 October 1950, 17; and "New Deal for Reserves," *Newsweek,* 30 October 1950, 27. The Seattle business community rallied to find jobs for men "awaiting [their] country's call to duty," but elsewhere such generosity proved rare. "Jobs Pledged to Reservists," *Seattle Post-Intelligencer,* 2 September 1950, 3.

147. Robert D. Andre to Senator Robert A. Taft, 21 May 1951, Papers of Robert A. Taft Sr., Box 1077, Library of Congress (hereafter Taft Papers, LOC).

148. "New Deal for Reserves," 27, and Omori, *Quiet Heroes,* 12.

149. Initially the Senate Armed Services Committee "intended to recommend the discharge of all men called up in National Guard or Reserve units who had more than three dependents," but the military protested that the loss of those men was "not in the national interest at this time." Instead, the committee recommended against inducting enlisted men with more than three dependents. William S. White, "Senate Unit Votes GI Dependency Aid," *New York Times,* 22 August 1950, 1.

150. John Saddic in Berry, *Hey, Mac, Where Ya Been?* 161-62.

151. Harry VanZandt, Interview by Tara Liston and Tara Kraenzlin, 11 May 1996, New Brunswick History Department: Oral History Archives of World War II (Rutgers), http://fashistory.rutgers.edu/oralhistory/Interviews/Van_Zandt_harry.html.

152. "Reservists: Forgotten Men," 15-17.

153. The 1951 Universal Military Training and Service Act required that involuntarily recalled reservists be gradually released, starting with World War II veterans, and this was largely accomplished by January 1952. Still, 88% of officers in the Far East continued to be reservists or guardsmen. Kendall, "An Inflexible Response," 206-10, and "New Deal for Reserves," 28. As the war went on, and as volunteers and draftees were trained, some reserve troops were released from the obligation of going to Korea, a fact that did not sit well with those already in the war zone. Clarence Davis wrote his brother that new reserves were taken off the ship at Kobe to be returned to the United States, but "I had to come over here, and I think they should come on over and let the ones over here go on home first. That bit of news really pisses me off." See Jack to Bud, 21 May 1951, Clarence Jackson Davis (AFC2001/001/1644), Folder 1, VHPC, AFC, LOC.

154. Mulhausen and Alexander, *Korea: Memories of a U.S. Marine,* 3.

155. George H. Tsegeletos, *As I Recall: A Marine's Personal Story* (Bloomington, IN: 1st Books Library, 2003), 2.

156. Thomas C. Shay (AFC 2001/001/5807), Folder 3, Interview by Kent Fox, 24 February 2003, 1, VHPC, AFC, LOC. Early in the war even reservists still in high school, who had joined with the belief that they could request discharge at any time, were activated and deployed despite the pleas of parents and guardians for deferment. Randy K. Mills, "Unexpected Journey: Evansville's Marine Corps Reserve and the Korean War," *Traces of Indiana and Midwestern History* 12.3 (Summer 2000): 6 and 11. Celebrities like Ted Williams, a 34-year-old World War II veteran and player for the Boston Red Sox, also had to serve when recalled. See Berry, *Hey, Mac, Where Ya Been?* 259.

157. Frank Rowan mentions that his National Guard unit had only thirty-five of its authorized 160 men just before being federalized, but a recruitment drive brought the numbers up to ninety men by the time the 161st was actually federalized. Frank Rowan, "History of the 161st Ordnance Depot Company and the 502nd Ordnance Depot Platoon 1948/1952," 5. On how vacancies were filled, see William M. Donnelly, *Under Army Orders: The Army National Guard during the Korean War* (College Station: Texas A&M University Press, 2001), 13.

158. Many Korean veterans note the sense of déjà vu they had in leaving. They remembered the World War II departures and felt that in a sense history was repeating itself. Charles F. Cole, *Korea Remembered: Enough of a War; The USS Ozbourn's First Korean Tour, 1950-1951* (Las Cruces, NM: Yucca Tree Press, 1995), 29.

159. Paul L. Cooper, *Weekend Warriors* (Manhattan, KS: Sunflower University Press, 1996), 14.

160. Mulhausen and Alexander, *Korea: Memories of a U.S. Marine*, 4.

161. William M. Donnelley, "The Best Army That Can Be Put in the Field in the Circumstances," 815.

162. Email A. Pat Burris to Melinda Pash, 20 July 2005, in author's possession.

163. Berry, *Hey, Mac, Where Ya Been?* 205.

164. Omori, *Quiet Heroes*, 12.

165. Flynn, *The Draft*, 114.

166. Peter S. Kindsvatter, *American Soldiers: Ground Combat in the World Wars, Korea, and Vietnam* (Lawrence: University Press of Kansas, 2003), 14, and Harry VanZandt, Interview by Tara Liston and Tara Kraenzlin, 11 May 1996, 34.

167. Bevier, "Nearly Everyone Should Write a Book," 11.

168. During the Korean War era, as today, women were not subject to the draft, though many Americans (46% of men and 51% of women) supported the idea of drafting single women. Gallup, *The Gallup Poll: Public Opinion 2000*, 972.

169. *Annual Report of the Director of Selective Service for the Fiscal Year 1953 to the Congress of the United States Pursuant to the Universal Military Training and Service Act as Amended* (Washington, DC: United States Government Printing Office, 3 January 1954), 89.

170. Flynn, *The Draft*, 114.

171. *Annual Report of the Director of Selective Service for the Fiscal Year 1954 to the Congress of the United States Pursuant to the Universal Military Training and Service Act as Amended* (Washington, DC: United States Government Printing Office, 3 January 1955), 3.

172. *Ibid.* By the end of 1951, local boards delivered 5.5% more men than requested on average. Flynn, *The Draft*, 116.

173. Flynn, *The Draft*, 119. Also, Wool, "Military Manpower and Procurement and Supply," in Little, ed., *Social Research and Military Management*, 40.

174. Flynn, *The Draft*, 116.

175. Mrs. D. Caulkins to Senator Robert A. Taft, December 1951, Taft Papers, Box 1061, LOC.

176. The first man rounded up for draft evasion was Clarence White Jr., who had recently moved from the address to which his draft summons was mailed. Interestingly, White was classified 4-F in World War II, but the Korean War draft board claimed him as I-A. "First Man Seized as Draft Evader," *New York Times*, 21 September 1950, 8.

177. Newspapers and magazines frequently noted the lack of enthusiasm among draftable boys for both the military and the war. *Time* magazine noted in late 1951 that "hardly anyone wants to go into the Army; there is little enthusiasm for the military life, no enthusiasm for war." "The Silent Generation," from "The Younger Generation," *Time*, 5 November 1951, 45-52.

178. See Ira Peck, "A Night at Local Draft Board No. 14," *New York Times Magazine*, 29 October 1950, 15 and 47-49.

179. Blacks accounted for about 20% of those arrested for violating the Selective Service Act of 1948, the draft law under which the Korean War began. Plummer, *Rising Wind*, 207.

180. Telegram from Clara W. Spies to Harry S. Truman, 4 February 1951, Box 35 "Native Americans," folder 12, CFSOKW.

181. "Draft Dodger's Appeal Studied," *Pittsburgh Courier*, 22 March 1952, 5. Plummer, *Rising Wind*, 207.

182. Rudolph W. Stephens, *Old Ugly Hill: A GI's Fourteen Months in the Korean Trenches, 1952-1953* (Jefferson, NC: McFarland, 1995), 25.

183. Mickey Scott in Murdock, *Forgotten War*, 113.

184. Korean draft boards posted low satisfaction rates. In January 1951, only 60% of Americans polled believed the draft was being handled fairly in their communities. Criticisms included boards granting too many deferments or exemptions, drafting men at too young an age, ignoring the problems of inductees, and showing favoritism. Gallup, *The Gallup*

Poll: Public Opinion 2000, 1124. Conversely, at the end of World War I, 79% concluded that draft boards were fair. Only during the Vietnam War did pollsters find less satisfaction. In June 1966, only 43% supported the boards. Charles C. Moskos Jr., ed., *Public Opinion and the Military Establishment* (Beverly Hills, CA: Sage, 1971), 235. Also see John Whiteclay Chambers II, *To Raise an Army: The Draft Comes to Modern America* (New York: Free Press, 1987) on the draft.

185. *Annual Report of the Director of Selective Service for the Fiscal Year 1952 to the Congress of the United States Pursuant to the Universal Military Training and Service Act as Amended* (Washington, DC: United States Government Printing Office, 3 January 1953), 37; *Annual Report of the Director of Selective Service for the Fiscal Year 1953*, 27; *Annual Report of the Director of Selective Service for the Fiscal Year 1954*, 30; and Flynn, *The Draft*, 125-26.

186. Tom Clawson in Tomedi, *No Bugles, No Drums*, 148.

187. Draft resistance to the World War I draft is ably presented in Jeanette Keith, *Rich Man's War, Poor Man's Fight: Race, Class, and Power in the Rural South during the First World War* (New York: Macmillan, 2004).

188. See Flynn, *The Draft*, 127 and 167, for one version of this argument.

189. Wool, "Military Manpower Procurement and Supply," in Little, ed., *Social Research and Military Management*, 40.

190. "Induction Statistics," History and Records online (http://www.sss.gov/induct.htm), 1-2.

191. Jimmie L. Clark, Memoir (KWE), 1. See also John J. Dwyer, Army Service (Korean War) Questionnaire, 1, 5th Regimental Combat Team, Carlisle Barracks.

192. Joseph Gerald Fabiani, Army Service (Korean War) Questionnaire, 1, 2nd Division, 23rd Regiment, Alphabetical Box 1, Carlisle Barracks.

193. Gerald. R. Hanacek, Army Service (Korean War) Questionnaire, 1, 2nd Division, 23rd Regiment, Alphabetical Box 2, Carlisle Barracks.

194. Mickey Scott in Murdock, *Forgotten War*, 113.

195. Stephens, *Old Ugly Hill*, 25. During the Korean War, the average sentence for draft violations peaked at thirty-one months, only one month short of World War II's high. Not until the late 1960s did sentences surpass this mark. Michael Useem, *Conscription, Protest, and Social Conflict: The Life and Death of a Draft-Resistance Movement* (New York: Wiley, 1973), 129.

196. Jimmie L. Clark, Memoir (KWE), 1.

197. Inductees often disagreed with local boards and appealed their classification in hope of deferment. Selective Service Appeal Boards heard 2,232 cases in 1950, 31,923 cases in 1951, 49,289 cases in 1952, and 51,123 cases in 1953. *Annual Report of the Director of Selective Service for the Fiscal Year 1953*, 81. Selective Service standards became strict during the Korean War, and only 30% could expect reclassification from an appeal, a lower percentage than in either World War II (35%) or the Vietnam War (32%). Robert B. Smith, "Disaffection, Delegitimation, and Consequences: Aggregate Trends for World War II, Korea, and Vietnam," in Moskos, ed., *Public Opinion and the Military Establishment*, 235.

198. Exemptions provided permanent shelter from the draft while deferments only shielded men temporarily. Also, most men who received some kind of deferment agreed to extend their draft vulnerability to age thirty-five rather than the usual twenty-six. *Annual Report of the Director of Selective Service for the Fiscal Year 1953*, 5-7 and 15-16. A wide variety of physical defects could bar one from military service, such as alcoholism, circulatory problems, the loss of one eye, old fractures, flat feet, goiters, a history of rheumatic fever, and sex perversion. *Annual Report of the Director of Selective Service for the Fiscal Year 1951 to the Congress of the United States Pursuant to the Universal Military Training and Service Act as Amended* (Washington, DC: U.S. Government Printing Office, January 3, 1952), 50-54. The percentage of men deferred rose with educational level. Only 20% of men with less than an eighth grade education qualified for deferment, but 51% of graduate students did. Those with less education more often received rejections, however, based on physical

and mental exams. The Army rejected 54% of candidates with less than an eighth grade education but only 29% of those in graduate school. Albert D. Klassen Jr., *Military Service in American Life since World War II: An Overview* (Chicago: National Opinion Research Center/University of Chicago, September 1966) (Report No. 117), 235 and 240.

199. "Selection Process," 16, Bradley Commission: Records, 1954-1958, A69-22 and 79-6, Box 58, DDE Library.

200. Men in class IV-F were deferred in that their status could change as mental or physical test standards changed. Various reclassifications took place throughout the Korean War. In August 1951, the Department of Defense started reexamining 250,000-300,000 men because the acceptable mental exam score had been lowered. In September 1951, childless husbands deferred for dependency reasons became subject to reclassification, as did some men classified IV-F. *Annual Report of the Director of Selective Service for the Fiscal Year 1953*, 16 and 61.

201. Typically the order of call was (1) registrants delinquent in fulfilling their obligations under the draft law; (2) volunteers for the draft; and (3) men aged 19-25. Once the Universal Military Training and Service Act of 1951 lowered the age of induction to 18.5, those younger men could only be called after all older I-A males. Wool, "Military Manpower Procurement and Supply," in Little, ed., *Social Research and Military Management*, 53.

202. Dan Spence Grimes, 1, Army Service (Korean War) Questionnaire, 1, 2nd Division, 23rd Regiment, Alphabetical Box 2, Carlisle Barracks.

203. Lowell D. Truex to Robert Taft, 27 October 1951, Taft Papers, Box 1061, LOC.

204. Between 1950 and 1962, the Selective Service disqualified 32.5% of all registrants, one-third for mental test scores alone. During that same period, 60% of African American registrants were disqualified, over two-thirds for mental test scores alone. Bernard Karpinos, "Results of the Exams of Youth for Military Service, 1966," Supplement to *Health of the Army*, Medical Statistics Agency, Office of the Surgeon General, Department of the Army (Washington, DC: U.S. Government Printing Office, March 1967), 14-15. Standards rose again between the Korean War and Vietnam, and Selective Service became a target for champions of the underprivileged who claimed that high minimum exam scores barred too many Americans from the benefits of military service. Appy, *Working-Class War*, 30.

205. From 1950 to 1966, 54.1% of blacks were rejected by the Selective Service based on AFQT scores. Paul T. Murray, "Blacks and the Draft: A History of Institutional Racism," *Journal of Black Studies* 2.1 (September 1971): 58, 63, and 70.

206. The practice of lowering standards began during the Second World War when Selective Service dropped literacy standards to allow large numbers of functionally illiterate individuals to qualify for service. In turn, Korea provided a model for Vietnam when Robert McNamara's Project 100,000 waived supplementary aptitude tests for high school graduates in Category IV and allowed men with remedial conditions to muster in. Still, the early years of Vietnam posted a higher rejection rate than the Korean War. From July 1950 to July 1953, only 23.6% of registrants faced disqualification compared to 35.2% in 1963 and 29.5% in 1966. Wool, "Military Manpower Procurement and Supply," in Little, ed., *Social Research and Military Management*, 42-44. Also Appy, *Working-Class War*, 32.

207. "Processing Procedures, 1950-1953," 53 (Bradley Commission): Records, 1954-1958, A 69-22 and 79-6, Box 58, DDE Library.

208. *Annual Report of the Director of Selective Service for Fiscal Year 1953*, 83.

209. A broader base of males was also more likely to be retained by the services as manpower pressures resulted in a sharp decline in the numbers of Americans rejected or discharged for homosexuality. From 1947 to 1950, the military tossed about one thousand homosexuals a year out of service, twice as many as during the Korean War. Allan Berube, *Coming Out under Fire: The History of Gay Men and Women in World War II* (New York: Free Press, 1990), 262.

210. By 1953, over sixty thousand ministers and divinity students held exemptions. *Annual Report of the Director of Selective Service for the Fiscal Year 1953*, 21 and 26. Drafting COs

probably cost more than it was worth. Selective Service filed a report claiming the greatest difficulty "is almost universal refusal of members [COs] . . . to accept any work assignment." *Annual Report of the Director of Selective Service for the Fiscal Year 1953*, 15 and 26.

211. The Universal Military Training and Service Act of 1951 provided that in lieu of noncombatant service, COs could do civilian tasks in national service. Harry A. Marmion, "Historical Background of Selective Service in the United States," in Roger W. Little, ed., *Selective Service and American Society*, 43.

212. "Draft Evader Draws Three-Year Term," *Daily Oklahoman*, 2 April 1952, 1.

213. Robert E. Dudgeon to Robert A. Taft, 18 January 1951, Taft Papers, Box 1061, LOC.

214. The minimum service time necessary for determent ranged from six to twelve months. See *Annual Report of the Director of Selective Service for the Fiscal Year 1953*, 20, and *Annual Report of the Director of Selective Service for the Fiscal Year 1954*, 10.

215. Raymond S. Johnston to Robert A. Taft, 24 July 1951, Taft Papers, Box 1061, LOC.

216. Clipping "Draft Beckons Vet of 33 Months," included with letter Raymond S. Johnston to Robert A. Taft, 24 July 1951, Taft Papers, Box 1061, LOC.

217. Pfc. Doug Brown to Robert A. Taft, 11 November 1951, Taft Papers, Box 1061, LOC.

218. Some estimate that 2.7 million veterans received exemption. Flynn, *The Draft*, 114. According to the *Annual Report of the Director of Selective Service for Fiscal Year 1953*, 21, that number was exempted in 1950. Others assert that half of those in the draft pool, or roughly four hundred thousand, were exempt due to veteran status. Donald D. Stewart, "The Dilemma of Deferment," *Journal of Higher Education* 24.4 (April 1953): 187. A report on the classification of men from 1948 to 1953 notes that during those years at least 3,868,919 veterans had to be taken out of the pool of registrants due to previous service. *Annual Report of the Director of Selective Service for the Fiscal Year 1953*, 1. Americans were split on whether veterans should have to serve again or not. In a 1951 Gallup Poll, 41% of Americans thought that veterans with less than one year of service should be drafted while 40% thought they should not. Gallup, *The Gallup Poll: Public Opinion 2000*, 965.

219. *Annual Report of the Director of Selective Service for the Fiscal Year 1953*, 17.

220. For an example, see Lewis B. Hershey to Robert A. Taft, 29 April 1951, Taft Papers, Box 1061, LOC.

221. Louis A. Perrino to Robert A. Taft, 21 July 1951, Taft Papers, Box 1061, LOC.

222. Despite fears that students would "pyramid" deferments by marrying and having children at the end of their academic deferments, such cases were fairly rare during the Korean War. A 1953 sampling showed that only 3% of registrants classified as II-S (deferred as students) on April 30, 1953, were deferred for dependency exactly one year later. *Annual Report of the Director of Selective Service for the Fiscal Year 1954*, 9, 20, and 49. Graduate students were more likely than undergraduates to try to avoid the draft by pyramiding deferments. Flynn, *The Draft*, 145 and 149.

223. "Prospective Father of Triplets Due for a Rude, and GI, Shock," *Daily Oklahoman*, 19 February 1951, 4.

224. *Annual Report of the Director of Selective Service for the Fiscal Year 1953*, 16.

225. The National Farmers' Union was especially active in protesting the draft, usually on the grounds that it destroyed family farms. Flynn, *The Draft*, 130-31.

226. John William "Bill" Dallas, Memoir (KWE), 1.

227. Earl F. Brause to Senator Robert Taft, 6 January 1951, Taft Papers, Box 1061, LOC.

228. Wilvin R. Long to Senator Robert Taft, 10 September 1951, Taft Papers, Box 1061, LOC.

229. Many accounts exist of farmers wrangling to get deferments for their sons rather than for the tenant workers actually doing the farming or of farm boys who got farm deferments but ended up working in factories where they could earn more money. For an example, see Edith Dean to Senator Taft, 24 July 1951, Taft Papers, Box 1061, LOC.

230. Close to one hundred thousand men per year were deferred for agriculture in 1952 and 1953. *Annual Report of the Director of Selective Service for the Fiscal Year 1953*, 19.

231. Relatively high numbers of men did receive deferment based on occupation, but very few government officials seem to have fit into the parameters of draft vulnerability. In 1953, only nineteen men were classified II-B. *Annual Report of the Director of Selective Service for the Fiscal Year 1953*, 20.

232. *Annual Report of the Director of Selective Service for the Fiscal Year 1951*, 55. About thirty thousand such men received deferment in 1952 and 1953. *Annual Report of the Director of Selective Service for the Fiscal Year 1953*, 20.

233. Student deferment dates back to World War I's 1917 Student Army Training Corps, devised to allow students under twenty-one to complete three years of college before beginning military service. After many revisions, the virtually unused system puttered out with peace. Marmion, "Historical Background of Selective Service in the United States," in Little, ed., *Selective Service and American Society*, 39-40. Post–World War II conditions helped ripen the Korean War era for a new student draft deferment system. During the late 1940s and early 1950s, the federal government gave vast amounts of money to universities for research and development, so much so that colleges like Stanford University became dependent upon federal patronage and expanded into applied research to meet military and government needs. Rebecca S. Lowen, *Creating the Cold War University: The Transformation of Stanford* (Berkeley: University of California Press, 1997), 120-22. This link convinced Americans that university-trained men were essential to the nation's security and that drafting future scientists and engineers put the country at considerable risk.

234. After the passage of the Universal Military Training and Service Act in 1951, men 18.5 could be inducted and the number of men in I-S classification began to rise. By 1953, local boards began classifying younger registrants in earnest and class I-S grew even larger. *Annual Report of the Director of Selective Service for the Fiscal Year 1953*, 18. Selective Service placed strict limits on college registrants. College students who had already had their induction postponed because of student status, had been previously occupationally deferred, or already had some sort of educational deferment were not eligible for a Korean War student deferment. *Annual Report of the Director of Selective Service for the Fiscal Year 1951*.

235. *Annual Report of the Director of Selective Service for the Fiscal Year 1954*, 20. Flynn, *The Draft*, 145. Also, Benjamin Fine, "Colleges Urge Student Deferment, Citing Need for Future Leadership," *Special to the New York Times*, 11 January 1951, 16.

236. George Q. Flynn, "The Draft and College Deferments during the Korean War," *Historian* 50 (May 1988): 374. Truman was not alone in his belief that student and other deferments became "class legislation." Edward R. Murrow asserted in 1951 that draft policies gave preferential treatment to an "intellectual elite." *Saturday Review of Literature*, 21 April 1951, 23.

237. *Annual Report of the Director of Selective Service for the Fiscal Year 1953*, 17. Bachelor's degree and doctoral students had up to four years to finish their degrees, while master's students had only two. Flynn, *The Draft*, 142.

238. A limerick in the Selective Service quoted in Flynn, *The Draft*, 150.

239. *Annual Report of the Director of Selective Service for the Fiscal Year 1954*, 19. About 850,000 students total during the war held student deferment classifications. Paul M. Edwards, *To Acknowledge a War: The Korean War in American Memory* (Westport, CT: Greenwood Press, 2000), 109, and Flynn, "The Draft and College Deferments during the Korean War," 384. College students passed and failed the SSCQT along clear geographic lines. Students in Mid-Atlantic, New England, West North Central, Pacific, East North Central, and Mountain states were most likely to qualify for deferment while those in East South Central, West South Central, and South Atlantic states were least likely to make the grade. Also, engineering, physical science and math, biological science, and social science majors had a very high pass rate while students of business and commerce, agriculture, and especially education failed with great frequency. Still, of 482,403 examinees, 62% scored 70% or higher on the exam and those who did not could still hope to qualify for student

deferment based on class rank. Educational Testing Service, "Statistical Studies of Selective Service Testing, 1951-1953," SR-55-30, Princeton, NJ: ETS, November 1955.

240. Baskir and Strauss, *Chance and Circumstance*, 21. For every industrial worker deferred during the war, three students received a deferment. Flynn, "The Draft and College Deferments during the Korean War," 382.

241. This sharply contrasts with the Vietnam War, when young men of prosperous families expected to avoid military service altogether. Appy, *Working-Class War*, 6-12.

242. "Section I: Selection Process (Korean Conflict)," 14, Bradley Commission: Records, 1954-1958, A 69-22 and 79-6, Box 58, DDE Library.

243. Robin M. Williams Jr., Edward A. Suchman, and Rose K. Goldsen, "Reactions of College Students to Manpower Policies and the Military Service Prospect," *Educational Record* 34 (April 1953): 102.

244. Flynn, *The Draft*, 144.

245. William D. Dannenmaier, *We Were Innocents: An Infantryman in Korea* (Chicago: University of Illinois Press, 1999), 11.

246. James Brady, *The Coldest War: A Memoir of Korea* (New York: Orion Books, 1990), 222.

247. Mrs. Fern Brakefield to Robert A. Taft, 10 October 1951, Taft Papers, Box 1061, LOC.

248. Mrs. Jack Carter to Senator Taft, 17 August 1951, Taft Papers, Box 1061, LOC. See also Mrs. Ida Vordenberg to Senator Taft, 11 October 1951, Taft Papers, Box 1061, LOC.

249. Academics writing on Korean War draft policies stress that Americans accepted and even supported the deferment system because it protected American values like home, family, and education. However, had Korea lasted as long as the Vietnam War, people might have more actively protested the system that herded poorer boys into military service while men who could afford college or who had been able to train for protected occupations remained outside its reach. Through opinion polls, one can see the decline in public support for student deferments. In April 1951, 55% of those polled believed that college students passing a test should be allowed to complete college before entering the armed forces, but in April 1952, only 24% thought students making good grades should be able to graduate before being drafted. Gallup, *Gallup Poll: Public Opinion 2000*, 985 and 1067.

250. Donald D. Stewart, "The Dilemma of Deferment," *Journal of Higher Education* 24.4 (April 1953): 188. Some foundation for criticisms of the Korean War draft existed. In 1950, half of American families earned less than $3,000 a year, clearly too little to afford the $700-$1,000 a year tuition demanded by universities across the country. So, most young men of meager means could not have hoped for a college deferment. Flynn, "The Draft and College Deferment during the Korean War," 380.

251. Quoted in Flynn, *The Draft*, 126. Richard K. Kolb, "Korea's 'Invisible Veterans' Return to an Ambivalent America," *Veterans of Foreign Wars Magazine* 85.3 (November 1997): 25.

252. A selective sampling shows that as the educational level rose, the percent of those entering active service through the draft fell. Thus, 56% of men with less than an eighth-grade education entered the armed forces because they were drafted, but only 39% of high school graduates and 23% of college graduates who entered were drafted. Klassen, *Military Service in American Life since World War II*, 250.

253. Flynn, "The Draft and College Deferments during the Korean War," 384. Appy, *Working-Class War*, 18 and 30.

254. Eligible males twenty-six and under could be called by either draft. One father wrote to the director of Selective Service to make him aware that doctors such as his son were being forced to enter the Army as privates under the regular draft. Clarence M. Salzer to Colonel Richard H. Eames, 19 November 1951, Taft Papers, Box 1061, LOC.

255. Flynn, *The Draft*, 156.

256. Flynn, *The Draft*, 154-59; Otto F. Apel Jr. and Pat Apel, *M*A*S*H: An Army Surgeon in Korea* (Lexington: University Press of Kentucky, 1998); and Dorothy G. Horwitz, *We Will*

Not Be Strangers: Korean War Letters between a M.A.S.H. Surgeon and His Wife (Chicago: University of Illinois Press, 1997).

257. See Donnelley, "The Best Army That Can Be Put in the Field in the Circumstances," 824-27.

258. During World War I, men were drafted by geographical area. In World War II, units trained and served together. For the first time in American history, during the Korean War, most men mustered in on an individual basis, went to training alone, and were sent to replace individual troops in established units. Then, they were replaced and rotated out one at a time according to a point system. Edwards, *To Acknowledge a War*, 109.

259. The July 1863 draft riots proved the greatest incident of domestic violence to that time. See Mark E. Neely Jr., *The Fate of Liberty: Abraham Lincoln and Civil Liberties* (New York: Oxford University Press, 1991), 69 and 133.

260. Jimmie L. Clark, Memoir (KWE), 1. Also, T. R. Fehrenbach, *This Kind of War: A Study in Unpreparedness* (New York: Macmillan, 1963), 91.

261. While there is little debate that World War II provided a generational experience for men and women of many ethnic, racial, social, economic, and educational backgrounds, scholars still argue over the nature of the Vietnam War. Traditionally, Vietnam has been depicted as a class war in which the sons of poor men served while the wealthy protected their boys through educational deferments or other means. See Appy, *Working-Class War*, and Myra MacPherson, *Long Time Passing: Vietnam and the Haunted Generation* (Garden City, NY: Doubleday, 1984). Recently, some revisionists have tried to dispel the idea that Vietnam was class or race biased. See Burkett, *Stolen Valor*.

262. The 1951 UMT&SA lowered the age of induction to 18.5, causing much debate in Congress. Ultimately, unable to change the policy, some members of Congress fought to lower the voting age, "enabling every one of those boys, whom they are going to draft . . . to vote regardless of age. If they are old enough to fight they are old enough to vote." Congressman Edwin Arthur Hall in *Congressional Record* (House), 82d Congress, 1st sess., 97:2, 2605. Such legislation did not pass until 1971 when the voting age was lowered to eighteen. Appy, *Working-Class War*, 27.

263. Mrs. A. E. Erickson to Robert A. Taft, 3 March 1952, Taft Papers, Box 1196, LOC.

264. Roger W. Little, "Buddy Relations and Combat Performance," in Morris Janowitz, ed., *The New Military: Changing Patterns of Organization* (New York: Russell Sage Foundation, 1964), 196.

265. During the Civil War the average age of soldiers was 25.54, and in World War I it was 24.89. In World War II, the average enlisted man was twenty-six, while in Korea he was only twenty-three. Offsetting the general youth of the Korean War military, officers during the Korean period had an average age of thirty-three, three years older than the average World War II officer. "Section 11," 7-8, Bradley Commission: Records, 1954-1958, A 69-22 and 79-6, Box 61, DDE Library.

266. Some scholars place the average age of Korean War soldiers at twenty. Stokesbury, *A Short History of the Korean War*, 45. This seems possible in light of available data. In 1955, the Bradley Commission estimated that almost half of Korean War veterans with no World War II service were twenty-two years old or younger during the Korean War. Of 3,188,000 such veterans, twenty-six thousand were under age eighteen, and another 1,406,000 were age 18-22. "Veteran Population—General," folder "Estimated Age of Veterans in Civil Life, June 30, 1955," Bradley Commission: Records, 1955-1958, A 69-22, Box 85, DDE Library. Also, a 1987 survey of veterans found that 79% of those who served in Korea were between the ages of sixteen and twenty-five in 1953. "1987 Survey of Veterans (conducted for the Department of Veterans Affairs by the U.S. Bureau of the Census) (July 1989)," 19, NA, Record Group 015, Box 1.

267. Office of the Assistant Secretary of Defense, Memorandum for the Advertising Council, "Information about Women in the Armed Services," 3 December 1952, 5, Staff Files,

Files of the Special Assistant Relating to the Office of Coordinator of Government Public Service Advertising (James M. Lambie Jr.), Women in the Services—Correspondence 1952-1953, Box 9, folder "Women in the Service (Policy Material)," DDE Library.

268. After World War II, the average age of enlistees continued to decline until it reached low but stable levels during the Vietnam War. Anne Hoiberg, "Military Staying Power," in Sam Sarkesian, ed., *Combat Effectiveness: Cohesion, Stress, and the Volunteer* (Beverly Hills, CA: Sage, 1980), 218.

269. In 1940, the median years of school for those age twenty-five and over was only 8.4. By 1950 that figure had risen by almost a year of schooling, to 9.3. Bureau of the Census Library, Prepared under the direction of Morris B. Ullman in the Office of the Assistant Director for Statistical Standards, *Statistical Abstract of the United States 1953* (Washington, DC: U.S. Government Printing Office, 1953), 115. Women wishing to join any of the services had to have graduated high school or passed an equivalent test so all service-women had a degree of one sort or another. "Policy Guide for Women in the Armed Services Information Program, 1953, U.S. Army, U.S. Navy, U.S. Air Force, U.S. Marine Corps," 9 February 1953, 4, Staff Files, Files of the Special Assistant Relating to the Office of Coordinator of Government Public Service Advertising (James M. Lambie Jr.), Box 9, DDE Library.

270. About 54% of men with less than an eighth grade education were rejected as compared to 12% of high school graduates and 14% of men with some college but no degree. Klassen, *Military Service in American Life since World War II*, 240. During the Korean War, Selective Service disqualified 7.9% of draft-liable men for mental exam failure compared to 3.2% during World War II. Wool, "Military Manpower Procurement and Supply," in Little, ed., *Social Research and Military Management*, 43. Despite higher rejection rates, 40% of the Army's accessions during the Korean War were classified below mental group III, compared to the Marine Corps (34%), Navy (27%), and Air Force (27%). "Section I: Selection Process," 20, Bradley Commission: Records, 1954-58, A 69-22 and 79-6, Box 58, DDE Library.

271. Hoiberg, "Military Staying Power," in Sarkesian, ed., *Combat Effectiveness*, 214. Charles C. Moskos Jr., *The American Enlisted Man: The Rank and File in Today's Military* (New York: Russell Sage Foundation, 1970), 196. Perhaps because of draft pressures, those in the Korean War military averaged more years of education than their civilian peers. The 1950 Census found that 50.3% of Americans age 18-20 had less than a high school diploma and 46.5% of those 21-24 had no degree. *Statistical Abstract of the United States 1953*, 114. Comparing Selective Service registrants with the general population, George Flynn found that the pool of registrants reflected the larger society. However, the percent classified I-A (available for service) went up as the educational level of the registrant went up. Flynn, *The Draft*, 144.

272. The percent of troops with high school degrees fluctuated throughout the Vietnam War from a low of 56.9% in 1970 to a high of 65.5% in 1968. Overall, though, 60.3% of those who served in the Vietnam years had completed high school. Reports and Statistics Service, Office of the Controller, Veterans Affairs, *Bringing the War Home* (Washington, DC: U.S. Government Printing Office, 11 April 1972), 303. Also Appy, *Working-Class War*, 25-26.

273. Hoiberg, "Military Staying Power," in Sarkesian, ed., *Combat Effectiveness*, 214. A Department of Defense study places the rate of college-degreed enlisted men much lower for the Korean and Vietnam wars. It found that in 1952 only 2.8% of enlisted personnel had college degrees, still higher than in 1965 when only 1.3% did. Moskos, *The American Enlisted Man*, 196.

274. The Air Force provides one possible exception to this. From July 1946 to December 1947, 77% of fourteen thousand regular commissions went to officers without college degrees. In 1948, 75.4% of regular Navy officers and 62.8% of Army officers possessed a baccalaureate degree compared to only 37.05% of those in the Air Force. Struggling with low

educational levels, the Air Force instituted a number of college-credit programs on the eve of 1950, but the outbreak of war served to keep educational levels low throughout the early 1950s. John Darrell Sherwood, *Officers in Flight Suits: The Story of American Air Force Fighter Pilots in the Korean War* (New York: New York University Press, 1996), 11-13.

275. Moskos, *The American Enlisted Man*, 196. Some sources estimate that 55% of all Korean War–era officers had college degrees. Klassen, *Military Service in American Life since World War II*, 255.

276. The rate for specialized training for this category of men was highest in the Army during the Korean War. During World War I, a greater percentage of men in this classification received training than during either the Korean War or World War II—129,000 out of 791,548. In part this might be a reflection of changes taking place in American society as young people received more years of education with each passing generation. It might also reflect mental qualification standards for service. "Section 3: Training (2)," Tab E-1, Tab E-2, Tab E-3, and Tab E-4, Bradley Commission: Records, 1954-1958, A 69-22 and 79-6, Box 58, DDE Library.

277. Klassen, *Military Service in American Life since World War II*, 230. Also, Flynn, *The Draft*, 126.

278. During the Vietnam War, those with low income had a greater chance of military service than those with either middle or high income. Baskir and Strauss, *Chance and Circumstance*, 9. Some scholars claim that 80% of those who served during Vietnam were working class or poor. Appy, *Working-Class War*, 6-7 and 24-30.

279. Edward R. Murrow in *Saturday Review of Literature*, 21 April 1951, 23.

280. John Hannah in *United States News*, 20 February 1953, 18-20.

281. Klassen, *Military Service in American Life since World War II*, 232. Also, Flynn, *The Draft*, 126. In some ways it is easier to estimate the social class of Korean War servicemen by their fathers' occupations as the relative youth of the troops meant that many had not yet settled on career paths of their own before entering service. About 26% of Korean War soldiers mustered in straight out of school. President's Commission on Veterans' Pensions, *Readjustment Benefits: General Survey and Appraisal; A Report on Veterans' Benefits in the United States* (Washington, DC: U.S. Government Printing Office, 1956), 75-76.

282. See Frank O. Pruitt, entry at United States of America Korean War Commemoration Site (http://korea50.army.mil/history/remember/index.shtml), 16. Also Appy, *Working-Class War*, 30.

283. Memo John Folger to Burke Marshall, "Conversation with Morris Janowitz, University of Chicago," 19 August 1966, NA, Record Group 220, File C.10.1, 6.

284. Albert J. Mayer and Thomas Ford Hoult, "Social Stratification and Combat Survival," *Social Forces* 34.2 (December 1955): 155-59.

285. In particular the study divided Detroit into wealthy and poor neighborhoods and then plotted the numbers of casualties per neighborhood. Poorer neighborhoods, though, tend to have denser populations than wealthier neighborhoods because of small lot sizes and multifamily housing structures. Also, wealthier areas often consist of older residents rather than of parents with draft-age kids. One might well expect a higher participation rate from a younger, more populated area than one with older and fewer people. So, the casualty rate of neighborhoods might not accurately reflect the class composition of the troops as compared to the home community. Still, many scholars make the claim that the lower classes were overrepresented in combat units in Korea. See Moskos, *The American Enlisted Man*, 10, and Morris Janowitz and Roger W. Little, *Sociology and the Military Establishment*, 3rd ed. (Beverly Hills, CA: Sage, 1974), 112.

286. "Section I: Selection Process (Korean Conflict)," 20, Bradley Commission: Records, 1954-1958, A 69-22 and 79-6, Box 58, DDE Library.

287. Both the Air Force and the Navy conducted personnel surveys in 1951 to find out what careers servicewomen had pursued before entering the armed forces. In the Air Force,

only 1% had been engaged in domestic service and 3% in food service, the professions at the lower end of the social scale. In the Navy, .002% were domestic workers, .003% were in agriculture or horticulture, and 5.2% claimed personal service. Office of the Assistant Secretary of Defense, Memorandum for the Advertising Council, "Information about Women in the Armed Services," 8 December 1952, 4-5, Staff Files, Files of the Special Assistant Relating to the Office of Coordinator of Government Public Service Advertising (James M. Lambie Jr.), Women in the Services—Correspondence 1952-1953, Box 9, folder "Women in the Service (Policy Material)," DDE Library.

288. In the Air Force survey, 31% of servicewomen said they came from clerical/secretarial jobs, 11% from sales, 9% from factory/plant work, and only 2% from one kind of school or another. In the Navy, 73% claimed a clerical background, 3% professional, 4.5% semipro-fessional, 2% managerial or office, 5.3% sales, and 9% skilled/semiskilled/unskilled. *Ibid.* For more on female recruits, see also Robert A. Rogers III, "These Boots Wear Skirts," *United States Naval Institute Proceedings* 75.9 (September 1949): 1024-25, and Gertrude Samuels, "It's 'Hup, 2, 3, 4' and 'Yes, Ma'am,'" *New York Times,* 3 September 1950, 88.

289. The great irony is that during World Wars I and II, quota systems prevented many blacks from enlisting but allowed local boards to draft black youths at a higher rate than their white counterparts. During World War I, blacks comprised 9.63% of the total population, but 13.08% of those drafted and 34.1% of black registrants were called to induction compared to only 24.04% of white registrants. Similarly, during World War II, many African Americans found the path to voluntary enlistment fraught with troubles, but at the same time had difficulty securing deferments from the draft. After 1950, Selective Service did not keep sta-tistics by race, so it is difficult to determine how many blacks actually received a Korean War deferment or to find out what types of deferments African Americans held. Murray, "Blacks and the Draft," 58, 63, and 68. See also Westheider, *Fighting on Two Fronts,* 22.

290. For more on the racial policies of the armed forces, refer to MacGregor, *Integration of the Armed Forces*; Richard Dalfiume, *Desegregation of the Armed Forces: Fighting on Two Fronts, 1939-1953* (Columbia: University of Missouri Press, 1969); Nalty, *Strength for the Fight;* and Bowers, Hammond, and MacGarrigle, *Black Soldier, White Army.*

291. Asked by a reporter whether equality of opportunity meant the eventual end of segrega-tion, Truman replied, "Yes." Bernard C. Nalty and Morris J. MacGregor, eds., *Blacks in the Military: Essential Documents* (Wilmington, DE: Scholarly Resources, 1981), 240.

292. *Ibid.,* 296. Also, MacGregor, *Integration of the Armed Forces,* 312.

293. Only in the Navy did the percentage of blacks decrease from 4 to 3.2% in these years. The Air Force went from 4.5% to 7.5% African American, and the Marine Corps rose from 1.9 to 5.9%. Moskos, *The American Enlisted Man,* 214. While integration meant that more blacks could find their way into service via the draft because they could be used to fill out any unit, enlistments also shot up once quotas were lifted. In April 1950, African Americans accounted for about 10.2% of enlisted personnel, but by December 1952 that ratio had gone up to 13.2%. MacGregor, *Integration of the Armed Forces,* 430. Some scholars claim that by mid-1951 one in four new Army recruits was black. Westheider, *Fighting on Two Fronts,* 22.

294. Moskos, *The American Enlisted Man,* 214. The rising ratio of black servicemen seems to be further substantiated by veteran surveys. The "National Survey of Veterans, 1979" found that the proportion of black veterans increased over successive wars, from 6.9% of World War II veterans to 7.4% of Korean Conflict veterans to 8.4% of Vietnam veterans. "National Survey of Veterans, 1979," 10, NA, Record Group 015, Box 1.

295. During World War II, many African Americans were relegated to support units, and blacks were far less likely than whites to serve overseas. In the Korean War and the Vietnam War, however, blacks were more likely than whites to serve outside of the United States. "1987 Survey of Veterans (conducted for the Department of Veterans Affairs by the U.S. Bureau of the Census) (July 1989)," 12, NA, Record Group 015, Box 1. Westheider,

Fighting on Two Fronts, 22. Appy, *Working-Class War*, 18-19. About 13% of troops serving in the Far East were black. Kolb, "Korea's 'Invisible Veterans,'" 24. Puerto Ricans were also more likely to see combat in Korea than during either of the world wars, when many of them were sent to guard the Panama Canal. Matthew Hay Brown, "New Generation Fights for 65th," *Orlando (FL) Sentinel*, 27 May 2002, A1.

296. These figures come from averaging the percentage of men from metropolitan areas, small towns, and rural residences from each section of the country who served. Klassen, *Military Service in American Life since World War II*, 234.

297. Of men living in rural areas, 14% of northerners, 15% of midwesterners, 15% of southerners, and 24% of men in the Far West received deferments. *Ibid.*, 239.

298. *Ibid.*, 9.

299. *Statistical Abstract of the United States 1953*, 117.

300. Southern states topped the list in terms of IV-F classification rates. The highest rates were as follows: Puerto Rico 43.5%, Mississippi 24.1%, Virgin Islands 21.4%, North Carolina 20.9%, Georgia 18.4%, Alabama 18.3%, South Carolina 18.2%, and Louisiana 18.1%. By contrast, the lowest rates were as follows: South Dakota 7.1%, Utah 7.3%, Kansas and Minnesota 7.6%, Wyoming 7.7%, Indiana 7.9%, and New Hampshire 8.2%. Southern states also had higher preinduction exam rejection rates. The highest rates were Puerto Rico 70.3%, South Carolina 62%, Virgin Islands 56.3%, Mississippi 56%, Alabama 54.8%, Louisiana 54.5%, Arkansas 52.6%, and Georgia 50%. The lowest rates were Kansas 19.6%, North Dakota 19.7%, Panama Canal Zone 20.5%, Minnesota 20.6%, Utah 21.3%, Iowa 21.2%, South Dakota 22.2%, and Nebraska 23.2%. Southern states even accounted for the highest rates of induction exam rejections. *Annual Report of the Director of Selective Service for the Fiscal Year 1953*, 74-75, 84, and 91.

301. In the middle, 14.3% of midwesterners and 15.3% of far westerners were rejected. Klassen, *Military Service in American Life since World War II*, 244.

302. Oklahoma had a rate of 4.29%. *Congressional Record, Appendix*, 86th Congress, 1st sess., 1959, vol. 105, A6153.

303. Only 1.94% of Alabama's population served during the Korean War era. Other states with low participation rates were Delaware (3.14%), New York (3.25%), New Jersey (3.37%), Ohio (3.41%), and Illinois (3.42%). *Ibid.* By the induction exam, weaker applicants had already been weeded out, but southern states still had a surprisingly high rate of rejection. With a rate of 9.4%, Arkansas actually surpassed Alabama, as did Louisiana (8%), South Carolina (7.6%), Texas (6.8%), and Oklahoma (6.4%). By way of contrast, Guam's rate was .5% and Nebraska's was 2.8%. *Annual Report of the Director of Selective Service for the Fiscal Year 1953*, 91.

304. As far as sheer numbers are concerned, New York (482,000), Pennsylvania (405,000), and California (379,000) had the most men in uniform. *Congressional Record, Appendix*, 86th Congress, 1st sess., 1959, vol. 105, A6153.

305. West Virginia claimed the honor of being the state with both the highest percentage of its military population killed in action and the highest percentage of its total population killed or wounded during the Korean War. The state with the lowest percentage killed or wounded was Alabama. The states with the most men killed or wounded were New York (8,786) and California (9,513). *Congressional Record, Appendix*, 86th Congress, 1st sess., 1959, vol. 105, A6153, and *Congressional Record*, 86th Congress, 1st sess., 1959, vol. 105, part 11, 13924.

306. Other states included Arizona, South Dakota, New Mexico, North Dakota, California, Minnesota, Maine, Wyoming, Indiana, and New Hampshire. *Congressional Record*, 86th Congress, 1st sess., 1959, vol. 105, part 11, 13924.

307. Klassen, *Military Service in American Life since World War II*, 259.

308. A 1950 study showed that Army and Navy officers in 1950 overwhelmingly had been born in the South or had a southern affiliation. The same pattern was evident as late as 1964.

Wool, "Military Manpower Procurement and Supply" in Little, ed., *Social Research and Military Management*, 68.

309. A July 1951 Navy study found that most female Navy recruits came from the general areas of New York (12.2%), Boston (12%), Philadelphia (8%), Pittsburg (7.5%), Chicago (7.2%), Atlanta (7.1%), Los Angeles (6.5%), San Francisco (5.5%), and Detroit (5.5%). The rest hailed from areas around Cincinnati, Dallas, Washington, DC, Kansas City, Minneapolis, Seattle, New Orleans, Denver, and Honolulu. Office of the Assistant Secretary of Defense, Memorandum for the Advertising Council, "Information about Women in the Armed Services," 8 December 1952, 4, Staff Files, Files of the Assistant Relating to the Office of Coordinator of Government Public Service Advertising (James M. Lambie Jr.), Box 9, DDE Library.

310. *Ibid*. Also, "Policy Guide for Women in the Armed Services Information Program, 1953, U.S. Army, U.S. Navy, U.S. Air Force, U.S. Marine Corps," 9 February 1953, 5, Staff Files, Files of the Special Assistant Relating to the Office of Coordinator of Government Public Service Advertising (James M. Lambie Jr.), Box 9, DDE Library.

311. In part, lenient agricultural deferments during the Korean War explain why more small town and rural boys did not end up in the military and in Korea. With regard to Vietnam, see Appy, *Working-Class War*, 14.

312. James Hamilton Dill, *Sixteen Days at Mungol-li* (Fayetteville, AR: M&M Press, 1993), 402.

313. Boris R. Spiroff, *Korea: The Frozen Hell on Earth; A Platoon Sergeant's Diary, Korean War, 1950-1951* (Baltimore, MD: American Literary Press, 1998), 9.

314. President's Commission on Veterans' Pensions, *Readjustment Benefits: General Survey and Appraisal; A Report on Veterans' Benefits in the United States* (Washington, DC: U.S. Government Printing Office, 1956), 161.

315. U.S. Department of Veterans Affairs, Assistant Secretary for Planning and Analysis, Office of Program and Data Analyses, *Data on Veterans of the Korean War*, June 2000 (online publication at http://www.va.gov/vetdata/demographics/KW2000.doc), 2.

CHAPTER 3

1. Newspaper articles described women boarding troop trains while their husbands remained behind as well as servicewomen heading one direction for military training or duty while their husbands went another for the same. "Several Hundred Seattle, Everett Men Bid Good-bys to Families," *Seattle Post-Intelligencer*, 10 August 1950, 1, and "Boy Friends Cheer Girls Off to War, *New York Times*, 16 September 1950, 5.

2. Sometimes hometown folks refused to say goodbye. Friends and relatives followed the Oklahoma 45th Division all the way to Camp Polk, Louisiana. William M. Donnelly, *Under Army Orders: The Army National Guard during the Korean War* (College Station: Texas A&M University Press, 2001), 35-38, and "Furnishings for Day Room? Incidental Now, Says Mother," *Daily Oklahoman*, 25 February 1951, 18A.

3. Harold L. Mulhausen, *Korean War Veteran Survey*, 4-5, CFSOKW.

4. James H. Putnam, Memoir (KWE), 3.

5. In August 1950, the Army's basic replacement training centers included Fort Dix, New Jersey; Fort Knox, Kentucky; Fort Jackson, South Carolina; Fort Riley, Kansas; Fort Ord, California; Camp Chaffee, Arkansas; Camp Breckinridge, Kentucky; and Fort Leonard Wood, Missouri. "Army Ready to Open 11 Training Centers," *New York Times*, 17 August 1950, 16. The Marine Corps' boot camps included Parris Island, South Carolina, and San Diego, California. The Navy offered boot camp at Great Lakes, Illinois, but moved female recruits to Bainbridge, Maryland, in 1951. Jean Ebbert and Marie-Beth Hall, *Crossed Currents: Navy Women from World War I to Tail Hook* (Washington, DC: Brassey's, 1993), 129. Most Air Force recruits trained at Lackland Air Force Base in San Antonio, Texas, the only Air Force basic training location at the start of the war. E. W. Kenworthy to Eric Severeid, 24 February 1950, Box "Desegregation of the Armed Forces, Box 1," CFSOKW.

6. Mary Robinson, *Korean War Veteran Survey*, 5, CFSOKW.

7. Segregation also affected Native Americans, Puerto Ricans, and other dark-skinned groups who were subject to local southern laws and practices. Peter A. Soderbergh, *Women Marines in the Korean War Era* (Westport, CT: Praeger, 1994), 59.

8. Richard Dalfiume, *Desegregation of the Armed Forces: Fighting on Two Fronts, 1939-1953* (Columbia: University of Missouri Press, 1969), 209.

9. Americans came into contact with many different types of people for the first time at basic training. Hawaiian veterans recall boot camp first introducing them on a personal basis to mainland "haoles" and blacks. Louis Baldovi in Louis Baldovi, ed., *A Foxhole View: Personal Accounts of Hawaii's Korean War Veterans* (Honolulu: University of Hawai'i Press, 2002), 18. Guy Bishop notes that he never met a Catholic before entering the Army. Guy C. Bishop, *Korean War Veteran Survey*, 4-6, CFSOKW. Marian Nicely recalls black and white interaction among WACs at Ft. Lee. Marian Nicely, *The Ladies First Army* (Ligonier, PA: Fairfield Street Press, 1989), 17.

10. Prior to 1948, the Army assigned recruits to a specific branch at enlistment and recruits took specialized rather than general basic training. "New Soldiers for New Tasks," *New York Times*, 23 July 1950, 4.

11. Louis Baldovi in Baldovi, *A Foxhole View*, 18. Also, Shelley Stewart and Nathan Hale Turner Jr., *The Road South: A Memoir* (New York: Warner Books, 2002), 168-69.

12. Nicely, *The Ladies First Army*, 14. None of the services explicitly forbade women from wearing their hair short, but concerns about homosexuality that surfaced as early as World War II led training cadre to keep a close eye on "mannish" or "athletic" women and to interrogate and harass those suspected of lesbianism. Soderbergh, *Women Marines in the Korean War Era*, 61; Mary Ann Humphrey, *My Country, My Right to Serve: Experiences of Gay Men and Women in the Military, World War II to the Present* (New York: Harper-Collins, 1990), 11-20; Allan Berube, *Coming Out under Fire: The History of Gay Men and Women in World War II* (New York: Free Press, 1990), 260-65; and Leisa D. Meyer, "The Regulation of Sexuality and Sexual Behavior in the Women's' Army Corps during World War II," *Feminist Studies* 18.3 (Autumn 1992): 581-601. Also, Leisa D. Meyer, *Creating GI Jane: Sexuality and Power in the Women's Army Corps* (New York: Columbia University Press, 1996), 153-56.

13. John E. Williams to Melinda Pash, email, 7 May 2004, in author's possession.

14. Some trainees attempted to escape the military during processing-in. One man tried to convince officials he was crazy by pretending to be driving a car wherever he went. *Ibid.* At Fort Knox, Kentucky, eight recruits committed suicide by jumping off a water tower. Kenneth R. Kendall, Memoir (KWE), 4-5.

15. Literature on basic training emphasizes the primary function of tearing down the individual Boot and refashioning him or her into a soldier. See "Report on Training," December 1955, 35, Bradley Commission: Records, 1954-58, A69-22 and 79-6, Box 58, DDE Library; Peter S. Kindsvatter, *American Soldiers: Ground Combat in the World Wars, Korea, and Vietnam* (Lawrence: University Press of Kansas, 2003), 27; and James R. Ozinger, *Altruism* (Wesport, CT: Praeger, 1999), 58.

16. Of Selective Service registrants taking their preinduction exam from July 1950 to July 1953, 1,177,000 served in the Navy, 424,000 in the Marine Corps, and 1,285,000 in the Air Force. The Marine Corps also received 84,447, or 6%, of draftees. The Navy and Air Force did not participate in the draft. "Report on Conditions of Military Service, Section 1, Selection Process," 14, Bradley Commission: Records 1954-58, A 69-22 and 79-6, Box 58, DDE Library.

17. After World War II, the military also stored equipment that, without proper maintenance, had become unusable by the Korean War, further hindering training efforts. William T. Bowers, ed., *The Line: Combat in Korea, January–February 1951* (Lexington: University Press of Kentucky, 2008), 5. Also William M. Donnelley, "'The Best Army That Can Be

Put in the Field in the Circumstances': The U.S. Army, July 1951–July 1953," *Journal of Military History* 71 (July 2007): 814-16.

18. Korean War Army planners no doubt looked back to World War II when manpower shortages had been alleviated by reducing boot camp to six weeks. Also, shortening basic training must have seemed an appropriate response to the Senate Preparedness Subcommittee's charges of "inexcusable and indefensible waste" in the "valueless repetition of basic." "Waste in Training Laid to Army Units," *New York Times*, 26 December 1951, 1.

19. "Fort Dix Training Shorter, Tougher," *New York Times*, 12 August 1950, 4; Daniel Zimmerman, *Fort Dix* (Mount Pleasant, SC: Arcadia, 2001), 8; "Report on Training," December 1955, 36, Bradley Commission: Records, 1954-58, A69-22 and 79-6, Box 58, DDE Library; and U.S. Department of Commerce, *Historical Statistics of the United States*, vol. 2 (Washington, DC: U.S. Government Printing Office, 1975), 101.

20. Betty J. Morden, *The Women's Army Corps, 1945-1978* (Washington, DC: Center of Military History, U.S. Army, 2000), 101.

21. In 1953, basic training briefly lengthened to twelve weeks, but training generally stayed at six to eight weeks. "Army to Let GI's Pick Buddies to Live and Fight in 4-Man Teams," *New York Times*, 5 July 1953, 1.

22. There were some exceptions to this. National Guard and Reserve troops often arrived at training as a group. Also, late in the Korean War, in an effort to restore camaraderie within the ranks, a new program allowed men to train, eat, sleep, and fight with three buddies of their own choosing. "Army to Let GI's Pick 'Buddies' to Live and Fight in 4-Man Teams," *New York Times*, 5 July 1953, 1. Courting female enlistment, the Army and Air Force promised high school coeds and girls' clubs that the corps would make sure friends enlisting together went through basic training together. "Armories Sought for Reserves' Use," *New York Times*, 4 December 1950, 20.

23. James C. Shelburne and Kenneth J. Groves, *Education in the Armed Forces* (New York: Center for Applied Research in Education, 1965), 28-29, and Dave Moniz, "Army Updates Training" (online at www.usatoday.com), posting 5 January 2004.

24. Rudolph W. Stephens, *Old Ugly Hill: A GI's Fourteen Months in the Korean Trenches, 1952-1953* (Jefferson, NC: McFarland, 1995), 15.

25. John R. Kamperschroer, *Korean War Veteran Survey*, 5, CFSOKW.

26. Robert Shields, *Korean War Veteran Survey*, 5, CFSOKW.

27. Stephens, *Old Ugly Hill*, 15.

28. Merle Wysock describes these conditions at Camp Breckinridge, Kentucky, in *Korean War Veteran Survey*, 3, CFSOKW. Also "Training at Fort Dix," *New York Times*, 5 July 1955, 12.

29. Thus describing Indiantown Gap, Daniel Wolfe went on to say that in order to earn weekend passes trainees had to thoroughly clean these old structures. If the barracks failed inspection, the men paid by spending the weekend on "toilet drill," running back and forth on the command of a whistle from the bunks to the bathroom to raise or lower the toilet seats. Daniel Wolfe, *Cold Ground's Been My Bed: A Korean War Memoir* (New York: iUniverse, 2005), 19 and 27-28. Women describe similar experiences. See Nicely, *Ladies First Army*, 11, and Dorothy Rechel, Oral History by Eric Elliott, 22 January 2001, 14, WVHP, OHC, UNCG.

30. Morden, *The Women's Army Corps*, 76-79.

31. Wolfe, *Cold Ground's Been My Bed*, 28.

32. *Ibid.*, 21, and Rechel, Oral History by Eric Elliott, 22 January 2001, WVHP, OHC, UNCG, 14.

33. Margie Jacob, *Korean War Veteran Survey*, 5, CFSOKW.

34. Wolfe, *Cold Ground's Been My Bed*, 25-27.

35. Major General John M. Devine in "New Soldiers for New Tasks," *New York Times*, 23 July 1950, 4.

36. Despite efforts to ensure trainees not flee boot camp, some went AWOL and a larger number thought about it. At Fort Dix, 90% of trainees complained to chaplains and another 5% consulted psychiatrists during their basic training. "New Soldiers for New Tasks," *New York Times*, 23 July 1950, 4.

37. Harold Selley, Memoir (KWE), 2-3. Some trainees refused to shower daily, causing the entire barracks to fail inspection. Trainees were not above administering a "GI shower," painfully scrubbing the offender with stiff brushes to remind him to stay clean. William E. Anderson, Memoir (KWE), 4.

38. Nicely, *Ladies First Army*, 12-13.

39. Donald Chase, Memoir (KWE), 2; LeRoy Eaton, Memoir (KWE), 3-4; Robert Fernandez in Baldovi, *A Foxhole View*, 184; and Nicely, *Ladies First Army*, 14. During postwar basic training, the Army tackled the topic of homosexuality. Reversing earlier policies, the Army and other branches of the armed forces started explicitly lecturing against homosexuality and encouraging soldiers to turn in anyone they suspected of being gay. Berube, *Coming Out under Fire*, 263.

40. Wolfe, *Cold Ground's Been My Bed*, 24-25.

41. Kenneth R. Kendall, Memoir (KWE), 6.

42. Seymour Bernstein, *Monsters and Angels: Surviving a Career in Music* (Milwaukee, WI: Hal Leonard, 2002), 201. Despite no small amount of griping, soldiers in some locales could not drink alcohol. The New Jersey liquor law required men to be age twenty-one or older and a great number of Fort Dix soldiers had to limit their good times to root beer. "New Soldiers for New Tasks," *New York Times*, 23 July 1950, 4.

43. Harold Selley, Memoir (KWE), 2.

44. Robert Popenhagen, *Korean War Veteran Survey*, 5, CFSOKW.

45. Nicely, *Ladies First Army*, 13.

46. Frank Faculjak remembers that after turning left instead of right in drill he was issued stone to be carried at all times in his right pocket. Frank J. Faculjak, *Korean War Veteran Survey*, 5, CFSOKW.

47. Bernstein, *Monsters and Angels*, 193.

48. Wolfe, *Cold Ground's Been My Bed*, 37-41.

49. Shelburne and Groves, *Education in the Armed Forces*, 29; "New Soldiers for New Tasks," *New York Times*, 23 July 1950, 4; and Bernstein, *Monsters and Angels*, 198-200.

50. "Fort Dix Training Shorter, Tougher," *New York Times*, 12 August 1950, 4, and Wolfe, *Cold Ground's Been My Bed*, 53.

51. Kelly C. Jordan, "Right for the Wrong Reasons: S. L. A. Marshall and the Ratio of Fire in Korea," *Journal of Military History* 66.1 (2002): 147, and James H. Toner, "American Society and the American Way of War: Korea and Beyond," *Parameters* 11.1 (1981): 80. During World War II, the Army tried to reduce the gap between training and combat, but ended these efforts after the war. John T. Collier, "Military Training: World War II and Korea," *Army Information Digest* 8 (May 1953): 26.

52. Toner, "American Society and the American Way of War," 83; "Army Going Back to Tough Training," *New York Times*, 15 August 1954, 45; "Rougher Training Planned by Army," *New York Times*, 21 August 1950, 11; and "Need for Training Revealed in Korea," *New York Times*, 3 November 1950, 4.

53. Collier, "Military Training," 26.

54. Bernstein, *Monsters and Angels*, 195-97, and "Fort Dix Training Shorter, Tougher," *New York Times*, 12 August 1950, 4.

55. *Ibid.*, 196.

56. "4 Month Soldiers Stand under Fire," *New York Times*, 5 February 1952, 25.

57. William Abreu in Baldovi, *A Foxhole View*, 193.

58. One newspaper article claimed that recruits at Fort Dix spent three times as much time learning how to fire various weapons as on anything else in the program. "New Soldiers for New Tasks," *New York Times*, 23 July 1950, 4. Women trainees learned how to disassemble, clean, and reassemble the M-1, but firing weapons on the range generally took place on a voluntary basis. Nicely, *Ladies First Army*, 14.

59. *Ibid.*, and "Training at Fort Dix-II," *New York Times*, 6 July 1955, 12.

60. Robert Fernandez in Baldovi, *A Foxhole View*, 184-88; Wolfe, *Cold Ground's Been My Bed*, 47-50; Bernstein, *Monsters and Angels*, 193; Charles L. Brown, Memoir (KWE), 5; and "Fort Dix Training Shorter, Tougher," *New York Times*, 12 August 1950, 4.

61. "GI 'Very Sorry' He Slew Buddy on Maneuvers," *Daily Oklahoman*, 7 April 1952, 2, and Bernstein, *Monsters and Angels*, 200.

62. "War's Grief Besets Couple in Everett," *Seattle Post-Intelligencer*, 19 August 1950, 1.

63. Jim Whittaker, *A Life on the Edge: Memoirs of Everest and Beyond* (Seattle, WA: Mountaineers, 1999), 56.

64. Stephens, *Old Ugly Hill*, 20. Similarly, James Draught notes, "We learned a simple skill, how to make war and how to murder and how to hate and how to obey orders no matter what." Quoted in Philip K. Jason and W. D. Ehrhart, eds., *Retrieving Bones: Stories and Poems of the Korean War* (Piscataway, NJ: Rutgers Press, 1999), 147. For a sociological assessment of this aspect of basic training, see David P. Barash and Charles P. Webel, *Peace and Conflict Studies* (Thousand Oaks, CA: Sage, 2002), 139-40.

65. Bernstein, *Monsters and Angels*, 195. Sometimes women were driven to the bivouac site or excused from it because of bad weather.

66. William Abreu, quoted in Baldovi, *A Foxhole View*, 192.

67. See Wolfe, *Cold Ground's Been My Bed*, 56-59. Wolfe's unit was supposed to learn the .45 caliber pistol while camping, but the temperature was so cold that the pistol froze to the instructor's hand and he had to be rushed to an aid station.

68. William Abreu in Baldovi, *A Foxhole View*, 193.

69. "Draftee Duty Set," *New York Times*, 13 July 1950, 1. Army spokesmen admitted that some recruits might be sent over later but insisted the number would not be large, "nor will that happen soon."

70. "Army Denies Use of Green Troops," *New York Times*, 10 September, 1950, 6.

71. Men already in service could go overseas after one year in a noncombat job in the United States. Previously, lieutenants and captains got three years between overseas assignments. "Army Duty in U.S. Cut," *New York Times*, 20 November 1951, 20.

72. Wolfe, *Cold Ground's Been My Bed*, 59.

73. Only about 27% of Korean War–era Army troops received specialized training after basic training. This figure compares favorably with World War I and the post–Korean War period, when only 18% and 16.8% of troops, respectively, received such training, but it lags behind the 28.4% of World War II. "Report on Training," December 1955, Tab C, Bradley Commission: Records, 1954-58, A69-22 and 79-6, Box 58, DDE Library. Bernstein, *Monsters and Angels*, 199.

74. "Need of Training Revealed in Korea," *New York Times*, 3 November 1950, 4. After the war, Colonel F. W. Gibb agreed, asserting that forces in 1957 were better trained than those during the Korean War because "when you train a large number of people in a short length of time . . . you actually put more people through, but you do not give them the degree of training that we feel is required." Congress, House of Representatives, Subcommittee of the Committee on Appropriations, *Department of the Army Appropriations for 1957: Hearings*, 84th Congress, 2d sess., 1956, 494.

75. Marguerite Higgins, *War in Korea: The Report of a Woman Combat Correspondent* (Garden City, NY: Doubleday, 1951), 221.

76. "Army Going Back to Tough Training," *New York Times*, 15 August 1954, 45.

77. Lewis H. Carlson, *Remembered Prisoners of a Forgotten War: An Oral History of Korean War POWs* (New York: St. Martin's Press, 2000), 8, and General Upham in House of Representatives, *Department of the Army Appropriations for 1957: Hearings before the Subcommittee of the Committee on Appropriations*, 437.

78. "Army Going Back to Tough Training," *New York Times*, 15 August 1954, 45. In his memoirs, General Mark Clark argued that no matter how stringent military training might be, it could never completely erase lessons learned from civilian life. He remembered responding to a mother who asked him to make a man of her son that "his military service would help him, but that . . . we would have him for eighteen months and she had had him for eighteen years." Mark W. Clark, *From the Danube to the Yalu* (New York: Harper, 1954), 192-93. On the difficulty of transforming civilians into soldiers and the impact of civilian life on military training, see Toner, "American Society and the American Way of War," 79-90, and Bernstein, *Monsters and Angels*, 199.

79. Bernstein, *Monsters and Angels*, 199, and Wolfe, *Cold Ground's Been My Bed*, 50.

80. Kevin Cowherd, "One Came Home: Still Haunted by Missing Twin," *Baltimore Sun*, 22 March 1998, 3 (reprinted at United States of America Commemoration Site—www.Korea50.army.mil/media/interviews/ krepps/shtml).

81. Walter Ogasawara and Pedro Behasa in Baldovi, *A Foxhole View*, 28.

82. Merle Wysock, *Korean War Veteran Survey*, 4, CFSOKW.

83. Roy Appleman in Toner, "American Society and the American Way of War," 81. Also, T. R. Fehrenbach, *This Kind of War: A Study in Unpreparedness* (New York: Macmillan, 1963), 100.

84. Before 1948, the Army sent men to the branch in which they would serve for basic training. "New Soldiers for New Tasks," *New York Times*, 23 July 1950, 4. By 1949, the Army began a new training initiative to establish combat readiness, but the Korean War came before its completion. Some scholars argue, though, that this initiative got the Eighth Army in shape before Korea. Thomas E. Hanson, "The Eighth Army's Combat Readiness before Korea: A New Appraisal," *Armed Forces and Society* 29.2 (Winter 2003): 167-84.

85. When the Army reduced its basic training to eight weeks, it primarily dropped field training exercises, physical fitness programs, and lessons in marksmanship and weapons familiarization. Unfortunately, for men stationed in Japan, mundane duties and civilian relief efforts hindered participation in training before they went to Korea. Also, personnel turnover in Japan (about 50% annually) and special duty assignments prevented the conduction of meaningful larger unit exercises. Bowers, *The Line*, 7-8.

86. Addison Terry, *The Battle for Pusan: A Korean War Memoir* (Novato, CA: Presidio, 2000), 1. Sworn into the military on the basis of a graduate degree with no military training or active duty service since ROTC in 1948, Terry shipped to Japan immediately after swearing in. Also, Susumu Shinagawa in Baldovi, *A Foxhole View*, 4-5; "Waste in Training Laid to Army Units," *New York Times*, 26 December 1951, 1; and "New Soldiers for New Tasks," *New York Times*, 23 July 1950, 4.

87. David K. Holland in Donald M. Buchwald, ed., *Tales from the Cold War: The 13th Armored Infantry Battalion on Freedom's Frontier* (Victoria, Canada: Trafford Publishing, 2004), 116.

88. Quoted in Toner, "American Society and the American Way of War," 80.

89. Arthur L. Kelly, interview by Russell Harris, 16 December 1993, Kentuckiana Digital Library (http://kdl.dyvl.org), 9. Also Clarence Young in Baldovi, *A Foxhole View*, 8-9, on the physical state of soldiers.

90. Robert Fernandez in Baldovi, *A Foxhole View*, 181.

91. "Mortality and Combat Service," 2, Bradley Commission: Records 1954-58, A 69-72 and 79-6, Box 61, DDE Library. The deaths per one thousand men due to disease in the Korean War was only 1.0, the same as World War II, but far less than in the Spanish American War (29.5) and World War I (17.0).

92. Barash and Webel, *Peace and Conflict Studies*, 139, and Jordan, "Right for the Wrong Reasons," 137. S. L. A. Marshall claimed in his 1947 landmark study that 25% or less of American combat infantrymen fired their weapons in World War II. Marshall, *Men against Fire: The Problem of Battle Command* (Norman: University of Oklahoma Press, 2000). Marshall's work and methods became the subject of intense scrutiny and criticism, however. John Whiteclay Chambers II, "S. L. A. Marshall's *Men against Fire*: New Evidence Regarding Fire Ratios," *Parameters* (Autumn 2003): 113-21.

93. William A. Pickett, *Korean War Veteran Survey*, 5, CFSOKW; Robert Fernandez in Baldovi, *A Foxhole View*, 181; and "Waste in Training Laid to Army Units," *New York Times*, 26 December 1951, 1. The Army assigned returning combat soldiers from Korea to basic training camps and other schools for this very purpose. Korean War veterans provided valuable insight into the current war and helped alleviate the shortage of qualified trainers. "Report on Training," December 1955, 39, Bradley Commission: Records, 1954-58, A69-22 and 79-6, Box 58, DDE Library.

94. "4 Month Soldiers Stand under Fire," *New York Times*, 28 February 1952, 25.

95. "Waste in Training Laid to Army Units," *New York Times*, 26 December 1951, 1.

96. Marine Boots were called "Sand Fleas" because Parris Island sat atop a sandy flatland in South Carolina. Marines who went through Parris Island often note in their memoirs that while they were drilling, sand fleas would bite their legs. Gene Dixon, Memoir (KWE), 5-6; Donald Joseph Loraine, Memoir (KWE), 3-4; and Robert B. Campbell, Memoir (KWE), 2.

97. For descriptions of Parris Island, see Robert B. Campbell, Memoir (KWE), 2, and Daniel Da Cruz, *Boot* (New York: St. Martin's, 1987), 54.

98. Ralph Cutro, *Korean War Veteran Survey*, 5, CFSOKW. Also, Robert B. Campbell, Memoir (KWE), 2, and Donald Joseph Loraine, Memoir (KWE), 3.

99. Huston Wheelock in Dawn Scher Thomae, "Wisconsin Warriors: Interviews with Native American Veterans," *LORE* 43.3 (September 1993): 5.

100. Marine boot camp varied in length from eight to fourteen weeks for males. Shelburne and Groves, *Education in the Armed Forces*, 28. Women reservists and enlistees, however, attended abbreviated boot camps, lasting only six weeks. "Boy Friends Cheer Girls Off to War," *New York Times*, 16 September 1950, 5, and "Women Volunteers Asked," *New York Times*, 26 August 1950, 3.

101. Women's Marine Corps boot camp proved a bit easier, and few female veterans remember excessive physical training or corporal punishment. Rather, "I sometimes thought we were just like civil service members in uniform." Marie Kevensky, Interview by Hermann J. Trojanowski, 3 November 1999, WVHP, OHC, UNCG, 3.

102. Norman D. Weibel, *Korean War Veteran Survey*, 5, CFSOKW, and Robert B. Campbell, Memoir (KWE), 2-3.

103. Robert B. Campbell, Memoir (KWE), 3.

104. James H. Putnam, Memoir (KWE), 5.

105. Robert B. Campbell, Memoir (KWE), 3.

106. James H. Putnam, Memoir (KWE), 5.

107. Cadre had great latitude in disciplining trainees, but the Marine Corps punished overzealous trainers for the maltreatment of recruits. Veteran Glenn Potts remembers a drill instructor (D.I.) being convicted of charges stemming from his mistreatment of trainees. Glenn Potts to Melinda Pash, 5 July 2004, in author's possession.

108. James H. Putnam, Memoir (KWE), 4.

109. Ralph Cutro, email to Melinda Pash, 28 February 2006, in author's possession.

110. Leonard G. Sewell, *Korean War Veteran Survey*, 6, CFSOKW.

111. John "Jack" Orth, *Korean War Veteran Survey*, 5, CFSOKW.

112. Gene Dixon, Memoir (KWE), 5.

113. Colonel Frash in Congress, Senate, *Communist Interrogation, Indoctrination, and Exploitation of American Military and Civilian Prisoners: Hearings before the Permanent Subcommittee on Investigations of the Committee of Government Operations*, 84th Congress, 2d sess., June 1956, 182-83.

114. Norman D. Weibel, *Korean War Veteran Survey*, 5, CFSOKW. Also Ralph Cutro, *Korean War Veteran Survey*, 5, CFSOKW, and Colonel Frash in Congress, Senate, *Communist Interrogation, Indoctrination, and Exploitation of American Military and Civilian Prisoners*, 182-83. Explaining why fewer marines succumbed to communist "brainwashing" than Army soldiers, Frash extolled the cohesiveness achieved by the Corps: "[The Marine] is trained to rely on his fellow Marine. He is trained to rely on his non commissioned officers."

115. Harlee Lassiter, attachment to *Korean War Veteran Survey*, CFSOKW. Also, James H. Appleton, *Korean War Veteran Survey*, 5, CFSOKW, and Boyce Clark, Memoir (KWE), 4.

116. Combat veterans who completed boot camp in an earlier era had to have at least four weeks of refresher training. "Army Denies Use of Green Troops," *New York Times*, 10 September 1950, 6. The Marine Corps, like the Army, though, did not always follow its own rules and, especially early in the war, reserve troops shipped out to the war zone without the requisite training.

117. Lee Ballenger, *The Final Crucible: U.S. Marines in Korea*. Vol. 2, *1953* (Washington, DC: Brassey's, 2001), 6-11.

118. *Ibid.*, 7.

119. *Ibid.*

120. Brady, *The Coldest War*, 7.

121. Near Sonora Pass, Pickel Meadows proved an ideal training ground for the Korean War. Mountainous and isolated, Pickel Meadows remained frigid almost year round with snow blanketing the landscape. Daytime temperatures ranged from 10 to 48 degrees, but fell well below zero at night. Ballenger, *The Final Crucible*, 9.

122. *Ibid.*, 10-12.

123. Norman D. Weibel, *Korean War Veteran Survey*, 5, CFSOKW.

124. Once the Marine Corps set up the Staging Regiment, every Marine headed to Korea went through the Pickel Meadows exercise, even chaplains, doctors, officers, and corpsmen. Pilots went through a modified course where they were dropped out to live in the elements for a couple of days. Ballenger, *The Final Crucible*, 11.

125. Colonel William M. Frash in *Communist Interrogation, Indoctrination, and Exploitation of American Military and Civilian Prisoners*, 182-83. In fact, although in short supply in the war zone, all lieutenants, whether recruits or "mustangs" commissioned from the ranks, had to complete extensive training before deploying. Ballenger, *The Final Crucible*, 9.

126. Some scholars argue that the Marine Corps enjoyed greater success than the Army in Korea because men in command positions had been trained by combat, unlike Army officers, many of whom moved up the chain of command without any battlefield experience. Faris R. Kirkland, "Soldiers and Marines at Chosin Reservoir: Criteria for Assignment to Combat Command," *Armed Forces & Society* 22.2 (Winter 1995): 257-74.

127. "Report on Training," December 1955, 35, Bradley Commission: Records, 1954-58, A69-22 and 79-6, Box 58, DDE Library, and Shelburne and Groves, *Education in the Armed Forces*, 28.

128. Navy women learned standard military drill, but did so without rifles. Lt. Robert A. Rogers III, "These Boots Wear Skirts," *United States Naval Institute Proceedings* 75.9 (September 1949): 1025.

129. Early in the war, the Navy permanently cut boot camp from fourteen to eleven weeks. Heavy enlistments in December 1950 led to a temporary reduction to nine weeks. "Great Lakes 'Boot' Training Cut," *New York Times*, 7 January 1951, 64. Also, "Report on

Training," December 1955, 38, Bradley Commission: Records, 1954-58, A69-22 and 79-6, Box 58, DDE Library.

130. Tony Ybarra, Memoir (KWE), 3; Ralph David Fly, Memoir (KWE), 4; and Rogers, "These Boots Wear Skirts," 1025.

131. Glenn Schroeder, Memoir (KWE), 3.

132. *Ibid.*, and Ralph David Fly, Memoir (KWE), 5. In order to float, men took off their pants, tied knots in the end of each leg, and put the pants up over their shoulders in such a way that they filled with air.

133. Tony Ybarra, Memoir (KWE), 3.

134. "Report on Training," December 1955, 38, Bradley Commission: Records, 1954-58, A69-22 and 79-6, Box 58, DDE Library. The Air Force compressed basic or "Preflight" training for aviation cadets to four weeks to save time. Cadets, however, had to complete eighteen weeks of "Primary" training focused on navigation and instruments as well as on elementary flying time, eighteen weeks of "Basic," which despite the name consisted of advanced instruction in instruments and flying, and twelve weeks of "Advanced" training, where recruits specialized in a particular area. John Darrell Sherwood, *Officers in Flight Suits: The Story of American Air Force Fighter Pilots in the Korean War* (New York: New York University Press, 1996), 41-65, and Walton S. Moody and Warren A. Trest, "The Air Force as an Institution," in Bernard C. Nalty, ed., *Winged Shield, Winged Sword: A History of the United States Air Force.* Vol. 2, *1950-1997* (Washington, DC: Air Force History and Museums Program, 1997), 118.

135. Gertrude Samuels, "It's 'Hup, 2, 3, 4' and 'Yes Ma'am,'" *New York Times*, 3 September 1950, 88. Women found the Air Force particularly attractive. The Air Force guaranteed women they could enlist and stay together through basic training. "Armories Sought for Reserves' Use," *New York Times*, 4 December 1950, 20. WAFs could enter almost every aviation specialty. Deborah G. Douglas et al., *American Women and Flight since 1940* (Lexington: University Press of Kentucky, 2004), 134.

136. "Air Force to Cut Recruit Training," *New York Times*, 9 August 1955, 9, and "Air Drill Is Again Cut," *New York Times*, 7 May 1956, 6.

137. Glenn Schroeder, Memoir (KWE), 3.

138. Tony Ybarra, Memoir (KWE), 3.

139. Glen Schroeder, Memoir (KWE), 3. One veteran recalls that not all men completed Navy boot camp in their original companies. Some had difficulty with the rules and regulations while others had medical or dental problems or issues like bed wetting. These moved into the "Triple Zero Company," where they wore leggings or "boots" denoting their status. Email to Melinda Pash from Harry Matthews, 17 October 2006, in author's possession.

140. Rogers, "These Boots Wear Skirts," 1025, and Samuels, "It's 'Hup, 2, 3, 4' and 'Yes Ma'am,'" *New York Times*, 3 September 1950, 88.

141. Glen Schroeder, Memoir (KWE), 2.

142. "Air Officers Deny Hardships at Base," *New York Times*, 30 January 1951, 6, and "Training Program Collapse Is Blamed on Overcrowding Facilities at Lackland Base," *Daily Oklahoman*, 19 February 1951, 1. That the Air Force lacked adequate housing for recruits in the Korean War period is understandable given that the Corps more than doubled in size from 1950, when it had a strength of 411,000, to 1953, when it had 977,000 troops. Moody and Trest, "The Air Force as an Institution," in Nalty, ed., *Winged Shield, Winged Sword*, 110.

143. During World War II, military policy dictated silence on homosexuality as discussion might arouse curiosity. Also, throughout that war antigay regulations were enforced only haphazardly as a result of manpower shortages. Berube, *Coming Out under Fire*, 263, and Meyer, "Creating GI Jane," 592-93.

144. Loretta "Ret" Coller in Humphrey, *My Country, My Right to Serve*, 11-14. Similar tactics had been used earlier. See Meyers, *Creating GI Jane*, 173-75.

145. Allan Berube and John D'Emilio, "The Military and Lesbians during the McCarthy Years," *Signs* 9.4 (Summer 1984): 764-70.
146. Berube, *Coming Out under Fire*, 263-64.
147. Loretta "Ret" Coller in Humphrey, *My Country, My Right to Serve*, 14-17. Some women discharged for lesbianism contacted the American Civil Liberties Union for help, charging that the military denied them counsel and failed to advise them that they need not testify against themselves. The ACLU refused assistance on the basis that Army expulsion of homosexuals did not violate civil liberties. Berube and D'Emilio, "The Military and Lesbians during the McCarthy Years," 770-75.
148. Because of the sophisticated equipment used by the Navy and Air Force, specialized training beyond boot camp often proved indispensable for recruits. During the Korean War, 68.3% of Navy enlistees received specialized training of some sort. "Report on Training," December 1955, Tab C, Bradley Commission: Records, 1954-58, A69-22 and 79-6, Box 58, DDE Library. For some men, further training ensured release from the armed forces without draft liability. Until 1951, aviation washouts received immunity from the draft, so some men signed up as aviation cadets and then resigned after the first week. To fix the problem, the Air Force changed its policy so that all men who resigned after February 1951 had to serve four years wherever the Air Force put them. Sherwood, *Officers in Flight Suits*, 39-40.
149. Donnelly, *Under Army Orders*, 7. Also, Marshall Andrews, "'M-Day Force' Still Mainly on Paper," *Washington Post*, 30 July 1950, 3B.
150. Donnelley, "The Best Army That Can Be Put in the Field in the Circumstances," 815.
151. Donnelly, *Under Army Orders*, 17-18.
152. *Ibid.*, 19.
153. George W. Gatliff, Memoir (KWE), 2. Guardsmen were not required to attend basic training until the 1960s.
154. Donnelly,*Under Army Orders*, 18.
155. Relatives frequently served together in National Guard units. One veteran recalls that his unit had four sets of brothers and numerous cousins in it. Conrad Grimshaw, Memoir (KWE), 4.
156. Army Field Forces, "Report of Staff Visit to National Guard Units of Texas and Oklahoma," January 1950, 11, NA, Record Group 337, Box 26.
157. Marshall Andrews, "'M-Day Force' Still Mainly on Paper," *Washington Post*, 30 July 1950, 3B.
158. World War I veterans dominated the general officer ranks while World War II veterans made up the majority of field and company grade officers. World War II enlisted men also received a fair number of commissions in the postwar period. Donnelly, *Under Army Orders*, 13-15. In the Oklahoma 45th, 40% of officers commissioned after reactivation in 1946 had been wartime enlisted, 10% of the officers served with the T-Birds during World War II, and 20-21% of enlisted men were veterans of the Second World War. "45th Packed with Know-How," *Daily Oklahoman*, 8 August 1950, 3.
159. Frank Rowan, "History of the 161st Ordnance Depot Company and the 502nd Ordnance Depot Platoon 1948/1952," updated 9 October 2001, 1-5, included with *Korean War Veteran Survey*, CFSOKW," 1-5, and Arthur Smith, Memoir (KWE), 1.
160. Rowan, "History of the 161st Ordnance Depot Company and the 502nd Ordnance Platoon 1948/1952," 3-4.
161. Men in the Illinois 44th, a unit ranked low in Army evaluations, were surprised to be activated. Billy R. Smith, Memoir (KWE), 4-5. Also, Donnelly, *Under Army Orders*, 64.
162. Before the Korean War, National Guard units recruited heavily among high school boys, some as young as fifteen or sixteen years old. When it became clear that units were mobilizing for war, parents scrambled to get their kids out of the Guard and the Army discharged boys under age eighteen. George W. Gatliff, Memoir (KWE), 2-3, and Donnelly, *Under Army Orders*, 27.

163. In the Oklahoma 45th Division, only 60% of guardsmen activated for the Korean War had at least one summer camp and a year of armory training behind them. The rest presumably had far less. "45th Packed with Know-How," *Daily Oklahoman*, 8 August 1950, 3.

164. George W. Gatliff, Memoir (KWE), 3, and Frank Rowan, "History of the 161st Ordnance Depot Company and the 502nd Ordnance Depot Platoon 1948/1952," 10.

165. National Guard units conducted basic training until their overseas departures. As the Army took levies of individuals to be sent to Korea as replacements, units had to be replenished with reservists, enlistees, or draftees, most of whom needed to be given basic training. Some units lost and replaced as many as six thousand men in a year of training. "New Training Plan Is Set for Guard," *New York Times*, 11 October 1951, 27, and Donnelly, *Under Army Orders*, 22, 41, and 59-60. Additionally, the National Guard provided training for individual replacements. One division commander noted that it "was a sad day to see the draftees leave us for the Korean War, only after an inadequate fourteen weeks of military training with us." Quoted in Donnelly, *Under Army Orders*, 61.

166. Arthur L. Kelly, Interview by Russell Harris, 16 December 1993, 9-17 (Kentuckiana Digital Library at http://kdl.kyvl.org).

167. George Hubbard, Memoir (KWE), 3.

168. Forty-one nondivisional National Guard units served in Korea. Most arrived between January and March 1951, but a few shipped out only five months after the start of the war and others as late as 1952. Donnelly, *Under Army Orders*, 69.

169. "45th Will Keep Training, Grant Short Furloughs," *Daily Oklahoman*, 25 February 1951, 18A; "Untrained GI's to Stay," *New York Times*, 28 February 1951, 3; Frank Rowan, "History of the 161st Ordnance Depot Company and the 502nd Ordnance Depot Platoon 1948/1952," 10; and Donnelly, *Under Army Orders*, 61. Army rules also stipulated that men under the age of eighteen were to be weeded out of the unit before shipping overseas. The burden of proof of age, however, fell to the individual recruits, many of whom wanted to remain in service. Although ordered to write home for his birth certificate, sixteen-year-old Fred Rose Jr. managed to remain with his unit in Korea until he was killed by a sniper. George W. Gatliff, Memoir (KWE), 3.

170. "45th Will Keep Training, Grant Short Furloughs," *Daily Oklahoman*, 25 February 1951, 18A.

171. "Protests over 45th Assignment Cease," *Daily Oklahoman*, 4 March 1951, 1.

172. Joseph Popolo quoted in "2000 Guardsmen Back from Camp," *Philadelphia Inquirer*, 23 July 1950, 1.

173. William T. Craig, *Lifer! From Infantry to Special Forces* (New York: Ivy Books, 1994), 33, and Donnelly, *Under Army Orders*, 71.

174. Arthur R. May, Interview by Shawn Illingworth and Kevin Bing, 27 April 2004, 8-9, Rutgers Oral History Archives, Rutgers University, New Brunswick, NJ, available at http://oralhistory.rutgers.edu/Interviews/may_arthur.html. Regulars had good cause for their assumptions. When taking levies and shipping men from Guard units to the war zone, the Army did not always try to find a good match. Frank Rowan remembers that men from his outfit, an ordnance supply company, were attached to infantry companies in Korea although they had had little training in infantry tactics. Frank Rowan, "History of the 161st Ordnance Depot Company and the 502nd Ordnance Depot Platoon 1948/1952," 10.

175. A 1957 Gallup Poll showed that 65% of Americans favored requiring National Guardsmen to take six months of basic training in the regular Army before entering the Guard. Among Americans who knew that the Guard operated independently of the regular military, 48% thought it should be placed under the direct control of the Army. George Gallup Jr., *The Gallup Poll: Public Opinion, 1935-1971*(New York: Random House, 1972), 1471-72.

176. Marshall Andrews, "'M-Day Force' Still Mainly on Paper," *Washington Post*, 30 July 1950, 3B.

177. Active reserves met regularly while the inactive reserves rarely drilled or met before activation. Ironically, the inactive reserves were first in line for Korea because military planners feared a larger war with Russia and wanted to save better-trained active reserves for that possibility.

178. "136 Seamen Reserves End 2-Month Course," *New York Times*, 20 August 1950, 54, and "Shake Down Cruise," 1-2, as told to Milinda Jensen by Daniel A. Gallucci for the United States of America Commemoration Site (www.korea50.army.mil/media/interviews/gallucci.shtml). At least after the Korean War began, the Women Marine Corps Reserves also received basic training. See "Boy Friends Cheer Girls Off to War," *New York Times*, 16 September 1950, 5.

179. Letter from thirty-two enlisted reserve personnel in Korea, quoted by Congressman Williams in *Congressional Record,* 82d Congress, 1st sess., 97:4, 5285.

180. Randy K. Mills, "Unexpected Journey: Evansville's Marine Corps Reserve and the Korean War," *Traces of Indiana and Midwestern History* 12.3 (Summer 2000): 6-9. Summer camp attendance for Evansville's Marine Corps Reserve fell from just 54% in 1948 to an even lower 47% in 1949.

181. This only applied to recruits who did not owe the military some sort of service at the end of an enlistment.

182. Many of the veterans sent to Korea had not fired a weapon since World War II but were sent overseas within weeks of being called up. W. D. McGlasson, "Manpower for the Korean War," *VFW,* June/July 1990, 23, Article 0057, CFSOKW, 25.

183. To varying degrees, high school students were taken out of groups headed overseas. In Washington State, the newspaper reported that seventeen- and eighteen-year olds still in high school would be put into the inactive reserves at home while eighteen-year-old graduates would go with their squadrons to the war. "Uniformed Teen-Agers Told of War's Outlook," *Seattle Post-Intelligencer*, 18 August 1950, 19.

184. Especially for reservists activated early in the war, the turnaround time from orders to sailing was very short. The first man from the Evansville Marine Corps Reserve unit died just thirty-four days after leaving Camp Pendleton, where he had received two weeks of training. Mills, "Unexpected Journey," 12. Clyde Queen, who enlisted in the Marine Corps Reserves in July 1950, had only a couple of weeks of training under his belt when he landed at Inchon. Clyde H. Queen Sr., "Straight to Hell," as told to Milinda D. Jensen, 50th Anniversary Korean War Commemoration Committee (www.korea50.army.mil/media/interviews/ queen.shtml). Harry Van Zandt, a World War II veteran, received a two-week refresher course before flying to the Korean front. Harry Van Zandt, Interview by Tara Liston and Tara Kraenzlin, 11 March 1996, 27, Transcript by Donovan Bezer, Andrew Noyes, Shaun Illingworth, Harry Van Zandt, and Sandra Stewart Holyoak, Rutgers Oral History Archives for World War II, Rutgers University, New Brunswick, New Jersey, available at http://oralhistory.rutgers.edu/Interviews/van_zandt_harry.html. In 1955, General Shepherd admitted that during the Korean War the reserves were mobilized rapidly and "many men were in Korea within 6 weeks or 2 months after they were called to active duty." Quoted in U.S. Senate, *National Reserve Plan [No. 11]: Hearings before Subcommittee No. 1 of the Committee on Armed Services*, 84th Congress, 1st sess., February–March 1955, 1327.

185. In early 1950, the Army said all reservists with less than a year of Army service would be sent to training centers and that all reservists would get at least a three-week refresher course. "Army Denies Use of Green Troops," *New York Times*, 10 September 1950, 6.

186. Quoted in Mills, "Unexpected Journey," 12.

187. A. Pat Burris, email to Melinda Pash, 20 July 2005, in author's possession.

188. In addition to Air Force reservists, regular pilots ended up assigned to planes with which they had little experience as a result of the incomplete shift from propeller to jet aircraft. "Boots" Blesse, a jet pilot before the war, had one evening in country to qualify on a

propeller plane for a mission the next morning. Robinson Risner flew only seven and a half hours in the F-86 before being deemed "combat ready." Jennie Ethell Chancey and William R. Forstchen, eds., *Hot Shots: An Oral History of the Air Force Combat Pilots of the Korean War* (New York: HarperCollins, 2000), 39-41 and 158. Jim Kasler qualified in Korea to fly after only three flights in his plane. Perry D. Luckett and Charles L. Byler, *Tempered Steel: Three Wars of Triple Air Force Cross Winner Jim Kasler* (Dulles, VA: Potomac Books, 2005), 25-29.

189. Robert Smith in Henry Berry, *Hey, Mac, Where Ya Been? Living Memories of the U.S. Marines in the Korean War* (New York: St. Martin's Press, 1988), 152. Also J. Patrick Morrison, letter to Melinda Pash, 31 October 2004, in author's possession.

190. Martin Chamberlain, quoted in "Marine Corps, Navy Reserve Practice," *Seattle Post-Intelligencer*, 18 August 1950, 9A.

191. By 1952, 80% of Air Force pilots were reservists. Donald S. Luther, "The 1952 Strike against Combat Training," *Peace and Change* 12.1-2 (1987): 96 and 101.

192. *Ibid.*, 98-100.

193. "Standard Policies on Reserves Asked," *New York Times*, 3 July 1951, 4.

194. "Rougher Training Planned by Army," *New York Times*, 21 August 1950, 11.

195. "GI's in Korea Handicapped by Unawareness of Mission," *New York Times*, 13 August 1950, 1. Years later one veteran asserted that "I had absolutely no understanding of it [the war] at all. Zero." John Edward Nolan, interview by J. Cantwell, 29 December 1999, online at American Century Project, St. Andrews Episcopal School Library Archive (www.doingoralhistory.org), 4.

196. In Korea, Matthew Ridgway found the question "What the hell are we doing in this godforsaken place?" much on the minds of his men. Fehrenbach, *This Kind of War*, 300.

197. On American soldiers as a reflection of their society, see Toner, "American Society and the American Way of War."

198. Baron von Steuben in J. Lawton Collins, *War in Peacetime: The History and Lessons of Korea* (Boston: Houghton Mifflin, 1969), 394.

199. On the American soldier's need for a cause, see Robert H. Leckie, *Conflict: The History of the Korean War, 1950-1953* (New York: Putnam's, 1962), 89, and "GI's in Korea Handicapped by Unawareness of Mission," *New York Times*, 13 August 1950, 1.

200. "Armed Forces Get Citizenship Course," *New York Times*, 24 April 1951, 19.

201. In one instance, a nineteen-year-old National Guardsman who had previously been an undertaker's assistant was given the job of lecturing on foreign policy. Benjamin Fine, "'Information' Hour in Army Gives None," *New York Times*, 15 May 1951, 25. Also, Benjamin Fine, "Military Teaching on 'Why' Men Serve Termed a Failure," *New York Times*, 14 May 1951, 1.

202. After the war the military faced criticism for not adequately indoctrinating troops in why they were fighting, and Americans blamed the perceived high incidence of POW collusion in part on this. As a result, the *Code of Conduct for Members of the United States Armed Forces* was developed and the military was charged with presenting it in such a way that servicemen would take it to heart. United States Secretary of Defense's Advisory Committee on Prisoners of War, *POW: The Fight Continues after the Battle*, August 1955, 7 and 31-32, Bradley Commission: Records 1955-58, A 69-22, Box 82, DDE Library. Also, U.S. Senate, Committee on Armed Services, *Military Cold War Education and Speech Review Policies*, report prepared by the Special Preparedness Subcommittee, 87th Congress, 2d sess. (Washington, DC: U.S. Government Printing Office, 1962).

203. Family allowances originated during World War I but were not widely used until World War II. "Selection Process," xiv, Bradley Commission: Records, 1954-58, A69-22 and 79-6, Box 58, DDE Library, and "Military Training for Youth Studied," *New York Times*, 11 August 1950, 8.

204. Under the *Soldiers' and Sailors' Relief Act*, mortgage payments could be waived until a man was discharged and creditors were supposed to get court orders before

repossessing homes. Also, landlords could not legally evict servicemen's dependents from dwellings costing less than eighty dollars a month. The law was often ignored and dependents knew nothing of their rights. "GI Legal Aid Need Stressed," *Seattle Post-Intelligencer*, 23 August 1950, 5A, and "Act Protects Homes of GI's," *Seattle Post-Intelligencer*, 14 August 1950, 15.

205. Luckett and Byler, *Tempered Steel*, 25-26.

206. "D.A.V. Protests GI Kin Treatment," *Seattle Post-Intelligencer*, 12 August 1950, 1 and 4.

207. "Congress Action in Stopping Funds for Dependents Wrecks Homes," *Seattle Post-Intelligencer*, 11 August 1950, 1A, and "Reserve Answering Call Loses Home," *Seattle Post-Intelligencer*, 10 August 1950, 3.

208. "State Coming to Aid of GI Dependents," *Seattle Post-Intelligencer*, 18 August 1950, 1.

209. "Truman Asks Funds for GI Families," *Seattle Post-Intelligencer*, 16 August 1950, 1. Truman's plan called for families to receive up to $150 a month, part of which would come from the serviceman's paycheck and part of which would be paid by the government.

210. For coverage of different proposals for allotments, see "Military Training for Youth Studied," *New York Times*, 11 August 1950, 8; "House Votes $85 to $125 Monthly Allowances for GI's, Families," *Seattle Post-Intelligencer*, 25 August 1950, 4; and "Congress Units O.K. Payments for Enlisted Men's Families," *Seattle Post-Intelligencer*, 18 August 1950, 4.

211. "3 Percent Raise for Servicemen Passes Senate," *Daily Oklahoman*, 1 April 1952, 12.

212. Men had to provide documentation that they contributed to their parents' support, but wives, regardless of whether or not they had jobs of their own, automatically qualified for support. Restrictions prohibiting mothers of minor children from entering or remaining in service meant that servicewomen had no young dependents to support in the Korean War years.

213. Betsy B. McKenny, "Frontiero v. Richardson: Characterization of Sex-Based Classifications," *Columbia Human Rights Law Review* 6.1 (Spring 1974): 239-47.

214. Terry, *The Battle for Pusan*, 1.

215. Hank Litvin, email to Melinda Pash, 17 June 2004, in author's possession.

216. "2348 Medical Men Register in Draft," *New York Times*, 17 October 1950, 14.

217. Otto F. Apel and Pat Apel, *M*A*S*H: An Army Surgeon in Korea* (Lexington: University Press of Kentucky, 1998), 98.

218. Dr. Hermes Grillo, Interview by G. Kurt Piehler and Crystal Dover, 8 July 2002, 25-34, Veterans' Oral History Project, Center for the Study of War and Society, University of Tennessee, Knoxville, TN.

219. Rotation wreaked havoc on nonmedical units as well. Just as seasoned men reached a point where they could benefit from their experience, they rotated out of the war zone, replaced by men without their skills or expertise. Donnelley, "The Best Army That Can Be Put in the Field in the Circumstances," 823.

220. Richard F. Haynes, *The Awesome Power: Harry S. Truman as Commander in Chief* (Baton Rouge: Louisiana State University Press, 1973), 91.

221. *Ibid.*, 90-92, and Morris J. MacGregor Jr., *Integration of the Armed Forces, 1940-1965* (Washington, DC: Center of Military History, U.S. Army, 1981), 461.

222. Haynes, *The Awesome Power*, 91. By February 1950, 71% of African Americans in the Air Force belonged to mixed units. Dennis Cushman, *African-Americans and the Quest for Civil Rights, 1900-1990* (New York: New York University Press, 1991), 101, and E. W. Kenworthy to Eric Severeid, 24 February 1950, Box "Desegregation of the Armed Forces, Box 1," CFSOKW.

223. The Fahy Committee elicited concessions, but stateside integration increased because of the need to train large numbers of men for Korea. Segregation posed administrative challenges that in wartime became dangerously burdensome and inefficient. In 1950 the Navy integrated everything from basic training to messes and sleeping quarters. Sean Cushman, *African-Americans and the Quest for Civil Rights*, 101. In January 1950, the Army abolished

racial quotas, and by August local commanders independently and haphazardly began integrating training. Dalfiume, *Desegregation of the Armed Forces*, 201-3, and Major Steve G. Davis, Human Relations and Research Branch, Military Personnel Management Division, G-1, Memo, "Integration of Negro Personnel," 1-2, NA, Record Group 319, Box 7. The Marine Corps began assigning men according to their specialty in 1949 and eliminated segregation in basic training in 1950, but continued to maintain separate black units in the field. MacGregor, *Integration of the Armed Forces*, 461, and Haynes, *The Awesome Power*, 92. Unlike the regular services, the National Guard delayed integration longer and in 1950 had few black members, most belonging to segregated units. Donnelly, *Under Army Orders*, 12.

224. Leo Bogart, ed., *Project Clear: Social Research and the Desegregation of the United States Army* (New Brunswick, NJ: Transaction Publishers, 1992), 39.

225. W. Thompson, Memo to Mr. Nash, "The Confidential Report of the Survey of Troop Attitude toward Integration," 20 March 1950, 12, "Desegregation of the Armed Forces, Box 2 of 2," Box 20, CFSOKW.

226. Eighteen-year-old recruit quoted in *ibid.*, 11. Also, Bogart, *Project Clear*, 181.

227. See Bogart, *Project Clear*, 98-99.

228. Bernard Nalty, *Strength for the Fight: A History of Black Americans in the Military* (New York: Free Press, 1986), 271.

229. See Bogart, *Project Clear*, 95-96 and 180.

230. *Ibid.*, 182.

231. *Ibid.*, 181.

232. *Ibid.*

233. Charles C. Moskos Jr., "Has the Army Killed Jim Crow?" *Negro History Bulletin* 21 (November 1957): 28.

234. Bogart, *Project Clear,* 226.

235. Quoted in "Letter from a Neophyte Infantryman of the 5th Division," GI Interviews, NA, 319, Box 011.

236. Studies commissioned by the military in the 1940s and 1950s back up this assertion. A May–June 1945 survey found that before serving alongside blacks, 64% of white officers and noncommissioned officers expressed skepticism about working with African Americans. Seventy-seven percent of those, however, became more favorable after actually working with blacks. Army Service Forces, Information and Education Division, "Opinions about Negro Infantry Platoons in White Companies of 7 Divisions," 3 July 1945, 2, "Desegregation of the Armed Forces," Box 1, CFSOKW. *Project Clear* found that mixed training made men more favorable toward integration later. Of whites in all-white units who had prior exposure, 38% favored integration versus 32% of men without mixed training experience. Of whites in integrated units who had prior mixed training, 44% supported integration versus 37% of those who had not gone through mixed training. Bogart, *Project Clear*, 92. Other factors such as educational level, premilitary exposure to other races, and combat experience also influenced whether or not one supported integration.

237. Private J. B. Black quoted in "GI Integration Answers Governor Jimmy Byrnes," *Pittsburgh Courier*, 27 March, 1954, 17.

238. Nalty, *Strength for the Fight*, 267.

239. S. Thorne Harper, "All-Black Ranger Unit Recalls Fighting for America during Segregation," *Ledger-Enquirer* (Columbus, GA), 28 July 2002, A1.

240. Williams, a reserve officer returned to duty for the Korean War, was expelled from the Air Force after this incident. The NAACP charged the Air Force with continuing to reprimand African Americans who failed to bow to southern customs despite Supreme Court rulings such as that against segregation in interstate travel. "Press Release for Monday Morning, November 23, 1953, NAACP," NA, Record Group 319, Box 8.

241. The rioters were paratroopers from Fort Benning, and newspaper accounts suggest that their training had prepared them to deal fearlessly with any situation. "Brutalities Reported in Columbus, GA," *Pittsburgh Courier*, 12 May 1951, 1.

242. Collins S. George, "Jim Crow Is Still King at Fort Bragg," *Pittsburgh Courier*, 12 May 1951, 1. Fort Dix and Fort Leonard Wood also proved slow to embrace integration. Robert C. Doty, "Moon Still Bright as Rookies Arise," *New York Times*, 1 September 1950, 6, and Bill Smith, "Black Soldiers Fully Shared Korean War's Bloody Cost," *St. Louis Post-Dispatch*, 20 February 2002, A1. In March 1951, white and black troops engaged in a fight at Camp Rucker, Alabama. "Army Won't Punish GIs in Ala. Riot," *Pittsburgh Courier*, 24 March 1951, 3. Despite problems, successes in integration existed. By October 1951, Fort Bragg boasted the South's first integrated elementary schools. "Army Runs Unsegregated School at Ft. Bragg, N.C.," *Pittsburgh Courier*, 27 October 1951, 20.

243. Bogart, *Project Clear*, 167.

244. "Convict Non-Coms for Abuse of GI," *Pittsburgh Courier*, 6 March 1954, 5, and "Army OKs Uniforms of 'Rebels,'" *Pittsburgh Courier*, 10 May 1952, 5.

245. Stanley Stone to his mother, 7 December 1950, NA, Record Group 319, Box 7.

246. Bogart, *Project Clear*, 240-48.

247. *Ibid.*, 227.

248. Moskos, "Has the Army Killed Jim Crow?" 28.

249. Quoted in Kimberley L. Phillips, "All I Ever Wanted Was a Steady Job," in John Russo and Sherry Lee Linkon, eds., *New Working-Class Studies* (New York: Cornell University Press, 2005), 48. Also see "Race GIs Taking Advantage of Armed Forces Training," *Pittsburgh Courier*, 5 January 1952, 12.

250. Curtis James Morrow, *What's a Commie Ever Done to Black People? A Korean War Memoir of Fighting in the U.S. Army's Last All-Negro Unit* (Jefferson, NC: McFarland, 1977), 4.

251. In an interesting 1955 case, white draftee James Staebler won a general discharge under honorable conditions. Staebler, sent as part of a May 1953 initiative to integrate an all-black laundry company, protested Army efforts to resegregate the 200-member group, saying that integration worked. In response, the Army declared Staebler a threat and gave him an "undesirable security risk discharge." Peter Kihss, "Discharge Ruling Changed by Army," *New York Times*, 25 September 1955, 19.

252. Gilbert M. Branche, Interview by Melinda Pash, 3 March 2005.

253. A white southern politician in 1951 quoted in Peter Karsten, *Soldiers and Society: The Effects of Military Service and War on American Life* (Westport, CT: Greenwood Press, 1978), 96-97.

254. William A. Fowlkes, "Brutalities Reported in Columbus, GA," *Pittsburgh Courier*, 12 May 1951, 1.

255. "GI Victim of Dixie Mob Rule," *Pittsburgh Courier*, 27 January 1951, 1.

256. GIs usually received a two-week "delay en route" before having to arrive at a new duty station.

257. "Most of 45th to Get Leave before Sailing," *Daily Oklahoman*, 27 February 1951, 1.

258. Men leaving from Schofield Barracks remember that time was so short that dentists simply pulled teeth instead of filling cavities. See Irwin Cockett in Baldovi, *Foxhole View*, 8.

259. As in World War II, the Korean War hurried nuptials. Feeling that their time was short, couples quickly tied the knot before men shipped overseas. Jessica Weiss, *To Have and to Hold: Marriage, the Baby Boom, and Social Change* (Chicago: University of Chicago Press, 2000), 22. For a personal account, see Martin Pestana in Baldovi, *A Foxhole View*, 10.

260. The Marine Corps used "cattle cars"—semitrailers with wooden benches along each side and down the middle that held about forty-five men with packs and rifles—to transport men from the Staging Regiment at Camp Pendleton to the Navy Pier in San Diego. Ballenger, *The Final Crucible*, 12.

261. Merle Wysock, email to Melinda Pash, 29 December 2008, in author's collection.

262. Wolfe, *Cold Ground's Been My Bed*, 73.
263. Many personal accounts give great detail about life aboard the troop ship. Bernstein, *Monsters and Angels*, 217-49; Ballenger, *The Final Crucible*, 12-14; and George Tsegletos, *As I Recall: A Marine's Personal Story* (Bloomington, IN: 1st Books, 2003), 2-3.
264. Harold L. Mulhausen and James Edwin Alexander, *Korea: Memories of a U.S. Marine* (Oklahoma City, OK: Macedon, 1995), 14.

CHAPTER 4

1. Seymour Bernstein, *Monsters and Angels: Surviving a Career in Music* (Milwaukee, WI: Hal Leonard, 2002), 265-67; Mattie Donnell Hicks, Interview by Hermann J. Trojanowski, 25 February 1999, WVHP, OHC, UNCG, 5; Raymond Sturgeon in John Darrell Sherwood, *Officers in Flight Suits: The Story of American Air Force Fighter Pilots in the Korean War* (New York: New York University Press, 1996), 118-20; and Aubrey Loving, Interview by Natalie Shocklee, in Virginia Havard, ed., *By Word of Mouth* (Lufkin, TX: Lufkin High School, Kwik Kopy Printing, 1990), 20-21.
2. Richard J. H. Johnston, "GI's in Korea Handicapped by Unawareness of Mission," *New York Times*, 13 August 1950, 1, and Frank Bifulk in Joseph R. Owen, *Colder Than Hell: A Marine Rifle Company at Chosin Reservoir* (Annapolis, MD: Naval Institute Press, 1996), 175.
3. Private First Class Peter Santella in Henry Berry, *Hey, Mac, Where Ya Been? Living Memories of the U.S. Marines in the Korean War* (New York: St. Martin's Press, 1988), 220.
4. Quoted in Johnston, "GI's in Korea Handicapped by Unawareness of Mission," *New York Times*, 13 August 1950, 1.
5. The statistics vary somewhat in different sources. Tom Heuertz, "The Korean War + 50: No Longer Forgotten, Teaching Resources," Box FF "A.0957-A.0986," Folder A.0974 (CFSOKW), and "Section XI: Mortality and Combat Service," "Section 11," 1, Bradley Commission: Records, 1954-58, A 69-22 and 79-6, Box 61, DDE Library.
6. James L. Stokesbury, *A Short History of the Korean War* (New York: Morrow, 1988), 21-24; Walter LaFeber, "Truman and Foreign Policy: The Korean War," in Robert D. Marcus and David Burner, eds., *America since 1945*, 2d ed. (New York: St. Martin's Press, 1977), 39; T. R. Fehrenbach, *This Kind of War: A Study in Unpreparedness* (New York: Macmillan, 1963), 10-11; and Captain Janice Albert, "Air Evacuation from Korea: A Typical Flight," *The Military Surgeon* 112.4 (April 1953): 256.
7. Rhee employed fraud and repression to remain in power, but his government remained friendly to the United States.
8. For more detail, see Fehrenbach, *This Kind of War*, 18-33; Stokesbury, *A Short History of the Korean War*, 24-31; Jerald A. Combs, *The History of American Foreign Policy* (New York: Knopf, 1986), 340-45; and Max Hastings, *The Korean War* (New York: Simon & Schuster, 1987), 23-45.
9. See Fehrenbach, *This Kind of War*, 42-49; Walter J. Boyne, *Beyond the Wild Blue: A History of the United States Air Force, 1947-1997* (New York: St. Martin's Press, 1997), 56-57; Stokesbury, *A Short History of the Korean War*, 33-49; and Hastings, *The Korean War*, 46-53.
10. Contemporaries blamed Acheson for the Korean War and some called for his resignation. Remarks and press release by Senator Malone in *Congressional Record, Appendix*, 81st Congress, 2d sess., September 1950–January 1951, vol. 96:18, A7207. Many scholars similarly argue that the omission of Korea from plans for an Asian defense perimeter emboldened Kim Il Sung and convinced the Russians and Chinese that Americans would not interfere there. For one version of this reasoning, see David Halberstam, *The Coldest Winter* (New York: Hyperion, 2007), 48.
11. Marcus, *America since 1945*, 40.
12. *Ibid.*, 42.
13. Harry Truman in a copy of a press address to be given 1 September 1950, Box "(43) Korean War: North Korea's Invasion of South Korea," CFSOKW.

14. Corporal Harrison Lee in Louis Baldovi, ed., *A Foxhole View: Personal Accounts of Hawaii's Korean War Veterans* (Honolulu: University of Hawai'i Press, 2002), 3.
15. Albert J. Glass, "Psychiatry in the Korean Campaign," *U.S. Armed Forces Medical Journal* 4.10 (October 1953): 1388.
16. Quoted in Baldovi, *A Foxhole View,* 36.
17. The 29th planned to conduct six weeks of training in Japan before shipping to Pusan but instead went directly to Korea, where they immediately entered battle. Thus thrust into the war, these battalions had no time to clean their machine guns (which were still packed in Cosmoline) or test-fire any weapons. William T. Bowers, ed., *The Line: Combat in Korea, January–February 1951* (Lexington: University Press of Kentucky, 2008), 22.
18. See Arsanio Vendiola and Private First Class Pete Behasa in Baldovi, *A Foxhole View,* 35 and 38; Nick Tosques quoted in Rudy Tomedi, *No Bugles, No Drums: An Oral History of the Korean War* (New York: Wiley, 1993), 220; and Addison Terry, *The Battle for Pusan: A Korean War Memoir* (Novato, CA: Presidio, 2000), 1.
19. Bowers, *The Line,* 23.
20. Colonel John "Mike" Michaelis in Hastings, *The Korean War,* 96.
21. See Corporal Irwin Crockett in Baldovi, *A Foxhole View,* 88-89.
22. Halberstam, *The Coldest Winter,* 369.
23. The Joint Chiefs of Staff and President Truman cautioned MacArthur to take a step-by-step approach and to keep American troops away from any province bordering China, but, "they did not effectively rein him in." Stokesbury, *A Short History of the Korean War,* 81-83. Also, Halberstam, *The Coldest Winter,* 11-12; Hastings, *The Korean War,* 20-28; Bowers, *The Line,* 29; and Lisle Rose, *The Cold War Comes to Main Street: America in 1950* (Lawrence: University Press of Kansas, 1999), 258.
24. Chinese Foreign Minister Chou En-lai to Indian ambassador Sardar K. M. Panikkar on 3 October 1950, quoted in Fehrenbach, *This Kind of War,* 187. China conveyed that it would intervene in the war if troops other than those of the Republic of Korea pushed above the 38th Parallel. MacArthur, still thinking of China as a backward feudal society, underestimated the threat. David Halberstam, *The Fifties* (New York: Villard Books, 1993), 86.
25. Fehrenbach, *This Kind of War,* 193. The Chinese had far greater numbers in North Korea than the United Nations. The Marines who had to fight their way out of Chosin Reservoir numbered about 15,000 but were surrounded by 120,000 Chinese volunteers. Michael Kernan, "Chosin Survivors and the 78-Mile Nightmare," *Washington Post,* 1 December 1984, Vertical Files, "Chosen," CFSOKW.
26. Early encounters with Chinese troops did not always indicate to Americans that the Chinese had entered the war or what their participation meant. Sherman Pratt recounts how his patrol made contact with a Chinese unit near the Yalu River and both groups simply waved at each other. Later, a second patrol got fired on by the Chinese, but when a third patrol went to recover wounded Americans, they found that the Chinese had bandaged them, covered them in warm blankets, and put them on litters for the Americans to pick up. Pratt in Tomedi, *No Bugles, No Drums,* 63-64.
27. Corporal Bertram Sebresos and Private First Class Nick Nishimoto in Baldovi, *A Foxhole View,* 98. In addition to winter uniforms, infantrymen lacked sleeping bags and supplies. Certain the war was won, the upper echelons deemed further shipments of goods to the war zone unnecessary. MacArthur, acting on a request from General Walton Walker, diverted Korea-bound shipments of ammunition to Japan and Hawaii. Halberstam, *The Coldest Winter,* 16-21.
28. Captain Norman Allen in a letter to his mother, 24 January 1951, in Donald Knox, with additional text by Alfred Coppel, *The Korean War: An Oral History.* Vol. 2, *Uncertain Victory* (New York: Harcourt, Brace, Jovanovich, 1988), 23.

29. Corporal Robert Fountain, with Task Force Smith at the beginning of the war, realized in the winter of 1950-1951 that he was taking shelter in the same building he had been in at the start of the war in July. Hastings, *The Korean War,* 176-77.

30. Some concluded, "Never have American men fought in a more useless war." Letter to the editor of the Ft. Wayne *News Sentinel* from Lt. Gale O. Buuck in *Congressional Record, Appendix,* 82nd Congress, 1st sess., January 1951–October 1951, vol. 97, A1834.

31. Andy Barr in Tomedi, *No Bugles, No Drums,* 77.

32. Description of the line by a replacement in Lee Ballenger, *The Final Crucible: U.S. Marines in Korea.* Vol. 2, *1953* (Washington, DC: Brassey's, 2001), 34.

33. John A. Sullivan, *Toy Soldiers: Memoir of a Combat Platoon Leader in Korea* (Jefferson, NC: McFarland, 1991), 19.

34. Ballenger, *The Final Crucible,* 205-6.

35. Bute Findley to Robert A. Taft, 8 December 1951, Taft Papers, Box 1061, LOC.

36. Stokesbury, *A Short History of the Korean War,* 129-59.

37. William M. Donnelley, "A Damn Hard Job: James A. Van Fleet and the Combat Effectiveness of the Eighth Army, July 1951–February 1953," paper presented at the Society for Military History Conference, "Warfare and Culture," Murfreesboro, Tennessee, 2-5 April 2009.

38. Sullivan, *Toy Soldiers,* 17-18. See also Lt. General Sidney Berry, Oral History by Dr. Orley Caudill, 1980, volume 198, Mississippi Oral History Program, University of Southern Mississippi, Hattiesburg, Mississippi (MOHP), 36.

39. General James A. Van Fleet wanted to take a more aggressive approach in Korea but was restrained by President Truman's decision to abandon the idea of conquering North Korea and to emphasize the peace talks. General Ridgway reminded Van Fleet that his primary mission was to inflict as many casualties on the enemy as possible with as few losses of his own as possible. In a letter to Van Fleet Ridgway wrote that gaining ground in the war "in itself is of little or no value." Quoted in Donnelley, "A Damn Hard Job." Also see Ballenger, *The Final Crucible,* 262.

40. By October 1952 ammunition was in short supply as domestic manufacturers reduced their production in the belief that the war was almost at an end. In 1953, the Marine Corps ordered marines to "pick up your brass," meaning that after a battle they would comb the field for spent cartridges to be sent back by tank to be recycled. Ballenger, *The Final Crucible,* 45-47. Also see Fehrenbach, *This Kind of War,* 439.

41. Sergeant William Janzen in Ballenger, *The Final Crucible,* 48. For similar sentiment, see Boris R. Spiroff, *Korea: The Frozen Hell on Earth; A Platoon Sergeant's Diary, Korean War, 1950-1951* (Baltimore, MD: American Literary Press, 1998), 36.

42. From an extract from a letter sent home from a GI in Korea, quoted in U.S. Senate, *Congressional Record,* 82nd Congress, 2nd sess., 8 January 1952-25 February 1952, vol. 98, part 1, 979.

43. Quoted in William C. Barnard, "Jet Pilots Joke about Exploits, but Yalu Border Angers Them," reproduced in U.S. House, *Congressional Record,* 82nd Congress, 1st sess., 26 April 1951-24 May 1951, vol. 97, part 4, 5284.

44. U.S. House, *Congressional Record,* 82nd Congress, 1st sess., 26 April–24 May 1951, vol. 97, part 4, 5284-5286.

45. Arthur L. Kelly, Interview by Russell Harris, 16 December 1993, 54 (Kentuckiana Digital Library at http://kdl.kyvl.org). Also, Sullivan, *Toy Soldiers,* 19.

46. Fehrenbach, *This Kind of War,* 447-48, and Stokesbury, *A Short History of the Korean War,* 249-51.

47. Dwight D. Eisenhower, "Radio and Television Address to the American People Announcing the Signing of the Korean Armistice," *Public Papers of the Presidents of the United States, Dwight D. Eisenhower: Containing the Public Messages, Speeches, and Statements of the President, 1953* (Washington, DC: U.S. Government Printing Office, 1960), 520.

48. For the chronology of events, see Hastings, *The Korean War,* 345-50.

49. The first naval activity in country began the day after Truman's order when the USS *Juneau* fired on positions near Samchok on June 28, 1950. Paul M. Edwards, *To Acknowledge a War: The Korean War in American Memory* (Westport, CT: Greenwood Press, 2000), 110.

50. The Navy, Air Force, and Marine Corps all supplied airmen for the Korean War. Tomedi, *No Bugles, No Drums,* 161.

51. Rose, *The Cold War Comes to Main Street,* 253.

52. Jeanne Holm, *Women in the Military: An Unfinished Revolution* (Novato, CA: Presidio, 1982), 149.

53. Halberstam, *The Coldest Winter,* 21-22.

54. "U.S. Troop Transfer Is Smooth," *Daily Oklahoman,* 1 July 1950, 5; Robert Roy in Tomedi, *No Bugles, No Drums,* 3; and Baldovi, *A Foxhole View,* xvii. Some men died in Korea before their wives and families were notified of their deployment. Sidney Berry remembers that his wife boarded the last transport for dependents of men stationed in Japan and by the time she arrived the husbands of some of the women she traveled with already had been killed in Korea. Berry, Oral History by Caudill, 24.

55. Susumu Shinagawa in Baldovi, *A Foxhole View,* 10.

56. Robert F. Hallahan, *All Good Men: A Lieutenant's Memories of the Korean War* (New York: iUniverse, 2003), 13-14.

57. Ballenger, *The Final Crucible,* 14.

58. Ferries were uncomfortable, but troop ships proved more unpleasant at disembarkation. Marines landing at Inchon Harbor (not during the famed September invasion) had to climb down the sides of the ships on net ropes while carrying field packs, rifles, and helmets and drop into landing craft that carried them to the dock. See Ballenger, *The Final Crucible,* 15.

59. Terry, *The Battle for Pusan,* 4-6.

60. Bernstein, *Monsters and Angels,* 264.

61. *Ibid.,* 265.

62. Stanley Weintraub in Tomedi, *No Bugles, No Drums,* 188, and Ballenger, *The Final Crucible,* 14.

63. Private First Class Arnold Winter in Tomedi, *No Bugles, No Drums,* 25.

64. A. Vendiola in Baldovi, *A Foxhole View,* 30.

65. Arthur L. Kelly, Interview by Russell Harris, 16 December 1993, 24.

66. Ballenger, *The Final Crucible,* 15-18.

67. Peter S. Kindsvatter, *American Soldiers: Ground Combat in the World Wars, Korea, and Vietnam* (Lawrence: University Press of Kansas, 2003), 71. By late 1951, the Army sometimes provided several days of orientation in Japan before men shipped over to Korea. Icle G. Davis, "A Soldier Reminisces about Koje," unpublished memoir included with *Korean War Veteran Survey* (1965), 1, CFSOKW, and author's collection.

68. Tom Clawson in Tomedi, *No Bugles, No Drums,* 149. Men in the Air Force eventually joined their Army and Marine brethren in country as the line stabilized and the military repaired or rebuilt air fields. However, Air Force personnel headed straight to compounds shared by crew members, and the nature of their assignments lessened the impact of arrival in country and of the land front.

69. John Edward Nolan, interview by J. Cantwell, 29 December 1999, online at American Century Project, St. Andrews Episcopal School Library Archive (www.doingoralhistory. org), 2.

70. Private Taro Goya in Baldovi, *A Foxhole View,* 216.

71. Ronald J. Landry, "Excerpts," in "Chosin House: Poems and Prose," Box FF, Folder A0964, CFSOKW.

72. M. Vendiola in Baldovi, *A Foxhole View,* 36.

73. Landry, "Excerpts," in "Chosin House."

74. A 1987 survey found that 48.5% of veterans served in Korea and 35.2% experienced combat; thus 72.5% of men in country saw action. "1987 Survey of Veterans (conducted for the Department of Veterans Affairs by the U.S. Bureau of the Census) (July 1989)," 16, NA, Record Group 015, Box 1. A 2001 survey concluded that 42.4% served in Korea and 34.8% experienced combat, meaning 82% of men in Korea experienced battle. "2001 Survey of Veterans" (online at www.va.gov/vetdata/surveyresults/final.htm).

75. Of deaths in Korea, naval personnel accounted for 1.4% and Air Force personnel accounted for 3.6%. The Army, of course, supplied 82.4% of the fatalities and the Marine Corps the other 12.7%. Steven L. Canby, *Military Manpower Procurement: A Policy Analysis* (Lexington, MA: Lexington Books, 1972), 65.

76. American Air Force pilots flew over 700,000 missions, Marine units 100,000, and Navy pilots 170,000. Together these dropped 700,000 tons of ordnance and 30,000 tons of napalm and expended more than 100 million rounds of machine gun ammunition. Jennie Ethell Chancey and William R. Forstchen, eds., *Hot Shots: An Oral History of the Air Force Combat Pilots of the Korean War* (New York: HarperCollins, 2000), 237-38. Also Edwards, *To Acknowledge a War*, 112.

77. During the war, the Navy fired four million rounds of ammunition, damaging 3,334 buildings, 824 vessels, and numerous trucks, locomotives, tanks, bridges, and supply dumps. Navy personnel also inflicted almost 30,000 enemy casualties. When the Chinese entered the war, the Navy took part in the largest evacuation in U.S. history, carrying hundreds of thousands of soldiers and refugees out of North Korea in December 1950. Edwards, *To Acknowledge a War*, 110-12, and Jean Ebbert and Marie-Beth Hall, *Crossed Currents: Navy Women from World War I to Tail Hook* (Washington, DC: Brassey's, 1993), 128.

78. Reporter Bill Mauldin described distance in Korea as "up and down" and asserted that "when they say this is a young man's war, they aren't kidding." See Mauldin, *Bill Mauldin in Korea* (New York: Norton, 1952), 63.

79. Private First Class Arnold Winter in Tomedi, *No Bugles, No Drums,* 24.

80. Corporal Jay Hidano in Tomedi, *No Bugles, No Drums,* 60.

81. Baldovi in Baldovi, *A Foxhole View,* 263. Baldovi further notes that the rugged terrain of Korea made it a young man's war.

82. Stokesbury, *A Short History of the Korean War,* 21.

83. Faris R. Kirkland, "Soldiers and Marines at Chosin Reservoir: Criteria for Assignment to Combat Command," *Armed Forces & Society* 22.2 (Winter 1995): 257-59, and "Out Front: Aging World War II, Korea Vets Finally Compensated for Frostbite Ills," *Boston Globe Online,* 6 April 1997, 4.

84. Bowers, *The Line,* 94 and 103.

85. Behasa in Baldovi, *A Foxhole View,* 94.

86. Kindsvatter, *American Soldiers,* 41-42. Also Owen, *Colder Than Hell,* 230.

87. Richard Suarez in Tomedi, *No Bugles, No Drums,* 94-95. In his poem, "I Remember," William Wantling describes the rediscovery of a comrade listed missing in action and buried all winter in a snow bank, "preserved like a side of beef all winter." See Philip K. Jason and W. D. Ehrhart, eds., *Retrieving Bones: Stories and Poems of the Korean War* (Piscataway, NJ: Rutgers Press, 1999), 188.

88. Men sometimes went AWOL (absent without leave) because of the cold. Lieutenant Barnes of 2d Battalion, 38th Infantry describes how three men of Company F went AWOL after being left in the cold with no bedding. Bowers, *The Line,* 93-94.

89. "Navy News Release," *Dixie Times-Picayune,* 7 December 1952, 1-2, NA, Record Group 319, Box 007. Also Colonel "Pancho" Pasqualicchio in Chancey and Forstchen, *Hot Shots,* 83-84.

90. James Michener, "The Forgotten Heroes of Korea," *Saturday Evening Post,* 10 May 1952, 20. Also Jim Service in Tomedi, *No Bugles, No Drums,* 159.

91. Ent in Tomedi, *No Bugles, No Drums,* 19.

92. Nolan, interview by Cantwell, 29 December 1999, 6.

93. Colonel Cecil Foster and Robinson Risner in Chancey and Forstchen, *Hot Shots,* 148 and 158.

94. Foster, Risner, and General Frederick C. "Boots" Blesse in *ibid.,* 40-42,148, and 158.

95. Bob Ennis in Tomedi, *No Bugles, No Drums,* 161-62. Risner in Chancey and Forstchen, *Hot Shots,* 158.

96. M. Vendiola in Baldovi, *A Foxhole View,* 37. Veterans recall the Chinese doing this also. See M.Sgt. William Price, quoted in Harold L. Keith, "Sarge Volunteers for Korea Duty, Wants to See His Pals," *Pittsburgh Courier,* 7 February 1953, 2.

97. Van Scarborough, Interview by Robin Morris in Havard, *By Word of Mouth,* 34.

98. Fred Lawson in Tomedi, *No Bugles, No Drums,* 87.

99. Baldovi and Sebresos in Baldovi, *A Foxhole View,* 108 and 208.

100. Lawson and George Zonge in Tomedi, *No Bugles, No Drums,* 87 and 99; Arnold Del Castillo in Don Boxmeyer, *A Knack for Knowing Things: Stories from St. Paul Neighborhoods and Beyond* (St. Paul: Minnesota Historical Society Press, 2003), 153; and Sebresos in Baldovi, *A Foxhole View,* 107.

101. Kindsvatter, *American Soldiers,* 50.

102. See Jack to Bud, 21 May 1951, Clarence Jackson Davis (AFC2001/001/1644), Folder 1, VHPC, AFC, LOC.

103. Korean War–era soldier quoted in R. W. Apple, "U.S. Study Calls a Night Army Essential for Victory in Vietnam," *New York Times,* 6 August 1967, 6.

104. Due to logistical issues, the Chinese at most could attack for about seven days before retreating. Major General John T. Carley, Oral History by Dr. Orley B. Caudill, 2 February 1978, Volume CVII (1979), transcript, Mississippi Oral History Program, University of Southern Mississippi, Hattiesburg, Mississippi, 24. Also Lewis Millett in Tomedi, *No Bugles, No Drums,* 115, for comments on the brevity of battle. Harry Van Zandt, Interview by Tara Liston and Tara Kraenzlin, 11 March 1996, 31, Transcript by Donovan Bezer, Andrew Noyes, Shaun Illingworth, Harry Van Zandt, and Sandra Stewart Holyoak, Rutgers Oral History Archives for World War II, Rutgers University, New Brunswick, NJ, available at http://oralhistory.rutgers.edu/Interviews?van-zandt_harry.html, and Clawson in Tomedi, *No Bugles, No Drums,* 150.

105. Ground troops frequently noted their appreciation of air support, crediting pilots with bringing them out of impossible situations alive. Carley, Oral History by Caudill, 24, and Bowers, *The Line,* 160.

106. Lawson in Tomedi, *No Bugles, No Drums,* 87. Also, Baldovi in Baldovi, *A Foxhole View,* 209-10. Hand-to-hand combat was common in the Korean War. Kindsvatter, *American Soldiers,* 210.

107. Some 53% of Korean War soldiers fired their weapons compared to 15% of men in World War II. Kelly C. Jordan, "Right for the Wrong Reasons: S. L. A. Marshall and the Ratio of Fire in Korea," *Journal of Military History* 66.1 (2002): 146 and 160.

108. Ed Simmons in Tomedi, *No Bugles, No Drums,* 33.

109. Private Donald F. Russell in Bowers, *The Line,* 271-72.

110. Lieutenant Jacobs and Private Reed in *ibid.,* 198-200.

111. Sergeant Copenhaver in *ibid.,* 203.

112. Terry, *The Battle for Pusan,* 31. Enemy troops capitalized on the weakness of American communications. One lieutenant described how an English-speaking enemy soldier used a radio abandoned by the 3rd Platoon to try to fool another unit into believing that the 3rd remained in position. Bowers, *The Line,* 150-52. Fans of the television series *M*A*S*H* might remember Radar contacting one location through another.

113. Jay Hidano in Tomedi, *No Bugles, No Drums,* 61, and Baldovi in Baldovi, *A Foxhole View,* 263.

114. Nolan, interview by Cantwell, 29 December 1999, 3. Also Ent in Tomedi, *No Bugles, No Drums,* 20, and Sergeant First Class Al Kaff in "45th Tastes Blood on Korean Hillside," *Daily Oklahoman,* 27 January 1952, 1.

115. Berry, Oral History by Caudill, 26.
116. Luckily for Corporal Wall, the grenade hit the enemy gunner, knocking him unconscious. See Captain Leonard Lowry in Bowers, *The Line*, 178.
117. Moses Pakaki in Baldovi, *A Foxhole View*, 13.
118. No Gun Ri remains hotly contested. Partly on the basis of a falsified eyewitness account, the Associated Press released a series of articles in 1999 alleging that civilians at No Gun Ri were intentionally massacred by Americans. The number of civilian deaths and the circumstances surrounding them are disputed by participants, the U.S. government, and reporters. See Robert L. Bateman, *No Gun Ri: A Military History of the Korean War Incident* (Mechanicsburg, PA: Stackpole Books, 2002); Sahr Conway-Lanz, *Collateral Damage: Americans, Noncombatant Immunity, and Atrocity after World War II* (New York: Taylor & Francis Group, 2006); and Charles J. Hanley, Sang-Hun Choe, and Martha Mendoza, *The Bridge at No Gun Ri: A Hidden Nightmare from the Korean War* (New York: Holt, 2001). Another news article suggests that marines shot North Korean POWs at a hotel in Seoul. Eric Longabardi, Kit R. Roane, and Edward T. Pound, "A War of Memories," *U.S. News and World Report*, November 2003, 28-35. More recently, South Korean investigators began probing other instances in which the "U.S. military [possibly] indiscriminately killed large groups of refugees and other civilians early in the Korean War." "Seoul Probes Massacres," *Fayetteville (NC) Observer*, 4 August 2008, 5A.
119. Lewis Millett in Tomedi, *No Bugles, No Drums*, 110-15.
120. Vernon L. Warren in Bill Smith, "Black Soldiers Fully Shared Korean War's Bloody Cost," *St. Louis Post-Dispatch*, 20 February 2002, A1. Also Richard Suarez in Tomedi, *No Bugles, No Drums*, 95, and Sergeant McGregor in Bowers, *The Line*, 82.
121. Thomas W. McLain (AFC 2001/001/256), Folder 1, "Remembering Korea, 28 June 1950-3 December 1951," an unpublished memoir, 51, VHPC, AFC, LOC. Also Uzal Ent and Fred Lawson in Tomedi, *No Bugles, No Drums*, 20 and 88, and Sergeant First Class Al Kaff in "45th Tastes Blood on Korean Hillside," *Daily Oklahoman*, 27 January 1952, 1. "No person can see an entire battle." Harold DeVries, Interview by Kirk Mathis in Havard, *By Word of Mouth*, 8.
122. Blaine Friedlander in Tomedi, *No Bugles, No Drums*, 195-96. The 24th Infantry Regiment has long stirred debate, with some scholars claiming the 24th performed uniquely badly and others suggesting it fared no worse than other units entering the conflict early in the war. For a full-length study of the 24th, see William T. Bowers, William M. Hammond, and George L. MacGarrigle, *Black Soldier, White Army: The 24th Infantry Regiment in Korea* (Washington, DC: Center of Military History, United States Army, 1996). Individual American soldiers working closely with ROK troops often came to regard them highly, but Americans generally disparaged ROKs. The command system proved problematic as regular Army officers had little or no authority over ROK units or soldiers and stories of ROK incompetence circulated freely among American troops. Describing a February 1951 engagement, Captain Searls noted that "ROK soldiers had to be beaten as they tried to drag the wounded off the trucks and climb aboard." Bowers, *The Line*, 185-86 and 212-13.
123. Quoted in Martin Binkin, Mark J. Eitelberg, Alvin J. Schexnider, and Marvin M. Smith, *Blacks and the Military* (Washington, DC: Brookings Institution, 1982), 29.
124. Marines fared better in general than Army infantrymen when the ranks broke. For soldiers, the situation often ended up being one of "every man for himself," with men refusing to take charge or bickering about what direction to take. Marines, conversely, because of indoctrination during training, usually regrouped with someone in command. Bob Roy and Richard Suarez in Tomedi, *No Bugles, No Drums*, 6-7 and 96, and Vendiola in Baldovi, *A Foxhole View*, 139.
125. Vendiola in Baldovi, *A Foxhole View*, 134-35.
126. Nolan, interview by Cantwell, 29 December 1999, 14. Also, Uzal Ent in Tomedi, *No Bugles, No Drums*, 22.

127. Rudolph W. Stephens, *Old Ugly Hill: A GI's Fourteen Months in the Korean Trenches, 1952-1953* (Jefferson, NC: McFarland, 1995), 78, and Jack to Bud, 21 May 1951, Clarence Jackson Davis (AFC2001/001/1644), Folder 1, VHPC, AFC, LOC.

128. Clarence Jackson Davis (AFC2001/001/1644), Folder 1, VHPC, AFC, LOC.

129. Many veterans recount feelings of guilt both during and after the war. See Peavy, interview by Holt, in Havard, *By Word of Mouth*, 29-30; Arthur W. Wilson in Cooper, "Vets Still Conflicted over Korea," *Los Angeles Times*, 19 January 2000, 1; Kindsvatter, *American Soldiers*, 166; and Seymour "Hoppy" Harris, "Confessions" and "When Sleep Comes," Box EE, Folder A0956, CFSOKW.

130. Nolan, interview by Cantwell, 29 December 1999, 9.

131. Terry, *The Battle for Pusan*, 142-43.

132. Korea had a lower incidence of psychiatric casualties than World War II, when 23% of men suffered battle fatigue. Roger J. Spiller, "Shell Shock," *American Heritage*, May/June 1990, 77. Of about 1.6 million men who served in Korea, only 48,002 entered military medical facilities for psychiatric treatment. Kolb, "Korea's 'Invisible Veterans,'" 26. This might be explained by the rotation system, which moved men out of the war zone in a matter of months rather than years, or by the fact that a smaller percentage of Korean veterans endured frequent or extended combat.

133. For information on shell shock and Korea, see Glass, "Psychiatry in the Korean Campaign," 1387-1400; Kindsvatter, *American Soldiers*, 157-58 and 170; Spiller, "Shell Shock," 75-87; and Edgar Jones and Lt. Col. Ian P. Palmer, "Army Psychiatry in the Korean War: The Experience of 1 Commonwealth Division," *Military Medicine* 165 (April 2000): 256-60. The treatment of combat fatigue continues to evolve. Just as George Washington supplied the troops with rum rations at Valley Forge and the U.S. military provided amphetamines to men during the Vietnam War, soldiers in Iraq and Afghanistan today receive prescription antidepressants to help them continue to function in the war zone. Mark Thompson, "America's Medicated Army," *Time*, 16 June 2008, 38-42.

134. Nolan, interview by Cantwell, 29 December 1999, 9.

135. Charles M. Bussey, *Firefight at Yechon: Courage and Racism in the Korean War* (Lincoln: University of Nebraska Press, 2002), 148.

136. This is not unique to Korea. See Glen H. Elder Jr. and Elizabeth C. Chipp, "Wartime Losses and Social Bonding: Influences across 40 Years in Men's Lives," *Psychiatry* 51 (May 1988): 177-82.

137. Fred Lawson in Tomedi, *No Bugles, No Drums*, 87.

138. Sergeant Martin L. Stephens, "I Returned," unpublished memoir, 30 May 1953, NA, Record Group 319, Box 007.

139. Note by Basil Humphrey included with letter from Douglas Humphrey to Bec, John, and Basil, 17 April 1951, 1st Cavalry Division, Surnames A-L, Carlisle Barracks. In a similar example, a first lieutenant refused to quit fighting after being wounded, ultimately being killed while rushing a machine gun position. See Lieutenant Kader in Bowers, *The Line*, 134-35.

140. Baldovi in Baldovi, *A Foxhole View*, 270. Many authors stress the importance of comrades to men in battle. S. L. A. Marshall went so far as to say, "I hold it to be one of the simplest truths of war that the thing which enables an infantry soldier to keep going with his weapons is the near presence of a comrade." Quoted in Jordan, "Right for the Wrong Reasons," 158. See also William L. Hauser, "The Will to Fight," in Sam Sarkesian, ed., *Combat Effectiveness: Cohesion, Stress, and the Volunteer* (Beverly Hills, CA: Sage, 1980), 192.

141. Theodore S. "Ted" Williams in Berry, *Hey, Mac, Where Ya Been?* 260.

142. Kindsvatter, *American Soldiers*, 208.

143. Corporal Clyde Queen in "No Nice Words as Wounded Sooner Tells of Korean War," *Daily Oklahoman*, 3 September 1950, 1.

144. Uzal Ent in Tomedi, *No Bugles, No Drums*, 18.

145. For an example, see Seymour "Hoppy" Harris, "KIA's," Box EE, Folder A0956, CFSOKW.

146. Lawson and Ent in Tomedi, *No Bugles, No Drums,* 18 and 88.

147. Airmen did not always use this time to prepare for combat. Pilots often drank heavily the night before a mission, reporting for duty with a hangover. Some had to throw up on the taxiway before takeoff. However, almost all airmen did visit the latrines just before flying and with good reason. Planes afforded no restroom facilities and word of frequent in-flight "problems" had caused flight suits to acquire the nickname "poopsuits." Sherwood, *Officers in Flight Suits,* 82.

148. Navy pilot Jim Service, in Tomedi, *No Bugles, No Drums,* 159.

149. Sherwood, *Officers in Flight Suits,* 90.

150. See Pasqualicchio in Chancey and Forstchen, *Hot Shots,* 79.

151. Pilots had to provide evidence of kills, photographs, or confirmation by a wingman in order to get credit for them. Sherwood, *Officers in Flight Suits,* 71-72 and 88-89. Also, Bob Ennis in Tomedi, *No Bugles, No Drums,* 163.

152. Pasqualicchio in Chancey and Forstchen, *Hot Shots,* 79. F-86 pilots flew three missions a week and one hundred missions per tour of duty. After every thirty missions, pilots received an Air Medal. After one hundred, they got a Distinguished Flying Cross. Ace status was awarded to men with a certain number of kills and Silver Stars to men with spectacular service. In the Air Force, rank came as a direct result of performance in combat and number of missions flown. Sherwood, *Officers in Flight Suits,* 85-86.

153. In World War II, pilots received a one-ounce shot of "mission whiskey" upon returning from a combat flight. Initially, Korean pilots did not receive a liquor ration, but later crews either got large volumes of alcohol at the end of the month or small quantities after each completed mission. Lieutenant Colonel Duane E. "Bud" Biteman in Chancey and Forstchen, *Hot Shots,* 24, and Sherwood, *Officers in Flight Suits,* 84.

154. Extract from a letter from a GI in Korea, U.S. Senate, *Congressional Record,* 82nd Congress, 2nd sess., 8 January 1952-25 February 1952, vol. 98, part 1, 979. Sherwood, *Officers in Flight Suits,* 98-108. Almost twelve hundred Air Force personnel died in air combat and thirty-six died in ground actions. Thirty-five men captured remained in enemy hands a year after the war ended. Chancey and Forstchen, *Hot Shots,* 239-40.

155. Biteman in Chancey and Forstchen, *Hot Shots,* 36.

156. Colonel Harold Fischer in *ibid.,* 170.

157. Biteman in *ibid.,* 31. Also Arthur W. Wilson in Richard T. Cooper, "Vets Still Conflicted over Korea," *Los Angeles Times,* 19 January 2000, 1.

158. Sherwood, *Officers in Flight Suits,* 89-91, and Jim Service in Tomedi, *No Bugles, No Drums,* 159.

159. Arthur L. Kelly, Interview by Russell Harris, 16 December 1993, 41.

160. Terry, *The Battle for Pusan,* 53.

161. Walter C. Benton in Richard T. Cooper, "Vets Still Conflicted over Korea," *Los Angeles Times,* 19 January 2000, 1.

162. Jessie Forrest, interview by Heather Barge in Havard, *By Word of Mouth,* 10.

163. James H. Appleton to Melinda Pash, 17 August 2004, in the author's possession.

164. On atrocities committed by North Koreans against United Nations soldiers early in the war, see Lloyd Kreider, Bill Chambers, and Arnold Winter in Tomedi, *No Bugles, No Drums,* 25, 48, and 52-53; "Five Massacred GIs Buried," *Daily Oklahoman,* 12 July 1950, 11; "No Nice Words as Sooner Tells of Korean War," *Daily Oklahoman,* 3 September 1950, 1; and Kindsvatter, *American Soldiers,* 208.

165. Bill Smith, "Black Soldiers Fully Shared Korean War's Bloody Cost," *St. Louis Post-Dispatch,* 20 February 2002, A1.

166. Arned L. Hinshaw, *Heartbreak Ridge, Korea, 1951* (New York: Praeger, 1989), 51.

167. Jessie Forrest, Interview by Heather Barge, in Havard, *By Word of Mouth,* 10.

168. Sherwood, *Officers in Flight Suits,* 5.

169. Available at www.history.navy.mil/faqs/faq82-4.htm.

170. Letter James H. Appleton to Melinda Pash, 17 August 2004, in the author's possession.

171. Richard C. Bevier to Melinda Pash, undated, in the author's possession.

172. Lt. Rolly G. Miller to his mother, quoted by John O. Pastore, *Congressional Record*, Appendix, 82nd Congress, 1st sess., 1951, vol. 97, A5860.

173. Doug Michaud in Knox, *The Korean War: Pusan to Chosin*, 670. See also Glen H. Elder Jr. and Elizabeth C. Clipp, "Wartime Losses and Social Bonding: Influences across 40 Years in Men's Lives," *Psychiatry* 51 (May 1988): 177-98, and Kindsvatter, *American Soldiers*, 127.

174. Jack Little in Ballenger, *The Final Crucible*, 20.

175. William D. Dannenmaier, *We Were Innocents: An Infantryman in Korea* (Chicago: University of Illinois Press, 1999), 1.

176. Raymond Myers, diary entry for 9 October 1951 in Hinshaw, *Heartbreak Ridge*, 110.

177. Higgins, *War in Korea*, 196.

178. Hinshaw, *Heartbreak Ridge*, 11-12.

179. Arthur W. Wilson in Richard T. Cooper, "Vets Still Conflicted over Korea," *Los Angeles Times*, 19 January 2000, 1.

180. Arnoldo A. Muniz in Linda Granfield, *I Remember Korea: Veterans Tell Their Stories of the Korean War, 1950-1953* (New York: Clarion Books, 2003), 33-35. Major James Kiser, an Air Force pilot, echoes this same sentiment, talking about moments, not months, of terror. See Kiser in Chancey and Forstchen, *Hot Shots*, 85.

181. Thomas W. McLain (AFC 2001/001/256), Folder 1, "Remembering Korea, 28 June 1950-3 December 1951," an unpublished memoir, 60, VHPC, AFC, LOC.

182. Stephens, *Old Ugly Hill*, 72.

183. Sherwood, *Officers in Flight Suits*, 120-22, and Biteman in Chancey and Forstchen, *Hot Shots*, 20.

184. Some veterans recall that only officers got heaters for their quarters and that everyone else had to stay warm as best they could. See Arthur L. Kelly, Interview by Russell Harris, 16 December 1993, 23.

185. Sherwood, *Officers in Flight Suits*, 122.

186. Both male and female veterans mention slit trench latrines. Hicks, Interview by Trojanowski, 25 February 1999, 8, and Baldovi in Baldovi, *A Foxhole View*, 206.

187. Sherwood, *Officers in Flight Suits*, 116.

188. Jack to Bud, 21 May 1951, Clarence Jackson Davis (AFC2001/001/1644), Folder 1, VHPC, AFC, LOC.

189. Ballenger, *The Final Crucible*, 34.

190. Ballenger, *ibid.*, 35.

191. Tomedi, *No Bugles, No Drums*, 176, and Kindsvatter, *American Soldiers*, 44. Some men contracted Hantavirus from exposure to rodents. See Bernstein, *Monsters and Angels*, 293.

192. Van Zandt, Interview by Liston and Kraenzlin, 11 March 1996, 31.

193. Ballenger, *The Final Crucible*, 38.

194. *Ibid., 38.*

195. Tom Clawson in Tomedi, *No Bugles, No Drums*, 150.

196. Corporal Harrison Lee in Baldovi, *A Foxhole View*, 44.

197. Corporal Elgin Fujimoto in Baldovi, *ibid.*, 275.

198. Sergeant First Class Charles Chang in *ibid.*, 261.

199. Private First Class Robert Hamakawa in *ibid.*, 234-35; Bernstein, *Monsters and Angels*, 283; and Kindsvatter, *American Soldiers*, 44.

200. Kindsvatter, *American Soldiers*, 41, and Jay Hidano, Nick Nishimoto, and Bertram Sebresos in Baldovi, *A Foxhole View*, 84, 94, and 98.

201. "They're Hungry, GIs Tell Folks," *Daily Oklahoman*, 16 February 1951, 22. Men in this article wrote about the amount, not quality, of food received, but it is difficult to determine whether the military furnished too little food or whether GIs overstated their hunger to

compel folks from home to send food. None of the memoirs consulted by this author claim that the military failed to feed men properly except in cases where they could not be resupplied readily, such as in North Korea in the winter of 1950.

202. Sullivan, *Toy Soldiers*, 58-61. In another instance, a unit got new heavy machine guns and spindles but none of the devices necessary for their operation. As a result, the guns had to be hauled around without ever being used. Sergeant Rena F. Lattorre-Lopez in Bowers, *The Line*, 85.

203. Arthur L. Kelly, Interview by Russell Harris, 16 December 1993, 57.

204. Colonel Ralph Parr in Chancey and Forstchen, *Hot Shots*, 105.

205. Talking about time in reserve, Robert Fernandez notes that almost everything was terrible, but they got hot meals twice a day. See Fernandez in Baldovi, *A Foxhole View*, 255.

206. Ted White and Tom Clawson in Tomedi, *No Bugles, No Drums*, 126 and 150, and Granville Cox in Havard, *By Word of Mouth*, 5-6. The quartermaster in Korea did not provide equipment to carry hot meals forward, so hot food reached the line via Korean laborers who carried the food and trays up and then returned to the kitchen with the dirty dishes. See House of Representatives, Committee on Appropriations, *Department of the Army Appropriations for 1957: Hearings before the Subcommittee of the Committee on Appropriations*, 84th Congress, 2d sess., 1956, 232-33.

207. Kindsvatter, *American Soldiers*, 46; Ted White in Tomedi, *No Bugles, No Drums*, 126; Terry, *Battle for Pusan*, xiii; and Ballenger, *The Final Crucible*, 41.

208. Dannenmaier, *We Were Innocents*, 225; Baldovi in Baldovi, *A Foxhole View*, 198; and Howard Matthias, *The Korean War: Reflections of a Young Combat Platoon Leader*, revised edition (Tallahassee, FL: Father & Son Publishing, 1995), 176. Boris Spiroff dropped from 170 to 150 pounds and noted that in his company there were no longer any fat people. See Spiroff, *Korea*, 66.

209. Mauldin, *Bill Mauldin in Korea*, 63. For examples of these leaflets, see Sgt. Maj. Herbert A. Friedman (retired), "Communist North Korea War Leaflets" (online at http://www.psywarrior.com/NKoreaH.html).

210. One young American felt so affected by this ritual that he made a point of killing the Chinese bugler and taking the bugle. See Jim "Bill" Peavy, interview by Melissa Holt in Havard, *By Word of Mouth*, 29-30.

211. Ballenger, *The Final Crucible*, 176-78. Ballenger goes on to say that Americans also employed psychological warfare against the Chinese, noting that a South Korean woman flew above the Chinese lines encouraging them to surrender, which some subsequently did.

212. Roy E. Appleman, *South to the Naktong, North to the Yalu* (Washington, DC: Center of Military History, U.S. Army, 1992), 351n.; Herbert A. Friedman, "Communist North Korea War Leaflets" (online at http://www.psywarrior.com/NKoreaH.html); and Edwards, *To Acknowledge a War*, 79. See also an account of Peiping Polly in Brenda Gayle Plummer, *Rising Wind: Black Americans and U.S. Foreign Affairs, 1935-1960* (Chapel Hill: University of North Carolina Press, 1996), 206.

213. Grant Hauskins, Interview with Nathan Stanley, 25 April 1997, 3 (online at http://mcel.pacifcu.edu/as/students/stanley/hoskins/html).

214. Many combat veterans mention the inability to sleep while in Korea although survival depended upon the ability to remain alert. Matthias, *The Korean War*, 133, and Harold Devries, Interview by Kirk Mathis in Havard, *By Word of Mouth*, 7-8. Underscoring the dangers of sleeping, Corporal Gary Hashimoto recounts the story of a young replacement who arrived at dusk, dug in, and was found dead the next morning from knife wounds. Hashimoto in Baldovi, *A Foxhole View*, 151.

215. Ballenger, *The Final Crucible*, 44.

216. Spiroff, *Korea*, 56.

217. Owen, *Colder Than Hell,* 203; Curtis James Morrow, *What's a Commie Ever Done to Black People? A Korean War Memoir of Fighting in the U.S. Army's Last All-Negro Unit* (Jefferson, NC: McFarland, 1977), 60; and Stephens, *Old Ugly Hill,* 171-72.

218. Arthur L. Kelly, Interview by Russell Harris, 16 December 1993, 40.

219. Quoted in Sherwood, *Officers in Flight Suits,* 118.

220. "Send a Xmas Gift to Korea," *Pittsburgh Courier,* 14 November 1953, 20.

221. Matthias, *The Korean War,* xiii.

222. Don Harrington, *Korean War Veteran Survey,* 3, CFSOKW.

223. Lt. Rolly G. Miller to his mother, quoted by John O. Pastore, *Congressional Record, Appendix,* 82nd Congress, 1st sess., 1951, vol. 97, A5860.

224. Extract from a letter from a GI in Korea, U.S. Senate, *Congressional Record,* 82nd Congress, 2nd sess., 8 January 1952-25 February 1952, vol. 98, part 1, 979

225. Morrow, *What's a Commie Ever Done to Black People?* 34.

226. *Ibid.,* and Grant Hauskins, Interview by Nathan Stanley, 25 April 1997 (online at http://mcel.pacificu.edu/as/students/stanley/hoskins.html).

227. See Berry, *Hey, Mac, Where Ya Been?* 4; Ballenger, *The Final Crucible,* 78; and Kindsvatter, *American Soldiers,* 152.

228. Van Zandt, Interview by Liston and Kraenzlin, 11 March 1996, 33. One soldier even wrote President Truman a letter asking, "How many years are you going to let American manpower, materials, and money drain into this Korean sewer? How many more of my men must die on account of your stubborn refusal to pull out of Korea?" Letter to President Truman from Lt. Gale O. Buuck in extension of remarks of Clare E. Hoffman, *Congressional Record, Appendix,* 82nd Congress, 1st sess., January 1951-October 1951, vol. 97, A1834. Sullivan, *Toy Soldiers,* 20.

229. Marguerite Higgins, *War in Korea: The Report of a Woman Combat Correspondent* (Garden City, NY: Doubleday, 1951), 196.

230. See "Gifts for GIs Wanted" and "Please Write This Lonely GI," *Pittsburgh Courier,* 15 March 1952, 3.

231. In 1955, one newspaper article thanked ten women for sending goods to hometown servicemen in Korea over a four-year period. See "Thanks from the Outposts of Korea," *Nutley Sun,* 17 February 1955, printed in the Extension of Remarks of Peter W. Rodino Jr., *Congressional Record, Appendix,* 84th Congress, 1st sess., January 1955-August 1955, Vol. 101, A1167.

232. These relationships often proved temporary. One woman complained publicly that her soldier pen pal dumped her once he rotated out of Korea. "Girl's Heart Broken by Soldier in Korea," *Baltimore Afro-American,* 22 August 1953, 20.

233. Victor Fox in Knox and Coppel, *The Korean War: Uncertain Victory,* 27. Learning of a devastating flood in Kansas and Missouri, one machine gun platoon sent a five hundred dollar check to a relief fund. "Combat GIs Help Victims of Floods," *Daily Oklahoman,* 13 August 1951, 8.

234. Edgar L. Miller in Granfield, *I Remember Korea,* 112-14.

235. From a young soldier's letter to his wife, quoted in Ballenger, *The Final Crucible,* 50-51. Also see Charles King in Bill Smith, "Black Soldiers Fully Shared Korean War's Bloody Cost," *St. Louis Post-Dispatch,* 20 February 2002, A1; Spiroff, *Korea,* 18; and Kindsvatter, *American Soldiers,* 108.

236. Bussey, *Firefight at Yechon,* 96-97.

237. Ralph Hammersmith wrote to Senator Robert Taft on behalf of his son in Korea who learned his wife was pregnant by another man and wanted a divorce so that he could declare a new beneficiary for his insurance should he be killed. The Army said the soldier would have to wait until he returned home to get a divorce. Ralph Hammersmith to Robert A. Taft, 20 February 1953, Taft Papers, Box 1077, LOC.

238. Owen, *Colder Than Hell,* 171. After receiving "Dear John" letters, many men broke down. They "deserted, committed suicide, became fatally careless in battle." Kindsvatter, *American Soldiers,* 109.

239. Thomas W. McLain in a letter dated 16 February 1951 (AFC 2001/001/256), Folder 1, "Remembering Korea, 28 June 1950-3 December 1951," an unpublished memoir, 47, VHPC, AFC, LOC.

240. In "Korea Blues," a GI mourns, "I was just sittin' here wonderin', who you gonna let lay down in my bed? / What hurt me so bad, think about some man has gone in your bed." Quoted in Doris Schmidt, "Americans Change Their Tune," 47-48, Box "A.0776 to A.0806," folder 0784, CFSOKW.

241. For a discussion of the interplay between the soldier and the home front and the soldier's perception that combat changed him, refer to Gerald F. Linderman, *The World Within War: America's Combat Experience in World War II* (New York: Free Press, 1997), chapter 8.

242. Bussey, *Firefight at Yechon,* 96.

243. Matthias, *The Korean War,* 87.

244. Hinshaw, *Heartbreak Ridge,* 13.

245. James Wallace, "Bloody Chosin: The Blind Lead the Brave," *U.S. News and World Report,* 9 December 1950, 37-43, AR 0070, CFSOKW.

246. Sent to clear a "deserted" village, Herbert Ikeda found a large enemy force whom he persuaded to surrender without firing a single shot by promising them food, tobacco, and candy. Afterward, he took the stars off a North Korean uniform and sewed them onto his own cap and shirt. His explanation quoted above was to a colonel who asked about the makeshift uniform. Ikeda in Baldovi, *A Foxhole View,* 57-58.

247. Ronald J. Landry, "Appropriateness," in "Chosin House." M. Vendiola in Baldovi, *A Foxhole View,* 36.

248. Matthias, *The Korean War,* 46.

249. On soldiers sanitizing their correspondence for hometown readers during World War II, see Linderman, *World within War,* 308.

250. Pfc. James Cardinal to his parents, 7 January 1950, quoted in Hastings, *The Korean War,* 176. Hastings records the date of this letter as 1950, but given the events described in it, including the entrance of the Chinese into the war, and the Eighth Army's retreat south, the letter must have actually been written in January 1951.

251. Sergeant Edward W. Moffett, Sergeant First Class William H. Bloss, and Sergeant Wade H. Beans to Senator Robert A. Taft, 15 May 1951, Taft Papers, Box 1077, LOC, and Spiroff, *Korea,* 24. See also Private First Class Sal Pultro to Mrs. Rogers in *Congressional Record, Appendix,* 82nd Congress, 1st sess., January 1951-October 1951, vol. 97, A3333.

252. Sergeant D. S. Ray to Senator Robert A. Taft from Korea, the frontlines, 16 May 1951, and R. C. Kash to Taft, 14 May 1951, Taft Papers, Box 1077, LOC.

253. Corporal Henry Orphal to Senator Robert A. Taft, 14 May 1951, Taft Papers, Box 1077, LOC.

254. "Korea: The Forgotten War," *U.S. News and World Report,* 5 October 1951, 21.

255. Mauldin, *Bill Mauldin in Korea,* 10.

256. A 53-day strike in the summer of 1952 cost men in the field necessary equipment such as 105 mm artillery shells. Richard K. Kolb, "Korea's 'Invisible Veterans' Return to an Ambivalent America," *Veterans of Foreign Wars Magazine* 85.3 (November 1997): 27.

257. Extract from a letter from a GI in Korea, U.S. Senate, *Congressional Record,* 82nd Congress, 2nd sess., 8 January 1952-25 February 1952, vol. 98, part 1, 979. The letter went on to say, "I know myself when I was over there [in the States] I didn't think much of the Korean War, except maybe as some sort of police action."

258. "Report on Korea and the Far East," remarks of a seven-month Korean War vet, entered into record by Mr. McClellan, U.S. Senate, *Congressional Record* , 82nd Congress, 2nd sess., 28 June 1952-7 July 1952, vol. 98, part 7, 8818. One GI noted, "America is a free country.

That's why we're fighting. But long strikes of essential industries are as bad as Communist propaganda or sabotage." Corporal Robert R. Kubick, "To Bolster GI Morale," *New York Times,* 1 September 1952, 16.

259. Edwin Phipp, "Forgotten Men in Korea Fight with Second-Hand Equipment," *Washington Star,* 14 May 1952, quoted in *Congressional Record, Appendix,* 82nd Congress, 2nd sess., January 1952-July 1952, vol. 98, A2973.

260. Richard C. Bevier, "Nearly Everyone Should Write a Book," 42, account attached by the author to *Korean War Veteran Survey,* CFSOKW.

261. James F. Boden, Army Service (Korean War) Questionnaire, 20, 2nd Division, 23rd Regiment, Alphabetical Box 1, Department of the Army, Carlisle Barracks.

262. Eismann in Bowers, *The Line,* 125.

263. Fictional character Lieutenant Anderson from Ernest Frankle's *Band of Brothers,* quoted in Kindsvatter, *American Soldiers,* 154.

264. Extract from a letter from a GI in Korea, U.S. Senate, *Congressional Record,* 82nd Congress, 2nd sess., 8 January 1952-25 February 1952, vol. 98, part 1, 979.

265. See Edwin Arthur Hall in U.S. House, *Congressional Record,* 82nd Congress, 1st sess., 22 February–26 March 1951, vol. 97, part 2, 2605.

266. Anthony Leviero, "Truman Asks Rush on GI Voting Bill," *New York Times,* 20 June 1952, 15.

267. During the Korean War, a few states allowed people younger than twenty-one to vote. Georgia, for instance, allowed eighteen-year-olds the privilege. During the Vietnam War, another conflict fought using young conscripts, the minimum voting age in all states finally was lowered from twenty-one to eighteen with the ratification of the Twenty-Sixth Amendment in July 1971.

268. The Indian Citizenship Act of 1924 converted all noncitizen Native Americans into citizens (some Native Americans received citizenship earlier either by privately farming their land or through World War I military service), entitling them to vote. However, since voting depended upon state law until voting rights legislation enacted in the 1950s and 1960s, many Native Americans were barred from voting.

269. C. P. Trussell, "GI-Vote Bill Sped through Senate," *New York Times,* 21 June 1952, 8, and "Light Vote Seen by Absentee GIs," *New York Times,* 2 November 1952, Republican National Committee, Additional Files of News Clippings, A-65-12/1, Box 636, DDE Library.

270. "Many GIs Stationed Overseas Are Denied Vote, Others Find Secrecy of Ballot Threatened," *St. Louis Post-Dispatch,* 2 October 1952, Republican National Committee, Additional Files of Newsclippings, A-65-12/1, Box 636, DDE Library. This process differed greatly from the process in 1944, when soldiers and sailors were given a ballot, marked it secretly, and then dropped it into a ballot box on the ship.

271. Extension of Remarks, S. J. Crumpacker Jr., *Congressional Record, Appendix,* 82nd Congress, 1st sess., January 1951-October 1951, vol. 97, A1914.

272. Paul Hood, "Officer School Discovers GIs Pull Fast One," *Daily Oklahoman,* 24 January 1952, 1, and "OCS No Longer a Ticket Home," *Daily Oklahoman,* 11 March 1952, 4. Likewise, men stateside found ways to avoid shipment to Korea. Men originally needed nine months' active duty left on their enlistments for an overseas posting, so they would go AWOL for twenty-nine days, then return to their units for courts-martial in hope that after their trials they would lack the requisite time to be sent to Korea. The Army closed this loophole in 1953, ordering sentences suspended and offending soldiers sent to Korea. William M. Donnelley, "'The Best Army That Can Be Put in the Field in the Circumstances': The U.S. Army, July 1951–July 1953," *Journal of Military History* 71 (July 2007): 837.

273. Arthur L. Kelly, Interview by Russell Harris, 16 December 1993, 44, and Ballenger, *The Final Crucible,* 47.

274. The USO had a slow start during the Korean War, but eventually put on 5,400 shows in Korea and by the end of the war boasted 113,394 volunteers and 300 USO centers overseas.

Peter A. Soderbergh, *Women Marines in the Korean War Era* (Westport, CT: Praeger, 1994), 86.

275. Matthias, *The Korean War,* 149, and Arthur L. Kelly, Interview by Russell Harris, 16 December 1993, 58. Not everyone received regular rations, and eventually the rations were stopped altogether. James H. Toner, "American Society and the American Way of War: Korea and Beyond," *Parameters* 11.1 (1981): 87, and Carl V. Tyozandlak, Army Service (Korean War) Questionnaire, 5, 1st Cavalry Division, surnames M-Z, Carlisle Barracks.

276. Sherwood, *Officers in Flight Suits,* 123-29.

277. Ballenger, *The Final Crucible,* 41; Matthias, *The Korean War,* 151; and Arthur L. Kelly, Interview by Russell Harris, 16 December 1993, 60-61. Richard Bevier describes the "raisin jack" produced by one of the men in his unit. Bevier, "Nearly Everyone Should Write a Book," 51.

278. Kindsvatter, *American Soldiers,* 97-98. While a number of veterans' memoirs, letters, diaries, and oral histories discuss the prevalence of smoking and drinking during the war, few mention drug addiction or substances like codeine and marijuana. For mention of drugs, see Douglas G. Anderson and Donald E. Barton, Army Service (Korean War) Questionnaire, 5 (for both sources), 2nd Division, 23rd Regiment, Alphabetical Box 1, Carlisle Barracks. Some accounts, however, suggest men developed addictions to prescription drugs in the war zone or mention Korea as their first experience with drugs. Peter Santella in Berry, *Hey, Mac, Where Ya Been?* 225.

279. Some servicewomen and Red Cross workers probably had romantic liaisons while stationed in country, but these are less well documented than the affairs of male servicemen, perhaps because of the strict rules of behavior imposed on women by both the Red Cross and the military. Also, many servicewomen felt that the men they encountered overseas held a low opinion of women in uniform. See Anita Bean, *Korean War Veteran Survey,* 6, CFSOKW. Many American men in country felt that "Round Eyes" (non-Asian women) were off-limits. Sherwood, *Officers in Flight Suits,* 129-31. It should also be noted that aside from R & R, many American soldiers had no time to think about starting a relationship or to mix with the local population. See Matthias, *The Korean War,* 22.

280. For more on treatment of gays in Cold War America, see David K. Johnson, *The Lavender Scare: The Cold War Persecution of Gays and Lesbians in the Federal Government* (Chicago: University of Chicago Press, 2004).

281. One author argues that gays tended to self-select themselves "to the medic, administrative . . . and cooks branches of the services," where comrades not only accepted but admired them. Selika M. Ducksworth, *What Hour of the Night: Black Enlisted Men's Experiences and the Desegregation of the Army during the Korean War, 1950-1951* (Ph.D. diss., Ohio State University, 1997), 152.

282. Ric Mendoza-Gleason (AFC2001/001/4939), Interview by Katia Bore, 22 January 2003, Transcribed and edited by Lara Ballard, February 2003, Folder 2, 9-10, VHPC, AFC, LOC, and Jim Tee in Mary Ann Humphrey, *My Country, My Right to Serve: Experiences of Gay Men and Women in the Military, World War II to the Present* (New York: HarperCollins, 1990), 51-54.

283. Several sources allude to the situational homosexuality that occurred in the war zone. See Gleason (AFC2001/001/4939), Interview by Bore, 10, VHPC, AFC, LOC, and Richard H. Waltner, *Men in Skirts: An Army Medic's Account of the Korean War and After* (New York: Author's Choice Press, 2000), 85.

284. Tony Lankford in Humphrey, *My Country, My Right to Serve,* 31.

285. Kindsvatter, *American Soldiers,* 94; Sherwood, *Officers in Flight Suits,* 116 and 131-33; and William T. Craig, *Lifer! From Infantry to Special Forces* (New York: Ivy Books, 1994), 48-49.

286. Sherwood, *Officers in Flight Suits,* 133, and Waltner, *Men in Skirts,* 76-77. Waltner asserts that only men with gonorrhea were kept for treatment, as genital warts were not yet

recognized as a form of venereal disease. Presumably, then, this would be the way genital warts made their way to the United States, through untreated Korean War veterans.

287. Bevier, "Nearly Everyone Should Write a Book," 40.

288. Sherwood, *Officers in Flight Suits,* 142.

289. The State Department remained especially slow to sign off on interracial marriages even after applications made it through all the military channels. Bussey, *Firefight at Yechon,* 65; Craig, *Lifer!* 49; and Barnett R. Wilson (AFC 2001/001/2783), Folder 1, *A Korean Cruise: Magic Moments of Life, Love, and War* (1981), an unpublished memoir, 153, VHPC, AFC, LOC. Certain states also discouraged these marriages. A Georgia state attorney warned a veteran that to marry a Japanese woman was illegal and Mississippi did not recognize marriages with "Mongolians." Plummer, *Rising Wind,* 209. Also, Thomas Bostlemann, *The Cold War and the Color Line: Race Relations in the Global Arena* (Cambridge, MA: Harvard University Press, 2001), 82.

290. Bussey, *Firefight at Yechon,* 65, and Craig, *Lifer!* 49.

291. It is interesting to note that while U.S. policy in 1952 permitted soldiers to recognize their children by German mothers and allowed German women the right to sue to establish paternity, the government expended little or no effort to aid war orphans in Japan and Korea. GIs and individuals did, however, try to raise funds to assist American offspring there. Plummer, *Rising Wind,* 207-9.

292. Addison Terry recalls being taken to the Pea Patch for a bit of rest in 1950. See Terry, *Battle for Pusan,* 134-35.

293. Fehrenbach, *This Kind of War,* 347-48.

294. Harold DeVries, Interview by Kirk Mathis, in Havard, *By Word of Mouth,* 8.

295. Supposedly, this particular soldier, once in Japan, talked himself onto a plane headed to his hometown, where he spent his R & R. Murray Schumach, "GI's Can Laugh Even in Korea," *New York Times,* 13 May 1951, SM23.

296. Nick Nishimoto in Baldovi, *A Foxhole View,* 63.

297. Matthias, *The Korean War,* 131.

298. Fehrenbach, *This Kind of War,* 348, and Kindsvatter, *American Soldiers,* 94.

299. Anita Bean, *Korean War Veteran Survey,* 6, CFSOKW.

300. Many National Guardsmen, particularly retreads, resented the Army's plans for rotating them out of Korea. Under the Army plan, men received no credit for service in World War II, placing them on an even footing with men who had served much less time in the Guard. Wayne Mackey, "National Guard Discharge Plan Irks 45th Men," *Daily Oklahoman,* 13 August 1951, 8.

301. *Ibid.,* 347. In October 1952 the military, facing another manpower shortage, raised the number of points for rotation to thirty-nine, but criticism proved so sharp that the 36-point minimum was quickly restored. Donnelley, "The Best Army That Can Be Put in the Field in the Circumstances," 818. Eligibility for rotation did not necessarily mean one would be able to rotate out as men had to wait for a replacement to fill their spot. Beverly Scott, for instance, had fifty-two points before he finally got to leave Korea. Scott in Tomedi, *No Bugles, No Drums,* 182. Additionally, the Army could raise the number of points required. See Stephens, *Old Ugly Hill,* 168; Charles W. Dryden, *A-Train: Memoirs of a Tuskegee Airman* (Tuscaloosa: University of Alabama Press, 1997), 293; and Daniel Hallock, *Hell, Healing, and Resistance: Veterans Speak* (Farmington, PA: Plough Publishing House, 1998), 98.

302. Ballenger, *The Final Crucible,* 34; Kindsvatter, *American Soldiers,* 86; and Arthur L. Kelly, Interview by Birdwhistell, 16 April 1985, 9 (Kentuckiana Digital Library at http://kdl.kyvl. org).

303. W. D. McGlasson, "Manpower for the Korean War," *VFW,* June/July 1990, 23, Article 0057, CFSOKW, 25.

304. Sullivan, *Toy Soldiers*, 20, and Hanson W. Baldwin, "Handicaps in Korea War," *New York Times*, 24 February 1953, 4. On the negative effects of rotation on unit cohesiveness and effectiveness, see Edwards, *To Acknowledge a War*, 109-10, and Roger Little, "Buddy Relations and Combat Performance," in Morris Janowitz, ed., *The New Military: Changing Patterns of Organization* (New York: Russell Sage Foundation, 1964), 195-223.

305. Sullivan, *Toy Soldiers*, 20. Desperate for officers and NCOs in Korea, the Army reduced the amount of time required in grade before promotion. Berry, Oral History by Caudill, 35. On rotation and the crisis in leadership see Donnelley, "The Best Army That Can Be Put in the Field in the Circumstances," 823.

306. Morris Janowitz and Roger W. Little, *Sociology and the Military Establishment*, 3rd ed. (Beverly Hills, CA: Sage, 1974), 99, and Van Zandt, Interview by Liston and Kraenzlin, 11 March 1996, 35.

307. Kindsvatter, *American Soldiers*, 73-74, and Baldovi and Clayton Murakami in Baldovi, *A Foxhole View*, 198 and 223-24.

308. Kindsvatter, *American Soldiers*, 91; Elgen Fujimoto and Alan Takamiyahiro in Baldovi, *A Foxhole View*, 63 and 229; and Arthur L. Kelly, Interview by Russell Harris, 16 December 1993, 52.

309. Matthias, *The Korean War*, 164.

310. Iwao Yokooji in Baldovi, *A Foxhole View*, 279; "POWs Left in Korea Troubled Eisenhower Administration," *Kansas City Star*, 18 September 1996, A4; "Korean Casualties," *U.S. News and World Report*, 12 November 1954, 4; and Barbara Slavin, "Teams Start to Search for U.S. Remains at Chosin," *U.S.A. Today*, 10 September 2001, 11A. The bodies of Americans continue to find their way home. In 2008, China finally admitted to burying one American POW in China though for decades the Chinese insisted that "all POW questions were answered at the conclusion of the war in 1953 and that no Americans were moved to Chinese territory from North Korea." Robert Burns, "China Admits Taking POW," *Fayetteville (NC) Observer*, 20 June 2008, 7A.

311. G. Kurt Piehler, *Remembering War the American Way* (Washington, DC: Smithsonian Institution Press, 1995), 155.

312. Capts. Arnd Frie, Jamie Kiessling, Gerard L. McCool, Thomas Moody, Benett Sunds, Robert Uppena, and Garth Yarnell, "Fallen Comrades: Mortuary Affairs in the U.S. Army," *Quartermaster Professional Bulletin* (Winter 1998) (online at www.qmfound.com/fallen.htm), and Lt. Col.John C. Cook, "Graves Registration in the Korean Conflict," *The Quartermaster Review*, March–April 1953, 1, online at www.qmmuseum.lee.army.mil/korea/gr_korea.htm.

313. See Bill Chambers in Tomedi, *No Bugles, No Drums*, 46-49.

314. Cook, "Graves Registration in the Korean Conflict," 2.

315. *Ibid.*, 4, and Colonel John D. Martz Jr., "Homeward Bound," *Quartermaster Review*, May–June 1954, 1-2, online at www.qmfound.com/homeward_bound_korea.htm.

316. Bradley Lynn Coleman offers a thorough account and analysis of graves registration during the Korean War. See "Recovering the Korean War Dead, 1950-1958: Graves Registration, Forensic Anthropology, and Wartime Memorialization," *Journal of Military History* 72 (January 2008): 179-222.

317. Martz, "Homeward Bound," 2-3.

318. *Ibid.*, 3-4. After the war, Operation Glory strove to recover the remains of Americans killed in Korea. "'Operation GLORY,' condensed from Graves Registration Division, Korean Communications Zone (KCOMZ), Historical Summary, Jul–Dec 1954," at www.qmmuseum.lee.army.mil/korea/op_glory.htm. See also "Search and Recovery," *Quartermaster Review*, July–August 1954 (online at www.qmfound.com/search_and_recovery_korea.htm). Efforts continue today.

319. Robert Jamieson, Letter home, 29 July 1950, in Baldovi, *A Foxhole View*, 29.

320. Irwin Crockett in Baldovi, *A Foxhole View*, 151.

321. Spiroff, *Korea,* 69, and Clarence Jackson "Jack" Davis, postscript to letter dated February 1952, 177 (AFC2001/001/1644), Folder 1, VHPC, AFC, LOC.

322. Edmund Krekovian in Knox and Coppel, *The Korean War: Uncertain Victory,* 351.

323. David Brouchoud to Dad, 16 November 1952, Box A, folder A0005, CFSOKW.

324. Frank Almy in Knox and Coppel, *The Korean War: Uncertain Victory,* 354.

325. W. B. Woodruff Jr. and Floyd Baxter in Knox and Coppel, *The Korean War: Uncertain Victory,* 223 and 357-58.

326. Frank Almy in Knox and Coppel, *The Korean War: Uncertain Victory,* 353.

327. Stephens, *Old Ugly Hill,* 171. See also Bernstein, *Monsters and Angels,* 328; Leonard Korgie in Knox and Coppel, *The Korean War: Uncertain Victory,* 353; and Stephens, *Old Ugly Hill,* 168-71.

328. Early in the war, reserve units by and large came and went together, but, as original members filtered out and units filled with replacements, the same breaks in cohesion occurred. There were drawbacks to putting men from the same locale in the same units. Ross Dwyer remembers a reserve company from Arizona that ended up at Seoul and Chosin Reservoir. "This meant we'd zapped a whole community in Arizona. We were now trying not to have all the men in a reserve unit go to Korea in the same outfit." Dwyer in Berry, *Hey, Mac, Where Ya Been?* 249. Although some men in World War II left with their units, many rotated home with strangers like Korean veterans, as timing of departure depended upon a point system.

329. Hallock, *Hell, Healing, and Resistance,* 99; Spiroff, *Korea,* 71; and Ronald J. Landry, "Return" and "Rotation" in "Chosin House."

330. Edmund Krekovian in Knox and Coppel, *The Korean War: Uncertain Victory,* 352.

331. James Brady, *The Coldest War: A Memoir of Korea* (New York: Orion Books, 1990), 239.

332. Edmund Krekovian in Knox and Coppel, *The Korean War: Uncertain Victory,* 352.

333. Ronald J. Landry, "Walls," in "Chosin House."

334. Ronald J. Landry, "Rotation," in "Chosin House."

335. Samuel R. Woodham (AFC2001/001/1595), Interview by Brian T. Woodham Jr., 23 March 2002, 8, Folder 3, VHPC, AFC, LOC.

336. Brady, *The Coldest War,* 239, and Samuel R. Woodham (AFC2001/001/1595), Interview by Brian T. Woodham Jr., 23 March 2002, 20, Folder 3, VHPC, AFC, LOC.

337. "The Allies," *Time Magazine,* 16 July 1951, 22.

338. *Ibid.,* and Michael Lind, *Vietnam: The Necessary War; A Reinterpretation of America's Most Disastrous Military Conflict* (New York: Free Press, 1999), 254-55.

339. The number of men killed in the first fifteen months of the Korean War surpassed the number of men killed in the same time frame in World War II. "Korea: The Forgotten War," *U.S. News and World Report,* 5 October 1951, 21. The three years of war in Korea cost some $67 billion, and since 1953 the cost to maintain a U.S. presence at the 38th Parallel has cost $2.4 billion a year. Soderbergh, *Women Marines in the Korean War Era,* xxi.

340. Edwards, *To Acknowledge a War,* 5.

341. In October 1953, 53% of Americans said they would not support reentering the fighting in Korea should South Korea start the war up again, and 56% said that the United States should definitely not send soldiers back. George H. Gallup, *The Gallup Poll: Public Opinion 1953-1971.* Vol. 2, *1949-1958* (New York: Random House, 1972), 1183.

342. Van Zandt, Interview by Liston and Kraenzlin, 11 March 1996, 33, and Charles F. Cole, *Korea Remembered: Enough of a War; The USS Ozbourn's First Korean Tour, 1950-1951* (Las Cruces, NM: Yucca Tree Press, 1995), 271.

343. Mike Royko quoted in Soderbergh, *Women Marines in the Korean War Era,* xxii.

344. Walter A. Klein (AFC2001/001/220), Interview by Jamie Malone, 15 November 2001, 1, Folder 2, VHPC, AFC, LOC.

345. See Hinshaw, *Heartbreak Ridge,* 1.

346. John Toland quoted in Soderbergh, *Women Marines in the Korean War,* 132.

347. Brady, *The Coldest War,* 239.
348. Louis J. Lyons in Granfield, *I Remember Korea,* 67.
349. James Hamilton Dill, *Sixteen Days at Mungol-li* (Fayetteville, AR: M&M Press, 1993), 401, and Dannenmaier, *We Were Innocents,* 11. See also Howard Davenport in Ballenger, *The Final Crucible,* 267.

CHAPTER 5

1. Jennie Ethell Chancey and William R. Forstchen, eds., *Hot Shots: An Oral History of the Air Force Combat Pilots of the Korean War* (New York: HarperCollins, 2000), 76-77 and 79.
2. Rudy Tomedi, *No Bugles, No Drums: An Oral History of the Korean War* (New York: Wiley, 1993), 219.
3. Of American Korean War POWs, 6,656 came from the Army, 263 from the Air Force, 231 from the Marine Corps, and 40 from the Navy. Harry Spiller, ed., *American POWs in Korea: Sixteen Personal Accounts* (Jefferson, NC: McFarland, 1998), 1. The official count of POWs is udoubtedly low as some of the 8,177 persons listed missing in action probably perished in captivity the first winter, when the death rate reached an estimated 60%.
4. T. R. Fehrenbach, *This Kind of War: A Study in Unpreparedness* (New York: Macmillan, 1963), 444. Though agreeing to return the sickest prisoners at Little Switch, the communists tried to save face by passing off healthy American POWs as the most ill. Many of the POWs returned at Little Switch were so-called progressives, POWs who responded favorably to Chinese indoctrination and whom the Chinese expected to give a favorable account of captivity, rather than "moderates," who did not resist the Chinese openly but did not willingly contribute to the education program, or "reactionaries," who actively resisted.
5. At least 40% of American POWs in the Korean War died and some scholars put the mortality rate at 50 to 58%. Lewis H. Carlson, *Remembered Prisoners of a Forgotten War: An Oral History of Korean War POWs* (New York: St. Martin's Press, 2000), 3, and Fehrenbach, *This Kind of War,* 375. This rate is exceedingly high. At Andersonville, the much maligned Confederate prison, only 32% of prisoners died, as did 34% of POWs held by the Japanese in World War II. Only 4% of those held by Germans and Italians in the Second World War died. Raymond B. Lech, *Broken Soldiers* (Chicago: University of Illinois Press, 2000), 2.
6. Fehrenbach, *This Kind of War,* 450; Secretary of Defense's Advisory Committee on Prisoners of War, "POW: The Fight Continues after the Battle" (August 1955), 29, Bradley Commission: 1955-58, A69-22, Box 82, DDE Library; and David Lawrence, "Case of 944 Missing GIs Called Buck-Passing Fiasco," Republican National Committee (Additional Files of), Lamb, Richard, A 65-12/1, Box 695, DDE Library.
7. Lech, *Broken Soldiers,* 281-85; "Korean Casualties," *U.S. News and World Report,* 12 November 1954, 4; "POW: The Fight Continues after the Battle," 29; and U.S. Senate, *Communist Interrogation, Indoctrination, and Exploitation of American Military and Civilian Prisoners: Hearings before the Permanent Subcommittee on Investigations of the Committee on Government Operations* (Washington, DC: U.S. Government Printing Office, 1956), 38. The Pentagon publicly maintains that China returned all the POWs it held, but recently the 450 still missing have attracted much attention. In the 1990s, alleged sightings of middle-aged Caucasian farmers in North Korea and Boris Yeltsin's claims that the Soviet Union imprisoned at least twelve airmen sparked fresh debate, as did China's 2008 admission that an American POW was buried in China during the war. Clipping "Korea: An Old War's Dark New Secrets," 23 September 1996, Box FF, CFSOKW; "Korean War POW's in Siberia," 4 May 1996 (online at www.kimsoft.com/korea/mia-us1.htm); Melissa Healy, "Report: China Lab Tests Used U.S. POWs," *Kansas City Star,* 3 July 1992, A7; Mike Christensen, "Soviets Shot Planes Down, Held 12 Pilots," *Kansas City Star,* 13 June 1992, AR 0745, CFSOKW; "Experts Downplay POW Tale," *Kansas City Star,* 18 June 1992, AR 0748,

CFSOKW; and Robert Burns, "China Admits Taking POW," *Fayetteville (NC) Observer,* 20 June 2008, 7A. In 2000, one author filled an entire book identifying the possible whereabouts of American POWs. Philip D. Chinnery, *Korean Atrocity! Forgotten War Crimes, 1950-1953* (Annapolis, MD: Naval Institute Press, 2000).

8. "Telephone Conversation with Army Secretary Stevens," 22 December 1953, Papers of John Foster Dulles, Telephone Calls Series, A67-28, Box 2, DDE Library.

9. Telegram Charlie Duerson to President Eisenhower, 23 November 1954, and Telegram Eugene R. Guild to President Eisenhower, 27 November 1954, Central/General File, GF125-U-1, Box 938, DDE Library.

10. Since the United States previously had severed diplomatic relations with China, the government worked through the British to try to recover the men, generally focusing on the airmen. See Lech, *Broken Soldiers,* 281-85. Largely due to the efforts of Dag Hammarskjold, Swedish diplomat and secretary general of the United Nations, four airmen returned home in mid-1955. "The Release of Four Airmen from Peking Imprisonment," *United Nations Review* 2.1 (July 1955): 16.

11. "Parents Welcome First POW Home," *Baltimore Afro-American,* 22 August 1953, 1.

12. William E. Mayer, "Why Did So Many Captives Cave In?" *U.S. News and World Report,* 24 February 1956, and William Shadish with Lewis H. Carlson, *When Hell Froze Over: The Memoir of a Korean War Combat Physician Who Spent 1010 Days in a Communist Prison Camp* (New York: iUniverse, 2007), 87. In an effort to protect themselves, many repatriating progressives insisted everyone in the camps collaborated. Though these rumors were untrue, Mayer seized upon them, triggering an Army witch hunt for collaborators. Shadish with Carlson, *When Hell Froze Over,* 87-88.

13. Unless evacuated immediately for medical care, Korean War POWs moved from Freedom Village, the first stop after repatriation, to Inchon, where they received psychiatric evaluations. From there they boarded ships that became "floating interrogation centers for the Center Intelligence Corps (CIC) of the U.S. Army." See Lech, *Broken Soldiers,* 205.

14. The Marine Corps held one Court of Inquiry for a former POW. The Air Force and Navy declined to subject their former prisoners of war to prosecution. *Ibid.,* xii-viii and 212-26.

15. "Freed GI's 'Burned Up' by Reports They Succumbed to Red Ideology," *New York Times,* 3 May 1953, 1A. Also, Peter Whitney, "Ex-Captives Deny Disloyalty Taint," *New York Times,* 4 May 1953, 1.

16. Major David MacGhee with Peter Kalischer, "In Korea's Hell Camps: Some of Us Didn't Crack," *Collier's,* 22 January 1954, 82-84.

17. Some movies, such as *Prisoner of War* (1954), based on the real-life experiences of Captain Robert H. Wise, and *Bamboo Prison* (1954) depicted POWs sympathetically or heroically, but the line between collaborator and spy remained so narrow that such movies fueled anxiety among American audiences.

18. Numerous authors speculated on why POWs did not resist more actively. See Eugene Kinkead, "The Study of Something New in History," *The New Yorker,* 26 October 1957; Archie Cairns, "Andrew Fortuna: Whose Failure?" *Journal of the National Educational Association* 45 (December 1956): 583-84; Benjamin Spock, "Are We Bringing Up Our Children Too 'Soft' for the Stern Realities They Must Face?" *Ladies Home Journal,* September 1960, 20; Anthony T. Bouscaren, "Korea, Test of American Education," *The Catholic World,* April 1956, 24-27. Also Betty Friedan, *The Feminine Mystique* (New York: Norton, 1963), 285-86. Kinkead, a writer for *The New Yorker* and former World War II Navy war correspondent, proved especially instrumental in discrediting Korean War POWs, casting doubt on their integrity and patriotism. Eugene Kinkead, *In Every War but One* (New York: Norton, 1959).

19. "Washed Brains of POW's: Can They Be Rewashed?" *Newsweek,* 4 May 1953, 37; C. B. Palmer, "The War for the P.O.W.'s Mind," *New York Times Magazine,* 13 November 1953, 13; Anthony Leviero, "For the Brainwashed: Pity or Punishment?" *New York Times Magazine,*

14 August 1955, 12-18; and William Lowe, "What Is Justice for a Tortured GI?" *Look*, 28 June 1955, 28-32 .

20. In *Remembered Prisoners of a Forgotten War*, Lewis Carlson offers an excellent account of POW life in Korea and of past and present debates surrounding the POWs.

21. "Convention (III) Relative to the Treatment of Prisoners of War. Geneva, 12 August 1949," available online at http://www.icrc.org/ihl.nsf/7c4d08d9b287a42141256739003e63bb/6fef 854a3517b75ac125641e004a9e68. The Third Geneva Convention was later included in the larger 1949 Geneva Conventions.

22. Conversely, China signed the Geneva Conventions in 1949 and ratified them with reservation in 1956. http://www.icrc.org/ihl.nsf/WebSign?ReadForm&id=375&ps=P.

23. William Lindsay White, *The Captives of Korea: An Unofficial White Paper on the Treatment of War Prisoners; Our Treatment of Theirs, Their Treatment of Ours* (Westport, CT: Greenwood Press, 1957), 4-10.

24. Only 4% of American POWs held by Germans and Italians in World War II died in captivity. Americans would have done well, however, to take a closer look at history. Nazi Germany treated Americans relatively humanely, but 60% of Russian POWs held by them became war casualties. Also, subjected to terrible treatment in Japan's bamboo prisons, thousands of American POWs died and many others went insane. Fehrenbach, *This Kind of War*, 316, and Lech, *Broken Soldiers*, 2. Also, "Horrors in North Korea," *Pittsburgh Courier*, 22 August 1953, 6, for a comparison of Nazis and communists with regard to POWs.

25. Senate, Committee on Government Operations, *Senate Report No. 848: Korean War Atrocities: Report of the Committee on Government Operations Made through Its Permanent Subcommittee on Investigations*, 83d Congress, 2d sess., January 1954 (online at http://www.koreanwar-educator.org/topics/atrocities.htm). For another account of Taejon, see Private First Class Herman G. Nelson in Richard Peters and Xiaobing Li, *Voices from the Korean War: Personal Stories of American, Korean, and Chinese Soldiers* (Lexington: University of Kentucky Press, 2004), 67-68. Nelson found GIs buried under the floor in the prison and thrown into a well and claims that there were three hundred more murdered and left in the surrounding hills.

26. Lech, *Broken Soldiers*, 13-14. See also Private Paul H. Smith in Harry Spiller, *American POWs in Korea*, 97.

27. Lloyd Kreider in Tomedi, *No Bugles, No Drums*, 53-55.

28. Senate, Committee on Government Operations, *Senate Report No. 848*.

29. 1st Lieutenant Wadie J. Rountree in Peters and Li, *Voices from the Korean War*, 219.

30. For examples, see Lloyd Kreider in Tomedi, *No Bugles, No Drums*, 55; Paul Smith in Spiller, *American POWs in Korea*, 97; and Wadie Rountree in Peters and Li, *Voices from the Korean War*, 219.

31. See Paul Smith in Spiller, *American POWs in Korea*, 97.

32. Akira Chikami in Carlson, *Remembered Prisoners of a Forgotten War*, 39. Also Lloyd Kreider in Tomedi, *No Bugles, No Drums*, 55-56.

33. The North Koreans held POWs in temporary camps because the permanent camps along the Yalu River were not yet completed.

34. Wadie Rountree in Peters and Li, *Voices from the Korean War*, 219.

35. On the number of prisoners on the "Tiger Death March," Lewis Carlson explains there were between 756 and 758 POWs (or captured combatants) and 74 to 87 noncombatant and/or political prisoners. Carlson, *Remembered Prisoners of a Forgotten War*, 49-50 and 274.

36. Wadie Rountree in Peters and Li, *Voices from the Korean War*, 221.

37. Carlson, *Remembered Prisoners of a Forgotten War*, 63.

38. Larry Zellers in *ibid.*, 65.

39. Jack Browning in *ibid.*, 67, and Wadie Rountree in Peters and Li, *Voices from the Korean War*, 221.

40. Irv Langell in Carlson, *Remembered Prisoners of a Forgotten War*, 74.
41. Susumu Shinawaga in Louis Baldovi, ed., *A Foxhole View: Personal Accounts of Hawaii's Korean War Veterans* (Honolulu: University of Hawai'i Press, 2002), 89.
42. Irv Langell in Carlson, *Remembered Prisoners of a Forgotten War*, 74.
43. Susumu Shinawaga in Baldovi, *A Foxhole View*, 90.
44. Larry Zellers in Carlson, *Remembered Prisoners of a Forgotten War*, 80.
45. Wadie Rountree in Peters and Li, *Voices from the Korean War*, 223.
46. *Ibid.*, and Carlson, *Remembered Prisoners of a Forgotten War*, 81.
47. Lech, *Broken Soldiers*, 26.
48. Lloyd Kreider in Tomedi, *No Bugles, No Drums*, 59. On the Sunchon Tunnel Massacre, see Lloyd Kreider in Tomedi, *No Bugles, No Drums*, 53-58; Carlson, *Remembered Prisoners of a Forgotten War*, 97-105; and Senate, Committee on Government Operations, *Senate Report No. 848.*
49. Bill Chambers in Tomedi, *No Bugles, No Drums*, 49.
50. See Major Clarence Anderson in U.S. Senate, *Communist Interrogation, Indoctrination, and Exploitation of American Military and Civilian Prisoners*, 107.
51. Quoted in Lech, *Broken Soldiers*, 24.
52. Under the North Koreans, camps frequently lacked adequate provision for latrines, a problem that continued when the Chinese took over the camps in 1951. Major Clarence Anderson in U.S. Senate, *Communist Interrogation, Indoctrination. and Exploitation of American Military and Civilian Prisoners*, 108.
53. Lech, *Broken Soldiers.*, 25.
54. *Ibid.*
55. Major Clarence Anderson in U.S. Senate, *Communist Interrogation, Indoctrination, and Exploitation of American Military and Civilian Prisoners*, 107-10.
56. Quoted in Robert J. Lifton, "Home by Ship: Reaction Patterns of American Prisoners of War Repatriated from North Korea," *American Journal of Psychiatry* 110 (1954): 732-39.
57. Paul Smith in Spiller, *American POWs in Korea*, 98-99.
58. American POWs recall that North Korean or Chinese guards had to protect them from hostile civilians in North Korean villages and that Americans who fell into the hands of North Korean civilians were treated badly. Reaching a North Korean hut after ejecting from his plane, Major James Kiser became the "personal prisoner" of the resident family who tied him up in the middle of the village where everyone beat him with sticks. Kiser in Chancey and Forstchen, *Hot Shots*, 88. Villagers pelted Sergeant Kenneth F. Nevill with rocks when Chinese guards marched him through a North Korean village. Spiller, *American POWs in Korea*, 128.
59. It is difficult to understand why North Koreans treated UN prisoners abominably except that they themselves had been victims of Japanese brutality. Interestingly, the North Koreans mended their ways but little by 1968 when they seized the USS *Pueblo* and its crew. Those Americans were starved, beaten, and tortured before release. Reverend Rodney Duke, Oral History by Michael Garvey, 1981, volume 171, Mississippi Oral History Program, University of Southern Mississippi, Hattiesburg, Mississippi.
60. One veteran notes that watching the entry of the Chinese from his prison camp was "one of the saddest moments of my life." Wadie J. Rountree in Peters and Li, *Voices from the Korean War*, 220.
61. Bert Cumby in U.S. Senate, *Communist Interrogation, Indoctrination, and Exploitation of American Military and Civilian Prisoners*, 46.
62. Richard M. Bassett with Lewis H. Carlson, *And the Wind Blew Cold: The Story of an American POW in North Korea* (Kent, OH: Kent State University Press, 2002), 21-22.
63. Lt. William H. Funchess in Spiller, *American POWs in Korea*, 45. Also Charles Quiring in *Ibid.*, 145.
64. Shadish with Carlson, *When Hell Froze Over*, 23.

65. Clarence Young in Baldovi, *A Foxhole View,* 143, and Donald M. Elliott in Spiller, *American POWs in Korea,* 7.

66. Jay Hidano in Baldovi, *A Foxhole View,* 87.

67. Lawrence Bailey in Donald Knox, with additional text by Alfred Coppel, *The Korean War: An Oral History.* Vol. 2, *Uncertain Victory* (New York: Harcourt, Brace, Jovanovich, 1988), 328.

68. Bert Cumby in U.S. Senate, *Communist Interrogation, Indoctrination, and Exploitation of American Military and Civilian Prisoners,* 46-47, and Shadish with Carlson, *When Hell Froze Over,* 24-25.

69. This often remained the situation wherever a prisoner happened to be before 1952. Bassett with Carlson, *And the Wind Blew Cold,* 59.

70. William H. Funchess in Spiller, *American POWs in Korea,* 46.

71. William Shadish remembers marching back and forth across North Korea because permanent camps were not completed and estimates that a fourth of those who left the collection point died on the march. Shadish with Carlson, *When Hell Froze Over,* 25. A few POWs remember kinder treatment from the Chinese. Unable to walk, Billy Gaddy was transported by the Chinese to the camp on the back of a cow. Billy N. Gaddy in Spiller, *American POWs in Korea,* 77.

72. Carlson, *Remembered Prisoners of a Forgotten War,* 119. North Koreans initially continued to administer some of the temporary camps so that men captured by the Chinese were held by North Koreans. Early on, little difference existed in Chinese- and Korean-regu-lated camps. On the temporary camps, see Spiller, *American POWs in Korea,* 163-65, and Carlson, *Remembered Prisoners of a Forgotten War,* 107-19. By October or November 1951, the Chinese took over nearly all United Nations POWs, but North Koreans continued to supervise Pak's Palace, an interrogation center; Camp 9, also called the Caves; and Camp 12. Spiller, *American POWs in Korea,* 118; Peters and Li, *Voices from the Korean War,* 225; and Carlson, *Remembered Prisoners of a Forgotten War,* 121.

73. Senate, Committee on Government Operations, *Senate Report No. 848,* and "POW: The Fight Continues after the Battle: The Report of the Secretary of Defense's Advisory Committee on Prisoners of War," August 1955, 9, Bradley Commission, Records 1955-58, A69-22, Box 82, DDE Library.

74. Korean huts sometimes had floor heating systems but the scarcity of wood limited their use. In former mining camps, dwellings had no windows or doors, only crude openings that allowed the winter chill to filter in. Shadish with Carlson, *When Hell Froze Over,* 29-30.

75. Lawrence Bailey in Knox and Coppel, *The Korean War: Uncertain Victory,* 329. A victim himself, Bailey lost all the toes on his right foot, four on his left foot, and his right pinky finger.

76. Donald M. Elliott and William H. Funchess in Spiller, *American POWs in Korea,* 8 and 48.

77. See William H. Funchess in *ibid.,* 49. A constant refrain in POW memoirs and oral histories is "give-up-itis," the idea that in captivity men willed themselves to die. They became despondent and quit eating, ensuring their demise. Clarence Anderson in Kinkead, "The Study of Something New in History," *The New Yorker,* 26 October 1957, 157. This condition continued in the permanent camps. Glenn Reynolds in Carlson, *Remembered Prisoners of a Forgotten War,* 139.

78. See MacGhee with Kalischer, "In Korea's Hell Camps: Some of Us Didn't Crack," 88. MacGhee here refers to Death Valley under North Korean supervision and notes that the Chinese seemed troubled by the lack of order in the camp, but such conditions continued in some places even after the Chinese took over. Also, Clarence Anderson in Kinkead, "The Study of Something New in History," *The New Yorker,* 26 October 1957, 154.

79. Shadish with Carlson, *When Hell Froze Over,* 29.

80. Five numbered camps administered by the Chinese existed along the Yalu River and most, but not all American POWs ended up in one of these. Carlson, *Remembered Prisoners of a Forgotten War*, 121.

81. Few POWs found shelter from terrible scenes of death. In Camp 5, Bill Funchess remembers the bodies thrown outside his hut, "covered with blood, body waste, and snow." See William H. Funchess in Spiller, *American POWs in Korea*, 50.

82. Senate, Committee on Government Operations, *Senate Report No. 848*.

83. For examples, see Donald M. Elliott and Thomas B. Gaylets in Spiller, *American POWs in Korea*, 9 and 21.

84. See Wadie Rountree in Peters and Li, *Voices from the Korean War*, 226-28.

85. Donald M. Elliott in Spiller, *American POWs in Korea*, 11.

86. Donald M. Elliott and William H. Funchess in Spiller, *ibid.*, 9 and 56; Bassett with Carlson, *And the Wind Blew Cold*, 60-64; Wadie Rountree in Peters and Li, *Voices from the Korean War*, 226-29; and Robert Fletcher and Douglas Tanner, in Carlson, *Remembered Prisoners of a Forgotten War*, 127 and 131. In addition to the chicken liver treatment, Clarence Anderson describes the "needle doctor" who poked needles in the heads of POWs to cure headaches. U.S. Senate, *Communist Interrogation, Indoctrination, and Exploitation of American Military and Civilian Prisoners*, 111-12. On medicine in Korea, see Shadish with Carlson, *When Hell Froze Over*.

87. One veteran contends that most deaths occurred before September 1951. Clarence L. Anderson in U.S. Senate, *Communist Interrogation, Indoctrination, and Exploitation of American Military and Civilian Prisoners*, 107.

88. Bassett with Carlson, *And the Wind Blew Cold*, 63.

89. See C. A. Irvin, "Reds Segregated Negro GIs in North Korean Prison Camps," *Pittsburgh Courier*, 6 June 1953, 2, and Daniel L. Johnson Sr. in Spiller, *American POWs in Korea*, 27. By the time POWs reached permanent camps, they had already been stripped of much of their military order. Upon capture, POWs were advised that "rank no longer existed among them—that they were all equal as simple prisoners of war released from capitalist bondage." Clarence Anderson in Kinkead, "The Study of Something New in History," *The New Yorker*, 26 October 1957, 154.

90. See Donald L. Slagle in Spiller, *American POWs in Korea*, 107; James L. Stokesbury, *A Short History of the Korean War* (New York: Morrow, 1988), 191; Clarence Young in Baldovi, *A Foxhole View*, 150; and Lech, *Broken Soldiers*. Lech argues that few POWs in Korea survived without collaborating but that their actions are understandable and justifiable given the uniquely inhumane treatment they endured.

91. The idea that most POWs tried to "play it cool" in the camps forms a thread throughout much of the literature. Kinkead, "The Study of Something New in History," *The New Yorker*, 26 October 1957, 161-63, and Robert J. Lifton, "Home by Ship: Reaction Patterns of American Prisoners of War Repatriated from North Korea," *American Journal of Psychiatry* 110 (1954): 734.

92. William H. Funchess, Eugene L. Inman, and Donald L. Slagle in Spiller, *American POWs in Korea*, 54, 88, and 108; MacGhee with Kalischer, "In Korea's Hell Camps: Some of Us Didn't Crack," 84; Wayman Simpson in Carlson, *Remembered Prisoners of a Forgotten War*, 136; and Bassett with Carlson, *And the Wind Blew Cold*, 68.

93. Bob Carman in Carlson, *Remembered Prisoners of a Forgotten War*, 138. Also Robert Blewitt in *ibid.*, 136. Trying to kill a chicken, Blewitt noticed a guard and tried to kick the chicken back to life. Asked what he was doing, Blewitt said he was playing with the chicken. The guard responded, "The Chicken cannot play with you" and threw Blewitt in "the hole."

94. Wadie J. Rountree in Peters and Li, *Voices from the Korean War*, 229, and Clarence Young in Baldovi, *A Foxhole View*, 158-60.

95. Donald M. Elliott in Spiller, *American POWs in Korea*, 13.

96. Patricia B. Sutker, Daniel Windstead, Z. Harry Galina, and Albert N. Allain, "Cognitive Deficits and Psychopathology among Former Prisoners of War and Combat Veterans of the Korean Conflict," *American Journal of Psychiatry* 148.1 (January 1991): 70. Not uncommonly, "reactionaries" spent vast amounts of time in solitary or in the hole. Wayman Simpson spent sixty-two days at one stretch there. Quoted in Carlson, *Remembered Prisoners of a Forgotten War*, 136. Eugene Inman spent ninety days in solitary. Quoted in Spiller, *American POWs in Korea*, 88.

97. William H. Funchess and Wilfred Ruff in Spiller, *American POWs in Korea*, 54-58 and 156, and Senate, Committee on Government Operations, *Senate Report No. 848*.

98. Charles Quiring in Spiller, *American POWs in Korea*, 147. The Chinese interrogated 25% of POWs on military equipment and supplies and 15% on Army tactics and strategy. Dr. Julius Segal in U.S. Senate, *Communist Interrogation, Indoctrination, and Exploitation of American Military and Civilian Prisoners*, 94.

99. *Ibid.,* and Bert Cumby in U.S. Senate, *Communist Interrogation, Indoctrination, and Exploitation of American Military and Civilian Prisoners*, 47.

100. Meung Ho Kim in Carlson, *Remembered Prisoners of a Forgotten War*, 181.

101. Bert Cumby in U.S. Senate, *Communist Interrogation, Indoctrination, and Exploitation of American Military and Civilian Prisoners*, 47-50.

102. On how many men collaborated and their activities, see Julius Segal, "Were They Really Brainwashed?" *Look*, 26 June 1956, 101-2.

103. Kenneth F. Nevill in Spiller, *American POWs in Korea,* 129. Mentally tortured by the Chinese, airmen especially were pushed beyond their ability to withstand questioning, admitting "everything under the sun, up to but not including the crucifixion of Christ." Don Poirot in Carlson, *Remembered Prisoners of a Forgotten War*, 182. Colonel Frank Schwable, a Marine aviator who signed a confession saying the United States engaged in germ warfare, faced a court of inquiry after the war. The court and Marine Corps General Lemuel Shepard agreed that no disciplinary action should be taken because Schwable had endured "mental torture of such severity and such compelling nature as to constitute an excuse for his acts." Lemuel C. Shepard Jr., General USMC, "Opinion on Colonel Frank Schwable Case, 14 April 1954," Robert B. Anderson Papers, Box 26, DDE Library.

104. Bert Cumby and Dr. Julius Segal in U.S. Senate, *Communist Interrogation, Indoctrination, and Exploitation of American Military and Civilian Prisoners,* 48 and 93. Nearly every POW experienced interrogation in North Korea, but the Chinese targeted men in the Air Force because they deemed pilots privy to the type of intelligence they wanted and recognized that, even if these possessed little knowledge, they could be used for propaganda. The Chinese tried to get airmen to publicly admit the United States was using germ warfare in Korea. Most prisoners, like most historians today, believed the Chinese knew the allegation was false, but Bob Carman remembers that when B-29s dropped foil around Camp 2 the guards panicked, running to the hospital to wash their hands in iodine. Carlson, *Remembered Prisoners of a Forgotten War*, 134 and 182-83, and Harold Fischer in Chancey and Forstchen, *Hot Shots*, 209.

105. Through violence, intimidation, and offers of rewards during interrogation sessions, the Chinese coerced American POWs into making radio broadcasts, signing petitions or confessions, or otherwise supporting the communist propaganda machine. Some admitted to participating in germ warfare, wrote letters home asking their families to persuade the government to end the war, or publicly praised the kind treatment being received under the lenient policy. Lech, *Broken Soldiers*, 158-61. Like Colonel Frank Schwable, under communist pressure they "lost my sense of judgment." Schwable quoted in "Cracked under Mental Torture, Schwable Says," *Pittsburgh Post Gazette,* 12 March 1954, 6.

106. Lech, *Broken Soldiers*, 81-82. About 97% of Army POWs experienced indoctrination—83% attended group study periods after lectures, 43% participated in small discussion groups, and 27% went to spontaneous public gatherings called by the Chinese. Dr. Julius Segal in

U.S. Senate, *Communist Interrogation, Indoctrination, and Exploitation of American Military and Civilian Prisoners*, 89-90.

107. Charles Quiring in Spiller, *American POWs in Korea*, 147; Wadie J. Rountree in Peters and Li, *Voices from the Korean War*, 229; Kinkead, "A Study of Something New in History," 142; and Bert Cumby in U.S. Senate, *Communist Interrogation, Indoctrination, and Exploitation of American Military and Civilian Prisoners*, 47-51.

108. Clarence Adams, edited by Della Adams and Lewis H. Carlson, *An American Dream: The Life of an African American Soldier and POW Who Spent Twelve Years in Communist China* (Boston: University of Massachusetts Press, 2007), 54-56. Initially Adams thought the lectures were nonsense, but became persuaded when the Chinese discussed racism in the United States. Also, Bert Cumby in U.S. Senate, *Communist Interrogation, Indoctrination, and Exploitation of American Military and Civilian Prisoners*, 60, and Bill Worthy, "Some POWs Desert 'Land of Jim Crow,'" *Baltimore Afro-American*, 15 August 1953, 1. Lectures on race in America led some African Americans to remain with the Chinese after the war as, like Adams, they believed more opportunities existed for them in China.

109. Nick Tosques in Tomedi, *No Bugles, No Drums*, 226.

110. Charles Quiring in Spiller, *American POWs in Korea*, 147.

111. Kinkead, "A Study of Something New in History," 142.

112. The Chinese did not convince many Americans that the quality of life in China exceeded that of America. Like Susumu Shinagawa, they "just couldn't believe how ignorant they [the Chinese] were of western civilization." The communists scoffed at POWs' photos from home, saying the cars and houses featured were government propaganda, and bragged that in China every other family owned a bicycle. Shinagawa in Baldovi, *A Foxhole View*, 172-74.

113. For a description of "brainwashing" run in the popular press, see "Washed Brains of POW's: Can They Be Rewashed?" *Newsweek*, 4 May 1953, 37.

114. See Daniel L. Johnson and William Funchess in Spiller, *American POWs in Korea*, 28-29, and 52-53; Lech, *Broken Soldiers*, 92-96; Kinkead, "A Study of Something New in History," 142-43; and "POW: The Fight Continues after the Battle," 11-12.

115. Bassett with Carlson, *And the Wind Blew Cold*, 55.

116. "Horrors in North Korea," *Pittsburgh Courier*, 22 August 1953, 6.

117. Lech, *Broken Soldiers*, 92-93.

118. Kinkead, "A Study of Something New in History," 143.

119. Charles Quiring in Spiller, *American POWs in Korea*, 148.

120. Bert Cumby in U.S. Senate, *Communist Interrogation, Indoctrination, and Exploitation of American Military and Civilian Prisoners*, 52.

121. Susumu Shinagawa in Baldovi, *A Foxhole View*, 172-73.

122. William E. Mayer in Richard Severo and Lewis Milford, *The Wages of War: When America's Soldiers Came Home; From Valley Forge to Vietnam* (New York: Simon and Schuster, 1989), 335-37. Mayer hit the lecture circuit with his opinions and Harding College developed a kit for those who wanted to help Mayer spread his message. Ronald Reagan provided narration.

123. Lech, *Broken Soldiers*, 96. Men involved in voluntary study groups earned special privileges like being excused from bed check and having extra time in the camp library. Kinkead, "A Study of Something New in History," 141.

124. Dr. Julius Segal in U.S. Senate, *Communist Interrogation, Indoctrination, and Exploitation of American Military and Civilian Prisoners*, 90. By autumn 1953, Army officials had identified only ninety progressives and believed that "fewer than 30 of those showed themselves really susceptible to enemy propaganda." "The Tough Prisoners," *Time*, 21 September 1953, 28-29.

125. Clarence Anderson in *ibid.*, 115. Also Fehrenbach, *This Kind of War*, 317.

126. MacGhee with Kalischer, "In Korea's Hell Camps: Some of Us Didn't Crack," 83.

127. Michael Cornwell in Carlson, *Remembered Prisoners of a Forgotten War*, 142.
128. Walter G. Adelmann in Spiller, *American POWs in Korea*, 33.
129. Donald M. Elliott in *ibid.*, 9.
130. Robert Schaefer in Carlson, *Remembered Prisoners of a Forgotten War*, 143.
131. Henry Humphries Osborne in Spiller, *American POWs in Korea*, 70.
132. *Ibid.*, 71, and Wadie J. Rountree in Peters and Li, *Voices from the Korean War*, 231.
133. Glenn Reynolds in Carlson, *Remembered Prisoners of a Forgotten War*, 133. See also Frederic Sondern Jr., "U.S. Negroes Make Reds See Red," *Reader's Digest*, January 1954), 39, for more examples of POW pranks.
134. Carlson, *Remembered Prisoners of a Forgotten War*, 145, and Shadish with Carlson, *When Hell Froze Over*, 51.
135. Jim Crombie in Carlson, *Remembered Prisoners of a Forgotten War*, 129. See also Donald L. Slagle in Spiller, *American POWs in Korea*, 108, and Bassett with Carlson, *And the Wind Blew Cold*, 53. In Camp 1, 80% of POWs allegedly smoked marijuana and in Camp 5 some prisoners had pot gardens. Lech, *Broken Soldiers*, 157.
136. Robert A. Maclean in Carlson, *Remembered Prisoners of a Forgotten War*, 27.
137. William Shadish claims that at least two hundred men tried to escape permanent camps and that other POWs supported them by offering up a part of their own rations. Shadish with Carlson, *When Hell Froze Over*, 51.
138. William H. Funchess in Spiller, *American POWs in Korea*, 54-58.
139. Clarence Young in Baldovi, *A Foxhole View*, 158-59.
140. Shadish with Carlson, *When Hell Froze Over*, 51.
141. Nick Tosques in Tomedi, *No Bugles, No Drums*, 224. Some POWs managed to escape from the Chinese before reaching the permanent camps. John G. Hubbell, "The Long Way Home," *Reader's Digest* 60 (April 1952): 26-28.
142. Susumu Shinagawa told his captors that his $140 watch had been stolen and they replaced it. In Baldovi, *A Foxhole View*, 274.
143. Donald M. Elliott and William Funchess in Spiller, *American POWs in Korea*, 13-15 and 62-65.
144. Lee Ballenger, *The Final Crucible: U.S. Marines in Korea.* Vol. 2, *1953* (Washington, DC: Brassey's, 2001), 190.
145. Donald M. Elliott in Spiller, *American POWs in Korea*, 15.
146. Walter G. Adelmann in *ibid.*, 23.
147. Susumu Shinagawa in Baldovi, *A Foxhole View*, 224.
148. "Prisoners of War Released by Reds," *Pittsburgh Courier*, 15 August 1953, 1, and Lifton, "Home by Ship," 754. For a similar refrain, see "Witnessing the Return of U.S. POWs in Korea: Press Conference Statement by Secretary Dulles," *Department of State Bulletin*, 24 August 1953, 236, and "Prisoners Home," *New York Times*, 3 May 1953, 2E. Also see Severo and Milford, *The Wages of War*, 29.
149. "Witnessing the Return of U.S. POWs in Korea," 236.
150. An official in the Far East quoted in "Washed Brains of POW's: Can They Be Rewashed?" 37.
151. "Prisoners Home," *New York Times*, 3 May 1953, 2E.
152. Robert Fletcher in Carlson, *Remembered Prisoners of a Forgotten War*, 219.
153. Lifton, "Home by Ship," 732.
154. Yung Sik Chung and S. J. Chang, "Born on the 25th of June: The Story of Wilfred J. Ruff," Article 0783, Box A.0776-A.0806 "W," CFSOKW.
155. Ultimately, the Army concluded that 15% of Americans actively collaborated with the Chinese, 80% did not collaborate beyond minor acts, and 5% vigorously resisted the enemy. White, *The Captives of Korea*, 262-63.
156. William Allen notes that while not everyone who deserved justice got it, "We did a good job. There was a grand total of 14 walking wounded when the ship docked." William M.

Allen, *My Old Box of Memories: Thoughts of the Korean War* (self-published, c. 1999), 84. Also Lifton, "Home by Ship," 735.

157. From a poem jointly authored by three returning POWs and quoted in Lifton, "Home by Ship," 737.

158. For years after his discharge, the CIA sent agents to question Donald Slagle about POWs suspected of collaboration. Spiller, *American POWs in Korea*, 111. Using the Freedom of Information Act to get his POW file, Akira Chikami learned that the Army investigated him after he got home despite the fact that he remained in service. Before working with the Joint Chiefs of Staff, Michael Cornwell had to pass a lie detector test and his father-in-law, a colonel, had him investigated before the wedding. Carlson, *Remembered Prisoners of a Forgotten War*, 47 and 220. William Shadish cleared his name (and file), but the process involved several interrogations, the testimony of other POWs, and much review of the evidence. It took Shadish fourteen months to restore his reputation. Shadish with Carlson, *When Hell Froze Over*, 93-100.

159. Severo and Milford, *The Wages of War*, 326-29.

CHAPTER 6

1. Mary T. Sarnecky, *A History of the U.S. Army Nurse Corps* (Philadelphia: University of Pennsylvania Press, 1999), 301-3, and T. R. Fehrenbach, *This Kind of War: A Study in Unpreparedness* (New York: Macmillan, 1963), 40-41.

2. Sarnecky, *A History of the U.S. Army Nurse Corps*, 303, and Mary T. Sarnecky, "Mildred Ines Clark," in Vern L. Bullough and Lilli Sentz, eds., *American Nursing: A Biographical Dictionary*, vol. 3 (New York: Springer, 2000), 53.

3. Betty J. Morden, *The Women's Army Corps, 1945-1978* (Washington, DC: Center of Military History, U.S. Army, 2000), 108. Some sources claim that "Korean field commanders requested women soldiers, but were refused by the Pentagon." See Joni Wilson, "Unknown Women of a Forgotten War," unpublished paper, Box A, Folder A0938, CFSOKW, and June A. Willentz, *Women Veterans: America's Forgotten Heroines* (New York: Continuum, 1983), 33.

4. Mary T. Sarnecky, "The Army Nurse Corps in the Korean War," online at the United States of America Korean War Commemoration site (http://korea50.army.mil/history/factsheets/armynurses.shtml). For more detail on the nursing shortage, see Sarnecky, *A History of the U.S. Army Nurse Corps*, 281-82.

5. Public Relations Coordinator, Defense Advisory Committee on Women in the Services, Office of the Assistant Secretary of Defense (M&P), "Policy Guide for Women in the Armed Services Information Program, 1953, U.S. Army, U.S. Navy, U.S. Air Force, U.S. Marine Corps," 9 February 1953, 3, Staff Files, Files of the Special Assistant Relating to the Office of Coordinator of Government Public Service Advertising (James M. Lambie Jr.), Box 9, DDE Library. Office of the Assistant Secretary of Defense, Memorandum for the Advertising Council, "Information about Women in the Armed Services," 6 December 1952, 5, Staff Files, Files of the Special Assistant Relating to the Office of Coordinator of Government Public Service Advertising (James M. Lambie Jr.), Women in the Services— Correspondence 1952-1953, Box 9, folder "Women in the Service (Policy Material)," DDE Library. Jeanne Holm, *Women in the Military: An Unfinished Revolution* (Novato, CA: Presidio, 1982), 150.

6. No definitive number of women serving in the Korean War theater exists. Most sources estimate that 600-1500 women served in Korea and thousands more in Japan or the Philippines. Sarnecky, "The Army Nurse Corps in the Korean War"; Judith Bellafaire, "Volunteering for Risk: Black Military Women Overseas during the Wars in Korea and Vietnam," 2 (online at www.womensmemorial.org); and Frances Omori, *Quiet Heroes: Navy Nurses of the Korean War, 1950-1953; Far East Command* (St. Paul, MN: Smith House Press, 2000), 67. Calculating WAC strength in theater, Betty Morden puts the number at 626 in 1950, 2,604

in 1951, 1,711 in 1952, and 1,764 in 1953. Morden, *The Women's Army Corps,* 107. Compare this to World War II, when nearly half a million American women served overseas. Sharon Cohen, "Women in War," *Fayetteville (NC) Observer,* 3 December 2006, 17A.

7. Holm, *Women in the Military,* 149, and Sarnecky, "The Army Nurse Corps in the Korean War," 149.

8. Morden, *The Women's Army Corps,* 108.

9. Edith A. Aynes, "Hospital Trains in Korea," *American Journal of Nursing* 52.2 (February 1952): 166.

10. Janice Albert, "Air Evacuation from Korea: A Typical Flight," *Military Surgeon* 112.4 (April 1953): 256-59; Omori, *Quiet Heroes,* xix; and Jean Ebbert and Marie-Beth Hall, *Crossed Currents: Navy Women from World War I to Tail Hook* (Washington, DC: Brassey's, 1993), 128.

11. Holm, *Women in the Military,* 150; Bellafaire, "Volunteering for Risk," 2; and Omori, *Quiet Heroes,* xix.

12. Morden, *The Women's Army Corps,* 107.

13. No branch of the military assigned women other than nurses to the war zone. Holm, *Women in the Military,* 150, and Morden, *The Women's Army Corps,* 107.

14. Omori, *Quiet Heroes,* 1, and Eleanor Harrington, "Aboard a Hospital Ship," *American Journal of Nursing* 53.5 (May 1953): 585.

15. Sarnecky, *A History of the U.S. Army Nurse Corps,* 306, and Albert, "Air Evacuation from Korea: A Typical Flight," 257.

16. "With the Army Nurse Corps in Korea," *American Journal of Nursing* 51.6 (June 1951): 387.

17. Originally hospital trains carried a doctor, a nurse, and a medical aid man, but shortages as the war progressed resulted in nurses and aid men functioning alone on the long rides. Aynes, "Hospital Trains in Korea," 166. Also, Sarnecky, "The Army Nurse Corps in the Korean War."

18. Lt. Helen Ely, "The Most Wounded, the Most Sick, the Most Tired," *Reader's Digest,* June 1951, 9-10.

19. Morden, *The Women's Army Corps,* 107.

20. Ebbert and Hall, *Crossed Currents,* 132. Keating was, incidentally, an African American. William E. Alt and Betty L. Alt, *Black Soldiers, White Wars: Black Warriors from Antiquity to the Present* (Westport, CT: Praeger, 2002), 105.

21. "No Longer Forgotten: African American Servicewomen during the Korean War Era" (online at http://www.womensmemorial.org/H&C/Exhibits/afamkoreaexhibit/afamkore-asplash.html). In May 1951, Lt. Col. Marie Clark, the advisor for the Far East, reported, "WACS in the Far East Command are being efficiently utilized in assignments heretofore believed by some could only be performed by male personnel." Quoted in Morden, *The Women's Army Corps,* 107.

22. Sarnecky, *A History of the U.S. Army Nurse Corps,* 307, and "With the Army Nurse Corps in Korea," *American Journal of Nursing* 51.6 (June 1951): 387.

23. Sarnecky, *A History of the U.S. Army Nurse Corps,* 305. Catherine "Faye" Neville (AFC2001/001/113), Interview by Helen Roach and Win Wilbur, 25 February 2000, 10, Folder 2, VHPC, AFC, LOC; Mattie Donnell Hicks, Interview by Hermann J. Trojanowski, 25 February 1999, WVHP, OHC, UNCG, 8; and "Korean Assignment," *American Journal of Nursing* 53.6 (June 1953): 679.

24. Hicks, Interview by Trojanowski, 25 February 1999, 5.

25. Wayne Wangstad, "More Than One Female GI Was Reluctant to Report Harassment," *St. Paul (MN) Pioneer Press,* 7 September 1998, 3D.

26. Sarnecky, "The Army Nurse Corps in the Korean War"; Omori, *Quiet Heroes,* 6; and "With the Army Nurse Corps in Korea," 387.

27. Omori, *Quiet Heroes,* 6.

28. Hicks, Interview by Trojanowski, 25 February 1999, 5-6.

29. Lois Colgate Merritt, Lieutenant Helen Fable, and Nurse "Bing" (Commander Nancy J. Crosby) in Omori, *Quiet Heroes*, 18, 39, and 138-39. Conditions permitting, normal shifts lasted eight hours.

30. From Commander Haire's journal, 2 November 1950, in Omori, *Quiet Heroes*, 89.

31. "No Longer Forgotten: African American Servicewomen during the Korean War Era" (online at http://www.womensmemorial.org/H&C/Exhibits/afamkoreaexhibit/afamkore-asplash.html) and Albert, "Air Evacuation from Korea," 257.

32. Commander Emery in Omori, *Quiet Heroes*, 106.

33. From Commander Haire's Journal, 2 November 1950, in Omori, *Quiet Heroes*, 89.

34. Anita Bean, *Korean War Veteran Survey*, 6, CFSOKW.

35. From Commander Haire's Journal, 2 November 1950, in Omori, *Quiet Heroes*, 89.

36. Julia Baxter in Williams, "Retired Army Nurse Recalls Korean War Service," 30 March 2001 (online at http://www.defenselink.mil/news/mar2001/).

37. Omori, *Quiet Heroes*, 8, and Hicks, Interview by Trojanowski, 25 February 1999, 5.

38. Anita Bean, *Korean War Veteran Survey*, 6, CFSOKW.

39. See Nurse "Bing" (Commander Nancy J. Crosby) in Omori, *Quiet Heroes*, 138-39.

40. 1st Lt. Mary C. Quinn, Interview by Clara L. Adams-Ender, 13 April 1980, 35, United States Army Nurse Corps Oral History Program, Army Nurse Corps Historian Files, U.S. Army Center for Military History, Washington DC, quoted in Sarnecky, *A History of the U.S. Army Nurse Corps*, 310-11.

41. Anita Bean, *Korean War Veteran Survey*, back of page 6, CFSOKW.

42. During the Revolution, blacks and whites served side by side in many northern units of the Continental Army, and throughout the War of 1812 the U.S. Army possessed racially integrated units. However, in the 1820s an order by then secretary of war John C. Calhoun precluded African Americans from serving in the Army until the Civil War, when segregated units were formed.

43. Richard F. Haynes, *The Awesome Power: Harry S. Truman as Commander in Chief* (Baton Rouge: Louisiana State University Press, 1973), 90-93.

44. Anne Hoiberg, "Military Staying Power," in Sam Sarkesian, ed., *Combat Effectiveness: Cohesion, Stress, and the Volunteer* (Beverly Hills, CA: Sage, 1980), 225, and Morris J. Mac-Gregor Jr., *Integration of the Armed Forces, 1940-1965* (Washington, DC: Center of Military History, U.S. Army, 1981), 436. Conversely, black women often served in integrated outfits, as MASH units and hospitals in the Far East were integrated, as was the U.S. Army Nurse Corps. Sarnecky, *A History of the U.S. Army Nurse Corps*, 316, and Bellafaire, "Volunteering for Risk."

45. Martin Binkin, Mark J. Eitelberg, Alvin J. Schexnider, and Marvin M. Smith, *Blacks and the Military* (Washington, DC: Brookings Institution, 1982), 28-29.

46. Ray R. Deimler, Army Service (Korean War) Questionnaire, 5, 2nd Division, 23rd Regiment, Alphabetical Box 1, Department of the Army, Carlisle Barracks, and Michael A. Fletcher, "Korean War Veterans Seek to Block Book Critical of Black Unit," *Washington Post*, 19 January 1997, A4.

47. In *Black Soldier, White Army,* a study of the 24th Infantry Regiment that African Americans protested as biased, the authors blame poor performance among black units early in the war on deficiencies in leadership, training, supply, and support, the very same things credited with hampering the performance of white troops. They conclude that color was not a main factor. William T. Bowers, William M. Hammond, and George L. MacGarrigle, *Black Soldier, White Army: The 24th Infantry Regiment in Korea* (Washington, DC: Center of Military History, United States Army, 1996), vi.

48. James Monte in S. Thorne Harper, "All-Black Ranger Unit Recalls Fighting for America during Segregation on Two Fronts," *Columbus (GA) Ledger-Enquirer*, 28 July 2002, A1.

49. Charles M. Bussey, *Firefight at Yechon: Courage and Racism in the Korean War* (Lincoln: University of Nebraska Press, 2002), 148, and Curtis James Morrow, *What's a Commie Ever*

Done to Black People? A Korean War Memoir of Fighting in the U.S. Army's Last All-Negro Unit (Jefferson, NC: McFarland, 1977), 35.

50. Harper, "All-Black Ranger Unit Recalls Fighting for America during Segregation on Two Fronts," A1.

51. Morrow, *What's a Commie Ever Done to Black People?* 11, and Roy C. Wright, "Why Should Negroes Die for 2nd-Class Citizenship?" *Pittsburgh Courier,* 27 January 1951, 11. The mainstream press covered the actions of "Tan Yanks" at Yechon, but beyond that made little mention of African American sacrifices and contributions.

52. Harry Van Zandt, Interview by Tara Liston and Tara Kraenzlin, 11 March 1996, 35, Transcript by Donovan Bezer, Andrew Noyes, Shaun Illingworth, Harry Van Zandt, and Sandra Stewart Holyoak, Rutgers Oral History Archives for World War II. See also Lt. General Sidney Berry, Oral History by Dr. Orley Caudill, 1980, 37, volume 198, Mississippi Oral History Program, University of Southern Mississippi, Hattiesburg, Mississippi. Berry discusses the difficulty of getting officers for the 24th and the lack of black leadership.

53. Binkin et al., *Blacks and the Military,* 22.

54. Stouffer's conclusions that blacks preferred northern whites as officers can be found in Leo Bogart, ed., *Project Clear: Social Research and the Desegregation of the United States Army* (New Brunswick, NJ: Transaction Publishers, 1992), xix.

55. Beverly Scott in Rudy Tomedi, *No Bugles, No Drums: An Oral History of the Korean War* (New York: Wiley, 1993), 178.

56. Bowers, Hammond, and MacGarrigle, *Black Soldier, White Army,* 134.

57. Matthew Hay Brown, "New Generation Fights for 65th, Advocates Say a Puerto Rican Unit Was Treated Unjustly during the Korean War," *Orlando Sentinel,* 27 May 2002, A1.

58. Morrow, *What's a Commie Ever Done to Black People?* 34.

59. Hector J. Figueroa-Ruiz, Army Service (Korean War) Questionnaire, 5, 3rd Division, Alphabetical Box 1, Department of the Army, Carlisle Barracks.

60. Samuel L. Banks, "The Korean Conflict," *Negro History Bulletin* 36.6 (1973): 131.

61. Surveyed in 1987, only 34% of white Korean War–era veterans claimed combat exposure compared to 40% of black veterans. Hispanics had the highest rate of exposure at 43%. "1987 Survey of Veterans (Conducted for the Department of Veterans Affairs by the U.S. Bureau of the Census) (July 1989)," 24, NA, Record Group 015, Box 1.

62. Banks, "The Korean Conflict," 131, and Brenda Gayle Plummer, *Rising Wind: Black Americans and U.S. Foreign Affairs, 1935-1960* (Chapel Hill: University of North Carolina Press, 1996), 205.

63. Dan Spence Grimes, Army Service (Korean War) Questionnaire, 5, 2nd Division, 23rd Regiment, Alphabetical Box 2, Department of the Army, Carlisle Barracks.

64. Charles W. Dryden, *A-Train: Memoirs of a Tuskegee Airman* (Tuscaloosa: University of Alabama Press, 1997), 292.

65. Bussey, *Firefight at Yechon,* 117. At least one white officer with the 24th seemed agreed, noting, "there was a white officer in 1st [Battalion] who kept evading courts-martial because charges were never brought against him for one reason or another." John S. Komp in Bowers, Hammond, and MacGarrigle, *Black Soldier, White Army,* 186.

66. Bowers, Hammond, and MacGarrigle, *Black Soldier, White Army,* 186.

67. Plummer, *Rising Wind,* 205. On the courts-martial in Korea, see Bowers, Hammond, and MacGarrigle, *Black Soldier, White Army,* 185-87; Plummer, *Rising Wind,* 205-6; and Thomas Bostlemann, *The Cold War and the Color Line: Race Relations in the Global Arena* (Cambridge, MA: Harvard University Press, 2001), 82. The 24th suffered a high number of courts-martial, but the largest court-martial of the Korean War actually involved the Puerto Rican 65th Infantry Regiment. After suffering more than five hundred casualties and having their Puerto Rican commander replaced, almost two hundred Puerto Ricans walked away, ending up in the stockade. Of ninety-five who were tried, ninety-one were found guilty. Investigating the case in the 1990s, the Army found "bias in the prosecution

of Puerto Ricans," as many whites were not charged after refusing to fight in similar cir-cumstances. Brown, "New Generation Fights for 65th," *Orlando Sentinel*, 27 May 2002, A1.

68. "Capital Hypocrisy Making Mockery of GI Sacrifices," *Pittsburgh Courier*, 20 January 1951, 8.
69. William Weathersbee in S. Thorne Harper, "All-Black Ranger Unit Recalls Fighting for America," *Columbus (GA) Ledger-Enquirer*, 28 July 2002, A1.
70. Alt and Alt, *Black Soldiers, White Wars*, 104.
71. Banks, "The Korean Conflict," 132.
72. Dryden, *A-Train*, 283.
73. "Group of 92nd Division Vets Ban to Fight Job Bias in Wis.," *Baltimore Afro-American*, 19 August 1950, 15.
74. Alex M. Rivera Jr., "Dixie Justice!" *Pittsburgh Courier*, 2 February 1952, 1 and 4.
75. Morrow, *What's a Commie Ever Done to Black People?* 11.
76. Stanley Roberts, "Top Brass Silent as Alarm Spreads," *Pittsburgh Courier*, 29 September 1951, 5.
77. "Army OKs Uniforms of 'Rebels,'" *Pittsburgh Courier*, 10 May 1952, 5.
78. "Rebel Flags Still Flying In Korea . . . Unashamedly!" *Pittsburgh Courier*, 15 December 1951, 11, and Plummer, *Rising Wind*, 204.
79. Letter to the editor by "A Very Proud Veteran," "Believes MacArthur's Firing an 'Act of God,'" *Pittsburgh Courier*, 5 May 1951, 11. Thurgood Marshall noted of MacArthur's head-quarters that it was so segregated it had no blacks on duty. See Bernard Nalty, *Strength for the Fight: A History of Black Americans in the Military* (New York: Free Press, 1986), 258.
80. John Smith in Alt and Alt, *Black Soldiers, White Wars*, 104.
81. Donald Carter, Interview by Nathan Stanley, quoted in "When Black Is Burned: The Treatment of African American Soldiers during the Korean War," online at http://mcel. pacificu.edu/as/students/stanley/carter.html.
82. Captain Charles Bussey in Bowers, Hammond, and MacGarrigle, *Black Soldier, White Army*, 140.
83. Morrow, *What's a Commie Ever Done to Black People?* 1.
84. Sergeant William H. D. Brown, "Letters," *Baltimore Afro-American*, 26 October 1951, 4.
85. John E. Rousseau, "'War with Korea Not Cure,' Patterson Tells Louisiana Negroes," *Pittsburgh Courier*, 3 March 1951, 2.
86. Morrow, *What's a Commie Ever Done to Black People?* 34.
87. *Ibid.*, 8.
88. Bill Smith, "Black Soldiers Fully Shared the Korean War's Bloody Cost," *St. Louis Post-Dispatch*, 2 February 2002, A1; MacGregor, *Integration of the Armed Forces*, 433-34; Bostle-mann, *The Cold War and the Color Line*, 81; Charles C. Moskos Jr., "Racial Integration in the Armed Forces," *American Journal of Sociology* 72.2 (September 1966): 135; and Richard Dalfiume, *Desegregation of the Armed Forces: Fighting on Two Fronts, 1939-1953* (Columbia: University of Missouri Press, 1969), 204.
89. MacGregor, *Integration of the Armed Forces*, 433, and Military Personnel Management Division, Human Relations and Research Branch, "Integration of Negro Personnel," Memo by Steve C. Davis, 18 April 1952, NA, Record Group 319, Box 007.
90. MacGregor, *Integration of the Armed Forces*, 434-36 and 460. See also Bogart, *Project Clear*, 9.
91. William M. Donnelly, *Under Army Orders: The Army National Guard during the Korean War* (College Station: Texas A&M University Press, 2001), 120-21, and MacGregor, *Integration of the Armed Forces*, 436.
92. MacGregor, *Integration of the Armed Forces*, 449-50, and Dalfiume, *Desegregation of the Armed Forces*, 219.
93. Adam Clayton Powell Jr. to John Floberg, 29 June 1953, NA, Record Group 319, Box 007. Between 1948 and 1955, 51% to 66% of blacks in the Navy served in the Stewards' Branch.

U.S. Bureau of Naval Personnel, "Memo on Discrimination of the Negro," 24 January 1959, NA, Record Group 319, Box 7. ACLU investigators after 1956 continued to find "pockets of Negro segregation" in the Navy. Patrick Murphy Malin to Thomas S. Gates Jr., 26 November 1957, NA, Record Group 319, Box 007. By 1956, the Navy made a point of signing whites up for the Stewards' Branch, but until 1961, when the commandant set a racial quota ordering that half of all volunteers for steward service be white, these comprised only 10% of the total. MacGregor, *Integration of the Armed Forces,* 470-71.

94. Truman K. Gibson Jr., Civilian Aide to the Secretary of War, at a press conference, 9 April 1945, Box 1, "Desegregation of the Armed Forces," folder 4, CFSOKW. See also, Binkin et al., *Blacks and the Military,* 21.

95. Peter Karsten, *Soldiers and Society: The Effects of Military Service and War on American Life* (Westport, CT: Greenwood Press, 1978), 210.

96. White NCO quoted by Truman K. Gibson Jr. at a press conference, 9 April 1945, Box 1, "Desegregation of the Armed Forces," folder 4, CFSOKW.

97. Morrow, *What's a Commie Ever Done to Black People?* 35.

98. Negro Infantryman in Bogart, *Project Clear,* 129.

99. Banks, "The Korean Conflict," 132.

100. Richard W. Bass, Army Service (Korean War) Questionnaire, 5, 23rd Regiment, Alphabetical Box 1, Department of the Army, Carlisle Barracks.

101. Joseph R. Owen, *Colder Than Hell: A Marine Rifle Company at Chosin Reservoir* (Annapolis, MD: Naval Institute Press, 1996), 6.

102. Mark W. Clark, "Negro Battalions 'Weakened Battle Line," *U.S. News and World Report,* 11 May 1956, 55. After the war, Clark remarked that he did not believe "we should integrate then (1950) and I do not think so now." "Pentagon Aide Refutes Clark on Negro GIs," *New York Post,* 30 April 1956, 4.

103. James K. Donahue and Ray R. Deimler, 5 for both, Army Service (Korean War) Questionnaire, 5, 2nd Division, 23rd Regiment, Alphabetical Box 1, Department of the Army, Carlisle Barracks.

104. Selika M. Ducksworth, *What Hour of the Night: Black Enlisted Men's Experiences and the Desegregation of the Army during the Korean War, 1950-1951* (Ph.D. diss., Ohio State University, 1997), 1.

105. Negro Enlisted Man in Bogart, *Project Clear,* 51.

106. Negro MP (military policeman) in Bogart, *Project Clear,* 129.

107. William T. Craig, *Lifer! From Infantry to Special Forces* (New York: Ivy Books, 1994), 40, and White Infantryman in Bogart, *Project Clear,* 43.

108. Robert C. Bjork, 5, Army Service (Korean War) Questionnaire, 5, 2nd Division, 23rd Regiment, Alphabetical Box 1, Department of the Army, Carlisle Barracks.

109. Owen, *Colder Than Hell,* 34.

110. Howard Matthias, *The Korean War: Reflections of a Young Combat Platoon Leader,* revised edition (Tallahassee, FL: Father & Son Publishing, 1995), 104. See also Craig, *Lifer!* 40-41.

111. Beverly Scott in Tomedi, *No Bugles, No Drums,* 179.

112. Ronald H. Johnson, 5, Army Service (Korean War) Questionnaire, 5, 5th Regimental Combat Team, Department of the Army, Carlisle Barracks.

113. Sergeant Dale in Owen, *Colder Than Hell,* 34.

114. Sergeant Lyman D. Heacock in Bowers, Hammond, and MacGarrigle, *Black Soldier, White Army,* 218, and Raymond I. Delcambre, 5, Army Service (Korean War) Questionnaire, 5, 2nd Division, 23rd Regiment, Alphabetical Box 1, Department of the Army, Carlisle Barracks.

115. "GIs Riot in Japan," *Pittsburgh Courier,* 18 July 1953, 1. Problems with integration were most common outside the war zone. In 1951, in a clash that sent forty men to the hospital, nearly seven hundred black and white soldiers fought in a German café because black soldiers were publicly dating German girls. "Army Probes GI Race Riot," *Pittsburgh Courier,*

19 May 1951, 1. Less intense fights also broke out. See Douglas G. Anderson, Army Service (Korean War) Questionnaire, 5, 2nd Division, 23rd Regiment, Alphabetical Box 1, Department of the Army, Carlisle Barracks.

116. 1st Lieutenant Joseph Bracy in Berebitsky, *A Very Long Weekend*, 316. At most, troops of different colors self-segregated rather than mixing. Army officers, however, discouraged this. In Pusan, blacks demanded separate quarters and all-black gun crews, but Colonel Percy L. Wale, a southerner, refused on the grounds that orders said to integrate. Major Vernon Sikes in William Berebitsky, *A Very Long Weekend: The Army National Guard in Korea, 1950-1953* (Shippensburg, PA: White Mane, 1996), 253. Also, Sarnecky, *A History of the U.S. Army Nurse Corps*, 316, and Gilbert Charles Pfleger, Army Service (Korean War) Questionnaire, 5, 5th Regimental Combat Team, Department of the Army, Carlisle Barracks.

117. Don Ellwood to Melinda Pash, email, 12 May 2004, in author's possession.

118. Clentell Jackson in Chuck Haga, "Legacy of the Korean War: Blending Black and White; A Public Radio Documentary Examines How the Conflict 50 Years Ago Hastened Racial Integration of the United States," *Minneapolis Star-Tribune*, 7 July 2003, 1B.

119. White Regimental Staff Officer and White Infantryman in Bogart, *Project Clear*, 96-97.

120. Black Infantryman in *ibid.*, 99.

121. Bogart, *Project Clear*, 97-99.

122. White Infantrymen in *ibid.*, 97 and 43. Studies conducted after World War II and during the Korean War show that exposure to men of different races made soldiers more tolerant and less likely to support or participate in racism or discrimination. *Ibid.*, and Research Branch Information and Education Division, Headquarters, European Theater of Operations, under authority of The Commanding General, ETOUSA, "Opinions about Negro Infantry Platoons in White Companies of 7 Divisions," Information and Education Division Report no. B-157 (Washington, DC: Headquarters Army Service Forces, 3 July 1945), "Harry S. Truman Library Research File," Box 20, CFSOKW.

123. Dan Spence Grimes, Army Service (Korean War) Questionnaire, 5, 2nd Division, 23rd Regiment, Alphabetical Box 1, Department of the Army, Carlisle Barracks.

124. Frederick McClellan Sr., Oral History by Milinda D. Jenssen, no date, at United States of America Korean War Commemoration (http://korea50.army.mil/media/interviews/mcclellan.shtml).

125. Stan Jones to Melinda Pash, 6 May 2004, in the author's possession.

126. Robert C. Bjork, Army Service (Korean War) Questionnaire, continuation sheet, 2nd Division, 23rd Regiment, Alphabetical Box 1, Department of the Army, Carlisle Barracks, and Lyman Heacock in Bowers, Hammond, and MacGarrigle, *Black Soldier, White Army*, 218.

127. Gilbert Charles Pfleger, Army Service (Korean War) Questionnaire, 5, 5th Regimental Combat Team, Department of the Army, Carlisle Barracks.

128. Donald C. Dingee, Army Service (Korean War) Questionnaire, 5, 3rd Division, Alphabetical Box 1, Department of the Army, Carlisle Barracks. See also Lee Nichols in MacGregor, *Integration of the Armed Forces*, 447, and Icle Davis, *Korean War Veteran Survey*, 6, CFSOKW.

129. Clentell Jackson remembers a white friend in Korea hitting another white man who was calling Jackson names. Haga, "Legacy of the Korean War," 1B. Similarly, white troops of one unit had to be calmed down when they thought MPs were picking on black truck drivers. Berebitsky, *A Very Long Weekend*, 254.

130. Navy News Release, *Dixie Times-Picayune States ROTO Magazine*, 7 December 1952, NA, Record Group 319, Box 007.

131. Banks, "The Korean Conflict," 131.

132. White Artilleryman in Bogart, *Project Clear*, 97.

133. Frank Whisonant, "Yokota Air Base Is Perfect Model of Race Harmony," *Pittsburgh Courier*, 25 September 1950, 2.

134. At Gifu, however, social segregation marked life at the base though there was some integration in housing and among dependents below the high school level. Bowers, Hammond, and MacGarrigle, *Black Soldier, White Army*, 48-50.

135. Banks, "The Korean Conflict," 131.

136. GI in Ducksworth, *What Hour of the Night*, 104.

137. Lewis H. Carlson, *Remembered Prisoners of a Forgotten War: An Oral History of Korean War POWs* (New York: St. Martin's Press, 2000), 209-11; "Negro Deserters Blast Segregation in America," *Pittsburgh Courier*, 6 February 1954, 1; and Bill Worthy, "Some POWs Desert 'Land of Jim Crow,'" *Baltimore Afro-American*, 15 August 1953, 1.

138. "Pentagon Aide Refutes Clark on Negro GIs," *New York Post*, 30 April 1956, 4.

139. "Notes on Possible Declassification and Release of ORO Study 'The Utilization of Negro Manpower in the Army,' 'Confidential' (1954)," 3, NA, Record Group 319, Box 007.

140. "Negro Troops Rough on Reds," *Seattle Post-Intelligencer*, 20 August 1950, 6.

141. Bostlemann, *The Cold War and the Color Line*, 82-83, and Charles C. Moskos Jr., "Has the Army Killed Jim Crow?" *Negro History Bulletin* 21 (November 1957): 29.

142. Berry, Oral History by Caudill, 37.

143. Karsten, *Soldiers and Society*, 212.

144. Catherine Clinton, *The Black Soldier: 1492 to the Present* (Boston, MA: Houghton Mifflin, 2000), 82.

145. In a 1954 Gallup Poll, 92% of black veterans polled said they were better off for their Army service and found it rewarding. Not surprisingly, blacks increasingly made a career out of military service. Black reenlistment rates by 1965 in the Air Force outnumbered white ones more than two to one. Peter S. Kindsvatter, *American Soldiers: Ground Combat in the World Wars, Korea, and Vietnam* (Lawrence: University Press of Kansas, 2003), 13.

146. Jay Hidano in Louis Baldovi, ed., *A Foxhole View: Personal Accounts of Hawaii's Korean War Veterans* (Honolulu: University of Hawai'i Press, 2002), 61, and Blaine Friedlander in Tomedi, *No Bugles, No Drums*, 195-96.

147. Bertram Sebresos, Harrison Lee, and Clarence Young in Baldovi, *A Foxhole View*, 97, 44-45, 115, and 129.

148. Baldovi, *A Foxhole View*, 75.

149. Ben Nighthorse Campbell in "Native Americans in the Korean War," online at http://www.defenselink.mil/specials/nativeamerican01/korea.html.

150. Lt. Rolly G. Miller to his mother, quoted by John O. Pastore, *Congressional Record, Appendix*, 82nd Congress, 1st sess., 1951, vol. 97, A5860.

CHAPTER 7

1. Edmund Krekorian in Donald Knox, with additional text by Alfred Coppel, *The Korean War: An Oral History*. Vol. 2, *Uncertain Victory* (New York: Harcourt, Brace, Jovanovich, 1988), 354.

2. Russell C. Rodda, *Korean War Veteran Survey*, handwritten appendage, CFSOKW.

3. Wayne Mackey, "45th Veterans Dock in Seattle: Heading for Sill," *Daily Oklahoman*, 14 April 1952, 1.

4. Anthony B. De Angelis, Army Service (Korean War) Questionnaire, 17, 1st Cavalry Division, Surnames A-L, Carlisle Barracks.

5. Curtis James Morrow, *What's a Commie Ever Done to Black People? A Korean War Memoir of Fighting in the U.S. Army's Last All-Negro Unit* (Jefferson, NC: McFarland, 1977), 84.

6. Vincent Van Allen, Interview by Colin Pinkham, online at American Century Project, St. Andrews Episcopal School Library Archive (www.doingoralhistory.org).

7. Author's note in Knox and Coppel, *The Korean War: Uncertain Victory*, 356.

8. John A. Sullivan, *Toy Soldiers: Memoir of a Combat Platoon Leader in Korea* (Jefferson, NC: McFarland, 1991), 153. Also H. D. Buelow, typed papers, Box VV, Folder A.1467, CFSOKW, and James Putnam, Memoir (KWE), 35.

9. Floyd Baxter in Knox and Coppel, *The Korean War: Uncertain Victory*, 356.

10. Mrs. Lee in Frances Omori, *Quiet Heroes: Navy Nurses of the Korean War, 1950-1953; Far East Command* (St. Paul, MN: Smith House Press, 2000), 135.

11. Roy T. Gray, "Sniper Duty," 14, Box MMM, Folder A2202, CFSOKW.

12. Draftees, serving twenty-one to twenty-four months' active duty, entered the Reserves for five or six years and, instead of getting a discharge, got a Certificate of Service and a reservist identification card. Carl Peterson, "Difference," *New York Times*, 23 August 1953, SM4.

13. Some National Guard troops went home before processing. Officers of the Oklahoma 45th flew to Rogers Field in Oklahoma eight days before reporting to Ft. Sill for processing. "No Band, but Happy Families Are Plenty for 45th Arrivals," *Daily Oklahoman*, 15 April 1952, 1.

14. Jack Right in Knox and Coppel, *The Korean War: Uncertain Victory*, 355, and Seymour Bernstein, *Monsters and Angels: Surviving a Career in Music* (Milwaukee, WI: Hal Leonard, 2002), 333.

15. Billy Joe Harris in Lewis H. Carlson, *Remembered Prisoners of a Forgotten War: An Oral History of Korean War POWs* (New York: St. Martin's Press, 2000), 228, and Fernando Gandara, *Korean War Veteran Survey*, 7, CFSOKW.

16. Robert Jones in Carlson, *Remembered Prisoners of a Forgotten War*, 213.

17. Jack Right in Knox and Coppel, *The Korean War: Uncertain Victory*, 355. Most POWs, however, were warned not to talk with civilians about their experiences. Glenn Reynolds in Carlson, *Remembered Prisoners of a Forgotten War*, 230.

18. Thomas C. Shay (AFC2001/001/5807), Folder 3, Interview by Kent Fox, 24 February 2003, 7, VHPC, AFC, LOC.

19. These booklets stressed the need to safeguard military information and not disclose anything to unauthorized persons. Copies of Mark W. Clark, "Welcome Back!" and "What Has Happened since 1950" can be found at Edwin R. Meyers (AFC2001/001/3394), Folder 3, VHPC, AFC, LOC.

20. Bernstein, *Monsters and Angels*, 333-35.

21. Returnees chose their mode of transportation (bus, train, airplane) back to either their last duty station or the place where they entered service. Frank Almy in Knox and Coppel, *The Korean War: Uncertain Victory*, 356-57, and "Section 12: Mustering Out," U.S. President's Commission on Veterans Pensions, Bradley Commission: Records, 1954-58, A 69-22 and 79-6, Box 61, DDE Library.

22. Arthur L. Kelly, Interview by Russell Harris, 16 December 1993, 67 (Kentuckiana Digital Library at http://kdl.kyvl.org).

23. Frank Almy in Knox and Coppel, *The Korean War: Uncertain Victory*, 356-57.

24. Carl Stevens in William Berebitsky, *A Very Long Weekend: The Army National Guard in Korea, 1950-1953* (Shippensburg, PA: White Mane, 1996), 257.

25. Van Allen, Interview by Pinkham. The "incidental" that Van Allen chose not to think about as a black man was segregation.

26. Robert E. Baken (AFC2001/001/1443), Folder 2, Interview by Matthew Baken, 23 November 2001, 16, VHPC, AFC, LOC.

27. Story found in Catherine "Faye" Neville (AFC2001/001/113), Folder 2, Interview by Helen Roach and Win Wilbur, 25 February 2000, 10, VHPC, AFC, LOC.

28. Vincent Baron, *Korean War Veteran Survey*, 7, CFSOKW.

29. Edward H. Pykosz, Army Service (Korean War) Questionnaire, 18, 1st Cavalry Division, Surnames M-Z, Carlisle Barracks.

30. Edmund Krekorian in Knox and Coppel, *The Korean War: Uncertain Victory*, 354.

31. Paul Edwards in Janell Coppage, "Four Men: Stories of the War They Can Not Forget," unpublished history paper, 3-4, Box EE, CFSOKW.

32. Jack Wright in Knox and Coppel, *The Korean War: Uncertain Victory*, 355.

33. Clarence Jackson "Jack" Davis (AFC2001/001/1644), Folder 1, unpublished book of letters and postscript by author, 179, VHPC, AFC, LOC.

34. Edmund Krekorian in Knox and Coppel, *The Korean War: Uncertain Victory*, 358-59.

35. James Brady, *The Coldest War: A Memoir of Korea* (New York: Orion Books, 1990), 240.

36. Floyd Baxter in Knox and Coppel, *The Korean War: Uncertain Victory*, 356.

37. Berebitsky, *A Very Long Weekend*, 256; "A Small Town Honors Its Veterans," *New York Times Magazine*, 11 October 1953, 8-9; Walter G. Adelman in Harry Spiller, ed., *American POWs in Korea: Sixteen Personal Accounts* (Jefferson, NC: McFarland, 1998), 37; and Charles Ehredt, Army Service (Korean War) Questionnaire, 17, 1st Cavalry Division, Surnames A-L, Carlisle Barracks. Connecticut, Washington, Delaware, Indiana, Louisiana, Massachusetts, Michigan, New Hampshire, Alaska, South Dakota, Vermont, and Minnesota paid veterans a bonus. Harry Matthews to Melinda Pash, 11 October 2005, in author's possession; Patricia Sherman, *Korean War Veteran Survey*, 7, CFSOKW; Jim Cleary, "The Gulf War Veterans' Bonus: A Proposed Minnesota Constitutional Amendment," 9, online at www.house.leg.state.mn.us/hrd/pubs/cavetbon.pdf; Don Eastvold, "State Veterans' Bonus," online at http://www.atg.wa.gov/opinion.aspx?section=archive&id=10526; Delaware Veteran's Military Pay Commission, "Paid Korean War Bonus Claims," online at http://archives.delaware.gov/collections/guide/1400S/1470-000-010.shtml; and Congress, House, President's Commission on Veterans' Benefits in the United States, *State Veteran's Laws: Digests of State Laws and Related Statistical Data Regarding Rights, Benefits, and Privileges of Veterans, Their Dependents, and Their Organizations*, 2-13, 84th congress, 2nd sess., 16 May 1956, House Committee Print 246. See also "Rockefeller Bars Korea War Bonus," *New York Times*, 21 February 1962, 1, and "West Virginia Adopts Plan to Finance Korean Vets' $18 Million Issue," *Wall Street Journal*, 7 August 1957, 16.

38. Thomas B. Gaylets in Spiller, *American POWs in Korea*, 23.

39. POWs especially did not feel heroic. One writes, "People were calling me a hero and I really wanted to be one but I was not." Email Shorty Estabrook to Melinda Pash, 29 July 2004, in author's possession.

40. William M. Allen, *My Old Box of Memories: Thoughts of the Korean War* (self-published, c. 1999), 88; Jack Wright in Knox and Coppel, *The Korean War: Uncertain Victory*, 359; and email Shorty Estabrook to Melinda Pash, 5 August 2004, in author's possession.

41. Ralph Cutro, *Korean War Veteran Survey*, 7, CFSOKW. Korean War homecomings foreshadowed those of the Vietnam War. See Drummond Ayres Jr., "The Vietnam Veteran: Silent, Perplexed, Unnoticed," *New York Times*, 8 November 1970, 1.

42. Harlee W. Lassiter, *Korean War Veteran Survey*, attachment page, CFSOKW.

43. Charles Rice in Berebitsky, *A Very Long Weekend*, 256. Also Thomas C. Shay (AFC2001/001/5807), Folder 3, Interview by Kent Fox, 24 February 2003, 7, VHPC, AFC, LOC, and Bernstein, *Monsters and Angels*, 338.

44. Barnett R. Wilson (AFC2001/001/2783), Folder 1, *A Korean Cruise: Moments of Life, Love, and War*, unpublished memoir dated 1981, 160, VHPC, AFC, LOC. Also, Richared E. Merrill, *Korean War Veteran Survey*, 7, CFSOKW.

45. Some of these cases led to incidents of violence. See "Free GI's Wife in Slaying of Married Lover," *Pittsburgh Courier*, 14 February 1953, 1, and "Veteran Kills Wife's Lover," *Pittsburgh Courier*, 7 March 1953, 1.

46. "No Bands Playing," *Newsweek*, 15 August 1955, 21.

47. Floyd Baxter in Knox and Coppel, *The Korean War: Uncertain Victory*, 357.

48. Kelly, Interview by Harris, 16 December 1993, 69.

49. Allen, *My Old Box of Memories*, 87-88.

50. Jack Wright in Knox and Coppel, *The Korean War: Uncertain Victory*, 359.

51. Harvey J. Tompkins, "Korean Veterans with Psychiatric Disabilities," *Military Medicine* 117.1 (July 1955): 35.

52. Floyd Baxter in Knox and Coppel, *The Korean War: Uncertain Victory*, 357.

53. Edmund Krekorian in Knox and Coppel, *The Korean War: Uncertain Victory*, 363.

54. John M. Pitre, *Korean War Veteran Survey*, 7, CFSOKW.

55. Many veteran accounts mention marriage on the eve of one's departure for training or the war. See Jessica Weiss, *To Have and to Hold: Marriage, the Baby Boom, and Social Change* (Chicago: University of Chicago Press, 2000), 22.

56. Paul Foy, "Combat Can Kill Marriages, Study Finds," The Associated Press News Service (online at http://infoweb.newsbank.com), 19 December 2002. This study found that Vietnam veterans divorced at no higher rate than contemporaries. Studies of Vietnam War POWs indicate that POWs divorce at a higher rate than other veterans. Data from the 1970s revealed that by their third year home, 32% of Vietnam War POWs divorced compared to about 11% of a control group. Edna J. Hunter, "Treating the Military Captives' Family," in Florence W. Kaslow and Richard I. Ridenour, eds., *The Military Family: Dynamics and Treatment* (New York: Guilford Press, 1984), 191-92. Of combat veterans interviewed in 1970 (including but not exclusively Korean War veterans), only 43% were still married to their original wife. Glen H. Elder Jr. and Elizabeth C. Clipp, "Wartime Losses and Social Bonding: Influences across 40 Years in Men's Lives," *Psychiatry* 51 (May 1988): 191. Also William Ruger, Sven E. Wilson, and Shawn L. Waddoups, "Warfare and Welfare: Military Service, Combat, and Marital Dissolution," *Armed Forces and Society* 29.1 (Fall 2002): 85-107. On divorces after World War II, see William M. Tuttle Jr., *"Daddy's Gone to War": The Second World War in the Lives of America's Children* (New York: Oxford University Press, 1993), 220.

57. Gilbert Towner, *Korean War Veteran Survey*, 6, CFSOKW.

58. See Kelly, Interview by Harris, 16 December 1993, 69, and Charles M. Bussey, *Firefight at Yechon: Courage and Racism in the Korean War* (Lincoln: University of Nebraska Press, 2002), 259.

59. Kelly, Interview by Harris, 16 December 1993, 69.

60. Bussey, *Firefight at Yechon*, 259.

61. Lee B. Philmon in in Linda Granfield, *I Remember Korea: Veterans Tell Their Stories of the Korean War, 1950-1953* (New York: Clarion Books, 2003), 111.

62. Veterans of World War II also felt out of place and had difficulty dealing with children or spouses after returning home. See Robert J. Havighurst, Walter H. Eaton, John W. Baughman, and Ernest W. Burgess, *The American Veteran Back Home: A Study of Veteran Readjustment* (New York: Longmans, Green, 1951), 23, and Tuttle, *"Daddy's Gone to War,"* 215-23.

63. Ronald Ransom in Berebitsky, *A Very Long Weekend*, 257; James C. Becker, *Korean War Veteran Survey*, 7, CFSOKW; and "Wounded Veteran Weds," *New York Times*, 15 June 1951, 20.

64. "Korean War Orphan Adopted by Captain," *Pittsburgh Courier*, 14 February 1953, 1, and "Korean Tot's Dad Remains on Stateside," *Pittsburgh Courier*, 21 February 1953, 5. Concerned about war orphans fathered by American servicemen, the public and legislators agitated to ease the way for families in the United States to adopt children from Japan or Korea. Senator Richard L. Neuberger of Oregon, "Amendment of Refugee Relief Act of 1953," *Congressional Record* (Senate), 84th Congress, 2nd sess., volume 102, part 6 (27 April 1956-21 May 1956), 7247-7249; Senator Wayne L. Morse of Oregon, "Increase in Number of Visas to be Issued to Orphans under the Refugee Relief Act of 1953," *Congressional Record* (Senate), 84th Congress, 2nd sess., volume 102, part 11 (25 July 1956-27 July 1956), 14741-14743; and "Urge Adoption of Korean Babes," *Pittsburgh Courier*, 19 March 1955, 2.

65. Thirty-four percent of veterans of only the Korean War bought their first homes with VHA loans. This is probably a low estimate for total Korean War veterans as 53% of those who served in both Korean and Vietnam and 45% of those who served in both Korea and World War II used VHA funding to buy their first homes. "National Survey of Veterans, 1979," 209, NA, Record Group 015, Box 1.

66. David Stewart, "When a GI Buy$ Hi$ Dream Hou$e," *American Mercury* 89 (October 1959): 103-5.

67. Mickey Levine, "Report on Negro Veterans in the South," 15 March 1956, 1-4, Central Files, General File, GF 124-A-1, Box 912, DDE Library. In the South, only 4.2% of black veterans compared to 14.3% of white veterans held mortgages because of constraints put on them. African Americans had to provide a larger cash down payment (15% as opposed to 3%).

68. "Another Levittown!" *Pittsburgh Courier,* 5 February 1955, 6.

69. In the 1930s, redlining developed to rate neighborhoods on a block-by-block basis and record the findings in color on Residential Security Maps. The highest rating, green, generally went to white, middle-class areas while racially mixed or nonwhite neighborhoods received the lowest rating, red. Neither the FHA nor the VA would lend money to purchase or improve properties in red zones. Karen Brodkin, *How Jews Became White Folks and What That Says about Race in America* (New Brunswick, NJ: Rutgers University Press, 2006), 49-50.

70. "We've Been Asked: About Benefits for New GI's," *U.S. News and World Report,* July 1952, 82-83.

71. "GI Loan Gratuity to Be Suspended," *Baltimore Afro-American,* 29 August 1953, 13.

72. "Home Building Shift in New Jersey Seen," *New York Times,* 14 September 1952, R13, and "Korean Veterans Seek Homes," *Special to the New York Times,* 16 September 1951, 3. On a related note, see Walther H. Sterns "Korean Veterans in Mortgage Lead," *Special to the New York Times,* 10 November 1959, 80.

73. "'Negro' Market Is Newly Discovered," *Pittsburgh Courier,* 29 January 1955, 2. In Memphis, Tennessee, a claims service opened to help African Americans with claims for pensions, disability compensation, GI loans, and government employment. "New Memphis Claims Service Helps Solve Vets' Problems," *Pittsburgh Courier,* 8 June 1957, 4.

74. "Selling: After Sex, What?" *Time Magazine,* 2 November 1953, 95.

75. Herbert Mitgang, "A Pledge of Rememberance," *New York Times,* 17 December 1950, SM13.

76. *Congress and the Nation, 1945-1964: A Review of Government and Politics in the Postwar Years* (Washington, D.C.: Congressional Quarterly Press, 1965), 1364.

77. "We've Been Asked: About Job Rights of GI's," *U.S. News and World Report,* 20 July 1951, 46; Samuel R. Woodham (AFC2001/001/1595), Folder 3, Interview by Brian Woodham, 23 March 2002, 25, VHPC, AFC, LOC; and Barnett R. Wilson (AFC2001/001/2783), Folder 1, *A Korean Cruise: Magic Moments of Life, Love, and War,* unpublished memoir dated 1981, 200, VHPC, AFC, LOC. Resistance to hiring veterans surfaced after the war. In Terre Haute, Indiana, coal miners refused to work after a Korean War veteran was hired. See "250 Miners Stay Out," *New York Times,* 25 August 1953, 22. See also Harold L. Mulhausen, *Korean War Veteran Survey,* 6-7, CFSOKW.

78. "The New GI Bill: Who Gets What?" *Changing Times,* May 1953, 21-22.

79. U.S. Office of Personnel Management, "VetGuide Appendix D: A Brief History of Veterans Preference," online at www.opm.gov/veterans/html/vghist.asp, and *Congress and the Nation, 1945-1964,* 1369.

80. John David Skrentny, *The Ironies of Affirmative Action: Politics, Culture, and Justice in America* (Chicago: University of Chicago Press, 1996), 47. For examples of public dissatisfaction, see "Should Veterans Enjoy Job Preference for Life?" *Saturday Evening Post,* 30 May 1953, 10, and Stanley M. Rumbough Jr. to Charles F. Willis, 23 April 1953, Central Files, Official File, OF152-H, Box 819, DDE Library.

81. As with several benefit programs for Korean War veterans, this was not available to female veterans who married after coming home or to veterans dishonorably discharged.

82. Regulations forbade those seeking unemployment from collecting from more than one state, and federal benefits ended after payments reached $676. *Public Law 550,* Title IV, Section 408, 82nd Congress, 2nd sess., *United States Statutes at Large* (Washington, DC:

U.S. Government Printing Office, 1953), 687-88, and Congress, House, President's Commission on Veterans' Pensions, *Readjustment Benefits: General Survey and Appraisal; A Report on Veterans' Benefits in the United States,* 156-57, 84th Congress, 2nd sess., Committee Print 289, Staff Report No. IX Part A, 11 September 1956 (Washington, DC: U.S. Government Printing Office, 1956).

83. The waiting period was created because the government expected veterans to live off their mustering-out pay until they could find employment. "The New GI Bill: Who Gets What?" *Changing Times,* May 1953, 22; "Readjustment Pay or Bonus" in "Defense Department on Effect of GI Bill," 12 (Bradley Commission): Records 1954-1958, A69-22 and 79-6, Box 67, DDE Library; and Congress, House, Committee on Veterans Affairs, *The Historical Development of Veterans' Benefits in the United States,* report prepared by the President's Commission on Veterans' Pensions, 160, 84th Congress, 2nd sess., House Committee Print 244, Staff Report No. 1, 9 May 1956 (Washington, DC: U.S. Government Printing Office, 1956). Korean War veterans had a higher rate of unemployment (20.3%) than World War II veterans (17.1%), but had an easier time holding onto jobs. Once employed, only 18.9% of Korean War veterans versus 29.9% of World War II veterans subsequently lost their jobs. Harvey J. Tompkins, "Korean Veterans with Psychiatric Disabilities," *Military Medicine* 17.1 (July 1955): 36.

84. Congress, House, Committee on Veterans Affairs, *The Historical Development of Veterans' Benefits in the United States.* In their first year home, 17.8% of Korean War veterans used unemployment benefits compared to 37.5% of World War II veterans. As in World War II, younger veterans more readily used unemployment benefits than older veterans. Congress, House, President's Commission on Veterans' Pensions, *Readjustment Benefits: General Survey and Appraisal.*

85. Congress, House, Committee on Veterans Affairs, "Limitation on Application for Unemployment Compensation," report prepared by Congressman Olin E. Teague of Texas, 84th Congress, 1st sess., *House Reports, Volume 3: Miscellaneous Reports on Public Bills, II* (Washington, DC: U.S. Government Printing Office, 1955).

86. For an example, see "Ex-POW Joins U.S. Air Force," *Pittsburgh Courier,* 16 January 1954, 3. In a 1955 survey, Americans rated military officer lower in prestige than public school teacher. Career enlisted ranked sixteenth out of nineteen professions, above only barber, sales clerk, and truck driver. Further questioned, 12% of those polled suggested that most men who settled for a career as an officer did so because they were "either unwilling or unable to make a civilian living." Twenty-eight percent had the same opinion of enlisted men. Public Opinion Surveys, Inc., "Attitudes of Adult Civilians toward the Military Service as a Career," *Part I of a Study for the Office of Armed Forces Information and Education, Department of Defense* (Princeton, NJ: Public Opinion Surveys, 1955), 2 and 4.

87. "1987 Survey of Veterans (conducted for the Department of Veterans Affairs by the U.S. Bureau of the Census) (July 1989)," 9 and 17, NA, Record Group 015, Box 1. Service members with no service before the Korean War stayed in for more than twenty years at a rate slightly elevated above that of those who served only in World War II, .4% compared to .2%. Rates go up dramatically for men serving in more than one war. For instance, 30% of veterans who served in both World War II and Korea retired with more than twenty years, as did 86.9% who served in World War II, Korea, and Vietnam and 84.2% who served in Korea and Vietnam. "National Survey of Veterans, 1979," 149-50, NA, Record Group 015, Box 1.

88. Kelly, Interview by Harris, 16 December 1993, 62.

89. "Our Saddest Sacks," *Newsweek,* 26 May 1958, 28. In the cleanup, men like Major John Walker, an African American Korean War POW with only six years left to an Army retirement, found themselves on the street at the behest of a Department of Army Board. Letter Val J. Washington to Thomas E. Stephens, 8 March 1954; George S. Ives to Charles F. Willis Jr., 17 March 1954; and Paul T. Carroll to Val J. Washington, 25 March 1954, Central

Files, General File, GF 12-C 1954S, Box 241, DDE Library. After the Korean War, though, the military began studying ways to improve retention among career personnel, laying the foundation for things like health care for dependents and base housing. Sondra Albano, "Military Recognition of Family Concerns: Revolutionary War to 1993," *Armed Forces and Society* 20.2 (Winter 1994): 283.

90. Over the objections of Olveta Culp Hobby of the Department of Health, Education, and Welfare, Defense Secretary Charles E. Wilson ordered the military to end segregation in schools on post by September 1, 1955. Lee Nichols, "Night Lead Segregation," 31 January 1954, clipping, NA, Record Group 319, Box 007, and "Jim Crow in GI Schools Will End in Sept. 1955," *Pittsburgh Courier*, 13 February 1954, 5. Some authors argue that military desegregation paved the way for *Brown v. the Board of Education* by demonstrating that an integrated society could work. See Gerald Early in "Legacy of the Korean War: Blending of Black and White," *Minneapolis Star-Tribune*, Metro Edition, 7 July 2001, 1B. The Department of Defense also forbade the construction of any new schools to be operated on a segregated basis. C. E. Wilson, "Memo for the Secretary of Army/Navy/Air Force for Dependents of Military and Civilian Personnel," 12 January 1954, NA, Record Group 319, Box 8.

91. "Military Ending Pupil Color Line," *New York Times*, 21 August 1955, clipping attached to Carter L. Burgess, Memorandum for the Secretary of Defense (and others), "Status of Racial Integration in Schools on Military Installations for Dependents of Military and Civilian Personnel," 25 August 1955, Robert B. Anderson Papers, 1933-89, Navy-Defense, Special Problems M-N, Box 26, DDE Library. Generally, integration of base schools worked well, perhaps in part because the numbers of African Americans remained small or because those involved were accustomed to obeying orders. Department of Defense Office of Public Information, Memo for Mr. Burgess from C. Herschel Schooley, 10 November 1955, NA, Record Group 319, Box 007.

92. Letters between President Eisenhower and Harvey Higley released by Press Secretary James C. Hagerty, 26 October 1954, Files of Administrative Officer—Special Projects (Morrow), Inter-racial Affairs 1956-1954, Box 11, DDE Library, and "The Vet's Hospital Scandal," *Pittsburgh Courier*, 3 October 1953, 6.

93. American Legion Red River Post No. 118, *Resolution*, 2 December 1956, Central Files, General File, GF 124-A-1 1956, Box 912, DDE Library. A 1956 AVC audit concluded that veterans' hospitals were integrating despite some problems. In Mississippi, local veterans' organizations opposed integration, and elsewhere, as in Montgomery, Alabama, hospitals tried to shift black patients to black hospitals. Mickey Levine, "Report on Negro Veterans in the South," 15 March 1956, 4-5, Central Files, General File, GF 124-A-1, Box 912, DDE Library.

94. Letter Joan Bopp to President Eisenhower, 10 November 1953, Central Files, General File, GF 124-A-1 1954, Box 911, DDE Library.

95. International Public Opinion Research, "Chapter XVIII Army and Korea," in *The Integration of Social Activities on Nine Army Posts, Report of an Exploratory Study, Prepared for Human Resources Research Office*, August 1953, 1-7, NA, Record Group 319, Box 007. Men sometimes self-segregated, but Army policy upheld their right to frequent whatever clubs or other places they wanted. In the South, racial lines were drawn for activities involving members of both sexes.

96. Charles W. Dryden, *A-Train: Memoirs of a Tuskegee Airman* (Tuscaloosa: University of Alabama Press, 1997), 302 and 311.

97. "GI Tells of Bias in Army," *Pittsburgh Courier*, 9 January 1954, 1.

98. Collins C. George, "Fire Army Hostess at McCoy," *Pittsburgh Courier*, 22 December 1951, 1.

99. Grant Hauskins, Interview by Nathan Stanley, 25 April 1997, 3-4, online at http://mcel. pacificu.edu/as/students/stanley/hoskins.html.

100. Bernard Nalty, *Strength for the Fight: A History of Black Americans in the Military* (New York: Free Press, 1986), 273. Also Press Release for Monday Morning, 23 November 1953, Washington Bureau of the NAACP, NA, Record Group 319, Box 008. The Department of Defense prohibited the participation of service members in any type of civil rights demonstrations. David Sutton, "The Military Mission against Off-Base Discrimination," in Charles C. Moskos Jr., ed., *Public Opinion and the Military Establishment* (Beverly Hills, CA: Sage, 1971), 153-54.

101. Sutton, "The Military Mission against Off-Base Discrimination," 149-50.

102. Peter Karsten, *Soldiers and Society: The Effects of Military Service and War on American Life* (Westport, CT: Greenwood Press, 1978), 97.

103. Such was the case in Pulaski, Arkansas, where President Eisenhower proposed using eminent domain after the Board of Education refused to let it be integrated. See Nalty, *Strength for the Fight,* 275.

104. Southern whites overwhelmingly disapproved of efforts to desegregate facilities like trains, buses, and public waiting rooms. Polls in George H. Gallup, *The Gallup Poll: Public Opinion 1935-1971.* Vol. 2, *1949-1958* (New York: Random House, 1972), 1402 and 1572.

105. Quoted in Leo Bogart, ed., *Project Clear: Social Research and the Desegregation of the United States Army* (New Brunswick, NJ: Transaction Publishers, 1992), 263.

106. See the following in the *Pittsburgh Courier:* "Charleston, Mo., Veteran Beaten As Cop Watches," 11 October 1952, 4; "FBI, Army on Spot in GI Beating," 27 November 1951, 2; "Cops Beat GIs after Race Slur," 27 October 1951, 1; and "Half-Blind Vet Killed by 2 Cops," 23 December 1950, 1.

107. Ray Sprigle, "A Soldier Who Came Home to Die," *Pittsburgh Courier Magazine,* 28 April 1956, 3.

108. Morris J. MacGregor Jr., *Integration of the Armed Forces, 1940-1965* (Washington, DC: Center of Military History, U.S. Army, 1981), 468.

109. Mickey Levine, "Report on Negro Veterans in the South," 15 March 1956, 5-6, Central Files, General File, GF 124-A-1, Box 912, DDE Library.

110. Bill Smith, "Black Soldiers Fully Shared Korean War's Bloody Cost," *St. Louis Post-Dispatch,* 20 February 2002, A1.

111. Dryden, *A-Train,* 301.

112. "GI Awaits 'Permission' to Be Buried," *Pittsburgh Courier,* 12 January 1952, 1.

113. President Truman made Arlington National Cemetery available to Rice's family for his burial. Clipping "Iowa Cemetery Halts Burial of U.S. Indian Killed in Korea," Box 35 and Memo Haven Emerson to Harry Truman, 30 August 1951, Box 35, CFSOKW.

114. Mrs. Virginia Soule to President Eisenhower, undated, Central Files, General Files, GF 124-A-1 1957 (4), Box 913, DDE Library.

115. Samuel L. Banks, "The Korean Conflict," *Negro History Bulletin* 36.6 (1973): 132, and Dryden, *A-Train,* 392-93.

116. James G. Campbell, *Korean War Veteran Survey,* 7, CFSOKW.

117. Quoted in Bogart, *Project Clear,* 261.

118. Joe Robertson and Brian Burnes, "50 Years Ago Today, an Uneasy Truce Settled on Korea," *Kansas City Star,* A17, vertical file "Veterans' Recognition," CFSOKW.

119. When Adams returned to the United States a few years after refusing repatriation, he explained to HUAC that he chose China because "I'm black" and he wanted to improve his life. Carlson, *Remembered Prisoners of a Forgotten War,* 211.

120. "Ex-POW Donates to NAACP 'Freedom Fund,'" *Baltimore Afro-American,* 12 September 1953, 3, and "Veteran Takes Out 2nd NAACP Life Membership in Ind.," *Baltimore Afro-American,* 7 November 1953, 5. Also see Selika M. Ducksworth, *What Hour of the Night: Black Enlisted Men's Experiences and the Desegregation of the Army during the Korean War, 1950-1951* (Ph.D. diss., Ohio State University, 1997), 152.

121. The two white posts also wanted all Negro posts to expel all members who belonged to the NAACP. Letter Roy Wilkins to Martin B. McKneally, 23 December 1959; Memorandum to the Files from Mr. Current, 17 April 1958; and Medgar W. Evers to Roy Wilkins, 20 December 1957, all in the Records of the National Association for the Advancement of Colored People, Group 3, Box A197, Folder "Discrimination American Legion 1957-1964," LOC.

122. Ducksworth. *What Hour of the Night*, 152, and "FBI, Army on Spot in GI Beating," *Pittsburgh Courier*, 27 January 1951, 2.

123. The Records of the National Association for the Advancement of Colored People, Group 3, Box A197, Folder "American Veterans Committee 1956-1964," LOC; Clipping "Secretary Hobby Gets Brief Saying No Law Requires It," Central Files, Official Files, OF 142-A, Box 731, DDE Library; and American Veterans Committee, "Summary of Efforts to Make Uniform in the District of Columbia the Law against Racial Discrimination in Places of Public Amusement," 14 February 1956, and Paul Cook to E. Frederick Morrow, 2 September 1959, Staff Files of Administrative Officer—Special Projects (Morrow), Civil Rights Clippings and Data (3), Box 10, DDE Library. Also, Rodney G. Minott, *Peerless Patriots: Organized Veterans and the Spirit of Americanism* (Washington, DC: Public Affairs Press, 1962), 103-6.

124. "Resolutions Presented to the Platform Committees at the Democratic National Convention in Chicago and at the Republican National Convention in San Francisco by the Jewish War Veterans of the United States of America," Central Files, PPF 47, Jackson County Apple Festival Association, Box 822, DDE Library.

125. Greta de Jong, *A Different Day: African American Struggles for Justice in Rural Louisiana, 1900-1970* (Chapel Hill: University of North Carolina Press, 2002), 171.

126. Ducksworth, *What Hour of the Night*, 153.

127. Robert and Essie May Lewis, Interview by Greta de Jong (transcribed by Janna Robinson), 25 November 1996, 4700.0738, Session I, Special Collections, Hill Memorial Library, LSU Libraries, Baton Rouge, Louisiana.

128. Albert Turner, Memoir, online at www.crmvet.org/mem/alturner.htm.

129. William D. Dannenmaier, *We Were Innocents: An Infantryman in Korea* (Chicago: University of Illinois Press, 1999), 225.

130. Allen, *My Old Box of Memories*, 89.

131. Howard Matthias, *The Korean War: Reflections of a Young Combat Platoon Leader*, revised edition (Tallahassee, FL: Father & Son Publishing, 1995), 87. Many veterans report the difficulty they had keeping their language in check after returning from Korea. See also Robert Henderson, *Korean War Veteran Survey*, 10, CFSOKW.

132. Irwin Crockett in Louis Baldovi, ed., *A Foxhole View: Personal Accounts of Hawaii's Korean War Veterans* (Honolulu: University of Hawai'i Press, 2002), 152.

133. Kenneth Dixon, Videotaped Interview by Joe James, 20 August 2008, part of series "Remembering the Korean War: Wartime Wilmington Commemoration," held at University of North Carolina at Wilmington.

134. James H. Putnam, Memoir (KWE), 35, and Floyd Baxter in Knox and Coppel, *The Korean War: Uncertain Victory*, 357.

135. David Van Leeuwen (AFC 2001/001/4394), Folder 2, Interview by Grace Kay Van Leeuwen, 14 December 2001, 3, VHPC, AFC, LOC, and Arthur Smith, Memoir (KWE).

136. Bussey, *Firefight at Yechon*, 259, and Jack Wright in Knox and Coppel, *The Korean War: Uncertain Victory*, 359.

137. Edmund Krekorian in Knox and Coppel, *The Korean War: Uncertain Victory*, 362.

138. Williams's case is especially unusual in that when he committed this crime he was still a sergeant in the Army stationed at Ft. Benning. "GI Pays $3000 Fine," *Pittsburgh Courier*, 2 January 1954, 1.

139. "Youthful War Vet Kills Wife," *Pittsburgh Courier,* 4 June 1955, 1. Another article on the same day and page discusses the suicide of a 23-year-old airman after shooting his wife, but it is not clear whether or not he was a Korean War veteran. See "GI Shoots Wife, Kills Self," *Pittsburgh Courier,* 4 June 1955, 1."Brooklyn Man Held in Beating of Boy, 10," *New York Times,* 16 May 1955, 11.

140. Allen, *My Old Box of Memories,* 88.

141. Harlee W. Lassiter, *Korean War Veteran Survey,* attachment page, CFSOKW.

142. Gerald Gingery, Army Service (Korean War) Questionnaire, 18, 1st Cavalry Division, Surnames A-L, and Douglas G. Anderson, Army Service (Korean War) Questionnaire, 18, 2nd Division, 23rd Regiment, Alphabetical Box 1, Carlisle Barracks.

143. Bussey, *Firefight at Yechon,* 260, and Leonard Korgie in Knox and Coppel, *The Korean War: Uncertain Victory,* 373.

144. Hoppy Harris, "When Sleep Comes" in "Return to Heartbreak Ridge: A Journey into the Past," Box EE, Folder A0956, CFSOKW.

145. Ronald Landry, "Korea" in "Chosin House," Box FF, Folder 0964, CFSOKW.

146. Gilbert Towner, *Korean War Veteran Survey,* 9, CFSOKW, and Dannenmaier, *We Were Innocents,* 1.

147. Jack Wright in Knox and Coppel, *The Korean War: Uncertain Victory,* 359.

148. Ralph Cutro, *Korean War Veteran Survey,* 7, CFSOKW, and Edmund Krekorian in Knox and Coppel, *The Korean War: Uncertain Victory,* 362.

149. Charles V. Alioto, Army Service (Korean War) Questionnaire, 17, 2nd Division, 23rd Regiment, Alphabetical Box 1, Carlisle Barracks.

150. Bernstein, *Monsters and Angels,* 339.

151. Dannenmaier, *We Were Innocents,* 226.

152. Leonard Korgie in Knox and Coppel, *The Korean War: Uncertain Victory,* 371; Seymour Harris Jr., Army Service (Korean War) Questionnaire, 18, 2nd Division, 23rd Regiment, Alphabetical Box 1, Carlisle Barracks; Harold L. Mulhausen, *Korean War Veteran Survey,* 7, CFSOKW; Barnett R. Wilson (AFC2001/001/2783), Folder 1, "A Korean Cruise: Magic Moments of Life, Love, and War," 200, VHPC, AFC, LOC; Dannenmaier, *We Were Innocents,* 1.

153. Dannenmaier, *We Were Innocents,* 225.

154. Ralph David Fly, Memoir (KWE), 28.

155. Dannenmaier, *We Were Innocents,* 225.

156. Elmer "Palmer" Payne, *Korean War Veteran Survey,* 7, CFSOKW.

157. Floyd Baxter in Knox and Coppel, *The Korean War: Uncertain Victory,* 360-61. Also John M. Pitre, *Korean War Veteran Survey,* 7, CFSOKW, and Harlee W. Lassiter, *Korean War Veteran Survey,* attachment page, CFSOKW.

158. Clarence Jackson "Jack" Davis (AFC2001/001/1644), Folder 1, Unpublished letters and postscript, 180, VHPC, AFC, LOC.

159. Allen, *My Old Box of Memories,* 88.

160. *Ibid.,* and Harlee W. Lassiter, *Korean War Veteran Survey,* attachment page, CFSOKW.

161. *Ibid.*

162. Email Ted Hofsiss to Janell Coppage, 24 April 1999, Box FF, Folder A0958, CFSOKW, and Herman Aud McLeroy, Army Service (Korean War) Questionnaire, 18, 1st Cavalry Division, Surnames M-Z, Carlisle Barracks. Also see Gerald F. Linderman, *The World within War: America's Combat Experience in World War II* (NewYork: Free Press, 1997), 362.

163. Bussey, *Firefight at Yechon,* 260.

164. See Glenn Reynolds in Carlson, *Remembered Prisoners of a Forgotten War,* 230.

165. Spiller, *American POWs in Korea,* 111, and Richard Severo and Lewis Milford, *The Wages of War: When America's Soldiers Came Home; From Valley Forge to Vietnam* (New York: Simon and Schuster, 1989), 317-22. Army psychiatrist Major William E. Mayer claimed that

POWs had not been physically tortured and accused them of yielding because of "serious weakness in Americans' character." He publicized his findings in articles like "Why Did Many GI Captives Cave In?" *U.S. News and World Report*, 24 February 1956, 56-62. Celebrities such as Dr. Spock also weighed in, and a plethora of contemporary newspaper and magazine articles focused on the fears surrounding POWs. See "Washed Brains of POW's: Can They Be Rewashed?" *Newsweek*, 4 May 1953, 37, and "The Boys Come Home," *Time Magazine*, 11 May 1953, 30. Articles debunking brainwashing also appeared and a later congressional hearing helped set the matter straight, but in the minds of many, POWs remained tainted. See Congress, Senate, Committee on Government Operations, *Communist Interrogation, Indoctrination, and Exploitation of American Military and Civilian Prisoners: Hearings before the Permanent Subcommittee on Investigations of the Committee on Government Operations*, 84th Congress, 2nd sess., June 1956.

166. Carlson, *Remembered Prisoners of a Forgotten War*, 1.

167. See Donald L. Slagle in Spiller, *American POWs in Korea*, 111, and Akira Chikami in Carlson, *Remembered Prisoners of a Forgotten War*, 47.

168. Robert A. Maclean in Carlson, *Remembered Prisoners of a Forgotten War*, 29.

169. Richard T. Cooper, "Vets Still Conflicted over Korea," *Los Angeles Times*, 19 January 2000, 1.

170. Bussey, *Firefight at Yechon*, 260, and Walter G. Adelmann in Spiller, *American POWs in Korea*, 38.

171. In 1953, $3 million were trimmed from the VA budget. Consequently, the VA ordered a reduction of mental patient treatments at clinics outside regular VA facilities and abolished evening sessions created to accommodate working patients. Patients received notice of suspended treatment via telephone without prior warning. See remarks and articles provided by Congressman Isidore Dollinger of New York in *Appendix to the Congressional Record* (House), 83rd Congress, 2nd sess., volume 100 (Washington, DC: U.S. Government Printing Office, 1955), A5-A7.

172. For medical purposes, those returning from Korea were identified as war veterans before the war's end, but Congress did not designate the Korean War as a war until the late 1950s. Paul M. Edwards, *To Acknowledge a War: The Korean War in American Memory* (Westport, CT: Greenwood Press, 2000), 53. In December 1950, the American Legion redefined its membership eligibility rules to include Korean War veterans, but local chapters did not always abide by these. *Public Law 895*, 81st Congress, 2nd sess., *United States Statutes at Large* (Washington, DC: U.S. Government Printing Office, 1952), 1122.

173. Verlin Rogers, Army Service (Korean War) Questionnaire, 18, 1st Cavalry Division, Surnames M-Z, Carlisle Barracks. See also Minott, *Peerless Patriots*, 102-3.

174. Edwards, *To Acknowledge a War*, 32-34.

175. Email Shorty Estabrook to Melinda Pash, 5 August 2004, in author's possession. Also Morrow, *What's a Commie Ever Done to Black People?* 1.

176. Walter G. Adelmann in Spiller, *American POWs in Korea*, 37, and John "Jack" Orth, *Korean War Veteran Survey*, 8, CFSOKW.

177. *Ibid.* Many veterans of the Second World War also struggled with alcoholism after their return. See Tuttle, *"Daddy's Gone to War,"* 218-19.

178. Email Ted Hofsiss to Janell Coppage, 24 April 1999, Box FF, Folder A0958, CFSOKW, and Bill Smith, "Black Soldiers Fully Shared Korean War's Bloody Cost," *St. Louis Post-Dispatch*, 20 February 2002, A1.

179. L. Branchey, W. Davis, and C. S. Lieber, "Alcoholism in Vietnam and Korea Veterans: A Long Term Follow-Up," *Alcoholism: Clinical and Experimental Research* 8.6 (November/December 1984): 37. Also Keith A. Druley and Steven Pashko, "Posttraumatic Stress Disorder in World War II and Korean Combat Veterans with Alcohol Dependency," *Recent Developments in Alcoholism* 6 (1988): 89-101, and Grayson S. Norquist, Richard L. Hough,

Jacqueline M. Golding, and Javier I. Escobar, "Psychiatric Disorder in Male Veterans and Nonveterans," *Journal of Nervous and Mental Disease* 178.5 (May 1990): 328-35.

180. For a study of the long-term effects of veteran, particularly POW, use of alcohol, see William F. Page and Richard N. Miller, "Cirrhosis Mortality among Former American Prisoners of War of World War II and the Korean Conflict: Results of a 50-Year Follow-Up," *Military Medicine* 165.10 (October 2000): 781-85.

181. PTSD, called "shell shock" during World War I and "battle fatigue" during World War II, can afflict anyone who has been exposed to a frightening or life-threatening event, such as an earthquake, tornado, or battle. PTSD causes a wide range of problems such as emotional detachment, sleep disturbances, and fearfulness.

182. Ralph Cutro, *Korean War Veteran Survey*, 7, CFSOKW.

183. Richard T. Cooper, "Vets Still Conflicted over Korea," *Los Angeles Times*, 19 January 2000, 1, and Frances I. Snell and Edgardo Padin-Rivera, "Post-Traumatic Stress Disorder and the Elderly Combat Veteran," *Journal of Gerontological Nursing* 23.10 (October 1997): 17.

184. Robert C. Bjork, Army Service (Korean War) Questionnaire, continuation sheet, 2nd Division, 23rd Regiment, Alphabetical Box 1, Carlisle Barracks.

185. Some men complain about the lack of help available. See Billy Joe Harris in Carlson, *Remembered Prisoners of a Forgotten War*, 228.

186. Tompkins, "Korean Veterans with Psychiatric Disabilities," 36-37. A doctor, Tompkins also noted that Korean War veterans in general sought psychiatric help more readily than World War II veterans but then used it in a very limited fashion. Korean veterans who applied for treatment at mental clinics tended to be "more seriously and more severely disturbed than World War II veterans."

187. Spiller, *American POWs in Korea*, 30 and 66; Dannenmaier, *We Were Innocents*, 266; and Phillip N. Bailey and Robert C. Bjork, Army Service (Korean War) Questionnaire, 18, 2nd Division, 23rd Regiment, Alphabetical Box 1, Carlisle Barracks.

188. Rudolph W. Stephens, *Old Ugly Hill: A GI's Fourteen Months in the Korean Trenches, 1952-1953* (Jefferson, NC: McFarland, 1995), 171. Also, Morrow, *What's a Commie Ever Done to Black People?* 1. Studies demonstrate the longevity of these memories and PTSD. See Scott P. Orr, Roger K. Pitman, Natasha B. Lasko, and Lawrence R. Herz, "Psychophysiological Assessment of Posttraumatic Stress Disorder Imagery in World War II and Korean Combat Veterans," *Journal of Abnormal Psychology* 102.1 (February 1993): 158.

189. On heavy combat leading to "a much higher risk of emotional problems after the service," see Glen H. Elder Jr. and Elizabeth Colerick Clipp, "Combat Experience and Emotional Health: Impairment and Resilience in Later Life," *Journal of Personality* 57.2 (June 1989): 327. POWs continue to suffer from PTSD at alarmingly high rates. Some studies suggest as many as nine of ten POW survivors have PTSD. "Emotional Trauma Haunts Korean War POWs," *Science News*, 2 February 1991, 68.

190. "Emotional Trauma Haunts Korean POWs," 68. Also see Cynthia Lindman Port, Brian Engdahl, and Patricia Frazier, "A Longitudinal and Retrospective Study of PTSD among Older Prisoners of War" *American Journal of Psychiatry* 158 (September 2001): 1474-79, and Brian Engdahl, Thomas N. Dikel, Raina Eberly, and Arthur Blank Jr., "Posttraumatic Stress Disorder in a Community of Former Prisoners of War: A Normative Response to Severe Trauma," *American Journal of Psychiatry* 154.11 (November 1997): 1576-81.

191. Charles Davis in Carlson, *Remembered Prisoners of a Forgotten War*, 195.

192. Robert A. Maclean in *ibid.*, 29.

193. Email Shorty Estabrook to Melinda Pash, 5 August 2004, in author's possession.

194. Recent studies show that the manifestations of PTSD lessened over time, but reinvigorated as veterans aged, experienced health problems, or had memories triggered by external stimuli. Snell and Padin-Rivera, "Post-Traumatic Stress Disorder and the Elderly Combat Veteran," 18.

195. The return of Vietnam War veterans provided impetus for studying and treating PTSD although the condition had been long recognized. See Orr et al., "Psychophysiological Assessment of Posttraumatic Stress Disorder Imagery in World War II and Korean Combat Veterans," 152; Snell and Padin-Rivera, "Post-Traumatic Stress Disorder and the Elderly Combat Veteran," 13 and 16; and Joel Sadavoy, "Survivors: A Review of the Late-Life Effects of Prior Psychological Trauma," *American Journal of Geriatric Psychiatry* 5.4 (1997): 288.

196. Ralph David Fly, Memoir (KWE), 28. For an example of the kinds of articles they were reading, see David Gelman, "Treating War's Psychic Wounds," *Newsweek*, 29 August 1988, 62-64.

197. One study finds that only 19% of World War II veterans exhibit current PTSD compared to 30% of Korean War veterans. Avron Spiro III, Paula P. Schnurr, and Carolyn M. Aldwin, "Combat-Related Posttraumatic Stress Disorder Symptoms in Older Men," *Psychology and Aging* 9.1 (March 1994): 18. Snell and Padin-Rivera put the percentage lower for Korean War veterans, at 12%, but that estimate reflects all living veterans, not just those seeking treatment. See "Post-Traumatic Stress Disorder and the Elderly Combat Veteran," 14. Another study suggests that the adjustment problems of Korean veterans were more severe than those of World War II veterans. Edward W. McCranie and Leon A. Hyer, "Posttraumatic Stress Disorder Symptoms in Korean Conflict and World War II Combat Veterans Seeking Outpatient Treatment," *Journal of Traumatic Stress* 13.3 (2000): 436.

198. Robert A. Maclean in Carlson, *Remembered Prisoners of a Forgotten War*, 31.

199. See Billy Joe Harris and Robert A. Maclean in Carlson, *Remembered Prisoners of a Forgotten War*, 228 and 31, and Donald E. Barton, Army Service (Korean War) Questionnaire, continuation sheet, 2nd Division, 23rd Regiment, Alphabetical Box 1, Carlisle Barracks.

200. Tony Velasquez to Paul Edwards, 1 May 2002, Box AAA, CFSOKW.

201. Arthur Wilson in Richard T. Cooper, "Vets Still Conflicted over Korea," *Los Angeles Times*, 19 January 2000, 1.

202. Accounts of veteran suicides and attempted suicides appeared regularly in newspapers during and after the war. See "Man Long on High Ledge," *New York Times*, 11 May 1953, 16; "Sign of the Cross Halts Death Leap," *New York Times*, 3 June 1951, 34; "Vet in Death Leap from GW Bridge," *Pittsburgh Courier*, 8 March 1952, 1; and "Find Ex-GI's Body in Lake," *Pittsburgh Courier*, 13 February 1954, 1. Researchers note that Korean veterans "reported greater psychiatric distress . . . than both the World War II and Vietnam veterans" and had a greater tendency toward "suicidality." McCranie and Hyer, "Posttraumatic Stress Disorder Symptoms in Korean Conflict and World War II Combat Veterans Seeking Outpatient Treatment," 430, and Alan Fontana and Robert Rosenheck, "Traumatic War Stressors and Psychiatric Symptoms among World War II, Korean, and Vietnam Veterans," *Psychology and Aging* 9.1 (March 1994): 30-31. Fontana's article suggests a link between the greater distress of Korean War veterans and both the stigma placed on mental illness in the 1950s and the unpopularity of the conflict. POWs especially died young. When they first came home, almost every POW drank too much, had motorcycle accidents, went from woman to woman, or tried to kill himself. According to one source, 20% of them did not survive the first decade after their return home. Peggy Himmelheber in Carlson, *Remembered Prisoners of a Forgotten War*, 227.

203. "Find Ex-GI's Body in Lake," *Pittsburgh Courier*, 13 February 1954, 1. Hounded by the FBI, some POWs, like Jack Flanary, took their own lives. See "Tough Prisoners," *Time Magazine*, 21 September 1953, 28.

204. Clarence Jackson "Jack" Davis (AFC2001/001/1644), Folder 1, Unpublished letters and postscript, 180, VHPC, AFC, LOC.

205. Gilbert Towner, *Korean War Veteran Survey*, 6, CFSOKW.

206. Harold L. Mulhausen, *Korean War Veteran Survey*, 7, CFSOKW.

207. Clyde H. Queen Sr. (AFC2001/001/10115), Folder 2, Written answers to Interview Questions, 6 May 2003, 14, VHPC, AFC, LOC.

208. Douglas G. Anderson, Army Service (Korean War) Questionnaire, 18, 2nd Division, 23rd Regiment, Alphabetical Box 1, Carlisle Barracks. Coping mechanisms such as indulging in overwork to keep the mind busy and seeking jobs where one could be alone were typical. Snell and Padin-Rivera, "Post-Traumatic Stress Disorder and the Elderly Combat Veteran," 17.

209. Clarence Jackson "Jack" Davis (AFC2001/001/1644), Folder 1, unpublished letters and postscript, 179-180, VHPC, AFC, LOC, and Charles V. Alioto, Army Service (Korean War) Questionnaire, 18, 2nd Division, 23rd Regiment, Alphabetical Box 1, Carlisle Barracks.

210. Raymond Delcambre, Army Service (Korean War) Questionnaire, 18, 2nd Division, 23rd Regiment, Alphabetical Box 1, Carlisle Barracks. VA experts noted that many Korean War veterans seemed to be waiting for someone to tell them what to do. See George Barrett, "Portrait of the Korean Veteran," *New York Times Magazine*, 9 August 1953, 24.

211. Harry A. Matthews, *Korean War Veteran Survey*, 10, CFSOKW, and Leonard Korgie (on meeting a marine who had been at Chosin Reservoir while on leave) in Knox and Coppel, *The Korean War: Uncertain Victory*, 372.

212. Jack Wright in Knox and Coppel, *The Korean War: Uncertain Victory*, 359.

213. Ralph Cutro, *Korean War Veteran Survey*, 7, CFSOKW.

214. See Carlson, *Remembered Prisoners of a Forgotten War*, 225. No hard data exists to support the assertion that continued military service translated into an easier adjustment for veterans, but surveys, oral histories, and interviews show that men who remained in the military after wartime service feel more positively about their readjustment. Career military personnel often make comments such as, "I was still in the service, so there wasn't any readjusting to perform." Harry A. Matthews III, *Korean War Veteran Survey*, 11, CFSOKW. Also, Leonard DeBord, *Korean War Veteran Survey*, 5-6, CFSOKW, and Philip C. Bolte, Army Service (Korean War) Questionnaire, 18, 1st Cavalry Division, Surnames A-L, Carlisle Barracks. Military life had at least one major drawback in that one could not pick one's duty station. Seeking to draw on the experience of Korean War veterans for cold weather training, the Army stationed many returnees at Pine Camp, New York, where men complained about having to spend another winter in the cold. "Pine Camp Shifts Korea Veterans," *New York Times*, 29 November 1951, 18.

215. A good example of this is the drop in the percentage of men dying of penetrating and perforating wounds. In World War I, 27% of men with such casualties died, in World War II, 8.1% did, but at the Tokyo Army Hospital from 1950 to 1952, only .6% died. Furthermore, of those who survived during the Korean War, 80% recovered and were found fit for duty in ninety days or less. J. S. D. King and James H. Harris, "War Wounds of the Chest among Marine and Naval Casualties in Korea," *Surgery, Gynecology, and Obstetrics*, 210, AR 0021, CFSOKW.

216. In World War II, standard protocol for treating a severed artery was to tie it off so that a man did not bleed to death even though this usually resulted in amputation. MASH units in Korea instead employed arterial repair, lowering the mortality rate from 4% in World War II to less than .04% in Korea. Frank R. Denman, Interview by Jeffrey Albeldt in Virginia Havard, ed., *By Word of Mouth* (Lufkin, TX: Lufkin High School, Kwik Kopy Printing, 1990), 7, and Dr. Hermes Grillo, Interview by G. Kurt Piehler and Crystal Dover, 8 July 2002, 39, Veterans' Oral History Project, Center for the Study of War and Society, University of Tennessee, Knoxville, TN. Also Otto F. Apel Jr. and Pat Apel, *MASH: An Army Surgeon in Korea* (Lexington: University Press of Kentucky, 1998), 150-52.

217. Military medicine in Korea followed the same general pattern as in World War II, but advancements, including the placement of MASH hospitals near enough to the front to perform emergency surgery, lowered the mortality rate. On changes during the Korean

War, see "Section VIII: Medical Care" (Bradley Commission): Records 1954-1958, A69-22 and 79-6, Box 61, DDE Library, and Grillo, Interview by Piehler and Dover, 8 July 2002, 28-29.

218. Helicopter use probably increased survival rates. In World War II no rapid evacuation existed, in the Korean War 15% of the wounded were flown out by helicopter, and in Vietnam 90% were flown out. The mortality rate during the Vietnam War dropped to just 1% of those wounded. Len Morgan, "M*A*S*H Epilogue: The Story of the Popular TV Series Never Told, How the Helicopter Proved Its Worth," *Flying* 110 (March 1983): 160-63.

219. Richard K. Kolb, "Korea's 'Invisible Veterans': Return to an Ambivalent America," *Veterans of Foreign Wars Magazine*, November 1997, 26.

220. Once returnees quit taking pills to ward off malaria, many contracted the disease. Richard S. Homer, "Vivax Malaria without Primary Attack in Korean Veterans," *U.S. Armed Forces Medical Journal* 8.3 (March 1957): 427-30; Fred B. Rogers, "Vivax Malaria in a Returned Korean Veteran," *U.S. Armed Forces Medical Journal* 6.11 (November 1955): 1657-60; A. J. Moriarty, J. D. Lawrence, T. E. Hodgins, and B. C. Brown, "Vivax Malaria in Korean Veterans," *Treatment Services Bulletin* 7.8 (September 1952): 361-67; "Physicians Alerted on Soldiers' Malaria," *New York Times*, 10 August 1951, 13; and George W. Gatliffe, Memoir (KWE), 16. Other articles predicted leprosy outbreaks and charted intestinal parasites. "Predict Leprosy for Recent War Veterans," *Science New Letter*, 25 September 1954, 198, and Ryle A. Radke, "Incidence of Amebiasis in Korean Veterans," *U.S. Armed Forces Medical Journal* 3.2 (February 1952): 323.

221. Frank Muetzel in Knox and Coppel, *The Korean War: Uncertain Victory*, 367-69; Edward L. Beach, "Memorandum for the Record: Deactivation of the U.S.S. Williamsburg," 11 April 1953; J. T. Burke Jr., "Memorandum for the President," 28 April 1953; and Dwight D. Eisenhower to Commander J. T. Burke Jr., 1 May 1953, Central Files, Official File, OF 101-4 1956, Box 413, DDE Library.

222. Richard Newman in Berry, *Hey Mac, Where Ya Been?* 241.

223. Muetzel in Knox and Coppel, *The Korean War: Uncertain Victory*, 369-71.

224. National Academy of Sciences, National Research Council, *Study of Health Care for American Veterans* (Washington, DC: U.S. Government Printing Office, 1977), 4.

225. The commander of a Canton, Ohio, Amvets post, noting the increased number of men and women taken into the armed forces during the Korean War, wrote Senator Robert Taft about the need to keep the VA office there open. "We believe that the actual veteran population of Stark County is increasing rather than decreasing. Hence, it would seem that the need for medical and dental departments at the local Veterans Administration office is more necessary at the present time than ever before." Paul Beitzel to Robert Taft, 23 July 1951, Taft Papers, Box 1077, LOC.

226. On VA troubles and changes in veteran medical care in the 1950s see "Doctors' Revolt," *Newsweek*, 25 February 1952, 64-67; Lois Mattox Miller and James Monahan, "Veterans' Medicine: Back in the Doldrums," *Reader's Digest*, June 1951, 89-93; and "Section VIII: Medical Care (1)" (Bradley Commission): Records 1954-1958, A69-22 and 79-6, Box 61, DDE Library.

227. Emails Shorty Estabrook to Melinda Pash, 29 July 2004 and 5 August 2004, in author's possession.

228. See series of letters dealing with Richard J. Curtis, Central Files, General File 125-K 1958, Box 934, DDE Library.

229. "Veteran Denied VA Hospital Care, Dies," *Baltimore Afro-American*, 13 September 1952, 5.

230. Bruce Satra, *Korean War Veteran Survey*, 10, CFSOKW. Satra claims he signed a paper in basic training guaranteeing him lifetime medical care. In 2002, a federal appeals court denied the claims of World War II and Korean War veterans suing for the medical care promised them on the grounds that while the government conceded such promises were made, no valid contract existed because such assurances were not backed by law at the

time. Curt Anderson, "Appeals Court Denies Lifetime Health Care for WWII, Korean Veterans," *Associated Press News Service,* 20 November 2002, online at http://infoweb. newsbank.com.

231. Michael Doyle, "Veterans Win 'Cold War' for Health Benefits," *Fresno Bee,* 25 May 1997, A22, and "Out Front: Aging World War II, Korea Vets Finally Compensated for Frostbite's Ills," *Boston Globe Online,* 6 April 1997, Vertical Files, "Frostbite," CFSOKW.

232. Gilbert Towner, *Korean War Veteran Survey,* 9, CFSOKW.

233. "Loophole in the Law," *Newsweek,* 21 May 1951, 27.

234. "Korea G.I. Is 'War' Veteran," *Special to the New York Times,* 13 May 1951, B10, and "Benefits for Korea Veterans Voted after Hospital Bars an Ex-Marine," *Special to the New York Times,* 11 May 1951, 1. For another early effort in Congress on behalf of veteran health care, see Representative Sikes, *Congressional Record,* 84th Cong., 2d sess., vol. 102:8, 10718-10719.

235. "Undersecretary for Health's Information Letter: Recommendations for the Care and Examination of Veterans with Late Onset Effects of Cold Injuries," 31 December 1996, Vertical Files, "Frostbite," CFSOKW.

236. Jonathan Bor, "Korean War Cold Cripples Again," *Baltimore Sun,* 14 April 1996, 1A, and "Out Front: Aging World War II, Korea Vets Finally Compensated for Frostbite's Ills," *Boston Globe Online,* 6 April 1997, Vertical Files, "Frostbite," CFSOKW.

237. For examples of denied claims, see Augie Garcia in Don Boxmeyer, *A Knack for Knowing Things: Stories from St. Paul Neighborhoods and Beyond* (St. Paul: Minnesota Historical Society Press, 2003), 157, and Verlin N. Rogers, Army Service (Korean War) Questionnaire, 20, 1st Cavalry Division, Surnames M-Z, Carlisle Barracks.

238. Robert Rosenheck, "Wartime Military Service and Utilization of VA Health Care Services," *Military Medicine* 158.4 (April 1993): 223-28. Also, Bruce Satra, *Korean War Veteran Survey,* 8, CFSOKW. Of modern veterans, Vietnam veterans most often availed themselves of VA medical care, preferring it over other types of general care. JoAnn Damron-Rodriguez, Whitney White-Kazemipour, Donna Washington, Valentine M. Villa, Shawkat Dhanani, and Nancy D. Harada, "Accessibility and Acceptability of the Department of Veteran Affairs Health Care: Diverse Veterans' Perspectives," *Military Medicine* 169.3 (March 2004): 244. In 1957, only 89,000 Korean veterans compared to 385,000 World War II and 368, 000 World War I veterans occupied hospital beds. By 1986, Korean veterans in hospitals outnumbered World War I veterans 413,000 to 92,000, but World War II veteran patients numbered 1,399,000. "Table 7," IV-11, Central Files, Official File, OF55-B-1 1959-60, Box 246, Folder "55-B-1 1959-60," DDE Library.

239. Arthur Smith, Memoir (KWE), 18.

240. Email Ted Hofsiss to Janell Coppage, 24 April 1999, Box FF, Folder A0958, CFSOKW.

241. Pamela Moate to Dr. Edwards, 27 May 2001, Box VV, Folder A1485, CFSOKW.

242. Dannenmaier, *We Were Innocents,* 226.

243. Although studies of U.S. Korean War veterans are sparse, those conducted in other countries confirm a higher incidence of DDT and smoking-related cancers among Korean War veterans. Logically, one could assume that American soldiers were not immune to the health risks affecting men of other nations. See Chris Wattie, "Vets Demand Recourse for 'Abuse': Korean War Survivors; Soldiers Doused in DDT Denied Pensions, Dying 'Far Too Young,'" *National Post* (Canada), 5 May 2004, A4, and "Study Confirms Higher Incidence of Smoking-Related Cancers among Korean Veterans," M2 Presswire, 2 December 2003, available online at www.presswire.net.

244. Ernie "Pappy" Pappenheimer in Jonathan Bor, "Korean War Cold Cripples Again," *Baltimore Sun,* 14 April 1996, 1A.

245. Dr. Murray Hamlet in "Out Front: Aging World War II, Korea Vets Finally Compensated for Frostbite's Ills," *Boston Globe Online,* 6 April 1997, Vertical Files, "Frostbite," CFSOKW.

246. Michael Doyle, "Veterans Win 'Cold War' for Health Benefits," *Fresno Bee*, 25 May 1997, A22.

247. Robert J. Keehn, "Follow-Up Studies of World War II and Korean Conflict Prisoners," *American Journal of Epidemiology* 111.2 (February 1980): 194-211. This study also shows that the general mortality rate of Korean War veterans (1.03) was slightly higher than for World War II veterans (.99).

248. Korean War veterans generally felt entitled only to benefits related to recovery from service-related injuries or handicaps (physical, economic, etc.). The Bradley Commission found that 90% of men who served in the Far East believed they should receive free medical care for illnesses or injuries connected with their service, but only 22% felt entitled to free medical care for "any illness or injury whatsoever." Similarly, 83% thought their prewar jobs should be offered them on return, but only 35% favored veterans' preference in obtaining government jobs. Only 15% wanted pensions for life. "Study of Veterans Attitudes, Roper Poll (2)," (Bradley Commission): Records 1954-1958, A69-22 and 79-6, Box 63, DDE Library.

249. Congress, House, President's Commission on Veterans' Pensions, *Veterans in Our Society: Data on the Conditions of Military Service and on the Status of the Veteran*, 125, 84th Congress, 2nd sess., Committee Print 261, Staff Report No. IV, 21 June 1956 (Washington, DC: U.S. Government Printing Office, 1956). An earlier survey of World War II and Korean Conflict veterans reported that almost 96% of veterans favored extension of the GI Bill's educational benefits to Korean War veterans. Roy N. Chelgren, "An Attitude Survey concerning the Provision of Educational Benefits for Korean Veterans," *School and Society*, 13 September 1952, 170.

250. For an early call for benefits, see Senator Harry P. Cain of Washington in *Congressional Record* (Senate), 81st Congress, 2nd sess., volume 96, part 7 (14 June 1950-11 July 1950), 9790.

251. James L. Donnelly ? (name illegible), Executive Vice-President of the Illinois Manufacturers' Association to President Eisenhower, 1 September 1959, Central Files, General File, GF 125-I 1959 (3), Box 932, DDE Library.

252. Resentment toward veterans' benefits continued to build through the 1950s on this point. See John E. Booth, "Veterans: Our Biggest Privileged Class," *Harper's Magazine*, July 1958, 19-25.

253. Senators Lister Hill of Alabama and H. Styles Bridges of New Hampshire, Washington, in *Congressional Record* (Senate), 82nd Congress, 2nd sess., volume 98, part 7 (28 June 1952-7 July 1952), 8412-8413.

254. Congressman Thomas Lane of Massachusetts in *Congressional Record* (House), 82nd Congress, 2nd sess., volume 98, part 1 (8 January 1952-25 February 1952), 47.

255. Congress, House, President's Commission on Veterans' Pensions, *Readjustment Benefits: General Survey and Appraisal; A Report on Veterans' Benefits in the United States*, 150-51, 84th Congress, 2nd sess., Committee Print 289, Staff Report No. IX Part A, 11 September 1956 (Washington, DC: U.S. Government Printing Office, 1956).

256. George P. Perros, compiler, "Preliminary Inventory of the Records of the House Select Committee to Investigate Educational, Training, and Loan Guaranty Programs under GI Bill, 1950-52" (Washington, DC: National Archives and Records Services General Services Administration, 1957), 2.

257. The Teague Committee recommended time constraints for the start and completion of educational and training programs, the direct payment of money to veterans rather than to schools, limitations on school eligibility to receive GI Bill money, new standards on the type of schooling eligible for consideration under the GI Bill program, and more veteran accountability for making progress in a program. Congress, House, President's Commission on Veterans' Pensions, *Readjustment Benefits: General Survey and Appraisal: A Report on Veterans' Benefits in the United States*, 150-154,; Sidney Shalett, "How Our Tax Dollars

Are Wasted," *Saturday Evening Post*, 24 May 1952, 12; and Congress, House, House Select Committee to Investigate Educational, Training, and Loan Guaranty Programs under GI Bill, House Report No. 1375, 1-2 and 78-81, 82nd Congress, 2nd sess., 11 February 1952 in *House Reports*, vol. 5 (Washington, DC: U.S. Government Printing Office, 1952). Private colleges, fearful that veterans would choose less expensive public institutions if paying tuition themselves, lobbied hard for the "Springer Amendment," which would have required the government to split subsistence and tuition payments so that veterans only received their portion directly, but this failed to pass. See Congressman Olin E. Teague in *Congressional Record: Appendix* (House), 82nd Congress, 2nd sess., volume 98 (January 1952-July 1952), A3901-A3905 and 3993. For more on the evolution of the Korean GI Bill, see Melinda Pash, "'A Veteran Does Not Have to Stay a Veteran Forever': Congress and the Korean G.I. Bill," in Stephen R. Ortiz, ed., *Veterans' Policies, Veterans' Politics: New Perspectives on Veterans in the United States* (Gainesville: University of Florida Press, 2012).

258. The ninety days' active service requirement was waived for men discharged for injury or disability sustained as a result of their service. *Public Law 550*, 82nd Congress, 2nd sess., *United States Statutes at Large* (Washington, DC: U.S. Government Printing Office, 1953), 663. Men and women who remained on active duty seven or more years beyond the Korean service period lost their rights to the GI Bill. "Summary of Actions Which Have Had the Effect of Decreasing Incentives from Military Service," 4, Central Files, General File, GF 120, Box 700, DDE Library.

259. For Korean GI Bill specifics, see *Public Law 550*, 82nd Congress, 2nd sess., *United States Statutes at Large* (Washington, DC: U.S. Government Printing Office, 1953), 663-91; "The New GI Bill: Who Gets What," *Changing Times*, May 1953, 21-23; "We've Been Asked: About Benefits for New GI's," *U.S. News and World Report*, 11 July 1952, 82-83; and "Veterans under the New Law," *Personnel and Guidance Journal* 31 (October 1952): 42-43.

260. "More Billions for GI Schooling," *U.S. News and World Report*, 31 August 1951, 30-31. Many differences existed between the World War II and Korean GI Bills. Under the World War II GI Bill, the basic entitlement of veterans was one year plus active duty time instead of 1.5 times their active duty, the maximum basic entitlement was forty-eight months rather than thirty-six months, veterans had four years after their release from service to begin school instead of three, they were eligible for benefits for nine years rather than eight, they received up to five hundred dollars a year for tuition in addition to monthly subsistence payments ranging from fifty to seventy-five dollars, could change their course of study before commencement, were initially permitted to enroll in recreational courses, and were considered full-time students with only twelve credit hours rather than fourteen. Kenneth Edward Fisher, *A Comparative Analysis of Selected Congressional Documents Related to Educational Benefits Legislated for the Veterans of World War II, the Korean Conflict, and the Vietnam Era under the G.I. Bill* (Ph.D. diss., Florida State University, June 1975), table 9.

261. "333,000 Korea Vets Cast Fond Eye at GI Bill," *Army Times*, 4 July 1953, 1.

262. Paul P. Kennedy, "Korea G.I.'s Slow in Taking Benefits," *New York Times*, 30 August 1953, 8. See also Howard A. Rusk, "Public Apathy to Korea G.I.'s Slows Their Benefit Claims," *New York Times*, 27 September 1953, 4.

263. Charles F. Cole, *Korea Remembered: Enough of a War; The USS Ozbourn's First Korean Tour, 1950-1951* (Las Cruces, NM: Yucca Tree Press, 1995), 272-73. World War II veterans had a far greater sense of community and belonging when they returned to school. See Mary L. Dee, "We Lived in GI Town," *Coronet*, May 1952, 62-66.

264. Fisher, *A Comparative Analysis of Selected Congressional Documents Related to Educational Benefits Legislated for the Veterans of World War II, the Korean Conflict, and the Vietnam Era Under the G.I. Bill*, 32.

265. *Ibid.* The estimates vary somewhat. In 1956, the Bradley Commission found that only 35.5% of Korean War veterans had used educational benefits compared to 47.7% of World War II veterans, but separated out men and women who served in both wars, 52.2% of

whom had used their GI Bill for school. Congress, House, President's Commission on Veterans' Pensions, *Readjustment Benefits: General Survey and Appraisal: A Report on Veterans' Benefits in the United States,* 82, 84th Congress, 2nd sess., Committee Print 289, Staff Report No. IX Part A, 11 September 1956 (Washington, DC: U.S. Government Printing Office, 1956).

266. Howard A. Rusk, "Public Apathy to Korea G.I.'s Slows Their Benefit Claims," *New York Times,* 27 September 1953, L4.

267. See Congressman Olin E. Teague in *Congressional Record: Appendix* (House), 84th Congress, 2nd sess., volume 102 (January 1956-July 1956), A75.

268. The VBI helped veterans with all types of claims, including disability compensation, pensions, GI loans, insurance, and government employment. "New Memphis Claims Service Helps Solve Vets' Problems," *Pittsburgh Courier,* 8 June 1957, 4.

269. Benjamin Fine, "Few Korea G.I.'s Going to College," *New York Times,* 4 October 1954, 27, and Benjamin Fine, "Korean War Veterans Are Not Flocking to Colleges as They Were Expected to Do," *New York Times,* 24 October 1954, E9. Also Congress, House, President's Commission on Veterans' Pensions, *Readjustment Benefits: General Survey and Appraisal; A Report on Veterans' Benefits in the United States,* 164, 84th Congress, 2nd sess., Committee Print 289, Staff Report No. IX Part A, 11 September 1956 (Washington, DC: U.S. Government Printing Office, 1956).

270. John Walker Hatcher (AFC2001-001-1428), Letter to parents, 4 September 1952, Folder 1, *Mission Log and Letters from Korea 1952,* 62, VHPC, AFC, LOC

271. This injustice was corrected in 1972 with Public Law 93-540. June A. Willentz, *Women Veterans: America's Forgotten Heroines* (New York: Continuum, 1983), 193. In 1949 legislation passed by the House allotted disabled female veterans compensation for dependent spouses, but as late as 1951 the bill still languished in the Senate Finance Committee. *Congressional Record: Appendix (House),* 81st Cong., 2d sess., vol. 96:18, A7996.

272. See Henry Aldous Dixon in *Congressional Record: Appendix (House),* 84th Congress, 2nd sess., volume 102 (January 1956-July 1956), A2143. Also see Benjamin Fine, "Educators Back Korean Veterans," *New York Times,* 15 January 1954, 2, and Benjamin Fine, "Veterans of Korea Flock to Colleges under U.S. Grants," *New York Times,* 14 September 1953, 1.

273. Roy Willis to Senator Charles E. Bennett, 26 March 1953, NA, Record Group 233, Box 2022. See William E. Armstead to Charles E. Bennett, 26 March 1953; Roy Willis to Senator A. S. Herlong, 26 March 1953; C. E. Dye to George Long, 20 March 1953; Maurice Callum to Congresswoman Edith N. Rogers, 30 March 1953; and Nathan B. Spiro to Congresswoman Edith Nourse Rogers, 16 July 1954, in this same collection for further examples of men unable to enroll in the programs of their choice. A change of objective could mean going from a B.A. program to an M.A. program. This caused difficulties for men or women who completed one level of schooling and wanted to finish up another with the remainder of their GI Bill entitlement. See Senator Ralph Yarborough in *Congressional Record* (Senate), 86th Congress, 1st sess., volume 105, Part 11 (17 July 1959-30 July 1959), 14264.

274. See Charles E. Bennett to House Committee on Veterans Affairs, 4 December 1952, NA Record Group 233, Box 2022. Bennett gives the example of a black baking school in Tampa, Florida, with three hundred students enrolled, presumably under the World War II GI Bill, and not one paying his or her own tuition. Because of new restrictions on Korean War veterans, the school could not open to them and in fact "will no longer be in existence" once its present GIs finish. See also Trezzvant W. Anderson to Karl Standish, 5 March 1953, in the same collection. Blacks also reported problems with using the first GI Bill. See David H. Onkst, "'First a Negro . . . Incidentally a Veteran': Black World War Two Veterans and the GI Bill of Rights in the Deep South, 1944-1948," *Journal of Social History* 31.3 (Spring 1998): 517-43.

275. Mickey Levine, "Report on Negro Veterans in the South," 15 March 1956, 3, Central Files, General File, GF 124-A-1, Box 912, DDE Library. African American legislators early recognized the possible implications of the Korean GI Bill for African Americans. Representatives Adam C. Powell Jr. and William L. Dawson voted "present" in the House in protest of the nonveteran enrollment requirement, which they sensed would discriminate against black veterans in the South. C. P. Trussell, "New G.I. Rights Bill Is Passed by House," *New York Times*, 6 June 1952, 1.

276. *Public Law 550*, Title II, Part I, Sections 212-13, 664-65, 82nd Congress, 2nd sess., *United States Statutes at Large* (Washington, DC: U.S. Government Printing Office, 1953), 688-91.

277. Donald W. Dippe to President Dwight D. Eisenhower, 9 April 1959, Central Files, General File, GF 125-J (2), Box 933, DDE Library.

278. "Bill Aids Veterans of Korea," *New York Times*, 16 January 1962, 26, and Senator Richard L. Neuberger in *Congressional Record (Senate)*, 87th Congress, 2nd sess., volume 108, Part I (10 January 1962-1 February 1962), 154.

279. Sumner G. Whittier to David W. Kendall, 27 May 1959, Central Files, General File, GF 125-J (2), Box 933, DDE Library, and "G.I. Bill Extension Is Opposed by V.A.," *New York Times*, 19 March 1957, 20.

280. Chesty Puller in Richard K. Kolb, "Korea's 'Invisible Veterans' Return to an Ambivalent America," *Veterans of Foreign Wars Magazine*, November 1997, 30.

281. Christian G. Appy, *Working-Class War: American Combat Soldiers and Vietnam* (Chapel Hill: University of North Carolina Press, 1993), 246-47; Matthias, *The Korean War*, 93; and Executive Order 11016 (25 April 1962) at https://afls4.jag.af.mil/ARMY/BCMR/cy2002/2002077167C072.rtf . During the Korean War, Halsey McGovern became the first person to ever refuse to accept the Medal of Honor. With two sons killed in Korea, McGovern refused the Medal of Honor on the grounds that President Truman was unworthy to bestow it. Clipping "Hero's Scroll Rejected by His Parents" and "PA 163 Medal of Honor," Republican National Committee (Additional Files of) Richard Lamb, A65-12/1, Box 695, DDE Library.

282. Verlin N. Rogers, *Korean War Veteran Survey*, 8, CFSOKW.

283. Everett J. McFarland, *Korean War Veteran Survey*, 8, CFSOKW.

284. Fisher, *A Comparative Analysis of Selected Congressional Documents Related to Educational Benefits Legislated for the Veterans of World War II, the Korean Conflict, and the Vietnam Era Under the G.I. Bill*, 32, and Sar A. Levitan and Karen A. Cleary, *Old Wars Remain Unfinished: The Veterans Benefits System* (Baltimore, MD: Johns Hopkins University Press, 1973), 3.

285. Veterans of the Vietnam War also tended to do well in school after coming home. See Drummond Ayers Jr., "The Vietnam Veteran: Silent, Perplexed, Unnoticed," *New York Times*, 8 November 1970, 1.

286. "A Generation on Trial," *New York Times*, 28 August 1954, 14. Also F. Fraser Bond, "It's Fun to Teach GI's," *The American Mercury*, July 1958, 69-72.

287. Female veteran participation rates, though, were much lower than those of males. Robert H. Feitz, *Female Veterans' Usage of the Post–Korean Conflict GI Bill* (Office of Information Management and Statistics Statistical Policy and Research Service Research Division 711, March 1985), 12.

288. "Education of Veterans" in *Veterans in America*, Central Files, Official File, OF55 1959, Box 244, DDE Library, and Congress, House, President's Commission on Veterans' Pensions, *Readjustment Benefits: General Survey and Appraisal; A Report on Veterans' Benefits in the United States*, 78, 84th Congress, 2nd sess., Committee Print 289, Staff Report No. IX Part A, 11 September 1956 (Washington, DC: U.S. Government Printing Office, 1956).

289. The percentage of veterans attending college and earning degrees also rose among Korean veterans who did not use the GI Bill, but the climb was less dramatic, going from 16.1%

to 27.4% and 7.2% to 10.9%, respectively. "National Survey of Veterans, 1979," 2196-197, NA, Record Group 015, Box 1. One scholar argues that the trend toward increased formal education in America rather than the passage of the GI Bills accounts for the willingness of GIs to enter college. This might be true, but it should be noted that the GI Bills allowed that willingness to metamorphose into the ability to attend school. Charles B. Nam, "Impact of the 'GI Bills' on the Educational Level of the Male Population," *Social Forces* 43.1 (October 1964): 26-32.

290. George Pakkala, *Korean War Veteran Survey,* 12, CFSOKW, and Eugene R. Grace, *Korean War Veteran Survey,* 13, CFSOKW. See also Al Avisato Jr. in the Extension of Remarks of Senator Spessard L. Holland of Florida in *Congressional Record: Appendix* (Senate), 84th Congress, 2nd sess., volume 100 (January 1954-1 December 1954), A69.

291. "Education of Veterans" in *Veterans in America,* Central Files, Official File, OF55 1959, Box 244, DDE Library, and Congressman Radwan in *Congressional Record* (House), 84th Congress, 2nd sess., volume 102, part 2 (27 January 1956-17 February 1956), 2099.

292. "A Generation on Trial," *New York Times,* 28 August 1954, 14.

293. On the evolution of veterans' benefits beginning with the Revolutionary War, see Levitan and Cleary, *Old Wars Remain Unfinished.*

294. Howard A. Rusk, "Care for the Wounded," *New York Times,* 6 May 1956, 116, and "Statistical Summary of VA Activities," 31 December 1954, Bryce Harlow, Records 1953-61, Box 8, DDE Library. Paraplegics received yearly stipends of six thousand dollars for themselves and extra allowances of three hundred dollars for wives and two hundred dollars for children as well as monthly allotments to cover the cost of attendants, sixteen hundred dollars toward the purchase of a car if public transportation proved unsuitable, and a one-time ten thousand dollar grant to put toward a specially equipped house. John E. Booth, "Veteran against Veteran," *Atlantic,* October 1965, 89. Public Law 894, passed in December 1950, gave disabled veterans the same vocational rehabilitation benefits enjoyed by World War II disabled veterans, including counseling and GI Bill–type training or education. Sar A. Levitan and Joyce K. Zickler, *Swords into Plowshares: Our GI Bill* (Salt Lake City, UT: Olympus, 1973), 66, and Congress, House, *Record and Evaluation of the Vocational Rehabilitation Program for Service-Connected Disabled Veterans,* 84th congress, 1st sess., 8 July 1955, House Committee Print 109. Under the Federal Employees Compensation Act, National Guardsmen and Reservists recalled to duty during the Korean War and subsequently disabled received up to five times more in compensation and benefits than enlistees and inductees. Howard A. Rusk, "Public Apathy to Korea G.I.'s Slows Their Benefit Claims," *New York Times,* 27 September 1953, 4.

295. The *Combat Duty Act of 1952,* retroactive to the start of the war, entitled members of specially designated combat units to forty-five dollars a month for every month in which they had spent at least six days in duty. Richard K. Kolb, "Korea's 'Invisible Veterans': Return to an Ambivalent America," *Veterans of Foreign Wars Magazine,* November 1997, 25.

296. "You're Guilty but Don't Ask Why," *New Republic,* 13 February 1956, 9-10. Also Memo Roger W. Jones to Mr. Shanley, 8 February 1954, Central Files, Official File, Cross Reference Sheets, OF 154-6, Box 133, DDE Library, and Congressman Thomas Ashley of Ohio in *Congressional Record* (House), 84th Congress, 2nd sess., volume 102, part 1 (3 January 1956-26 January 1956), 445.

297. Pensions ranged from $15 to $150 a month based on the extent of disability. Amputees and the blind received more, but only those discharged with service disabilities could collect a pension. "We've Been Asked: About Aid to New Veterans," *U.S. News and World Report,* 8 June 1951, 58.

298. Cross Reference Sheet, Robert Mernit, 24 April 1953, Central Files, Official File, Cross Reference Sheets, OF154-1+, Box 133, DDE Library, and Disabled American Veterans (DAV), Resolutions 195, 295, and 293, Central File, PPF47, Order of Demolay, Box 808, Folder "47 Disabled American Veterans (1)," DDE Library.

299. Although using VA services less frequently than veterans of other wars, Korean War veterans accounted for a hefty percentage of those receiving pensions and service-connected compensation in March 2000. Of 370,200 veterans receiving pensions, 86,300 were Korean War veterans and another 172,600 were getting service-connected compensation. U.S. Department of Veterans Affairs, Assistant Secretary for Planning and Analysis, Office of Program and Data Analyses, *Data on Veterans of the Korean War*, June 2000 (online publication at http://www.va.gov/vetdata/demographics/KW2000.doc).

300. Amazingly, by June 30, 1972, the government had spent close to $100 billion on World War II veterans and their dependents and over $50 billion on World War I veterans and their dependents. And, though the Vietnam War was just ending, those veterans had already collected more than $7 billion. Levitan and Cleary, *Old Wars Remain Unfinished*, 3.

301. Alfred M. Mishos to Robert A. Taft, 27 April 1953, Taft Papers, Box 1282, LOC. Another combat veteran wrote Taft with the same problem. See Joseph P. Dew to Robert Taft, 13 April 1953, Taft Papers, Box 1282, LOC.

302. Arthur Smith, Memoir (KWE), 18.

303. As a result of veteran activism, Towner eventually did get a 100% rating for his cold injuries. "Cold Injury Report," *News Digest*, 8, Vertical Files, "Frostbite," CFSOKW.

304. Fernando Gandara, *Korean War Veteran Survey*, 7, CFSOKW.

305. Severo and Milford, *The Wages of War*, 329-33.

306. "You're Guilty but Don't Ask Why," *New Republic*, 13 February 1956, 9-10, and Congressman Thomas Ashley of Ohio in *Congressional Record* (House), 84th Congress, 2nd sess., volume 102, part 1 (3 January 1956-26 January 1956), 444-46.

307. Kutner asked to face his accusers but the Army denied his request. "Ex-P.O.W. Assails 'Kangaroo Trial,'" *New York Times*, 8 February 1956, 20.

308. Ultimately, POWs got special access to medical care and disability compensation for service-related diseases like beriberi and pellagra. "VA Expands Outreach to POWS," Vertical Files, "Frostbite," CFSOKW. Also, the courts ruled that the less than honorable discharges issued by the Army violated civil liberties, noting, "It would seem basic that a soldier has a right to an honorable discharge if his military record merits it" and "he cannot be held to answer for matters extraneous to his record." Many veterans did not realize the kind of discharge received until years later. Severo and Milford, *The Wages of War*, 329-30.

309. Men who served stateside also qualified for mustering-out pay, but it did not exceed two hundred dollars regardless of the length of their service. "The New GI Bill: Who Gets What?" *Changing Times*, May 1953, 21, and *Congress and the Nation, 1945-1964: A Review of Government and Politics in the Postwar Years* (Washington, DC: Congressional Quarterly Press, 1965), 1348. Also *Public Law 550*, Title V, Section 408, 501-6, 82nd Congress, 2nd sess., *United States Statutes at Large* (Washington, DC: U.S. Government Printing Office, 1953), 688-91. Some veterans mustered out before the act was passed, but Congress later extended the deadline for filing in order to make everyone who served in the Korean War eligible. See Sam A. Jaffe, "Uncle Sam's Bitter Nephews," *The Nation*, 29 December 1951, 567-68, and Congress, House, Committee on Veterans Affairs, "Extension of Time for Applying for Mustering-Out Payments," report prepared by Congressman Olin E. Teague of Texas, 84th Congress, 1st sess., *House Reports*, Vol. 3, *Miscellaneous Reports on Public Bills, II* (Washington, DC: U.S. Government Printing Office, 1955).

310. John Walker Hatcher (AFC2001-001-1428), Folder 1, *Mission Log and Letters from Korea, 1952*, 77, VHPC, AFC, LOC, and Anthony DeAngelis, Memoir, 80, attached to Army Service (Korean War) Questionnaire, 1st Cavalry Division, Surnames A-L, Carlisle Barracks.

311. Paul L. Cooper, *Weekend Warriors* (Manhattan, KS: Sunflower University Press, 1996), 219, and Apel and Apel, *MASH*, 209.

312. Robert Chappel (AFC2001/001/188), Folder 2, Interview by Laura M. Clifton, 23 November 2001, 13, VHPC, AFC, LOC, and Elmer P. Payne to Melinda Pash, 4 June 2004, in author's possession.

CHAPTER 8

1. "Dedication of Plaque Honoring Korean War Dead," *Department of State Bulletin*, 16 July 1956, 119-20; G. Kurt Piehler, *Remembering War the American Way* (Washington, DC: Smithsonian Institution Press, 1995), 158; and Richard K. Kolb, "Korea's 'Invisible Veterans': Return to an Ambivalent America," *Veterans of Foreign Wars Magazine*, November 1997, 30.

2. Piehler, *ibid.*, 157.

3. Charles F. Cole, *Korea Remembered: Enough of a War; The USS Ozbourn's First Korean Tour, 1950-1951* (Las Cruces, NM: Yucca Tree Press, 1995), 273.

4. Glen Lowery, Interview by Lisa Davis in Virginia Havard, ed., *By Word of Mouth* (Lufkin, TX: Lufkin High School, Kwik Kopy Printing, 1990), 22.

5. Louis J. Lyons in Linda Granfield, *I Remember Korea: Veterans Tell Their Stories of the Korean War, 1950-1953* (New York: Clarion Books, 2003), 67.

6. Eugene R. Manfrey, a former steelworker, in Sylvia Nasar, "Serving in Military May Cut Later Earnings, Studies Say," *New York Times*, 11 November 1991, D1.

7. Aubrey Loving, Interview by Natalie Shocklee in Havard, *By Word of Mouth*, 21; Harlee W. Lassiter, *Korean War Veteran Survey*, attachment page, CFSOKW; and Dick Munro in Henry Berry, *Hey, Mac, Where Ya Been? Living Memories of the U.S. Marines in the Korean War* (New York: St. Martin's Press, 1988), 277.

8. Edgar Miller in Granfield, *I Remember Korea*, 114. See also Joe Holland, Interview by Tamara Greening in Havard, *By Word of Mouth*, 18, and Samuel R. Woodham (AFC2001/001/1595), Folder 3, Interview by Brian Woodham, 23 March 2002, 28, VHPC, AFC, LOC.

9. Alan B. Krueger, "Economic Scene: For White Men, Military Service Does Not Pay in Later Life," *New York Times Online*, 11 November 2004.

10. On average, Vietnam veterans earned 10% less than civilian contemporaries after military service, World War II veterans (after factoring out nonveterans with mental or physical handicaps) 5-10% less, and post-Vietnam veterans 5% . *Ibid.*, and Alan B. Krueger, "Warning: Military Service Can Be a Drain on Later Earning Power in Civilian Life," *New York Times*, 11 November 2004, C2. Also, Saul Schwartz, "The Relative Earnings of Vietnam and Korean-Era Veterans," *Industrial and Labor Relations Review* 39.4 (July 1986): 564, and Stephen L. Mangum and David E. Ball, "The Transferability of Military-Provided Occupational Training in the Post-Draft Era," *Industrial and Labor Relations Review* 42.2 (January 1989): 234.

11. Advantages over other veterans remain obvious even after adjusting for demographic characteristics. Melanie Martindale and Dudley L. Poston Jr., "Variations in Veteran/Nonveteran Earnings Patterns among World War II, Korea, and Vietnam War Cohorts," *Armed Forces and Society* 5.2 (February 1979): 229.

12. "National Survey of Veterans, 1979," "Final Report," 11 and 68, NA, Record Group 015, Box 1. Of those who served in Korea, only 88.8% had bought or built a home compared to 87.3% of World War II veterans and 66.5% of Vietnam War veterans. Of those who served in both Korea and Vietnam, 90.9% owned homes, as did 95% of those who served in World War II, Korea, and Vietnam.

13. Schwartz, "The Relative Earnings of Vietnam and Korean-Era Veterans," 569, and Valentine M. Villa, Nancy D. Harada, Donna Washington, and JoAnn Damron-Rodriguez, "Health and Functioning among Four War Eras of U.S. Veterans: Examining the Impact of War Cohort Membership, Socioeconomic Status, Mental Health, and Disease Prevalence," *Military Medicine* 167 (September 2002): 785.

14. Mangum and Ball, "The Transferability of Military-Provided Occupational Training in the Post-Draft Era," 234, and Martindale and Poston, "Variations in Veteran/Nonveteran Earnings Patterns among World War II, Korea, and Vietnam War Cohorts," 238.

15. Krueger, "Warning: Military Service Can Be a Drain on Later Earning Power in Civilian Life," *New York Times*, 11 November 2004, C2.
16. "National Survey of Veterans, 1979," "Final Report," 13, NA, Record Group 015, Box 1.
17. "Two Support Mexican," *New York Times*, 21 March 1952, 45. This early effort failed, but later measures supported giving men who served in Korea the same naturalization rights as in other wars. "Naturalization Privileges for Korean War Veterans" in *Congressional Record* (Senate), 85th Congress, 2nd sess., volume 104, part 14 (14 August 1958-20 August 1958), 80, and "Proposed Citizenship Legislation for Veterans of Korean War" in *Congressional Record* (Senate), 85th Congress, 2nd sess., volume 104, part 1 (7 January 1958-30 January 1958), 531.
18. Harold L. Mulhausen and James Edwin Alexander, *Korea: Memories of a U.S. Marine* (Oklahoma City, OK: Macedon, 1995), i.
19. Many veterans note that they never told their children, or in some cases wives, that they had served in Korea. *Ibid.*, ii, and Glen Wilson in Steve Vogel, "After 50 Years, Veterans of Korea Are Still Haunted by Memories," *Washington Post*, 26 June 2000, B1.
20. Harlee W. Lassiter, *Korean War Veteran Survey*, attachment page, CFSOKW.
21. Email Shorty Estabrook to Melinda Pash, 29 July 2004, in author's possession.
22. Ted W. Peddycord, *Korean War Veteran Survey*, 12, CFSOKW.
23. On the healing effects of reunions, see Glen H. Elder and Elizabeth C. Clipp, "Wartime Losses and Social Bonding: Influences across 40 Years in Men's Lives," *Psychiatry* 51 (May 1988): 177-98, and Gilbert Towner in Richard T. Cooper, "Vets Still Conflicted over Korea," *Los Angeles Times*, 19 January 2000, 1.
24. Bob Barnett in Kelly O. Beaucar, "Korean War Vets . . . the Forgotten Ones," *The Herald* (New Britain, CT), 14 June 1998.
25. Many accounts note the impact of Vietnam veteran activism on Korean War veteran activism. Korean War veterans in part learned how to organize from this younger group and also became more desirous of recognition as they watched the country respond to Vietnam veterans. See Paul L. Cooper, *Weekend Warriors* (Manhattan, KS: Sunflower University Press, 1996), 219, and Albert J. Parisi, "Korean War: Memories, but . . . ," *New York Times*, 5 July 1987, NJ1.
26. Albert J. Parisi, "Korean War: Memories, but . . . ," *New York Times*, 5 July 1987, NJ1.
27. "KWVA History in Brief," online at http://www.kwva.org/brief_history.htm.
28. Piehler, *Remembering War the American Way*, 158, and Albert J. Parisi, "Korean War: Memories, but . . . ," *New York Times*, 5 July 1987, NJ1.
29. The Korean War Memorial had to be rededicated in 1999 as Washington weather had eroded much of the original memorial. Allan R. Millett, *Their War for Korea: American, Asian, and European Combatants and Civilians, 1945-1953* (Washington, DC: Brassey's, 2002), xviii. In his preface, Millett makes an interesting comparison of the Korean War Memorial in the United States and the one in South Korea.
30. William M. Allen, *My Old Box of Memories: Thoughts of the Korean War* (self-published, c. 1999), 92. Many veterans note the importance of the Korean War Memorial in their lives. See *ibid.*, 93-96, and Charles King in Bill Smith, "Black Soldiers Fully Shared Korean War's Bloody Cost," *St. Louis Post-Dispatch*, 20 February 2002, A1.
31. Michael Ollove, "A Soldier's Disgrace," *Baltimore Sun*, 28 April 1996, 1K; Michael A. Fletcher, "Korean War Veterans Seek to Block Book Critical of Black Unit," *Washington Post*, 19 January 1997, A4; and Charles M. Bussey, *Firefight at Yechon: Courage and Racism in the Korean War* (Lincoln: University of Nebraska Press, 2002), xvii.
32. Curt Anderson, "Appeals Court Denies Lifetime Health Care for WWII, Korean Veterans," Associated Press News Service, 20 November 2002, online at http://infoweb.newsbank.com, and Joe Galloway, "Vets Sue over Cuts in Benefits," *Fayetteville (NC) Observer*, 27 May 2005, 10A.

33. Jonathan Bor, "Korean War Cold Cripples Again," *Baltimore Sun,* 14 April 1996, 1A.

34. Michael Doyle, "Veterans Win 'Cold War' for Health Benefits," *Fresno (CA) Bee,* 25 May 1997, A22.

35. U.S. Congress, Senate, Bill S.2776, 108th Congress, 2nd sess., 7 September 2004, online at http://thomas.loc.gov/cgi-bin/query/z?c108S.2776. Also, Colonel John Zitzelberger continues to make "Cold Injury Information" packets available to veterans seeking to file a claim. Letter and packet Colonel John Zitzelberger to Melinda Pash, July 2004, in author's possession.

36. "Out Front: Aging World War II, Korea Vets Finally Compensated for Frostbite's Ills," *Boston Globe Online,* 6 April 1997.

37. Robert W. Chester, Sr., *Korean War Veteran Survey,* 10, CFSOKW.

38. South Koreans also expressed gratitude. In 2002, when South Korean activists protested against the United States, South Korean war veterans held pro-American rallies in front of a key U.S. Army base. Jong-Heon Lee, "Korean Veterans Block Anti-U.S. Rallies," United Press International, 3 January 2002, provided by COMTEX, online at http://www.comtexnews.com, article number A81238431. See also Clipping "Korean War Veterans Are Honored 50 Years Later," Vertical File "Veterans Recognized," CFSOKW.

39. "Church Bells to Salute Korean War," *Commercial News* (Danville, IL), 7 June 1988, Box MM, Folder 1311 B, CFSOKW.

40. Clipping "On Korean War Veterans," *The Examiner,* 15-16 July 2000, Box CC, Folder A0908, CFSOKW.

41. Sarah Lyall, "Act of Appreciation Assuages Korean War Vets," *New York Times,* 26 June 1988, 25, and James Barron, "A Korea War Parade Decades Late," *New York Times,* 26 June 1991, B1, and Peter A. Soderbergh, *Women Marines in the Korean War Era* (Westport, CT: Praeger, 1994), 131.

42. James Barron, "A Korea War Parade Decades Late," *New York Times,* 26 June 1991, B1.

43. The ban was lifted in 1954, but South Korea did not offer the medal again until the 1990s. Clipping, Robert Burns, "Pentagon Clears Way for Vets to Wear South Korean Medals," 23 June 2000, AR0664, CFSOKW.

44. For a list of Korean War memorials, see the KWVA site at http://www.kwva.org/memorials/index.htm.

45. Albert J. Parisi, untitled article, *New York Times,* 11 October 1987, NJ20.

46. Lee Ballenger, *The Final Crucible: U.S. Marines in Korea.* Vol. 2, *1953* (Washington, DC: Brassey's, 2001), 270, and William D. Dannenmaier, *We Were Innocents: An Infantryman in Korea* (Chicago: University of Illinois Press, 1999), 226-27.

47. Dannenmaier, *We Were Innocents,* 227.

48. Clipping, Bernard E. Trainor, "A Return to No Man's Land," AR0186, CFSOKW. See also Clyde H. Farnsworth, "Korea War Veterans Return for Another Look," *Special to the New York Times,* 27 October 1985, 16.

49. *Ibid.*

50. Dannenmaier, *We Were Innocents,* 229.

51. Ballenger, *The Final Crucible,* 267-68.

52. Lloyd A. Greening, *Korean War Veteran Survey,* 7, CFSOKW.

53. Eric Hansen in William Berebitsky, *A Very Long Weekend: The Army National Guard in Korea, 1950-1953* (Shippensburg, PA: White Mane, 1996), 260, and Mulhausen and Alexander, *Korea: Memories of a U.S. Marine,* i.

54. Richard G. Chappell and Gerald E. Chappell, *Corpsmen: Letters from Korea* (Kent, OH: Kent State University Press, 2000), 145, and Angelo J. Biviano, Army Service (Korean War) Questionnaire, 20, 1st Cavalry Division, Surnames A-L, Carlisle Barracks.

55. Angelo J. Biviano, Army Service (Korean War) Questionnaire, 20, 1st Cavalry Division, Surnames A-L, Carlisle Barracks

56. Arned L. Hinshaw, *Heartbreak Ridge, Korea, 1951* (New York: Praeger, 1989), 1.

57. John "Jack" Orth, *Korean War Veteran Survey*, 7, CFSOKW.

58. William S. Stegall, *Korean War Veteran Survey*, 12, CFSOKW, and Herman Lee Mingee, Interview by Wesley Miller in Havard, *By Word of Mouth*, 25.

59. Howard Matthias, *The Korean War: Reflections of a Young Combat Platoon Leader*, revised edition (Tallahassee, FL: Father & Son Publishing, 1995), 225.

60. William Wayne Montgomery, *The Mustache That Walks Like a Man* (Manchester Center, VT: Marshall Jones Company, n.d.), 175.

61. Gerald A. Willey, Army Service (Korean War) Questionnaire, 20, 3rd Division, Alphabetical Box 3, Carlisle Barracks, and Everett J. McFarland, *Korean War Veteran Survey*, 11, CFSOKW.

62. Burdette L. Thomsen, Army Service (Korean War) Questionnaire, 16, 1st Cavalry Division, Surnames M-Z, Carlisle Barracks, and Walter A. Klein (AFC2001/001/220), Folder 2, Interview by Jamie Malone, 15 November 2001, 14, VHPC, AFC, LOC.

63. Matthias, *The Korean War*, 226, and Montgomery, *The Mustache That Walks Like a Man*, 227.

64. James G. Campbell, *Korean War Veteran Survey*, 9. During the Vietnam War, some Korean War veterans participated in peace demonstrations. Ric Mendoza-Gleason was arrested protesting President John F. Kennedy's decision to send advisors to Vietnam. The judge let everyone go except five Korean War veterans whom he sent to jail, saying, "How could you as . . . veterans, now turn against your country?" Ric Mendoza-Gleason (AFC2001/001/4939), Folder 2, Interview by Katia Bore, 22 January 2003, Transcribed and edited by Lara Ballard, February 2003, 15, VHPC, AFC, LOC. A Korean War veteran, Ron Wolin, led a parade for peace through New York City in 1967. See John P. Callahan, "Parades for Peace, Brotherhood . . . (And Washington) Mark Holiday Here," *New York Times*, 23 February 1967, 24.

65. James L. Murphy, *Korean War Veteran Survey*, 12, CFSOKW.

66. Almost 41% of Korean War veterans desire a VA headstone or marker while 44% of World War II veterans do. "National Survey of Veterans, 1979," 238 and 245, NA, Record Group 015, Box 1. U.S. Department of Veterans Affairs, Assistant Secretary for Planning and Analysis, Office of Program and Data Analyses, *Data on Veterans of the Korean War*, June 2000 (online publication at http://www.va.gov/vetdata/demographics/KW2000.doc).

ABOUT THE AUTHOR

Originally from Oklahoma, Melinda L. Pash earned degrees at the University of Tulsa and University of Tennessee before settling in Fayetteville, North Carolina, with her husband and two boys. She has published several smaller works on the Korean War and spends her time teaching history at a local college where many of her students are veterans of the wars in Iraq and Afghanistan.